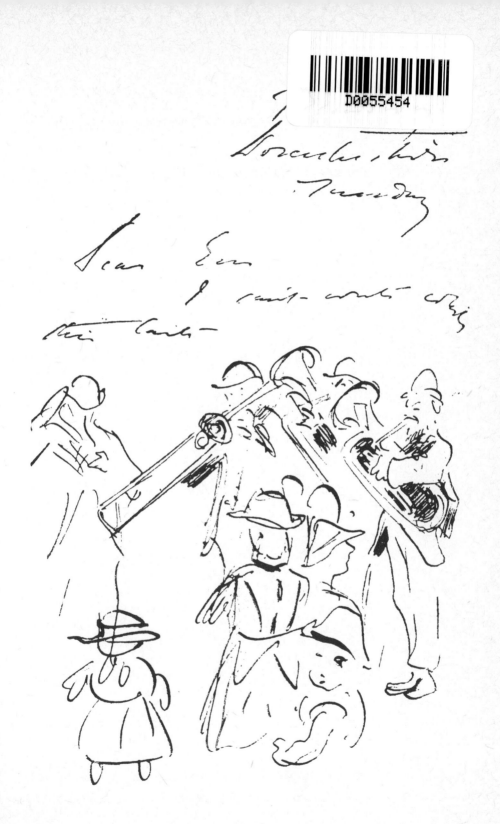

JOHN
SINGER
SARGENT

Other books by Stanley Olson

Elinor Wylie: A Life Apart
The Letters and Diaries of Harold Nicolson (ed.)

JOHN SINGER SARGENT

HIS PORTRAIT

STANLEY OLSON

St. Martin's Press
New York

Library of Congress Cataloging in Publication Data

Olson, Stanley.
  John Singer Sargent, his portrait.

  1. Sargent, John Singer, 1856-1925.   2. Painters—
United States—Biography.   I. Title.
ND237.S304   1986   759.13   [B]   86-6494
ISBN 0-312-44456-7

First published in Great Britain by Macmillan London Limited

First U.S. Edition

10 9 8 7 6 5 4 3 2 1

To Leonée and Richard

Contents

List of Illustrations

Acknowledgements

This book was made possible by the generous – and patient – help of the Ormond family, and I would like to express my thanks to Mr and Mrs David Housego, Mr and Mrs Lawrence Hughes, M. Jean Louis Ormond, Mr and Mrs John Ormond, Mr and Mrs Richard Ormond, Mr and Mrs Timothy Ormond, and Miss Jemima Pitman. Their assistance was offered freely, without any stipulations or qualifications, and therefore they must be excused from assuming any responsibility for my opinions about their uncle and great-uncle.

I would also like to thank the late Mr David McKibbin, who spent the best part of thirty-five years doing research on the life and works of the subject of this biography. Though, alas, I never met him, I do owe him a tremendous debt of gratitude, for the fruits of his efforts were made available to me both by the Boston Athenaeum and the Ormond family, who inherited his archive.

Others to whom I would like to acknowledge my gratitude are:

The Archives of American Art, The Smithsonian Institution; Authors' Aid; The Biltmore House Archives; The Library of the Boston Athenaeum; The Art Archives, Boston Public Library; The British Library; The Brooklyn Museum; Bryn Mawr College Library; Christie's; The Bancroft Library, University of California, Berkeley; The Coe Kerr Gallery; The Miller Library, Colby College; The Butler Library, Columbia University; The Library of Congress; The Corcoran Gallery of Art; Dartmouth College Library; Fogg Art Museum, Harvard University; Frick Art Reference Library; Glasgow University Library; Abo Akademi, Konsthistoriska Institutionen, Helsinki; Institute of History of Art, University of Helsinki; Grand Central Art Galleries; The Houghton Library, University Archives, and Harvard University Library (The Widener Library), Harvard University; Department of Art Archive, Imperial War Museum; Isabella Stewart Gardner Museum; The Brotherton Library, University of Leeds; Massachusetts Historical Society; The Grainger Museum, University of Melbourne; The Metropolitan Museum of Art; Museum of Fine Arts, Boston; National Academy of Design; National Museum of American Art, The Smithsonian Institution; The National Portrait Gallery; New York Historical Society; Messrs Pitt & Scott; The Library, University of Reading; Archives, Royal Academy of Arts; Royal Archives, Windsor Castle; The Sargent–Murray–Gilman–Hough House Association, Gloucester, Massachusetts; The Society of Authors; Sotheby's; The Sterling and Francine Clark Art Institute; Archives, The Tate Gallery; Humanities Research Center, University of Texas; City of Westminster Libraries (Marylebone Road); The Beinecke Rare Book and Manuscript Library, Yale University; Sterling and Francine Clark Art Institute, Williamstown, Massachusetts.

Lady Abdy, Mrs LaTrelle Brewster Adelson, Mr and Mrs Warren Adelson, Mr Michael Alcock, Mr Gregory d'Alessio, Lady Altrincham, Mr and Mrs Leonard Amster, Mr Gordon P. Anderson, Miss Sarah Anderson, Mrs Martha Shipman Andrews, Mrs Brigitta Appleby, Miss Josephine Appleby, Mrs Peter Balfour, Mrs Anne Balfour-Fraser, the Hon. Mrs Susan Baring, Miss Catherine Barnes, Dr Wendy Baron, Mr and Mrs Julian Barrow, Mrs Nicola Beauman, Mrs Sybille Bedford, Mrs Millicent Bell, Mr Gerard Bianco, Dr Jennifer Bienenstock, Mr John Bird, Lord Birdwood, The Hon. Mrs Mark Bonham-Carter, Miss Virginia Bonham-Carter, La Baronne de Bosmelet, M. Paul Brame, Mr H. C. Brewster, Mr Douglas Brown, Miss Juliet Brightmore, Mrs Ethel-Jane W. Bunting, Mrs Doreen Bolger Burke, Mrs M. Burnett, Mrs Rosalind Butler, Mr and Mrs James Byam Shaw, Miss Chita Campbell, the late Mr Robin Campbell and Mrs Robin Campbell, Miss Robin Carlaw, Mr Edward Cazalet, Miss Theresa Cederholm, Mr James W. Cheevers, Mr D. H. B. Chesshyre (Chester Herald), Mrs Tom Chetwynd, Mr A. Chisholm, The Dowager Marchioness of Cholmondeley, the late Mr John Churchill, Mrs Mary L. Clapp, Mr Alvord Clements, Mr Peter Cochoran, Mrs E. Mary Cockram, Mr J. Fraser Cocks, The Directors of the Coe Kerr Gallery, Miss Gill Coleridge, Dr Judith M. V. Collins, Miss Louise Collis, Mr Michael Congdon, Miss Angela Connor, Mr A. Coombes, Mr Richard Cork, Mr John Couper, Mrs Sally Crewe, Mr Ralph Curtis, Mr R. L. Davids, Mrs Russell W. Davenport, Miss Jeremyn Davern, the late Mr Terence Davies, Mr Whitney Davis, the late Mr and Mrs Bill Davis, the Hon. Mr George Dawnay, The Duke and Duchess of Devonshire, Mr Johnny Dewe-Mathews, Miss Ann Dex, Miss Katherine Dibble, Miss Edythe T. Donovan, Miss Kay Dreyfus, Mrs Patricia Ducas, Mme Odile Duff, The Marquess and Marchioness of Dufferin and Ava, Prof. Leon Edel, Mr A. E. Eldon-Edington, Mrs Carol Edwards, Mrs Nina Eloesser, Mrs Joyce Engelson, Mrs Mettha Westfeldt Eshleman, Miss Claudia T. Esko, Mrs Dorothy Evans, Miss Elizabeth C. Evans, Mrs Betty Eveillard, Dr Trevor Fairbrother, Mr Barry Fenby, Miss Linda S. Ferber, The Earl and Countess of Ferrers, Mr and Mrs Xan Feilding, Dr Lois M. Fink, Sir Brinsley Ford, Miss Anne

Gainsford, Dr Michèle Le Gal, Mrs Anne Galbally, Miss Carol Gardiner, Mrs Angelica Garnett, Mrs Henrietta Garnett, Mr Richard Garnett, Mrs Abigail Booth Gerdts, Mr and Mrs John Gere, Mr Christopher Gibbs, Mr Martyn Goff, Miss Deborah Gribbon, Mrs Christina Griffith, the Hon. Mr John Grigg, Miss Anne Greenshields, Mr Rollin van N. Hadley, Mrs Helen Hall, Mr Michael Hall, Mr and Mrs Stewart Hamilton, Mr Peter E. Hanff, Miss Francesca Hardcastle, Mrs Christine Harrison, Miss Sylvia Harrison, Mr John Hatt, Mr Francis Hazell, Mr Heywood Hill, Prof. Patricia Hills, Mr Sinclair Hitchings, Miss Caroline Hobhouse, Mrs D. E. Hodges, Mr Richard Holling, Mr Michael Holroyd, Mr Anthony Hopkins, Dr C. C. Houghton, Dr John House, Mme Paulette Howard-Johnston, Messrs Hudson & Williams, Mr T. Michael Huffington, Mr and Mrs Lawrence Hughes, Mr James-Crook, Mr Peter Jenkinson, Mr Graham Johnson, Mr George Jordan, Miss Sara C. Junkin, Dr David Kalstone, Mr and Mrs Peter H. Kaminer, Mr Anton Kamp, Mr and Mrs Robert Kee, Dr Richard M. Kenin, Miss Elaine Kilmurray, Miss Perjo Kivinem, Miss Sheila LaFarge, Dr Mary Lago, Miss Jane Langton, Mr Alan Lee, Mr William Lichtenwanger, Miss Doris B. Littlefield, Dr Franklin Loew, Mr James Lomax, Mr Deane W. Lord, Mr Justin Lowinsky, Mr Raymond Lucas, Mr J. Ludlow, Mr Jeremy Maas, Lord and Lady MacAlpine of West Green, Mrs Margueritte McBey, Dr Kenneth McConkey, Mrs Duncan MacDonald, Mr Mark MacDonald, Mr Nicholas McDowell, Mr Rory Maclaren, Mr Alan Maclean, Mr and Mrs Jamie Maclean, Mr Paul Magriel, Miss Synnöre Malmström, Mrs Maybelle Mann, Mrs Leslie Marple, Mrs Fiona Martin, Miss Deborah Masters, Mr Douglas Mathews, Mr and Mrs David Mathias, Mr Julian Mathias, Mr and Mrs Robert Mathias, Mr and Mrs R. Mehan, Miss Cynthia Millar, Sir Oliver and Lady Millar, Miss Selene Mills, Miss Marion Milne, Mrs Tessa Monroe, Mrs Moore, Miss Honor Moore, Lady Audrey Morris, Mr Michael Moss, Mrs L. H. Myers, M. Jean-Michel Nectoux, Mr Mark Newton, Mrs E. Q. Nicholson, Mr Nigel Nicolson, Mrs Stephen Nonack, Dr Barbara Novak, Dr Arlene Olson, Dr Norman Olson, Mr and Mrs Jaime Parladé, Mr John Pettus, Mr Geofrey Phillips, Mrs Diana Phipps, Mr David Pleydell-Bouverie, Mr Stewart Preston, Mr David Pryce-Jones, The Dowager Countess of Radnor, The Earl of Radnor, Mr Michael Ratcliffe, Mr and Mrs William Rathbone, Miss Aimo Reitala, Mrs Donald I. Renau, Sir Adam Ridley, Mr Sexton Ringbom, Mr Kirk Ritchie, Mrs Meg Robertson, Miss Hinda Rose, Mlle Elizabeth Royer, the late Mrs Maud Russell, Mr Roc Sandford, Mr Daniel Sargent, Mr C. S. Scott, Miss Donna Seldin, Mr Brian Sewell, Mrs Joyce Sharpey-Schafer, Miss Rosamond Sherwood, Mr. Richard Shone, Mr Marc Simpson, Mrs Sarah Krolle Simpson, Miss Susan Sinclair, Mr Peyton Skipwith, Mr John Saumarez Smith, Mrs N. W. Smith, Mr W. Smith, Mr Tom Söderman, Miss Anna Southall, Miss Karen Stafford, Mr Jeff Stell, Mrs Brenda Stephenson, The Earl of Stockton, Miss Robin Straus, Miss Susan Strickler, Miss Jean Strouse, Mr Denys Sutton, Major-General Sir John Swinton, Mr Chiam Tannenbaum, Mrs Barbara Tebbitt, the late Mr Lowell Thomas, Dr George P. Turner, Mr Robert Updegraff, Mr Raphael Valls, Mrs Patricia Curtis Vigano, Miss Gillian Vincent, Miss Mary Jo Viola, Mr James Wade, Mr John Walker, Mr Nicholas Ward-Jackson, Lady Warner, Mr Simon Watney, Sir Francis Watson, The Earl of Wemyss and March, Dr H. Barbara Weinberg, Mrs Rhu Weir, Dr Gabriel P. Weisberg, Mr Robert Werlich, Mrs Nancy Fisher West, the late Dame Rebecca West, Mrs Eileen Westcombe, Mr Monroe Wheeler, Mr and Mrs Terence de Vere White, Mr G. Patrick Williams, Miss Kate Williams, Mr and Mrs Jonathan Williams, Miss Elizabeth Winn, Mr S. Wright, Mr Paul York, Mr and Mrs Mark Zervudachi, Mr and Mrs Nolly Zervudachi, Mrs Virginia Zervudachi.

I would also like to thank the John Simon Guggenheim Memorial Foundation and the Phoenix Trust for valuable assistance.

And especial thanks to Lady Selina Hastings, Mrs Frances Partridge, Miss Miranda de Bush Jack York, and the late Prof. W. Olson.

Avant-propos

The history of Sargent biography has assumed a thirty-year cycle. The first, by the Hon. Evan Charteris, appeared in 1927, two years after Sargent's death. Though it is fair to say Sargent's sisters complained of inaccuracies and errors, it remains a very good book; if anything, perhaps a little clouded by affection and the urge to produce a record. The second, by Mr Charles Merrill Mount, was published first in 1957 and later revised. It too is an excellent book, more comprehensive and objective than the first, drawing on many documents and reminiscences which were not available to Evan Charteris. The present Sargent biography not only has the advantage of these two worthy predecessors, but also a freedom granted to neither of them because the ponderous machinery of the catalogue *raisonné*—to be produced by the Coe Kerr Gallery in New York—has been taken over by a team of scholars, allowing me to concentrate entirely on the life. Without such complementary research this biography would not have been possible.

*More and more it has seemed to me that
Sargent's life was absorbed in his painting;
and the summing up of the would-be
biographer must, I think, be:* he painted. *To
some of us he seemed occasionally to paint to
the exclusion of living. . . . But . . . I
recognize that his life was not merely in
painting, but in the more and more intimate
understanding and enjoying the world
around him. . . .*

Vernon Lee [Violet Paget], 1926

BOOK ONE

I am tired of this nomadic sort of life: — the Spring comes, and we strike our tents and migrate for the Summer: the Autumn returns, and we must again pack up our duds and be off to some milder region in which Emily and Mary can thrive. I wish there were some prospect of our going home and settling down among our own people and taking permanent root.

Dr FitzWilliam Sargent to his mother, from Florence,
10 October 1870

I

Dr FitzWilliam Sargent, his wife Mary and his mother-in-law docked at Liverpool on 13 September 1854, at the start of a European tour which was meant to be restorative, and brief. It turned out to be neither. Of course the Sargents never intended to stay, but they did omit to return. In truth they did not so much come to Europe as leave America. They were embarking on a life of unrelieved itineracy, chronic expatriation.[1]

Mary (née Singer) was twenty-eight, FitzWilliam thirty-four. Hitherto their married life had been a slightly uneasy example of the standard unrippled domestic order that was just manageable by a restless wife and a taciturn husband. All the correct elements seemed to be safely in place. They had a daughter within a month of their first anniversary. They were surrounded by a tight and interested community of friends and relatives. FitzWilliam's career adequately displayed his unthreatening sort of ambition, which relied on care rather than on speed. He had a small private practice; he wrote and edited texts; he had started to make investigations into disorders of the eye, and had risen to the post of Attending Surgeon at the Wills Hospital. Such solidity gave him a reputation for downright respectability. He and Mary had every reason to feel perfectly at home in Philadelphia, in the most usual and socially acceptable arrangement. But when their daughter died at the age of two the entire structure crumbled. Mary's spirit collapsed, her health gave way, and her taste for the conventional was lost. It was the end of three years of marriage and the start of a lifelong illness. She told her husband she could only recover abroad, he believed her, and once there they scarcely turned their heads away from thoughts of health. It was a campaign that remained undiminished for the next half-century, keeping them abroad, bound to a habit impossible to break.

They settled in Pau for their first winter abroad. FitzWilliam went back and forth to Paris to study French medical practices, in an attempt to keep warm the idea of his imminent return to his work at home. Mary and her mother found their retirement painfully uneventful, but exactly what her Parisian doctor had prescribed for her vague and unserious symptoms. They were extremely bored, liking neither their fellow-invalids nor the weather. They became restless. They plotted an ambitious summer progress through the thermal stations in the Pyrenees up to Paris. It was a brave plan, because Mary was pregnant.

Each stop on their itinerary was a *terminus a quo*; they stopped only in order to recover from the slight ailments contracted at the previous spa. In Luz, Mary had to recover from a cold. In Bagnères-de-Bigorre her husband had to rest after climbing the Pic de Bergons too hastily. In Bagnères-de-Luchon she again had a cold, this time brought on by the damp at Bagnères-de-Bigorre. By the time they reached Paris, Mrs Singer complained of a headache, and once in Paris they all suffered from the first bout of indecision that would dog them throughout their perpetually extended European visit: they had to determine where they would spend the following winter. First they favoured Nice, warmer than Pau, but hesitated because cholera was threatened. Italy was dismissed because of *reported* cholera. Winter always posed a threat to Mary's health, and the winter of 1855–6 loomed more crucial than most: Mary expected her second child at the turn of the year.

They did, however, go to Florence, at the end of October or the beginning of November. They rented Casa Arretini, in the Lungarno Acciaioli, a tall and much-windowed house next to the Palazzo Sperini on the left bank of the city. There, on Saturday, 12 January 1856, Mary gave birth to her second child, a son.*

His care was first entrusted to an English nurse, with whom he slept, and two days later he was handed over to an Italian peasant, his wet-nurse. The arrival of a wet-nurse (and there would be five of them) was trying for the Sargents. FitzWilliam had started to interview candidates in December and soon discovered that he had seen one woman twice – she had merely dyed her hair and lied with brazen skill throughout both meetings, thus confirming his and Mary's suspicions that Italian servants fell back on the truth only when lying would not help. By the end of February, when the three adults were ready to resume sightseeing, they were uneasy about leaving the house unguarded.

The baby's name was a problem. Mary wanted to call him FitzWilliam, and her mother agreed, pointing to the obvious fact that the boy was the

---

* The precise date of birth cannot be confirmed by any official document, though FitzWilliam claimed eighteen years later that he had registered the birth. At various times FitzWilliam, who was otherwise accurate about family birthdays, confused the date of his son's birth. On 3 September 1874 he wrote to a friend about the event and left the day of the month blank, later filled in an "11", and then changed it to "12" (Massachusetts Historical Society). In another letter, this time to his sister (2 December 1872) he wrote: "January is a memorable month in our family: – John's birth-day was on the 10th, *I believe* (I have a wretched memory for dates) – Emily's is on the 29th, mine on the 17th, Pa's on the 20th . . ." (Archives of American Art, Smithsonian Institution). Thirty-four years later another January anniversary could be added to the list: Mary Sargent died on the twenty-first.

John Sargent and his family always celebrated his birthday on the twelfth.

eldest son of an eldest son. (See Appendix I for the genealogy and family-tree.) FitzWilliam, however, wanted "John Singer", after the child's maternal grandfather and great-grandfather. Mrs Singer was flattered, but demurred: their first child had been named after her, her mother, and her grandmother, and that was sufficient honour to the maternal line. By the third week in February, Mrs Singer referred to her grandson as "fra Giovanni", an appropriate Italian version of John Singer Sargent.[2]

One year later, on 29 January 1857, Mary gave birth in Rome to another child, her second daughter: Emily, named after FitzWilliam's mother and elder sister. When Mrs Singer boasted about the new baby's beauty to relatives at home, Emily was classed as a rival to her brother John, who was himself often compared to the sister who had died.

Shortly after Emily's birth FitzWilliam submitted his resignation from the Wills Hospital. While Mrs Singer called the decision the joint alliance of prudence and morality – "He is quite convinced that it would not be wise or right to take Mary home at present"[3] – FitzWilliam was being coldly realistic. For two and a half years he had been ready to go home; for two and a half years he had lived in that hope and, paradoxically, for two and a half years he had moved with certainty away from that very potentiality. FitzWilliam relinquished his ambition, his career, the society of his parents, brothers and sisters, and without overmuch regret retired. His wife showed absolutely no sign of wishing to return home. She drew up a powerful list of obstacles, headed by her own health and that of her growing family. And for the two decades following her arrival in Liverpool she had good reason to avoid the dangers of returning home – she was pregnant five times. She had tremendous stamina for a woman who was too ill to recross the ocean. Three weeks after John's fifth birthday she gave birth to another daughter, in Nice, on 1 February 1861, named Mary Winthrop in keeping with the family tradition of being disconcertingly unoriginal about names. Thus the cool facts of genealogy suggest that Mary knew very well that John and Emily's survival to a less dangerous stage of childhood would naturally renew FitzWilliam's desire to return home. The arrival of other children ensured a further lease, at least for a few years, on Mary's own highly idiosyncratic version of liberty. There was another child born in 1867, and the last in 1870.

The Sargents evolved a pattern of life that ignored Mary's subtle intentions, that thrived because it was thought to be temporary – a wonderfully elastic notion. They never indulged in long-term plans. Their calendar only spanned the next few months. They never settled down for anything longer because they never needed to be anywhere specific. Their requirements were of the broadest measure, governed by general yet tenuous necessities. The only constant was a desire to avoid extremes of temperature: a vague plan that demanded mountains in the summer and sun in the winter. They reversed the natural course of the seasons because cold caused bronchitis and rheumatism, and heat caused malaria and cholera. They imposed on their lives an artificial sense of the temperate, which was little more than the enactment of an elaborate charade. Their allergy to permanence was threefold: FitzWilliam thought he was satisfying Mary's quest for health, Mary thought she was acceding to FitzWilliam's fading desire to return home, and both of them knew it was financial. Their existence balanced, somewhat precariously, on the limitations of a small income that could include constant travel but would not allow any substantial expenditure for a more stable variety of domesticity than rented accommodation by the season.

The Sargents were not wealthy. They did not stay in Europe in order to furnish a version of seemly life that, on their money, might have been threadbare in America. FitzWilliam's salary stopped the day they sailed for Europe, and he and his wife depended instead on assistance from Mrs Singer and the interest earned by Mary's small capital, which she had inherited after her father's death in 1850, shortly after her marriage to FitzWilliam. This inheritance was a $10,000 trust, on which she received interest twice a year. In other words, Mary had an income of approximately $700 a year. Added to this were the small dividends earned by FitzWilliam's few railway shares. When Mrs Singer died (in 1859), the Sargents' wealth did increase dramatically, without, however, making them rich. All her property and investments were left to Mary, her only child, amounting to $45,000. This money was eventually made over in 1862, when Mary approved the inventory drawn up by her uncle (William Henry Newbold) in Philadelphia.* Whether or not she invested the money and lived exclusively on dividends or drew freely on the capital is unknown. Yet after 1862 there appeared to be no radical improvement or change in the Sargents' standard of living. (When Mary died she left scarcely any money at all.) In his letters home FitzWilliam makes many veiled references to money. He was, above all else, extremely careful and vigilant, especially as the money they lived on was his wife's. "Mary's income", FitzWilliam wrote to his brother (24 November) [1869], "is only such as enables us to live on with a constant effort to spend as little as possible consistently with the requirements of rather delicate health in all of us, which makes it necessary to resort to places of residence which are more expensive than we should think of going to if we were well enough to avoid them."⁴ The Sargents had the luxury of being independent, but they never thought themselves wealthy or lived in a style consistent with wealth. For Mary, money was simply the means to buy health, and for her it was impossible to be well *and* settled. Health, it seemed, could only be achieved by the most unnatural conditions of nomadic constancy. And money was also for her a formidable ally in her battle to avoid America – the means to have her way.

*

* At present values approximately $242,000, or £193,000; and if invested at a yield of 5 per cent they would have earned an annual income of approximately $12,000, or £10,000.

Mary and FitzWilliam Sargent made a paradoxical couple. He looked nervous, but that quality belonged to her. He had the studied demeanour of ignorance of domestic life, but he was passionate about his wife and family. He was a scrupulous correspondent and never shed his deep affection for his brothers and sisters. He looked as if he radiated energy, but in truth he basked in lethargy. Every quality he looked the master of could neatly be assigned to his wife. Mary Sargent's appearance conveyed all the comfort of ardent maternity, steadfast domesticity. She was neither tall nor short; she had a round face with even, unremarkable features which were neither plain nor pretty. All of her physical characteristics seemed to stride between extremes. The only distinction she might lay claim to was a tendency towards stoutness no number of whalebone stays or tightly squeezed bodices could conceal; by middle age she turned this tendency into ample reality. She dominated the household both in size and tone.

FitzWilliam was tall and lean. He had a fine, prominent, broad forehead. His thinning, receding hair was drawn straightly and precisely over his scalp – a masculine counterpart to his wife's carefully dressed and woven tresses. He sported a dense walrus moustache that tended, if anything, to make his narrow head narrower and longer. His skin was pulled tightly over his face, as if there were not enough to make the complete journey. His neck was over-long and, because of his thinness, it appeared to incline slightly forward. His hands were long and tapering, as well suited for the piano keyboard as for the consulting-room. Strangely, his austere appearance inspired confidence, a confidence that was also based on his patients' awareness of his sound ability. His calm assurance was liked, but he had few friends.

Despite her comforting appearance, complacency had no place in Mary's nature. She was, on the other hand, wilful, and a safer reading would have been she was spoiled. She was driven by a strange abstract dissatisfaction, and was petrified by any notion of what people expected as her duty. She longed to escape the regular, unrelenting demands of children and home, and was shrewd enough to turn these very demands to advantage, to her own purpose. She suspected that if she had stayed in Philadelphia she would have enjoyed no release from keeping the shutters firmly drawn down on family life. At home she would have been surrounded by FitzWilliam's numerous family, and she had always been accustomed to having her own way. That is how she found the confidence to hatch the lie about her health, which was rather bold for a doctor's wife. She managed to find just enough illnesses to keep the myth alive.

FitzWilliam savoured no such optimism; he was burdened with an affection for the practical. He was logical and sensible to the point of being pessimistic. He favoured no extremes of emotion, and therefore he was well equipped to try to arrest his wife's imprudent flamboyance. He struggled, often unsatisfactorily, to steady a course of life that could never really embrace regularity. He tried to swim against the current his wife propelled through their lives, and altogether it proved a highly complimentary operation: his quiet manner avoided all confrontation, while at the same time refusing to dwell on the idea of sacrifice (which he could certainly lay claim to). Mary's robust, fertile imagination was tempered, lovingly and sympathetically, by his considerations for her, and her reckless schemes were always subject to his litmus paper of reasonableness. The only tension between them was the natural tension provoked by their opposing natures, which, miraculously, acted in harmony – either because of FitzWilliam's resignation or Mary's subtle determination – producing an atmosphere, by some odd concatenation of opposites, of security: security on the move, forever portable.

This quiet constant was sustained in a vacuum. They had no friends, few acquaintances, no occupations, in fact nothing apart from themselves and their children to monopolize them. Time weighed heavily upon them, and they awarded themselves every justification to plunge into an unnatural preoccupation with health. John Sargent's extreme youth began as it would continue for nearly twenty years, in a household that quivered on the brink of gloom. Everyone around him possessed a chilling aura of impending doom, of either waiting to be ill or struggling to recover. For him Europe was a warehouse stacked high with specimens of infirmity. First there was his grandmother, Mary's mother. After three years abroad with her daughter and son-in-law, and their two children, she decided it was time to go home. This return journey, like FitzWilliam's, was regularly postponed. By the time the Sargents moved to the Villino in the grounds of the Palazzo Sforza outside Rome for the summer of 1858, Mrs Singer was still with them, too ill to travel. What she suffered from was only reported as long and very painful. She died in Rome the following year, aged fifty-five.*

Then, after the drawn-out anxiety over Mrs Singer had ended, another began, longer and more harrowing, this time over Emily. Her back was injured, resulting in a spinal deformity. The precise cause cannot be verified, but family tradition records that she was dropped by her nurse. FitzWilliam frequently mentions her "disease" in his letters, which would have been an acceptable euphemism to shield the truth from his parents in America. Whatever afflicted Emily in Rome in the autumn of

---

* FitzWilliam's otherwise regular letters home have not survived from this period, nor have any of Mrs Singer's to her family. Twelve years later FitzWilliam only vaguely referred to his mother-in-law's death and previous illness. The only contemporary reference is found in the autobiography of Mrs Hugh Fraser (née Mary Crawford, the daughter of the sculptor Thomas Crawford and the sister of the novelist F. Marion Crawford), *A Diplomat's Wife in Many Lands* (1911), wherein she recalled being nursed for nose-bleeds by Dr FitzWilliam Sargent, who was then living upstairs in the Villino the summer before Mrs Singer died. Mary Singer died on 12 November 1859, while she was living with the Sargents at 13 Piazza de Spagna, in a second-floor apartment, in Rome.

1860 (when she was nearly four), the manifestation was painful, for her and for her parents. They were convinced she would die. She was forced to spend her waking hours lying down. At night she was strapped to her bed to prevent her from moving. When she travelled, her bed was placed on a sprung platform to reduce the sharp, harmful jolts of the carriage. And she endured these restraints with angelic, heartrending grace – for years. She did not complain; she sang. Her spirits soared in almost divine acceptance, making her illness all the more gruelling for observers. Finally, by the summer 1862, when the Sargents came to London, Emily was taken to consult surgeons and it became clear that what had been prescribed as a remedy – enforced immobility – had caused more damage to her vertebrae than the "disease"; disuse had created the lasting deformity. Her spine was twisted, causing one of her shoulders to be slightly higher and a little more prominently forward, and she appeared to bow forward. It was a minor but obvious feature that produced an air of stiffness in her movements throughout her life. By the time she was five she was allowed to crawl, allowed to resume the activities mistakenly arrested. A year later she began to walk.

The price Emily paid for this unfortunate fact of her childhood was apparent in almost every cell of her character. Her illness delayed the standard progress of her childhood and accelerated the development of her astonishing sensitivity. She had forfeited optimism at an early age. She had been forced to replace enthusiasm with bland acceptance. She became exaggeratedly, though understandably, embarrassed about her appearance, and later she explained she was ashamed less for herself than for the people around her. The potency of her feelings alarmed her father. Nearly a decade after she began to recover, FitzWilliam wrote to his father in America (20 May 1871): "She has grown up and is a good deal deformed, and is very sensitive to her deformity; and we often think that it would have [been] better for her, in view of this sensitiveness, had she been taken to heaven when she was a mere child, and been spared a great deal of unhappiness. But she seems to have a great fund of happiness within herself, is of a pious turn of mind. . . ."[5] She retired into herself, while at the same time she depended increasingly on her family – a feature well strained after five years.

During Emily's forced convalescence Mary Sargent became unaccountably healthy. The lie was suddenly exposed. The fundamental reason for these European wanderings evaporated and nothing stood in the way of their return – but for Emily, who now shouldered the great excuse for her mother. Emily paid a very high price to help keep her parents away from America. FitzWilliam's subsequent protestations about Mary's health sounded a little hollow, but they never ceased.

II

Emily endured her long confinement amidst John's unstoppable activity. While she stayed at home learning to knit and crochet, he was taken to a gymnasium in an attempt to blunt his unbridled animation. It was as if he were sufficiently active for both of them.

John's health and energy were totally novel to the Sargent household: for too long spontaneity had been substituted by caution and all excitement had been moderated. By the time John was five years old it was clear that a more robust version of life had bounded into the subdued regime. He was incapable of sitting still. The games he played outside were re-enacted inside for the benefit of his mother and sister. No attempt was ever made to dampen his enthusiasm; FitzWilliam positively enjoyed his son's rumbustious behaviour, but also knew that any lengthy reports of it in his letters were to little purpose – he never forgot that they were abroad to improve their health, not to enjoy themselves. The ill always starred in FitzWilliam's accounts, and the healthy were passed over. And, because a slightly biased picture had to be shown to America, John was given a less than prominent place.

The job of educating the children was assumed by FitzWilliam, who was ruled by equanimity in his approach; he had the ideal qualities for a teacher – patient and gentle, always encouraging. They started off with spelling, first taught in French in deference to the Swiss nurse and then later English. John's energy did not, however, make him an ideal pupil. Studying or any other indoor stationary discipline defeated him, and FitzWilliam never tried to master this unhelpfulness. "Johnny, particularly, is much more fond of climbing & kite-flying than he is of spelling," he wrote to his mother from Nice (16 September 1861), " – and, in truth, I like him all the better for it."[1]

He was much more excited being outdoors. His eyes were as active as his limbs. He loved looking at things even, he remembered, from the age of three. His first distinct memory, he later told his cousin Mary Hale, was a brilliant porphyry cobblestone he spotted in a Florence gutter which he begged his nurse to let him see on each of his daily walks. As he grew older he was equally keen on living things. Birds, flowers, animals stirred him to such a degree that the mere mention of them in hymns or Bible readings caught his interest, which would have otherwise strayed. "He is quite a close observer of animated nature," FitzWilliam wrote in another school report to America in 1863, "so much so that, by carefully comparing what he sees with what he reads in his books, he is enabled to distinguish the birds which he sees. . . . Thus, you see, I am enabled to cultivate his memory and his observing and discriminating faculties without his being bothered with the disagreeable notion that he is actually studying, which idea, to a child, must be a great nuisance."[2] FitzWilliam was so weary of imposing education by ordeal that he allowed them to skip the tedium of Catechism – "To me the dreariest of all books,"[3] he wrote in the same letter – handing over profusely illustrated volumes of Bible stories to deal with that instruction. It was a bold move, and showed up the sympathetic turn of his character, because FitzWilliam, like all of his family, was devoutly religious. They were stalwarts of the Presbyterian Church, and more: FitzWilliam's father spread the dogma by broadcasting pamphlets, bibles, sermons far and wide in his capacity as head of the Presbyterian Publications Office, and one of FitzWilliam's younger brothers became a minister. In almost every aspect of his life the Church was never far away. Once abroad, the little social life he could claim was the product of the minor posts he held in the American Church in Nice. He lost the refinement of sectarianism, but never his strong belief in God. Religion was a wide scaffolding round his existence, to be relied upon in the many moments of exaggerated emotion and throughout his long withdrawal from activity, but was not a steadfast way of life. He did not go to church with habitual regularity, he did not need institutionalized prayer, but he turned to the Bible often and he needed to believe in some divine sense of order. He allowed reason a little more space in his scheme of values, and perhaps common sense more room than reason. It was as if the shift to Europe disrupted and disturbed yet another aspect of his previous life. And, perhaps thanks to the scepticism that had intruded on the orthodox manifestation of his beliefs, his son strayed further and grew up with no religious feelings whatsoever, save ritual.

Because FitzWilliam's teaching was born of common sense and a lot of fatherly pride he was not parsimonious with encouragement, in or out of the schoolroom. John's affection for drawing can be overestimated. His earliest surviving sketch was done when he was nearly five – a portrait of his father. FitzWilliam enclosed it in his weekly letter to his father (18 December 1860, from Nice), adding the postscript: "While I was engaged in writing to you, John has had the impertinence to take my portrait, which I enclose, thinking you will prize it."[4] The scrap of paper was prized, as a family memento, as a token of fatherly pride and as a token of grandfatherly affection for the grandson he had never seen and would never see. But neither adult could or did attach much artistic precocity to the pencil sketch; it only had meaning in the family.

Tradition credits Mary Sargent for her son's later proof of artistic ability, and such credit is not altogether wide of the truth. She was herself a keen amateur artist, putting desire well ahead of ability. She drew and painted (watercolour) with the same tenacity that grips the performance of ornamental sewing or petit point – a gentle pastime, an afternoon diversion. Her view of sketching was one that ran closer to both playing patience and documentation than to creation. She used drawing to record what they had seen and where they had been on their walks. It had a purpose. But she did lay down one instruction that belied her own casual attitude: at least one picture must be finished, regardless of quality. It was an invaluable lesson. Mary's view was more potent than her husband's simply because she enforced it. FitzWilliam's skill was greater than hers and sadly discarded. When, in 1848, he published his *On Bandaging, and Other Operations of Minor Surgery* (for many years the standard text, which went into many editions and was used on the field of battle during the Civil War) he supplied the numerous illustrations which were models of precision and clarity. He showed that he, too, had a place – a minor place – in the history of his son's ability. After the appearance of the manual, it seems, FitzWilliam gave up drawing altogether. Still, both parents promoted the idea that there was nothing peculiar about drawing or painting, which was rare. To them such an activity was as much a part of life as reading or playing the piano – and, in their perpetual wanderings, a very important part of life. It helped to fill the time. It made up for the absence of friends. It was something to do. Yet it was inestimably valuable that they should smile on the pursuit; the oblique and indirect reason was unimportant. Mary gave her blessing less by example than by attitude, and it was an attitude she pushed while FitzWilliam quietly nodded. Her sponsorship was direct, even at this early stage. She gave John sketchbooks and later annotated his entries with the date and place. She led him to sights. She coaxed him to be ambitious, to sketch broad vistas, and not to be intimidated. This tuition, unlike FitzWilliam's role of teacher, also had a considerable importance for herself: it was a positive expression, more positive than her unquenchable restlessness and indistinct illnesses, that spoke loudly for everything she believed had been muffled, denied and sacrificed in her own life – her independence – but could only be regained second-hand, through her son. Though she had managed exile, she needed more, but she only had the sphere of family to enact whatever it might be. It was the first clue that the Sargents taught themselves the most indirect language to communicate motives and emotions. Sooner or later, her children subscribed to a vocabulary of codes; they, too, distrusted any direct statement of their feelings – it was the penalty of having been obliged to endure a life built on a lie.

The double edge ran through every aspect of the Sargents' history abroad. The artificiality that had been imposed upon the children was enacted as a contest between advantage and disadvantage; the gains and sacrifices of the parents were weighed and measured and never quite counterbalanced. John, alone among the children, was untainted by prolonged or serious illness. This good fortune made him peculiar. He was unique, in a family that was so tightly bound together there was a suffocating want of perspective. They were so self-absorbed they had no inkling of normality. His parents did not know what to make of him; they overestimated the speed and level of his development. Instead of being normal, he was perfect, and all because he was the only example of a healthy child FitzWilliam and Mary knew for nearly a decade and a half.

Mary's reaction to her children was strangely contradictory: while she depended on illness herself, she was incapable of facing it in them. During Emily's convalescence she withdrew, leaving them to the ministrations of her husband. FitzWilliam, it is fair to say, shook himself out of lethargy and came alive when confronted with illness. Emily's care was entrusted almost exclusively to him, with heartrending consequences. When he was preparing to sail home to see his parents again after eleven years (and, as it turned out, his mother for the last time) Emily grew increasingly distressed. "Poor little Emily, whose 'right-hand-man' I have been for so long," FitzWilliam wrote to his father from Biarritz (27 May 1865), "finds it difficult to understand that she is to exist without me; she spends most of the day asking, between her tears, how long I shall be gone, if the ocean will be very rough, if steamers are very strong. . . ."[5] Faced with illness, Mary shut herself off and FitzWilliam assumed his only occupation, with the net result that within the tiny orbit of the family opposites attracted. FitzWilliam displayed uncharacteristic energy, and his wife withstood another bout of her allergy to domestic and emotional obligation. And there was scarcely ever a break in this declension. They revolved in a steady, merciless cycle from illness to death. Five years after Mrs Singer died, they braced themselves for the inevitable loss of their second daughter. FitzWilliam noted with clinical exactness Minnie's pleurisy and bronchial infection that had left her weak, pale, thin – "a withered flower", he wrote to his mother.[6] They took her to be photographed so they might have some souvenir of her short life. Shortly after her fourth birthday they took her to Pau, where, alas, the weather was worse than Nice, and the prospect of any recovery quickly faded. John looked on helplessly. "Poor little Minnie is getting thinner every day," he wrote to a friend from Pau (16 April 1865). "She does not care for anything any more. Emily and I bought her some beautiful Easter eggs but she did not look at them. She never talks nor smiles now."[7] Two days later she died. The effect on the family was one of degree – they travelled even more, first to Spain, then to Biarritz where FitzWilliam left them for America, Switzerland, London, Luz, Paris, and finally Nice.

Minnie's death coincided almost to the day with the end of the American Civil War. For the Sargents, like other expatriate Americans, the great, emotionally charged spectator sport was at an end. For years they had lived on long-out-of-date newspaper reports, much interrupted transatlantic mail, and uncertain financial transactions. The connection to their native country, already made fragile by distance, became thinner during the years of crisis. Still, the expatriate reaction ran to extremes, displaying a keener sense of drama than understanding; partisan feelings were feverishly expressed. FitzWilliam told his mother of one American lady living in Nice who unfurled the Confederate flag from her window to celebrate each Union defeat – and mystify the Niçois. For FitzWilliam the war was yet another unhappy reminder of his separation from home, made sadder by the misunderstanding and ignorance he observed around him. His sense of patriotism was accentuated, and he rose to America's defence; in May 1863 he published a pamphlet entitled *England, the United States, and the Southern Confederacy* – what H. G. Wells later called a "Great Think". For someone who remained icily placid in personal turmoil, steadily unruffled, the appearance of such an elaborate argument was surprising. It was his reply to the popular and official support for the South in England which he read and heard about constantly in Nice.

He put on his most scholarly clothes to address his readers: "My desire is to evoke reason, not stir up passion and prejudice," he wrote in the middle of his treatise.[8] By 1863 he came to believe, and cherish the idea, that the war was being fought for the highest ideals: to abolish slavery and preserve the Constitution, which meant Union, though two years before he was so appalled by "this causeless war" he actively supported the idea of letting the southern states secede. English sympathy for the rebel cause, he claimed, was nothing more than lowly self-interest, in order to maintain the supply of cotton and save her emptying mills. FitzWilliam was shocked by this lack of vision and the historical inconsistency in England. He set about to correct the error, both by economic and political reasoning.

FitzWilliam was an unexpected spokesman, speaking from an unexpected quarter, "in so small a place as Nice",[9] relying on faulty sources: "I had not any surplus of materials," he confessed to his mother (12 May 1863), which did not matter as his intended audience was equally ill-informed: "It was intended particularly for English readers, in order to give them a more correct idea of the real questions involved in the contest than they seem to possess, or to be willing to acknowledge, as yet. It is my first attempt at political writing, and I shall not be surprised if it be not praised by the public at large."[10] His prediction was correct. The 125-page pamphlet was nearly totally ignored by the general public, though a second and much expanded edition, enlarging on the economic factors of slave labour, was published the following year, as well as a French translation, *Les états confédérés et l'esclavage*, which was a peculiar rendering of the original title, deliberately misleading in order to interest the French.

FitzWilliam's short, surprising "Great Think" was over. He never suffered another attack, and retired to the safety of domesticity once again, without ever re-emerging.

Mary looked on such a vigorous and brisk itinerary after Minnie's death as perfectly ordinary; after twelve years of such an unaltered routine she was eager for another twelve. Yet in the mid-1860s the Sargents' attachment to the idea of constant travel underwent a slight change; by their standards they "settled down", which only meant they returned to the same house for a few consecutive winters – a second-floor apartment in the Maison Virello, rue Grimaldi, Nice – and tried to limit their summer stops to three or four places. All their possessions still had to be packed and unpacked several times every year. Their rooms were heavy with the fragrance of camphor and peppercorns. FitzWilliam could not share his wife's appreciation for mobile quarterings nor did he think the reappearance of Nice much of an improvement. He held on to a fading belief that they would eventually return to Philadelphia and pick up where they had left off in 1854. Since then his family might have grown, but there was no other advance, and no replacement. He sighed to his brother (24 November) [1869] the vague summary of fifteen years abroad: "we lead a very quiet sort of life, balancing between winter-quarters and a summering place; we have very few acquaintances . . .".[11] There was no spark of enthusiasm behind his words, less pride, and only the weak timbre of resignation. And despite their parents' contradictory appreciation John and Emily calmly accepted their manner of life to be the natural state of affairs, untainted by any oddity or irregularity. Because they had known nothing else, it was also perfectly reasonable to find the same collection of people wherever they went, summer or winter. John and Emily spent their childhood surrounded by invalids and exiles, people expecting death at any moment and avoiding their native countries to do so. And such a population was rich in eccentricity, having drawn liberally on self-indulgence.

In 1866 the Sargents' narrow circle of acquaintances expanded when they met the Pagets and George Bemis. Matilda Paget (née Abadam) was a Scotswoman with an iron-clad, unattractive character, and she reserved its full strength for those least capable of dealing with her – her family. She had not found much pleasure in marriage and was strikingly unimaginative with her independence. She had been widowed soon after the birth of her son, and left England for the security of her brother in France. This tidy arrangement lasted for close on a decade, until her brother died, when she looked round for another source of protection and took the nearest candidate, unenterprisingly taking her son's tutor, Henry Ferguson Paget, for her second husband. A year later, at the age of forty-one, she gave birth to her second child, Violet (1856–1935), who became better-known as the writer Vernon Lee. Thereafter Mrs Paget reckoned she could be let off any further obligations, and forthwith ignored her husband, who was only too pleased to be let off. He found no difficulty making himself scarce: fishing, eating, walking, hunting were more than adequate compensations – so much so that few people knew what he looked like. And thus, more or less set free, Mrs Paget came into her own, which was not to say much. She detested the Church and society, the only features that might have populated her purposeless expatriate life. She said she came abroad to escape the injurious effects of the English Sunday. She saw no one and moved across the Continent in sublime isolation. Had she and her husband enjoyed more comfortable personalities their family life might not have been so deadly, which has been appropriately described as "Schopenhauerian hedgehogs coming together for warmth, all their prickles bristling".[12]

Mrs Paget was interested in nothing but her son, and made the fact painfully clear to her daughter. As a result, both her children took their revenge by odd methods. Eugene Lee-Hamilton first gained distinction by resigning from what looked to be a promising career as a diplomatist, and going to bed from 1875 to 1896. He turned his mother and sister into nurses, and turned himself into a poet as well as a friend of Henry James and Paul Bourget. When his mother died, he leapt out of bed, fully recovered, as if to confirm she alone had been his ailment.

His sister also scored a hollow sort of victory over her mother. Violet was energetic from the start. She threw herself at her books with overburdened conviction; she insisted that learning be the warmth and affection denied her. If anyone ever wore blue stockings, Violet Paget put on two pairs. She turned herself into one of the best-educated and most severely intellectual figures of her day – and one of the most obnoxious, in French, Italian or English. She had a talent for emptying rooms, a real gift for making enemies and very little ability in keeping friends, and all because she wanted attention. She was, quite simply, too eager or too desperate (or both) for her own good. Unwittingly, she more than satisfied her mother's opinion. Her appearance was not much of an asset either: she looked a sleek rodent, eyes glistening, nose twitching, hot on the trail of some tantalizing aroma, impatient and utterly singleminded. She produced some thirty books, a mountain range of fiction, philosophy, criticism, history, aesthetics – indeed, nothing was safe from her attack – all tremendously high-minded, long-winded, respected and now undusted on library shelves. She worked and fought hard for her niche in the history of English letters, and it was with a stamina developed from her early childhood.

Violet Paget met the Sargents in Nice in 1866; and, though Emily was three months younger and John ten months older, she and John affectionately referred to each other as "my twin". Violet was swift to latch on to them, not only because they seemed normal but because they, too, were desperate for friends. She won a place in their household and their hearts simply by the absence of competition. She was their only steady companion for the next couple of years.

The atmosphere at Maison Virello was a mirror-image of everything Violet had experienced in her own home. Where Violet's mother withered then disappeared at the prospect of entertaining her daughter, Mrs Sargent unexpectedly blossomed in the society of her children. Where Violet's father ambled to the station restaurant for his solitary lunch not to be seen for the rest of the day, FitzWilliam was an unavoidable (though silent) presence. The Sargents appeared to be doing the impossible: *enjoying* themselves. Violet joined in their family life as if she were another daughter. And Violet's intense appreciation started the wheels of Sargent mythology in motion, elevating Mrs Sargent higher than surrogate mother, to a nice combination of genius-heroine-goddess. Any warm memories Violet would keep of her childhood were the work of Mrs Sargent, and part of the elaborate revenge on her mother.

The three children played together easily, either in a neighbouring garden in rue Grimaldi or in the Pagets' garden. Some sixty years later Violet remembered that they performed historical charades of the execution of Mary Queen of Scots or the Earl of Essex. They sailed boats in the pond, and FitzWilliam took John to visit the American ships in port at Nice. After the Civil War the American Navy showed itself abroad to reassure unsteady allies worried about the future. The Sargents became acquainted with some of the officers, who were a welcome addition to Nice society. This interest led Violet to believe that John, aged ten, had a career in the Navy mapped out, though nothing could have been further from the truth. When the Pagets were in Rome the same winter as the Sargents (1868-9) the children trailed behind Mrs Sargent in the afternoons, painting. Violet's efforts had all the enthusiasm she could muster, which was a lot. Her attempts were ambitious and messy. She used up quantities of colour and paper. John, she recalled, was more subdued. He worked with care and patience, preferring to draw first, then colour. At home he copied illustrations from the *Illustrated London News*. Ships, broad landscapes, exotic animals and mountain ranges found in *Baedeker* caught his fancy. His outdoor work was much the same, following his mother's, recording what he saw as precisely as he could. The accuracy and attention to detail in these early drawings were remarkable, and inconsistent with the boisterous high spirits FitzWilliam recorded. These drawings show an ability for reproduction and an unwillingness to use imagination, or to take any short-cut away from precision. He took none of the leaps evident in probably all of Violet's pictures; he preferred exactness to originality.[13]

The appearance of George Bemis was less spirited than Violet Paget's, and beneficial mostly to FitzWilliam.* Bemis was a bachelor who had

---

* George Bemis (1816-78) was educated at Harvard College and Harvard Law School before being admitted to the Bar in 1839. Though he was obliged to give up his career, he never did so quite so comprehensively as FitzWilliam. Apart from Boston news, he and FitzWilliam shared an extreme interest in American politics, though most of FitzWilliam's information came through English newspapers.

Bemis's affection for FitzWilliam was expressed after his death. Dr Sargent attended him with devoted loyalty during his final illness, and as a token of appreciation Bemis left him $10,000, an enormous sum of money, nearly a quarter of a million by modern values. Another provision in Bemis's Will was the creation of the Bemis Professorship of International Law at Harvard.

come to Europe from Boston to die, or to help to postpone that eventuality, and while waiting he became one of FitzWilliam's closest companions. This friendship exposed the low relief of FitzWilliam's character, its utter uniformity in and away from his family. Bemis had the sort of mind FitzWilliam admired – clear, brilliant, unblurred by too much emotion and profoundly interested in gossip. He was four years older than FitzWilliam and had had a brilliant career in the law, reforming the Massachusetts penal system and becoming an expert in criminal law. In 1844 he established his reputation by using insanity as a defence for murder. In 1858, however, poor health compelled him to leave Boston and retire from practice. Once abroad, he turned his mind to international law and published several pamphlets on the legal foundation of American foreign policy. Unlike FitzWilliam, he frequently returned to Boston and Cambridge, and maintained a huge correspondence that kept him well informed of the activities and misdeeds of the relatives of the people he met abroad. His friendship had the added attraction of being a highly select newspaper. And he had the distinction of being FitzWilliam's *only* friend.

Bemis found FitzWilliam at best taciturn, and FitzWilliam himself was not one to deny this fault: "I am not, and never was, much given to talking," he wrote to his father (21 February 1865)[14] – which at least made him a good audience. Bemis was not able to admit that he found his new friend "a very lively or mirthful sort of man but [he] is always up to the level of equanimity & ready to do anything to improve my comfort or pleasure" as he wrote to his brother (18 February 1869).[15] But FitzWilliam did have the advantage of four years' European experience on Bemis, a sham domestic life, and no occupation to absorb his time. Bemis dined with the Sargents *en famille*, and went out riding with FitzWilliam every day, when not tortured by dizziness. Their friendship depended on the rarity of companionship, not on intimacy, and for FitzWilliam this alone was a welcome novelty, a diversion from the family life that had monopolized him for so many years.

But it was a temporary release. By the time John was ten and Emily nine, there was no apparent impediment to undertaking the homeward voyage – save that Mary was once again pregnant. Minnie's death the year before was fresh in her mind, and her optimism had collapsed. She instructed FitzWilliam, as her confinement approached, not to mention the fact in his letters. He shared her feelings. On 7 March 1867 he announced to his father from Nice the birth of their second son, adding ominously: "I think for his own sake, the sooner he goes to heaven the better. And yet I am very fond of babies."[16] The child was named FitzWilliam Winthrop; the first John had narrowly missed and the second, honouring his paternal grandfather, had also been Minnie's. Mary and FitzWilliam's forebodings were sadly realized. FitzWilliam Winthrop lived twenty-eight months. Seven months after his death, on 9 February 1870, Mary gave birth in Florence to another daughter. This time they strayed from family tradition, named her Violet, after Violet Paget, her godmother.

FitzWilliam had celebrated Emily's birth by resigning from the Wills Hospital; similarly, he honoured his youngest daughter by sending his microscope and medical books back to America, effectively giving up the pretence he would ever again resume his profession. Violet was fourteen years younger than John and thirteen years younger than Emily. She, too, thwarted mortality, outliving her brother by thirty years and her sister by seventeen. And through her alone Mary and FitzWilliam's line continued. As Mrs Francis Ormond she had six children, six grandchildren, and fifteen great-grandchildren.

III

John's education, like much of his childhood, was obscured by illnesses and deaths; it was also at the mercy of his parents' idea of stability, and their idea of stability was attached more to physical than to intellectual improvement. Though they continued to return to Nice each winter throughout the 1860s – for Emily's sake, FitzWilliam felt obliged to explain – such regularity made them so restless they could hardly wait for the spring to be off. In May 1867 they hastened to Paris for a month before embarking on a major tour of the Rhineland. The next year they left in March, for Spain and Gibraltar prior to retiring to the Pyrenees. In 1868 they could not last out the winter, and the following year they could not even face returning to Maison Virello to pack up: FitzWilliam was sent to dispatch their goods on to Florence.

In 1868, the year before Nice was given up altogether, John was given his first and highly abbreviated introduction to school. He was nearly thirteen. He attended a small establishment run by an English clergyman and his wife. FitzWilliam at once boasted (15 November 1868) "we think he is very well launch^d in the world"[1] and then withdrew him a week later when they moved to Rome. Thereafter John returned to education by *Baedeker* and *Murray's* for another year. His sketchbooks record a tourist's tuition: Rome, Tivoli, Frascati, Pompeii, Vesuvius, Capri, Naples, Sorrento, Ancona, Rimini, Pontresina, St Moritz, Alpine passes – all between the spring and early autumn of 1869.

The problem of educating John was one of the casualties of the larger conflict between his parents: the old exhausted argument of abroad versus America. Even by the time John was eleven, Mary heartily affirmed that Europe itself was sufficient education for her son. Sightseeing provided all the stimuli and nourishment he could need. In one of her rare letters to her mother-in-law (20 October 1867) Mary wrote that John "is getting old enough to enjoy and appreciate the beauties of nature and art, which are lavishly displayed in these old lands. He sketches quite nicely, & has a remarkably quick and correct eye. If we could afford to give him really good lessons, he would soon be quite a little artist. Thus far he has never had any instruction. . . ."[2] Mary relied on her own mother's belief that travel alone, without the larding considerations of health, *was* education. She never wavered from the conviction, which happened to be entirely compatible with what she herself wanted. FitzWilliam's more orthodox views were largely dismissed. By their eighth winter in Nice she declared the place had become denuded of all interest, educationally delapidated. Rome, she said, would renew the children's curiosity (while restoring her and FitzWilliam's health). Rome would become their school. So, the third week in November 1868, the Sargents returned to Rome after a decade's absence, settling into a one-storey house, full of windows looking over the panorama of the city, at 17 Trinità de' Monti, atop the Piazza di Spagna, near the apartment where Mrs Singer had died in 1859.

Rome enjoyed a compelling attraction for Americans. New Englanders were particularly susceptible to the intoxication of antiquity. They were able to overlook the filth and the malaria that raged in the warmer months. They found the Forum interesting under weeds, groundsel and ivy (the excavations were thirty years off). The Campagna was wild and desolate with foxes and pigs roaming freely, "where the soil is composed largely of the 'dust of ages'," FitzWilliam wrote (10 May 1869), "of dead mens' bones and all infirmities temperal & clerical".[3] The Vatican was in the death throes of absolute power and supplied the town with a wonderful show of ecclesiastical uniforms and carriages. Altogether Rome presented a potent draught of romanticism, a strong antidote to Boston severity. Hawthorne summed it up neatly in the preface to his novel *Transformation* (*The Marble Faun*) in 1860: "a sort of poetic or fairy precinct, where actualities would not be so terribly insisted upon as they are, and must needs be, in America. . . . Romance and poetry, ivy, lichens, and wall-flowers, need ruin to make them grow."[4] Americans came to become artists. They came to avoid the philistinism they sensed at home. They came, as Henry James explained half a century later in 1903, full of a "fine bewilderment". But most of all they came because "the fineness of Rome was exactly in the quality of amusement".[5] The atmosphere was generously hospitable to idleness – " 'dolce far niente' is not understood in Boston as it is practiced here", FitzWilliam confided to Bemis (20 August 1867)[6] – to the same degree that work dominated the climate at home. In Rome the Sargents witnessed the supreme example of expatriate American life, and it eventually sent them packing.

Still, Rome's major attraction was that it was not Nice. The Sargents found themselves surrounded by a society of displaced Bostonians used by Hawthorne for *The Marble Faun* a decade earlier. The community was superintended by William Wetmore Story (1819–95), lawyer turned sculptor, sculptor turned man of letters, who had set himself up in both suffocating luxury at the Palazzo Barbarini and an impenetrable region of pretension. Henry James was first dazzled by him, then forced to conclude: "his course . . . was almost the monotony of the great extremes of ease. Nothing really happened to him."[7] There was Harriet Hosmer (1830–1908) whose skill as a sculptor was outclassed by her eccentricity that entailed, among other things, importing hounds from England and riding through the streets at night at a cracking pace. There was Miss

Hosmer's singular friend, Charlotte Cushman (1816–76), an actress of uncompromising ugliness who began her stage career at eighteen playing Lady Macbeth, went on to play male roles convincingly, and gave farewell performances for the best part of a decade. Other residents were Randolph Rogers (1825–92), a sculptor given to celebrating great moments in American history in his Roman studio – the "Columbus Doors" for the Capitol in Washington and "Emancipation" for the Detroit Monument; John Rollin Tilton (1824–85), who executed gentle water-colours of European landscapes which sold like hot cakes to American tourists; and Henry Wadsworth Longfellow, who was taking a short break from his fame at home during the winter of 1868–9.

These artists were sustaining the tradition begun by Horatio Greenough and Thomas Crawford. All of them (save Longfellow) turned their backs on America, yet depended on her for commissions, success, fame and money. They remained abroad but found recognition in their native country. They tried to annex centuries of history, and only by employing the distinctly American qualities of brute perseverance and industry were they able to succeed. The surface of their lives was so engaging, the *Dictionary of American Biography* could not resist pointing out that Story was an indefatigable host to nobility and Harriet Hosmer was a friend of both the Queen of Naples and the Empress of Austria; in other words, they had triumphed in the great world and such social achievement refuted the incomprehensible "dolce far niente".

Violet Paget was sucked into this Roman world as if it were some great vacuum, designed to unsettle her. She was drawn in, excitedly hurtled around, and emerged, she claimed, never the same again. This swift transformation was entirely the work of Mrs Sargent – "the high priestess of them all [the *genius loci*], the most favoured and inspired votary of the Spirit of Localities, she who averred that the happiest moment in life was in a hotel 'bus – no other, in short, than the enchanting, indomitable, incomparable Mrs. S[argent]," Violet wrote two years after Mrs Sargent's death.[8] Mary Sargent merely continued to do in Rome what she had done across the entire continent of Europe: refuse to sit still. And for Violet, who was caught up in her wake along with John and Emily, it was an unending procession of delight, both outside and inside. Mrs Sargent dragged the children from church to museum, from palace to garden, and back again; she looked, she pointed, she stared, she talked, she sketched. It was perpetual motion, and it was a manifestation of boundless curiosity – precisely what Violet's own mother (and father) lacked. The Pagets had a gift for oblivion, no matter where they were. All of Europe fused into one vast ignored territory. When they went for walks their heads were buried in books, or with unerring skill they turned their backs on breathtaking scenery; "sights" were for other, less discriminating, travel-lers. Deifying Mrs Sargent might have been an exaggeration, but Violet was highly impressionable. She had not had, unlike John and Emily, a lifetime of this routine.

By comparison John's reaction to Rome was restrained. For him the town was just another stop on the vast itinerary that was his childhood. He repaid Violet's compliment to his mother by agreeing with *her* mother: for him Rome was no greater place than Nice, or Florence, or the Pyrenees, or Bohemia, or Spain – it was simply a great expanse of playground, slightly more interesting perhaps.

There were, however, amazing sights: "scamperings, barely restrained by responsible elders, through icy miles of Vatican galleries, to make hurried forbidden sketches of statues selected for easy portrayal"; smoky, dimly illuminated churches with an ethereal lilt of soprano and organ; early-morning mass crowded in St Peter's among the biscuit-chomping devout; an occasional glimpse of Pio Nono himself wrapped in an enormous white sash. From the Pagets' apartment the children were able to gape at other Vatican eminences attired in fantastic, near-pantomime splendour complete with scarlet umbrellas of state processing in and out of the Collegio di Propaganda Fide opposite. Or John, Emily and Violet studied the progress of the cookshop porter delivering their dinner. He weaved with great assurance, balancing on his head a tin hot-box crowned with a cream and savoy-finger confection of charlotte russe, ordered especially for them. Or Violet, accompanied by her nurse, ascended the Spanish Steps to 17 Trinità de' Monti to watch things she found more entrancing: a dinner-party. There she saw "cabs and *vetture di remessa*, drawn up outside", delivering Hawthorne's prototypes for *The Marble Faun*, the people "we children were perpetually reading about"[9] – Harriet Hosmer, Randolph Rogers, W. W. Story, who were as much a tourist attraction as the Sistine Chapel.

These visitors were also the very people Violet elevated beyond scenery to catalyst in John's education. Sixty years later (and four months after John's death) she wrote in her memorial essay, "J.S.S.: *In Memoriam*", an account of events that winter that strayed wide of the truth. She claimed Mary was uncertain about John's talent and FitzWilliam stuck fast to the idea of the Navy; in short, neither parent had sufficient vision to spot what was patently obvious to her at the age of twelve, and to these dinner-guests who unanimously voiced recognition of John's skill when his sketches were passed round the drawing-room. It was their intervention that steered John in the direction of the studio; it was a neat solution to a problem that never existed.[10] His parents were convinced of his potential, but this conviction was victim to their notions of more important things.

While in Rome, John's education lurched ahead along its haphazard, lazy course. He went to "study" in the studio of a "Germanico-American Artist of reputation", as FitzWilliam later referred to Carl Welsch.*[11] Years

* Welsch remains the sort of figure who gives a biographer nightmares. Very little is known about him; there is no proof that the Sargents actually did know him, and that he did instruct the thirteen-year-old Sargent as Charteris claims in his

later John explained the nature of this tutelage: he "made free of the studio . . . was kept busy fetching and carrying beer and wine from the nearest wine shops".[12] In the mornings, however, he copied his master's watercolours with painstaking care.

FitzWilliam wearied of trying to believe that trailing after Mary could possibly counterfeit real education. By 1869 he felt he had consented to it long enough. "I wish I was near a good school for boys," he wrote to his sister from St Moritz (20 September 1869), "for my boy is now thirteen years old and is tolerably advanced in ignorance."[13] He also knew that any solution would be difficult, and painful. "I shall have to pack him off from us soon to some good school somewhere . . . he will have to go to England or to Germany, I presume."[14] FitzWilliam was convinced that John must be exposed to some other influence than the exclusive atmosphere of family.

Mary flinched at the prospect. She "dreads the idea of sending her first-born son away from her", FitzWilliam explained to his mother (18 October) [1869], ". . . and I think it is a pity . . ."[14]. John stayed with them, through Italy, up and down the Alps, through Switzerland, and two more winters in Florence, where he did attend some classes at the Bargello.[15] FitzWilliam postponed taking action again for two years.

But Mary's eccentric version of education provided one unseen and scarcely apparent advantage – the advantage of dullness. As "home" followed unbracing climates, the Sargents roamed among the least-stimulating towns in Europe, with the attendant society of the infirm and elderly. Rome had been the glaring exception in nearly fifteen years. John and Emily grew up in total isolation. They had no idea who they might see again from one year to the next. They were nurtured on physical dislocation. They grew up in a strange vacuum, alone and restrained by the mere geography of their childhood. They could only depend upon themselves for entertainment and their parents for encouragement. Yet somehow they both thrived; they turned limitation to asset. What they

---

biography (p. 10): "Sargent used to spend the mornings in copying the water-colours of Welsch." Welsch was in Rome that winter, but if he did offer to teach John it was probably later, in Florence. Charteris *did* get his information from Emily, but after the biography appeared she complained to her sister of the numerous errors.

Charles Feodor Welsch (né Karl Friedrich Christian Welsch) was born in Wesel, 1828, the son of a painter and restorer and the brother of a muralist. He was first trained at home by his father, then in Brussels, The Hague, and in Paris under Ziem and Calamé. He went to America for eight years, and settled in Rome from 1866 to 1874. His subsequent itinerary covered Egypt, Venice, Paris, Karlsruhe, Baden Baden, Frankfurt and Dresden, where he died in 1904. He illustrated books and exhibited twice at the Royal Academy, in 1871 and 1873. He and John did go on a walking tour of the Tyrol in the summer of 1871. FitzWilliam's few references to him call him either an "Artist friend from Rome" or a "German landscape painter of reputation", but never by name.

lacked in systematic, formal education they made up in confidence, a confidence bred by independence. They had to look to themselves to satisfy curiosity. They had to supply their own excitement. They could rely on no one. And they were free of any artificial measure of success or failure, having no idea what was *expected*. They grew to appreciate this solitary condition to be normal. In adulthood John's devotion to independence was absolute and almost obsessive.

They learnt to negotiate loneliness; it was neither odd nor an enemy but, rather, the basic element of their childhood, which strengthened family ties to near-breaking. They learnt to value perseverance, developing private skills at a precocious age. John was highly literate even at the age of nine. His letters (in English) are stiffly precise, full of detail and observation, befitting travel-notes, like his sketchbooks. When Emily gave him a copy of *Paradise Lost* for Christmas 1869, he read it for pleasure, not as a duty. He mastered the mandoline and the piano, and he wrote to Violet Paget from Florence (23 April 1870), "On the piano (which I am getting to hate) I am playing Mendelsson, Beethoven, Schubert, etc. (superb isn't it!)"[16] He thought nothing of walking for hours to sketch a sight. And the only area in which he might have been accused of laziness was his vanity. He cared nothing for his clothes. They were constantly in disarray, torn, crumpled far too quickly for FitzWilliam's liking. And his cravats were a particularly vexing problem.

As "home" was also intensely mobile, ignorant of national frontiers, John and Emily did not know the impediment of "foreign" languages. Mary and FitzWilliam spoke English at home; the servants spoke French, Italian, German or Spanish. In Nice, John had been taught by an Englishman, and in Florence (1869–70) by a Frenchman in a small school for the sons of Italian aristocrats. He was undaunted by a new town or country. Each place unfolded before him, revealing new examples of architecture, landscape, art and flora. Whereas his mother looked at the map of Europe as an index to spas, John saw it as an index to museums, sights, excitement. His development, though guided in a disorderly fashion, was improved by the absence of schoolrooms. Mary's plan was bold, selfish, and on the whole appeared to be hugely successful. Mary could look at her son's pronounced accomplishments in music, literature, languages and art to dismiss FitzWilliam's persistent belief that "home" was not the best place for their son. The wonderfully subtle flaws and the grave failure of the system were not so obvious, would take years to surface, and then never resubmerge.

While he was a student at M. Joseph Domengé's day-school (located in the former Convent I Servi di Maria in the Piazza della SS Annunziata) John also took dancing lessons in the house at 43 via Romana. One day an elderly lady resident of the house was asked to play the piano for the class. "Presently a handsome old lady dressed in black silk came into the room. He [John] noted a certain faded elegance about her. . . ."[17] She was Claire Clairmont (1798–1879), Mary Shelley's stepsister, who had joined the Shelley household on their elopement from England in 1814. Two years later she met Byron, by whom she had a daughter, Allegra, in 1817. She took music lessons in Rome, was said to possess a beautiful voice, and eventually became music tutor to a Russian family in Moscow in 1824. For the twenty years before she settled in Florence she wandered across Europe, working as a governess.

A few years after John saw her, the events that James later immortalized in *The Aspern Papers* began to unfold. In 1876 she began to be pursued by a Shelley fanatic, an American, Captain Edward Augustus Silsbee (1826–1900), who longed to own papers.[18] He moved into via Romana, conscientiously copied out poems by Shelley and Mary Shelley, and made florid declarations of loyalty, complete with offers of financial support, to Miss Clairmont and her niece, Paula Clairmont (1824–?1885). As luck would have it, Silsbee was unfortunately in America when Claire Clairmont died, and he immediately rushed back to Florence. Paula inherited her aunt's papers and said they could be Silsbee's on one condition – Silsbee must marry her. He found this impossible.

The Sargents knew Silsbee slightly. FitzWilliam's cousin, Turner Sargent, wrote to George Bemis on 29 January 1877:

> Yes, I know Silsbee, living a false life: his father made the fatal mistake of sending all of his sons who are practical to College, & my friend who is thoroughly impractical, to Sea, & made him a Captain: the upshot of it was that Silsbee after 2 or 3 voyages of great length, pulled up at Trieste, sold the whole concern, & "flew to Venice" . . . & stayed a long time; when he returned, he talked of nothing but Art & Poetry & made his practical family mad, & was christened "Heavy Venice". . . . He had quite a gift of language, but as he has not been thoroughly educated he cannot become what his ambition desires, an Essayist, so he frets. . . . Italy is the best place for him.[19]

James got the Silsbee story from Eugene Lee-Hamilton, who had heard it from John.

FitzWilliam returned to the problem of John's education with a tenacity that had been born of frustration. "We are moving on in our usual grooves," he sighed to his mother (7 April 1870) with accuracy and a rare gift for the obvious.[20] These usual grooves were well worn. After having traded Nice for Florence in the winter, their energies were consumed by the tired predicament of trying to match temperature to health. They found Venice too hot and then rushed through the St Gothard pass to cooler air. John and his father went on a three-week walking tour of mountains and glaciers, stopping often enough to fill sketchbooks – later labelled by Mary "Splendid water-colours"[21] – before meeting up with the women of the family in Interlaken. Emily contracted remittent fever and Violet, scarcely six months old, was undergoing trial by wet-nurse – a standard feature of Sargent infancy – before graduating to cow's milk. The rest of the summer they moved up and down the Alps. Then back to

Florence, a new apartment, and more of the usual grooves at the beginning of October. The repeated pattern of their annual calendar was precisely why FitzWilliam had pressed for boarding-school. He and his wife allowed the education battle to go on for years because there had been no victory, or defeat, or stalemate – only sustained postponement. By the late summer of 1871, FitzWilliam took a radical step, displaying uncharacteristic strength, resolve and determination, and about the worst possible judgement: the whole family would move to Dresden for the winter.

The scheme cut straight across the long-standing excuse for not returning to America: the unsuitability of the harsh New England weather. The choice showed that he was now determined to indulge in long-term planning at the expense of health. Altogether, FitzWilliam's decision was startling. He selected Dresden over London (too expensive) and Paris (under siege) because Germany was reckoned to have the best schools in Europe and Dresden the best in Germany. Dresden also boasted a large expatriate community and was dubbed "German Florence". The same could not be said of the climate.

FitzWilliam's sudden resolution might have been produced entirely by battle-fatigue, or boredom with postponement especially as John was nearly sixteen, or by something totally unconnected with either condition. His mother died, aged seventy-nine, in April 1871. If eighteen years abroad had not cut him adrift from America, his mother's death more assuredly did so. It jolted him. The fading hope that John would, one day, return with him to America was finally extinguished. He had allowed that fanciful idea to obliterate practical reality for too long, and he was determined that his son's fate would not be determined by his own lethargy. This conviction called for action, and the entire family fell into line.

"The cold has not hurt any of us yet," FitzWilliam wrote to his father on 3 January 1872, addressing himself to the fundamental flaw in his experiment. But the fact that the school term began at Easter, and provided John could pass the entrance examination to Das Gymnasium zum heiligen Kreuz, surviving one winter would not be enough. "Indeed, Emily, who used to suffer a great deal from frost-bite, in the feet, has been quite free from it here."[22] She and John learnt to ice-skate. The apartment at 2 Weinerstrasse was kept comfortably warm on the coldest days by an enormous porcelain stove. John's course of tutoring – in Latin, Greek, mathematics, geography, history and German ("in which latter subject he is particularly deficient", FitzWilliam explained[23]) – progressed admirably, thus supplying reasons for optimism.

By the middle of January, nearly three months after their arrival in Dresden, hope foundered. Emily fell dangerously ill. Her remittent fever came back, added to which were peritonitis and inflammation of the tonsils. FitzWilliam and Mary nursed her day and night, and she only seemed to get worse. Emily and her parents prepared for the inevitable.

"She made various little dispositions of her goods & chattels," FitzWilliam wrote in his birthday letter, 17 January 1872, "told me that she had a 20 franc piece in her Porte-Monnaie which she would like me to give to the poor-box on the old market-place of Dresden; arranged for her Canary-bird . . . and said to her mother, 'Mamma, I have thought of a verse which I believe will comfort you, when I am gone, "In the world ye shall have tribulation; but be of good cheer, I have overcome the world." ' She said she was not afraid to die . . .".[24] Her astonishingly angelic resignation moved her family, while they grew more and more frightened. Mercifully, as in 1860, their forebodings were not realized. Towards the middle of February she began to recover. She was pitifully thin and feeble for weeks. The uncertainty of recovery lingered, however, and with it the growing certainty that FitzWilliam's plan had failed.

> I suppose we shall go back to Italy, probably, to Florence to winter. [Before moving to Dresden, FitzWilliam had disposed of the contents of their apartment in Maison Virello, Nice.] If Emily recovers, it will be a slow process, and her health & strength will be much less tried & taxed in Florence than in Germany. Educational advantages & facilities are less there than here for John, but if he acquires all the information there which *can* be acquired he will be sufficiently learned for all useful, or necessary, purposes.[25]

For FitzWilliam it was defeat. His large scheme failed because it had been forced into partnership with family life, with four other people. The burden had been too great. Almost from that moment on he gave up fighting for his son. For the first time John's requirements had been placed ahead of the others'. For the first time the family followed him. For the first time he enjoyed prominence; his future had been seen against everyone else's present. Dresden was a short, unhappy, sad flight neither buoyed by success nor downed by failure. It was merely truncated without conclusion, abruptly.

John was nearly seventeen years old, an age sufficient to reveal broad hints of what his character would become, and which qualities he intended to carry forward from his parents. If Mary and FitzWilliam were reduced to mere symbols in the mathematical arrangement of genealogy, then John's symbolic designation took equally and fairly from each parent. From FitzWilliam he took mostly outright appearance. He was as tall as his father, just over six feet, but it was a similarity too new, too hastily acquired; time alone would adjust movement to height, transforming awkwardness into assurance. He was a little stouter than his father, though still a good distance from being fat. Both parted their hair on the left, yet for FitzWilliam this honoured habit rather than necessity. Both had broad, smooth foreheads that gained prominence because of unfortunate retiring chins. His ears stuck out, his grey-blue eyes bulged slightly, and his other facial features paid little homage to beauty; they could not be summarized tidily because he had not quite grown into them, as if they had arrived too early. Still, he was neither handsome nor ugly. In a few years when he got to work improving on nature's gift, this compromise changed radically. He went a step further than his father's lip-obliterating moustache, to a beard, exchanging meek unobtrusiveness for unforgettable distinction.

From his mother John took the larger notations of his personality. He was wilful, curious, determined and strong – characteristics he found easier to handle than his mother had, because he did not have to resort to subterfuge to express them, and he had incorporated many of FitzWilliam's tempering additives, like modesty, restraint and shyness. It might have been a sorrowful combination of qualities, menaced by contradiction, but somehow it proved a magnificent union. John was precociously determined and touchingly shy. He was certain about himself and generous to others. It was an unfitful arrangement, flowing gracefully on the side of charm because his character was the fine achievement wrought from concentrated examples. Mary's vital forcibleness and FitzWilliam's languid restraint were never threatened by any competition. John had grown up in a distortion of ordinary life: one that stressed the importance of hospital-ward feelings and made no claim on any others. He developed within that peculiarity, knowing no other option, suspecting none: the classic argument of genetics versus environment was a little bit one-sided.

Violet Paget observed what she called John's "double nature" at the very moment it began to be apparent, in Bologna in the autumn of 1873. For Violet these days in Bologna were another instalment in the mythology of Mary Sargent and another occasion for near-swooning excitement. Still, she calmed herself enough to be soberly accurate in her appraisal of her friend. She noted John's lightly governed spontaneity, and his kindness: "It is characteristic of John Sargent's good-natured modesty and his willingness . . . to fall in with my fancies," she wrote, "that being a nearly grown-up painter, he readily set to copying some marvellously hideous portraits of the musicians . . . I idolized."[26] One portrait they saw at the music school inspired a story Violet wrote years later, "Winthrop's Adventure", which John praised. "You were quite right," John wrote to her [autumn 1881] "in not allowing your hero [Winthrop, a composite of the author and John] to indulge in analysing and labelling all his thrills as we did in rather a vainglorious way, probably, when we used to walk with the cold shivers under the Arcades of Bologna. We were not really awed enough not to take a great deal of pride and enjoyment in making the little catalogue of all the uncanny qualities of the portrait of Farinello."*[27]

* The history of Farinello [Carlo Broschi] (1705–82) could have inspired the least imaginative of writers. He possessed a voice of such rare beauty that he was able to achieve considerable power in the Spanish Court. Every night for ten years he sang the same six songs in order to calm Philip V's madness. Ferdinand VI, like his

John's language was unforgettable. He reeled off words such as "sphinx", "wizard", "weird", "fantastic", "serpent", "curious" – documents of sensation if not quite of precision. "That word *curious* was to me, at least," Violet explained, "his dominant word for many years,"[28] adding elsewhere, ". . . pronounced with a sort of lingering indefinable aspirate which gave it well! a *curious* meaning of its own, summing up that instinct for the exotic, the more-than-meets-the-eye, which plays so subtly through his audaciously realistic work . . .".[29] His entire nature reverberated in the word. It showed that he was drawn, like his mother, impetuously towards indefinable feelings provoked by odd, strange, mysterious sights, and at the same time was restrained, like his father, by an urge to understand, interpret. This word *curious* neatly encapsulated the two opposing impulses, attracting and repelling, leaving him somewhere between.

When he and his family returned to Florence (in September 1872) they also managed a relapse back to 1870. Nothing had changed. They moved into their old apartment in the Villino Torrigiani, 115 via de' Serragli (eight large rooms facing south, with a fine garden) and readdressed themselves to the same old problem that had sent them to Dresden. Again their solution was eccentric and original: the best policy would be to wait. It was as if the Dresden experiment had occurred in order to be ignored. John's education was again at the mercy of his parents; and Mary, once having made up her mind to be on the move again, left the details to FitzWilliam, whose opinions about geography rarely varied from high vacillation. John and his mother assumed they had come to Florence merely as a preparation to moving to Rome. In March 1873, FitzWilliam went to investigate, and returned to Florence having decided nothing save that Rome was too expensive. Seven months later Mary went back with him to Rome, found an apartment and returned to Florence to pack up. Then the owner changed his mind, refused them, and FitzWilliam calmly wrote to Bemis (from 15 via Magenta, Florence, on 1 November) [1873], "We shall do the best we can for John here, and I don't doubt that he will, for this winter, get on as well here as in Rome. However, it is somewhat of a disappointment to Mrs S. & John, to give up the latter place."[30] The plans for Rome were sacrificed for another year. FitzWilliam gave out the excuse of economy, but habit and procrastination were closer to the true reasons. John had to depend on the Accademia delle Belle Arti, an institution of uncompromising mediocrity and shameful organization. He would have to make do for yet another year.

---

predecessor, granted him the office of prime minister. Twenty-five years later Farinello retired to Bologna where he lived in "melancholy splendour". In Vernon Lee's story he becomes Rinaldi, a great singer who was assassinated. Winthrop spends a night in the deserted villa where the killing occurred, sees Rinaldi's ghost and hears his voice.

IV

"This boy of ours is on our minds," FitzWilliam confided to Bemis with admirable consistency (23 April 1874), "he has been improving a good deal this winter in his drawing, but we think that if [he] were under better direction than we can get for him here, he would do much better."[1] When John entered the Accademia delle Belle Arti, FitzWilliam believed he had achieved a modest victory – at least his son's education was not being *totally* neglected – and Mary was more or less content (though not happy) with a tolerable winter climate. It was a short-lived triumph. Almost at the very moment they shook the peppercorns from their clothes in the new apartment at via Magenta, the Accademia closed. The compromise had failed. FitzWilliam and Mary's gift for procrastination and oblivion was shown to be useless. They were forced to act, and sat out the winter debating what they would do.

John fell back into the tight grasp of his family. He was given his own studio at via Magenta. Emily continued to give him sketchbooks, the *Baedeker* education reasserted itself, and John was once more entirely on his own. It was the isolation FitzWilliam had always dreaded. Just as John had drawn from plaster casts in the Albertium in Dresden, so the job continued in Florence. And he showed remarkable ability to conduct his own education, swelling Mary's pride in her conviction that Europe itself was school enough. In Venice, the previous summer, he taught himself "to admire Tintoretto immensely and to consider him perhaps second only to Michael Angelo and Titian, whose beauties it was his aim to unite", as he wrote to a cousin (22 March 1874).*[2] He was acquiring knowledge, gaining experience and forming opinions. He was growing up.

Once determined to make some decision, FitzWilliam threw himself at the various possibilities, full of good intentions and almost entirely in

* Mrs Austin – "a sort of cousin", FitzWilliam described her – was born Elizabeth Turner Amory (1820–98), the eldest daughter of Esther Sargent and Thomas Coffin Amory. Her great-grandfather and FitzWilliam's great-great-grandfather was Epes Sargent (1690–1762), thus making them distant cousins. She and her husband Ivers James Austin (1808–89) lived for several years in Dresden. John later painted a portrait of her youngest child, Mary Turner Austin, in 1878.

ignorance. He sought opinions, which naturally counselled opposing solutions. He did not have far to cast for advice; Florence was crawling with advisers – expatriate painters.

The British were well represented, and their contingent appeared to be headed by the Pagets, who were once again resigned Florentines after a couple of winters in Rome. Their household welcomed callers primarily because Violet's half-brother, Eugene Lee-Hamilton, would neither get out of bed nor allow himself to be unsuperintended by his mother and half-sister. Violet herself was constantly poised to air some high-blown theory of art or brightly eager to be persuaded to explain away the mysteries of aesthetics. Her audience included Edward Clifford (1844–1907), who had been born in Bristol, studied at the Royal Academy Schools, and had turned his hand to complimentary portraits of Victorian worthies which he showed at the Academy. At other London galleries, however, he showed pictures closer to his heart – biblical scenes. Later these renditions were not enough, and he downed brushes to work for the Church Army. There was Arthur Lemon (1850–1912), who had been born on the Isle of Man but had spent most of his childhood in Rome with relatives. When Garibaldi was jeopardizing the tight hold of the Papal States and his uncle begged him to enlist in the defending Zouaves, Lemon would have none of it, and went off to California to try a cowboy's life. He spent the next eight years studying cattle, Indians and cacti (as well as working as a navvy), all of which made for strange qualifications to speak about art training. And there was Charles Heath Wilson (1809–82), a watercolourist who knew the most about academic discipline. In the 1840s, after teaching ornament-drawing and design in Edinburgh, he was appointed director of the Art Schools at Somerset House in London, before moving on, in 1849, to become headmaster of the Glasgow School of Design. He left Scotland for Italy in 1869 and became the biographer of Michelangelo (1879). He was the Sargents' prime adviser.

The expatriate American contingent had the Sargent household in via Magenta as its centre. The chief representative among them was Edwin White (?1817–77), whose biography remains largely vague. He was an early student at the National Academy of Design Schools (in New York) where he eventually returned in the 1860s as an instructor and a member of the Committee. He had also trained in Düsseldorf, and at the Ecole des Beaux-Arts in Paris where he studied under Picot. His large paintings of scenes from American history have earned him a highly uncertain perch in the catalogue of American art. Such reputation as he ever acquired came from his students, who went on to other teachers and greater fame than his own – a roundabout sort of distinction. White roamed about Rome and Florence, where he retired, before returning to Saratoga Springs to die. While in Florence he continued to teach, in a somewhat casual manner, finding his students among the American community: Frank Fowler, W. L. Palmer and John S. Sargent, all of whom had their eyes fixed elsewhere than on Florence, and were kicking to get out.*

Frank Fowler (1852–1910) had studied in Brooklyn before reaching Florence in 1873. When he left White's studio he went straight to Paris in 1875 to study with Carolus-Duran. In 1880 he returned to New York a portraitist and critic. He painted a distinguished list of sitters, got caught up in the Beaux-Arts movement, painting the vast ballroom ceiling of the Waldorf Hotel, and went on to write textbooks and protest that portraiture was insufficiently decorative. Other than this, Fowler's history is not loaded with helpful details.

Walter Launt Palmer (1854–1932) was kept in Florence by his family, who were traipsing after his father, the sculptor Erastus Dow Palmer, one of White's closest friends. Hitherto Palmer had been able, by some considerable demonstration of character, to withstand the lure of Europe that had enticed so many of his colleagues. The result of this immunity, however, left his work scarcely distinguishable from theirs, save in very slight modifications. He, too, produced neo-classic versions of abstract nouns using Red Indians instead of cupids, cherubs, nymphs and Roman Senators to reveal "truth", "hope", "peace", "sorrow", etc. And, though he had always thought that Albany, New York, was good enough for him, he believed his son needed Europe (or so he excused the present journey). W. L. Palmer, like Fowler, and like John, was biding his time in Florence. He wanted to move on; in fact he wanted to move back to America. Yet early in 1874 he went to Paris, entered Carolus-Duran's studio, had a quick look round, and shortly thereafter hastened back to America. His main interest was landscape painting, particularly land-scapes buried in winter. When he became too cold, he moved indoors to paint haunting interiors.

The best research can do for these two English-speaking groups of artists is place them in Florence at the same time. Once their influence was filtered through FitzWilliam's letters, it was as good as lost. But one cold fact must stand out: John was working with contemporaries for the first time, American contemporaries. White's leadership was not enough to make up for the failure of the Accademia in FitzWilliam's broad, though vague, scheme. Under the direction of his and Mary's uncertainty, they all put their heads together to determine where the compass should point for the next stop in John's education. One faction lined up behind London, hotly favoured by Heath Wilson (disregarding the minor detail that he himself had left); the other declared Paris, magically attractive to Americans. It was not much of a battle; scarcely a tepid skirmish: Paris had it, incontestably. "Every One says that Paris will be the best place to

---

* Just why Frank Fowler should be in Florence in 1873 remains unclear. I am grateful to Mrs Maybelle Mann, Walter Launt Palmer's biographer, for supplying me with the vital link between Palmer and John, and both of them with *atelier* Carolus-Duran.

find such advantages as we w^d like to give him," FitzWilliam wrote to Bemis (23 April 1874),

> and consequently we propose to take him to Paris & remain there as long as the weather &c will permit. And perhaps we may even ven[ture] on a winter there. If we can get him into the Atelier of some first rate painter we flatter ourselves (perhaps it is a parental delusion) that he will make something out of himself more than common.

If the Dresden experiment had been a gesture of hesitation, a mere short pause of certainty, then the Sargents' move to Paris in 1874 was a declaration, a loud confident announcement. For the second time in eighteen years John's future was elevated to the most important feature in itinerary calculations. The Sargents went to Paris quite simply for him. Their considerable stamina for postponement had given way.

Any recital of the Sargents' activities was constantly at odds with verb tense: FitzWilliam, despite his enormous affection for writing letters, only hastily noted what they *expected* to do, and was as quick to be vague about what they had done. As a result, events that seemed large in retrospect, like all others, slipped by unnoticed and unrecorded. It was as if the sheer weight of concentrated uncertainty which attended their every step dwarfed every detail to insignificance. The chain of events that led John to find himself in the rabbit warren of Paris studios by the late spring of 1874 eluded notation, first by FitzWilliam, then by John, then by observers, and eventually by memoirists.

But one detail remained clear – uncertainty and chance continued to document their progress. "We are packing up in order to leave in the first week in May," John wrote from Florence to Mrs Austin (25 April 1874),

> but the date of our departure is rendered rather uncertain by the provoking fact of my having sprained my ankle very severely two weeks ago on the stairs of the Academy. . . . Then our destination has been changed by reports of Cholera in Venice and of unique artistic training in Paris. . . . We go to Paris now for a short time to make enquiries about this, which will decide whether we go to Paris or not for next winter.

Leaving the Florence Academy had a greater attraction than the excitement of anything he might discover in Paris. The Accademia delle Belle Arti had resumed instruction in March after months of deliberation over reform; "when reopened the only perceptible change was that we, the students from the cast [drawing plaster casts], were left without a Master, while the former Professor vacillated and still vacillates between resigning and continuing his instructions".^{3}

The moment they were ready to set out for Paris, the natural order of Sargent preoccupations was reinstated. Health returned to the top of the list. Everyone, except FitzWilliam, came down with a bad cold. John had a sore throat and an attack of indigestion. Again their departure was postponed. By the time they got to Paris, on Saturday, 16 May, FitzWilliam suspected that his daughters were suffering from whooping cough, and that the others were likely candidates. Once in Paris, lodgings and weather joined the list of his major preoccupations. They did not seem much concerned by the relics of Paris' recent ordeal during the Franco–Prussian War. The town was only just beginning to pick itself up, like an invalid unsure of a new posture. Few trees remained for shade. There was an alarming amount of dust. Rubble and destroyed monuments produced a ghostly air of glory past, barren honours. Martial law continued. There was a lot to be done. The tourist excitement of the Sargents' last visit during the Exposition was gone.

For a family grievously committed to havering and constant indecision, John's speed in learning about and enrolling in a studio was refreshingly swift. The whole process took less than a fortnight. Four days after he arrived he met his friend Palmer who had been in Paris for the previous five months.[4] "He told me", John wrote to Heath Wilson (23 May 1874), "that he was himself in the atelier of M. Carolus Durand [sic] whom he prefers to any other artist in Paris, both as a teacher and as a painter. . . . I admired Durand's pictures immensely in the salon* and he is considered one of the greatest French artists. . . ."[5] On Friday, 26 May, John and his father went to Carolus-Duran's studio in the Boulevard Mont Parnasse.

When they arrived Carolus-Duran was making his rounds, criticizing his students' work. He then turned to assess the new candidate's work. The studies were shown one after another, the landscape pencil sketches, museum copywork, and the watercolours: it was a prodigious display. "Carolus-Duran said, 'You have studied much,' and then, with the caution which made 'not too bad' the highest praise lavished on a student's work, he added, 'Much that you have learned you must forget.' "[6] The students gathered round: "We were astonished", one of them remembered, "at the cleverness shown in the water-color and pencil work, and his début was considered a most promising one."[7] Carolus accepted John as pupil there and then. A week later FitzWilliam wrote to his father (30 May), "We have placed John in the Studio of a rising painter . . .".[8] Two weeks later John added, "I am quite delighted with the atelier . . .".[9]

Charles-Emile-Auguste Durand, restyled Carolus-Duran for considerations of professional refinement and vanity, was a potent influence on John Singer Sargent.† From a distance Carolus-Duran appeared a

---

* At the Salon that year (1874) Carolus-Duran showed *Dans la rosée* (661) and two portraits, one of his daughter, as well as a bronze bust.
† The surname Durand is to the French world what Smith or Jones is to the Anglo-Saxon. His students habitually mocked him, though not of course to his face, about his fancy adjustment of name. On the sign outside the studio, 'L'Atelier des Elèves de Monsieur Carolus-Duran', the fugitive *d* was frequently restored in chalk.

glamorous figure; close-up he was engaging: his character was highly magnetic. He had charm. He had warmth. And, above all, he was a superb but eccentric teacher, leaning unfortunately less on rudimentary preparation than on mere repetition of his own original version of how best to paint. But his students were drawn to him precisely for his originality, and they adored him. It was probably this extra bonus of affection that helped to produce so many immediately recognizable echoes of his painting on both sides of the Atlantic for several decades. Carolus' success was meteoric and bolted straight across the face of hallowed academic tradition. He was controversial, and quickly became the darling of the younger generation. He was witheringly talented, but somehow his visual language got arrested; he never seemed to move on from his brilliant achievements in the late 1860s and early 1870s. And in truth he did not look much like a painter; he looked like a very superior conjuror.

Carolus' history was remarkable only as a record of determination, precocity and astonishing fame quickly forgotten. He collected as many honours as France willingly dispensed, and his reputation remained undiminished throughout the final third of the nineteenth century. Today, however, he appears gifted only in repelling interest. He has been another casualty of fashion.*[10] This once-great name has been reduced to scarcely more than one short column in the *Dictionnaire de biographie française*, and the creaking groan of reluctance is evident throughout. His story is uncomplicated: country boy makes good, after three attempts. He was born in 1838, on 4 July – an appropriate day for the man who would later guide the progress of American portraiture – in Lille, which was perhaps the most fortunate detail in his biography. His home town always smiled favourably upon him. His education began when he was eight, and his parents were more determined to reveal his talent than his teacher. His early successes were always provincial, which he took to mean that he was ready for larger things. And with marvellous consistency he was wrong. In 1853 (three years before Sargent was born) he went to copy old masters at the Louvre, but poverty quickly sent him home. He won a local competition and used the prize-money for another assault on Paris. This second try was no better than the first, though he did earn himself a footnote in the history of art when he, with others, congratulated Manet in 1861 on the *Spanish Guitar Player*. He won another competition in Lille, promptly went to Italy for two years, and returned to Paris. Again failure and again he returned to Lille. But now the pattern altered. He sent a picture, *L'Assassiné*, to the 1866 Salon in Paris, won a

---

* Rebecca West wrote in *The Thinking Reed* (1936): "They walked through the rooms smiling up at the pictures, though these were Boldinis and de la Gandaras and Carolus-Durans, awful exhibitions of that facility with paint which has nothing to do with painting, which is closely akin to the Italian art of winding macaroni round the fork . . ." (p. 92).

medal, sold the picture to the museum in Lille, and went to Spain to examine Velazquez's paintings – a study that had lasting and enormous consequences.

Three years later he had his greatest triumph, the single achievement that promoted him from the status of talented provincial: a portrait of his wife Pauline-Marie-Charlotte Croizette, *La Dame au gant*.* It earned him a second-class medal in the 1869 Salon, went to the Musée de Luxembourg (now the Louvre) and earned him prime ranking among the most sought-after portraitists in France. Thereafter awards, recognitions and wealth piled up.

His idea of portraiture, if nothing else and if somewhat thin on the detail of profundity, was to be dramatic, hence his affection for startling colour. And he succeeded admirably. He abandoned his earlier affection for realism, which got him into hot water with Zola and other critics who were desperately trying to spread naturalism like limp butter across the face of the arts, favouring an altogether more complimentary approach to his sitters. Carolus-Duran, for his part, saw the whole process on a finer aesthetic plane: detail gave way to tone, and statement was reduced to a whisper. He played down the urge to place his sitters in a specific, well-defined place. Despite his heroic pursuit of the subtle, he could not withstand the allure of being theatrical, sometimes giving the starring role to the clothes of his sitters. Often satin, muslin, voile, lace stole the show. *La Dame au gant* (also known as *La Femme au gant*, but shown in the Salon under the title *Portrait de Mme ****) is a massive (2 metres by 1½ metres) and majestic study of an elaborate dress, languidly participating in a minor domestic suggestion produced by Madame Duran peeling a glove from her left hand, ready to join the other listlessly dropped on the floor. The picture might either be flagrant erotic implication or an episode in exhaustion. It would be hard to overestimate the brute skill involved in creating such a performance, and it would be equally hard to under-estimate Carolus-Duran's vision.

Carolus-Duran was suddenly famous. He was shoved from the exclusive and narrow world of painters where, by association alone, he enjoyed a certain importance. During his earliest days in Paris he was a fellow-copyist at the Louvre of Fantin-Latour. He was painted by Manet

* Pauline-Marie-Charlotte Croizette (or, alternatively, Croisette) married Carolus-Duran in 1868. She was born in St Petersburg to French parents. Her mother was Louise Croisette, first principal dancer at the Imperial Theatre, St Petersburg, and a prominent member of Russian aristocracy. She and her family went to France around the middle of the 1860s. She, too, was a painter, though at the other end of the scale practised by her husband: she worked in miniature and pastel, showing at the Salon between 1864 and 1875. Her sister was the celebrated comic actress at the Comédie-Française, Sophie Croisette, whom Carolus-Duran painted in Trouville in an equestrian portrait, *Au bord de la mer* (1873). She also toured England with Sarah Bernhardt.

and he painted Monet (1867). Paradoxically, he alone among his colleagues got his full ration of fame in his lifetime, and that was the end of it. His career, which soared so brilliantly and so lucratively, took off from this one picture. Thereafter his fortunes were more than handsomely reversed. If his name sparks recognition for only one picture, it is *La Dame au gant*. And, alas, even by the late 1870s his reputation slowly began its inevitable, but gradual, decline.

Almost to intensify the value of his achievement, he succeeded without any help. His independence was extraordinarily rare.* He had not enrolled in the Ecole des Beaux-Arts, the government institution created as a forcing-house of national talent. He had not known tuition under the great painter-teachers who enjoyed either the protection (and security) of the Ecole or powerful acclaim like Pils, Cabanel, Gérôme, Yvon, Gleyre or Picot. Duran achieved importance independently. Once there, however, he swam vigorously in the mainstream, all the way up to Grand Officier de la Légion d'Honneur and Director of the French Academy in Rome. Carolus-Duran's lasting significance depends more on what he represented than on what he actually did: ambition rewarded and an index to the extraordinarily high value France placed on her painters.

Though Carolus-Duran reached his position courtesy of persistence and completely by his own ability, he soon discovered – and, in all likelihood, not pleasantly – that his reputation carried obligations; the chief, ironically enough, was teaching and, worse still, the role of teacher was imposed upon him. Mystery surrounds the precise sequence of events that led him to open L'Atelier des Elèves de Monsieur Carolus-Duran in the spring of 1873. Carolus was first approached by a Frenchman, Paul Batifaud-Vaur, and later by a Bostonian, Robert C. Hinckley.†

---

* "La vie de M. Carolus-Duran est non seulement un modèle de vaillance et de foi, mais est aussi, pour les artistes, un example rare *d'indépendance*," the critic Arsène Alexandre wrote during Carolus' lifetime.
† Paul Batifaud-Vaur has been awarded very brief notice in Benizet's dictionary. Apart from the unembroidered facts that he was born in Paris, studied with Yvon and Carolus-Duran, showed at the Salon 1870–81, and was a portraitist, nothing else is revealed. He is mentioned in James Carroll Beckwith's diary (National Academy of Design, New York), 19 April 1874, as being among the top three students in Duran's studio.
    It is odd that Robert Cutler Hinckley (1853–1941) never thought his persuasive activities sufficiently important to mention. Hinckley was born in Northampton, Mass., and went abroad in 1872 after his father's death. Shortly thereafter he entered the Ecole des Beaux-Arts (*atelier* Bonnat). He showed at the Salon during the early 1880s, first mythological then less academic subjects. He returned to Northampton in 1884. Later he settled in Rehoboth Beach, Del.; a simple fact of geography that did little to spread his reputation as a portraitist. He taught at the Corcoran School in Washington 1894–7. His numerous portraits (approximately 350) are well represented at West Point and Annapolis, the United States Capitol and the Treasury. Perhaps his best-known painting is *The First Ether Operation* (Massachusetts General Hospital).

Carolus demurred, then agreed. A teaching studio was the ultimate affirmation of his success, if no contribution to his wealth.[11] He agreed to teach them on Tuesday and Friday mornings. He stipulated that the students must find a studio accessible to his own and must tend to the practical details of maintaining the studio. FitzWilliam outlined the general organization for his father (30 May): Duran "takes a limited number of pupils & looks after their work. He has his own private Studio, and another Studio for his pupils from whom he receives no compensation beyond what is necessary to defray the expenses connected with the public Studio; each pupil pays twenty francs a month, $4.00."[12] The entire operation was strikingly casual, and this quality filtered through to the other features of the *atelier* at 81 Boulevard Mont Parnasse. Few rules were imposed. No enrolment registers were filled in. Indeed, no records of any kind seem to have been kept. (And this, alas, explains why it is impossible to discover exactly who Sargent's contemporaries were in *atelier* Duran.)

The whole *atelier* system evolved into a complicated, though subtle, arrangement of mutual dependencies; an elaborate universe. In the centre was the Ecole des Beaux-Arts, an official body that had advanced from a whim of the kings of France to a political instrument of a couple of empires, before settling down as a constant and undeniable presence enjoying great prestige. Thus, it was looked upon as a standard. It was a measure. It was, above all else, the common denominator of all art training, and as such it stalwartly upheld outdated principles. Professors' appointments were for life. The power of the *chefs des ateliers* was absolute, and too long-lasting. "We hear that it is a common reproach", John wrote to Heath Wilson (12 June 1874), "among the artists against Cabanel & Gérôme that they should continue to hold the office and receive the salary of professors, while they only occasionally visit the studio in a stately manner without taking much individual interest in each of the pupils."[13] Private *ateliers* flourished mainly to counteract the Ecole's staleness. But the students of these fugitive studios felt the command of the Ecole all the same, for they, too, submitted to the official twice-yearly examinations, the *concours*, as well as the august Prix de Rome competition (though foreigners were ineligible).

In the broadest possible reading John enrolled in Carolus-Duran's *atelier* to prepare himself for the *concours*, which would prove, also in the broadest possible interpretation, the success of his apprenticeship with matriculation into the Ecole. As a student at the Ecole he simply had a more formal status and had the privilege of being crammed with the official line that might aid his standing in future *concours*. Yet his position as Carolus-Duran's apprentice would always remain infinitely more important. A teacher's success was evinced by his students' placing in the *concours*, and for many years his students were obliged to ride on the *patron*'s coat-tails. Testing the student via his teacher, and the teacher via his students, was a habit that only gradually faded away. The prime advertisement of this relationship was the Salon: the exhibition, as the title of the catalogue lengthily explains, of painting, architecture, engraving and lithography by living artists, held at the Palais des Champs-Elysées at the beginning of May. Each exhibitor was defined, after noting place of birth and address, by his teacher's name.

As *patron* Carolus-Duran bravely continued to taunt convention. He blithely waved his arm dismissing old aesthetic theories and practices that had corseted all training, that carried the heavy blessing of Ingres, and that ordered the declension of a young artist's career. He dropped the idea that painting was *only* an extension of drawing, which forced students of more orthodox training to put aside their palette for years. Duran did not see colour as an enemy. Out went the exhausting discipline of drawing endlessly from engravings ("from the flat") and from the antique or plaster casts ("from the round") – a practice that was thought to correct the inadequacies inevitably presented by a live model ("from the live"). Out went the whole copyist mentality. And in came a version of preparation that left his pupils wonderfully underqualified for the *concours*. They did particularly badly because they were so weak on drawing. After yet another reminder of this omission, Carolus bowed to necessity. "Duran I am pleased to observe", Beckwith wrote in his diary (6 December 1874), "is becoming much more severe in our drawing, somebody has awakened him to the realization of his neglect with us on this point . . . my only question of Duran's ability as a master. . . ."[14]

His blanket justification for rescaling the function of art training was consistent with his idea that painting was not just an imitative art. It was supremely expressive. It was individual. The Ecole's dogmatic blarings had ignored this fact, had abandoned this essential truth. Duran preferred anarchy (like Delacroix). He said, while not casting too far for support, the great "masters have interpreted nature, and not given a literal translation. . . . Without this individual point of view there can be no individual work. This shows how dangerous are those schools that, restricting the artists to the same methods, do not permit them to develop their individual feeling. These schools, however, make use of a very respectable motto: 'Tradition.' "[15]

As if this summary dismissal of the entire basis of ordinary training were not enough to enflame prudence, Carolus-Duran's specific approach to painting finished the outrage. His method kept to his creed of individuality. It encouraged, he hoped, confidence, and the habit of seeing things fresh, uncluttered and ungoverned by a mass of "flat" and "round" visions; the student needed his eyes, not the history of drawing, to see. Carolus-Duran believed that nature was composed of masses made up of planes. Their arrangement was ordered by light. Drawing only met the requirement of relationships and proportion and was, as such, only vaguely useful to painting. Hence he created a method which echoed in miniature the construction of nature as he saw it. First, the planes comprising an object were quickly and roughly discerned in charcoal on an unprepared canvas. Then basic sketching out was done with a broad brush: this would serve as a general guide, the overall pattern of the object. Now came the step that demanded acute analysis of vision, and relied heavily on the expressive quality Carolus-Duran tried to develop: the colour value of each plane of the object was diagnosed, the interrelationships of the surfaces were also calculated, and the planes were painted in subdued colour. This was the vital stage. From here one added, always in mosaic fashion, the next colour, the next value until the whole was created by an elaborate construction of parts. The process relied on accumulation, not filling in. The entire technique had at its core, and utterly depended upon, understanding half-tone – the unifying ingredient in a picture. " ' Cherchez la demi-teinte,' " Carolus-Duran instructed, and repeated like a war-cry to his students, " 'mettez quelques accents, et puis les lumières.' " He invoked, somewhat peculiarly, Velazquez's name drum-like; over and over again he shrieked "Velazquez", ordering ceaseless study of the master's painting. No other painter embraced Duran's creed so illogically, and eventually none more than Sargent adhered to the rules so magnificently. Years later he recognized the essential worthiness of Carolus-Duran's method and the undeniable fact that his teacher could not practise it himself – perhaps the final proof of a great teacher. He recited the process simply:

> "You must *classify* the values. If you begin with the middle-tone and work up from it towards the darks – so that you deal last with your highest lights and darkest darks – you avoid false accents. That's what Carolus taught me. . . . Of course, a sketch is different. You don't mind false accents there. But once you had made them in something which you wish to *carry far*, in order to correct them you have to deal with both sides of them and get into a lot of trouble."[16]

Carolus-Duran's technique was the art of achieving the maximum by use of the minimum. His perception demanded paring objects down to masses of reflected light. Altogether, as a variety of instruction, it was intensely personal with rather stunning historical precedents, most obvious in Franz Hals. It was severe and uncompromisingly harsh. A student had either to agree or leave. Perhaps to counteract his unbending theory, his manner of teaching was the reverse of the majestic visitations favoured by the *chefs des ateliers* at the Ecole. "Duran comes regularly twice a week to our atelier . . .," John wrote to Heath Wilson (12 June 1874),

> and carefully and thoroughly criticises the pupils' work staying a short time with each one. He generally paints a newcomer's first study, as a lesson, and as my first head had rather too sinister a charm, suggesting immoderate use of ivory black, he entirely repainted the face, and in about five minutes made a fine thing out of it, and I keep it as such.[17]

Inaccurately, though in keeping with the student–teacher connection important to art training, a false scent has been laid down leading back to Sargent's enormous debt to Carolus-Duran. It has always been a tempting line to draw. John's choice of Carolus-Duran was one of the happiest moments (and perhaps the only happy moment) in an education story aggrieved with miscalculation. However, the actual progression of events and motives that led John to 81 Boulevard Mont Parnasse was dramatically haphazard. The great appeal of *atelier* Duran was primarily its newness.

First, newcomers were not taunted. Carolus-Duran strictly forbade the practice widespread among the other studios. Of course hazing newcomers depended on time, permitting a hierarchy of students which gave those of long standing privilege and new arrivals no privilege. Hazing, and often cruel, gruesome, humiliating and savage teasing were absolutely standard procedure, save in another fairly new *atelier*, Académie Julien. John was repelled by the idea. It disgusted him, as he wrote shortly after he arrived in Paris (23 May);

> it appears that a newcomer is treated in the most brutal way in the studios of Gérôme and Cabanel; he is obliged to sing them a song, to do all their errands for soup and soap for the brushes, and sometimes they actually strip him and paint him blue all over, or shave one side of his head; you may imagine that I would not relish such jokes.[18]

Then there was the fact that the *atelier* Duran was easier to get into than well-established studios. The latter enjoyed more than just the reputation of the *patron*; they had a record of success. They were known. And since Ecole matriculation was the goal, prospective students naturally went first to the masters teaching there. When James Carroll Beckwith first arrived in Paris from New York (about six months before John) he went straight to Isadore Pils's studio but found it full. By comparison, Carolus-Duran as a teacher was unknown. Students did not flock to his side, despite his renown as a painter. Worse still, his radical approach to teaching was incompatible with *concours* adjudication. By May 1874, when John entered, Duran had a fair number of students, maybe as many as twenty-four, only two of whom were French – "two nasty little fat Frenchmen", John called them.[19] Foreigners were either more intoxicated by the *patron*'s reputation or less inclined to value the Ecole's blessing than their French contemporaries when it came to selecting a studio. (When W. L. Palmer entered *atelier* Duran it was out of a consideration of availability of a place as well as the *patron*'s fame; Palmer had no interest in portraiture.) For this reason *atelier* Duran was not full; there was room.

Finally, of all the studios in Paris, John learnt most about Carolus-Duran's within days of arriving in Paris. He owed this intelligence to W. L. Palmer, who was giving up his place at 81 Boulevard Mont Parnasse to return to America. Within six days of talking to Palmer, John enrolled: this was both surprising haste and a subtle precaution. John knew his family's tolerance for capital cities was so low that they could easily leave Paris before the problem of instruction was resolved. Therefore, formal enrolment had to be settled quickly before any danger of renewed postponement developed, as it had in Dresden and the year before in Rome. Such refinements as thorough research and suitability were less important, for the moment, than actual enrolment. Once he was attached to the *atelier* John's status was declared and settled.

His parents and sisters fell in with this certainty, uneasily. In order to preserve family life, no other choice was possible. John now set the pace and direction of their lives. He was a new compass for them and a steadying guide. After twenty years, almost to the day, one member of the family had an ambition and purpose outside their immediate and highly limited province.

For the first time the customary dithering about Alps, Venice, or the long list of spas for their summer visit never arose. They would follow John, FitzWilliam confidently told his father. John, in turn, fully anticipated following Carolus-Duran out into the country near Fontainebleau for the *plein air* antidote to so many months' lessons in the studio. A simplicity never known in itinerary calculations began, and almost as suddenly was discarded for reasons of illness. Mary, Emily and Violet's coughs persisted since they had arrived in Paris, and FitzWilliam's nervous anxiety turned on the youngest, Violet, who at the age of four was still referred to as the "Baby". Her illness worried him. He reported her condition to his sister with near-clinical insistence (admittedly after outlining John's developments): "The Baby is still coughing: She was much better of her Whoop a fortnight ago, but a slight fresh cold brought it all back again. But the tape-worm bothers me & her more than the cough. I hope that, when the time comes for the reptile to move again (in a month) we shall be able to get rid of him." When they left Paris at the beginning of July, it was not to follow Carolus-Duran; they went to a fishing village in Normandy – "We hope the sea-air will be of service to the Coughers of the family".[20]

Still, John's new position was more or less secure, and like the other subtle readjustments in the arrangement of family attitudes it coincided with another and seemingly unconnected event, as if to confirm that his family's activities were confined to a narrow, self-absorbed area, drawing on a finite reserve of energy. Just as Mary's determination never to return to America hardened when she inherited the means to stay abroad by her mother's legacy in 1865 and FitzWilliam's sudden, uncharacteristic insistence that they winter in Dresden in 1871 strengthened when his mother died, John's promotion occurred when his paternal grandfather Winthrop Sargent died in August 1874, aged eighty-two. John and his sisters had never even seen him. The last potent emotional cord tying FitzWilliam (and Mary) to America broke, leaving him and his family in the precise state he had struggled so hard to justify, in complete exile. Despite John's family's perplexingly expressed reactions to deaths in the

American branch of their relations, they were affected profoundly. There was more at work than coincidence: they were assailed by pre-Europe memories; they were haunted by sacrifice; they were reminded of the magnitude of their self-interest. They had no choice but to cling more feverishly to what they had constructed as their life abroad: a life composed of illness and death, and nothing more. It was dramatic and hollow, coasting along the knife-edge of emotion, but going nowhere. And because this life was so enclosed, so vacant of achievement, and so false the only reflection of their feelings was in shifting moods and attitudes – a subtle variation on an unspoken language. After eighteen years John had escaped to broader fields, and his parents looked on with vicarious pleasure.

V

The wide expanse of John's Paris years, the years of his apprenticeship, was played out largely unnoticed. He was settled, living to a regular pattern, and the novelty of such an occurrence slid by unnoticed, for many reasons. And to complicate John's history even more his character was emerging as a full-blown enigma.

His adjustment to this new order was the most complicated of all the family, and perhaps one that proved impossible. It was a radical change. His daily routine had a new centre and a new fullness. He went to the studio at seven every morning and returned home to the family apartment in rue Montaigne shortly before noon; in the afternoons he went off to galleries or back to the studio. And he was starting to make friends: "Amongst the other pupils", FitzWilliam wrote to his sister (25 June) [1874], "are two or three very good Americans, to whom he has taken kindly, and they to him."[*][1]

* The highly imprecise calculations regarding the number of John's fellow-students at *atelier* Duran yields a figure close to two dozen, which does not tally at all with FitzWilliam's letter or John's glancing references at the time. With some certainty it can be stated that the following were at Boulevard Mont Parnasse at the time of John's arrival: Robert C. Hinckley; Will Low (1853–1932), who was a friend of Erastus Palmer's, and many years later supplied scholars with memoirs of the period; Stephen Hills Parker (1852–1925), of whom almost nothing is known; John M. Tracy (1844–92), whose "Recollections of Parisian Art Schools" (a talk delivered at the Rembrandt Club in Brooklyn, 1883) reveals that he was knocking about Paris in the 1860s, studying under Yvon and Pils before being lured over the Boulevard Mont Parnasse, but otherwise remains mysterious; James Carroll Beckwith (1852–1917), whose extensive diary furnishes the best account of the art training and social life at the time. Beckwith became one of John's best friends, sharing a studio with him at 73 rue Notre-Dame-des-Champs from 1875. Others who *might* have been there were: Neville Cain (1855–1935), Eliot Gregory (1854–1915), C. M. Newton (unidentifiable) and Mountfort Coolidge (unidentifiable). They all were Americans. The other Frenchman, apart from Batifaud-Vaur, cannot be identified.

The traffic in *atelier* Duran was terrific. After 1874, the numbers did increase, but exactly who they were and when they arrived remains tantalizingly unclear. Memoirs are not reliable, and until students matriculated into the Ecole there was no other record of Carolus' pupils. And he had many students who either failed the *concours* or passed long after they became his students (or even were uninterested in the Ecole). So any reckoning is at best haphazard.

Every morning before he went off to Boulevard Mont Parnasse, John had breakfast with Emily. If anyone ever understood John, Emily did, and she was probably the only person who ever *could*. Her life was oddly parallel to his, but not emphatically similar. She, too, was the product of a highly irregular education, greatly reduced to accommodate her health and gender. She, too, had terrific energy, but it was forced to operate within a very confined space. Her growth was little more than a chronological advance on the total atmosphere of childhood. As if the great stop of continued family life were not enough to cripple her, her excessive modesty was. She accepted the fact that she was odd as easily as people accept the colour of their hair. Her deformity gave her the evidence, and her overweening sensitivity gave her the confirmation. In some ways such a frank interpretation simplified her shaded existence. She was able to protect herself. She restrained any ambition she might have had by sinking deeper and deeper into the ground marked out by her parents, sister and brother. She knew she would never stray beyond that boundary. She knew she would never marry. She knew there was nothing more for her. And she knew what John had accepted as part of his future: that he would always look after her. John could never really escape, had he wanted to, the work of eighteen years.

As John managed to inch out of the tight sphere of family influence, Emily was left behind. She could not leave home; such a desire was incompatible with every atom of her nature, and contradicted every aspect of her tuition. To her, it seemed, fell the nefarious job of preserving family life simply out of an absence of choice. By the joint alliance of injustice and contradiction Emily was forced to devote herself to the very activity Mary had successfully avoided. Mary's behaviour had left a vacuum which had to be filled, and though she had recoiled from the mere idea of family duty she unwittingly shoved her daughter into a life-long service. In time, Emily strode forward as the important figure, taking over from her parents. Mary did realize the strangeness of Emily's position, and perhaps even her part in its creation. Mary Sargent's will (1900) makes sad reading. She left her estate (by means of complicated administration) entirely to Emily, adding "my daughter Emily has no other provision for her future than that which I am making for her . . .".[2]

Emily needed John. She looked to him for any light in her shuttered existence, and such dependence was entirely consistent with the Sargent propensity to lean on each other and, more grievously, their habit of playing out their frustrated ambitions second-hand. John became, in a way, the filter between Emily and the outside world. And John needed Emily, because he, too, was incapable of leaving home. His parents and sisters had, for too long, obstructed the view. The borders of his life were also drawn by them, and he was content to go no further. But their obvious presence had created a marvellous shorthand for his emotions, because he, too, was well protected. All the menacing sensations of youth – doubt, fear, vulnerability – were banished by their airless formation

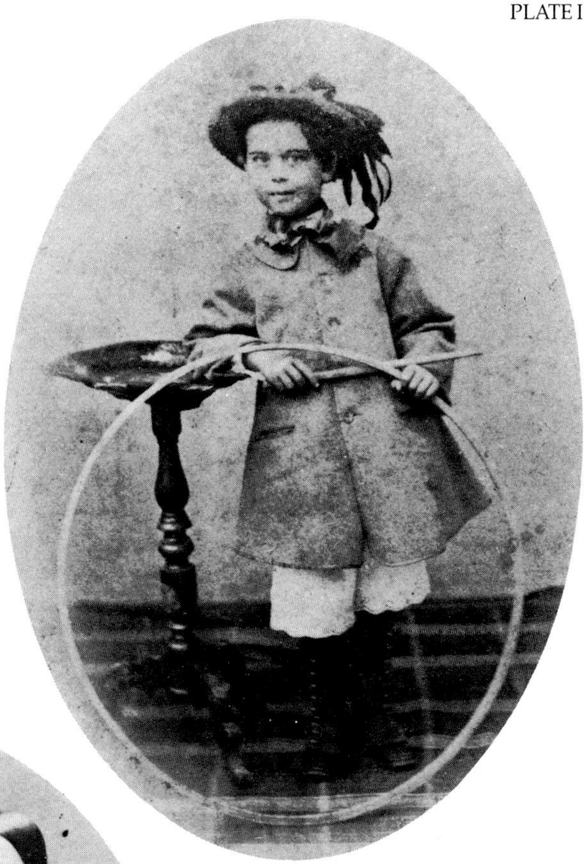

PLATE I

Right: John Singer Sargent aged nine – a souvenir portrait taken in France for his grandparents in America.

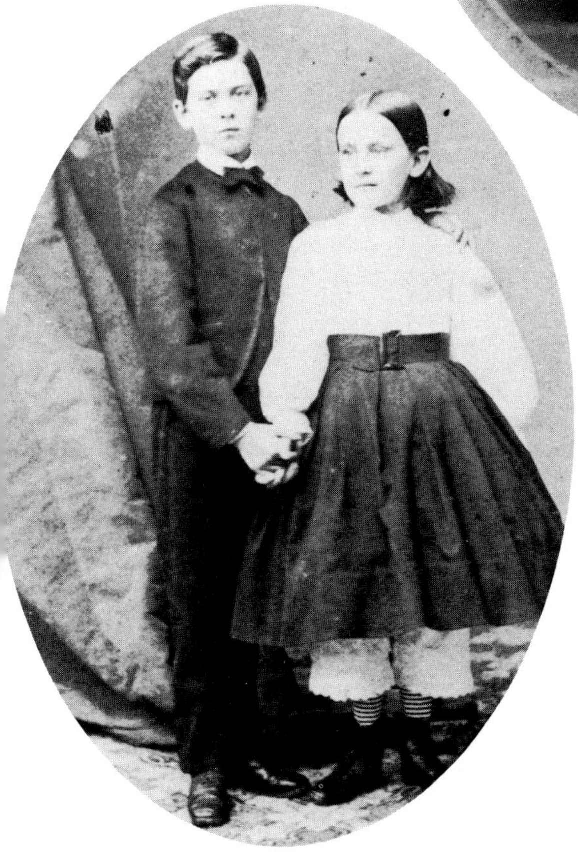

Left: John and his sister Emily (aged ten) taken two years later in Nice at the time of their sister Minnie's death.

PLATE II

Right: Mary Newbold Singer Sargent
(Mrs FitzWilliam Sargent) in her
mid-twenties.

Below: Mrs Sargent, aged sixty-one,
by her son, 1887.

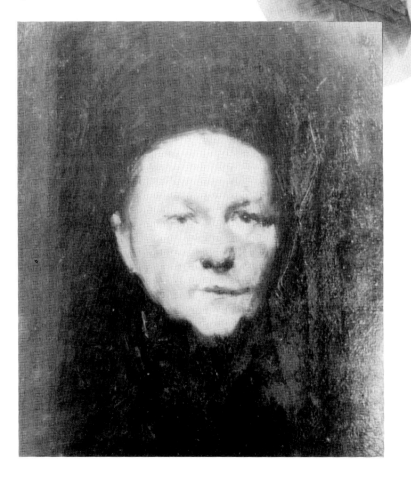

PLATE III

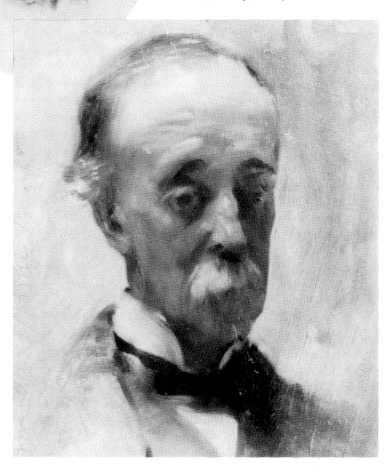

Left: Dr FitzWilliam Sargent in his late twenties, at the height of his career and shortly before his retirement.

Below: Dr Sargent by his son in 1886, three years before his death.

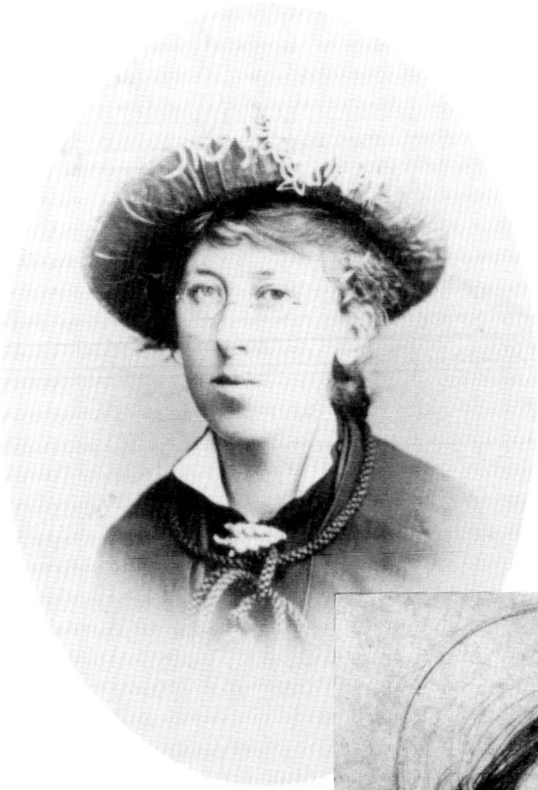

PLATE IV

Left: Violet Paget, later known as Vernon Lee, aged fourteen. She was one of John and Emily's few childhood friends.

Below: Vernon Lee, drawn by Sargent nineteen years later, when she was staying at Fladbury Rectory, Worcestershire.

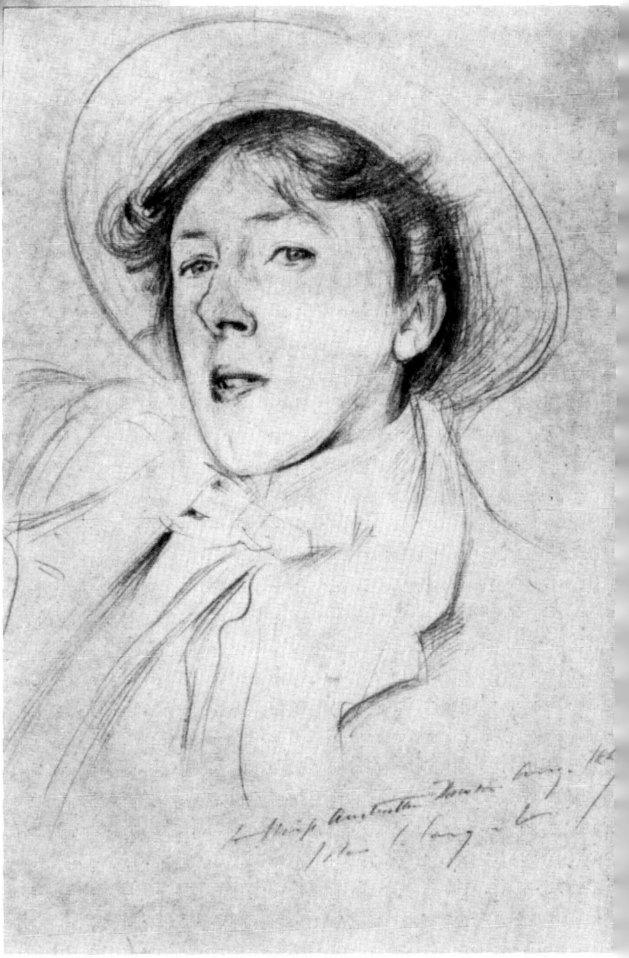

PLATE V

Right: Emily Sargent aged sixteen.

Below: Emily Sargent by her brother, painted in Paris, 1875.

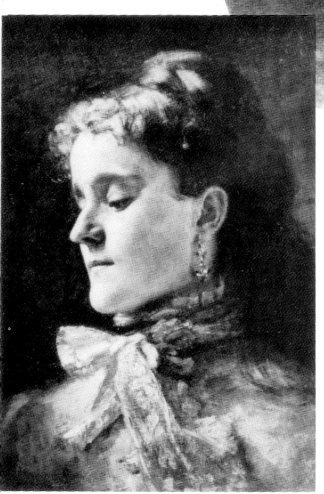

PLATE VI

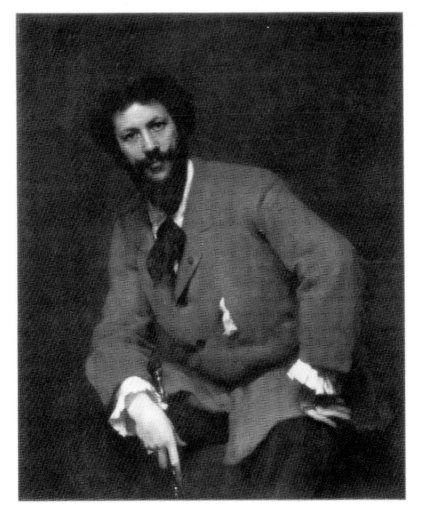

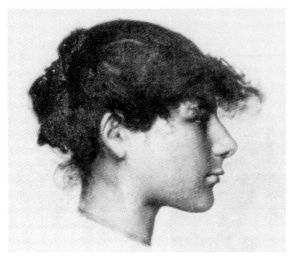

Above: Carolus-Duran, 1879, by his favourite student, Sargent.

Left: Rosina Ferrara, the model who banished dullness from Capri, by Sargent, 1879.

PLATE VII

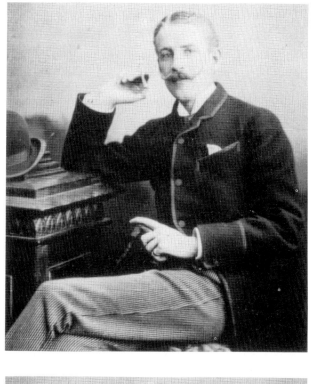

Sargent's Paris colleagues.
Right: *Ralph Curtis,*
Sargent's cousin, who
followed his parents abroad;
below: *a sketch by Sargent of*
Paul César Helleu, one of his
closest friends; **below right:**
James Carroll Beckwith, who
shared the studio at 73 bis rue
Notre-Dame-des-Champs.

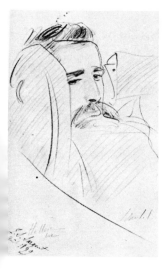

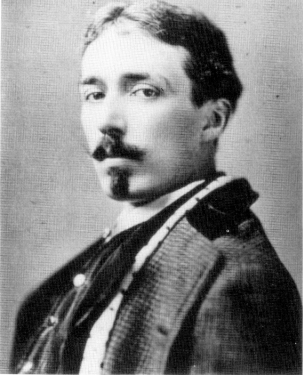

PLATE VIII

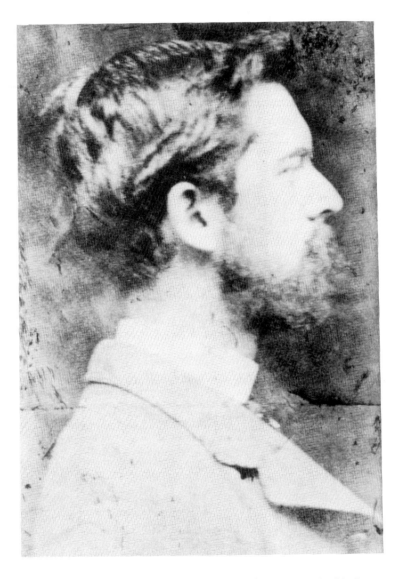

Sargent, aged twenty-two, nearing the end of his apprenticeship in Boulevard Mont Parnasse.

round him. He was safe, submerged in family life. It was perfectly natural; there was nothing odd, and nothing which inclined him to question the comfort of such a state. John never looked outside his family to satisfy his emotional needs. Such an arrangement supplied him with a weird, inhuman invulnerability. He seemed to operate on a different, uncluttered plane, apart from everyone else. And, as if this sophistication were not frightening enough, his maturity and talent dazzled onlookers into speechlessness.

John's arrival at Boulevard Mont Parnasse had attracted considerable attention, and a few months later his showing in the *concours des places* increased that impression. Before Carolus reopened the studio in October, his students sat the Ecole examinations. FitzWilliam, with his usual talent for simplification, explained the ordeal to Bemis (8 September) [1874]: "This concours is merely to enable those who pass . . . to spend a couple of hours every day in drawing from the nude at the Ecole des Beaux Arts. It is very doubtful if John [will] be able to pass . . . but worth his while to try."[3] The *concours* (repeated again in March every year) was a vital fixture in the art students' calendar. They flocked back to Paris from the country in September to prepare. The exams for a much-coveted place in Monsieur Yvon's class were exceptionally arduous and obnoxiously xenophobic – "only two foreigners got in last year out of 60 that tried", John wrote to Heath Wilson[4] – and very long, from 26 September until 16 October. First came perspective and anatomy (drawn from memory) – "unreasonably long difficult and terrible", John complained to Ben del Castillo – then ornament-drawing for three days, two hours each. "But the supreme moment is one of twelve hours wherein we must make a finished drawing of the human form divine."[5] The obstacles to confidence were pronounced: one's place in the hall for life drawing was determined by the skill shown in the previous three sections, the competition was greater than ever, and John had the singular disadvantage of never before having sat an examination. Altogether, the *concours* was excruciating. But John's level of self-training was high. On 27 October he was accepted into the Ecole. It was a remarkable distinction, and for a foreigner an honour. It was also proof, official proof of his ability. He was the only one of Carolus' students to matriculate that autumn.

John was clearly outpacing his colleagues. His success inevitably highlighted the advantages of his *Baedeker* education, as well as exposing its grave flaws. John found himself the product of a system highly tuned to accomplishments, skills and the accumulation of knowledge, and one that had thrived in isolation. Such training was also conducted with a sublime disregard of consequences, which never mattered in the concentrated society of home. But now the results were obvious and cruelly evident: he was too exquisitely prepared to be treated as an equal by his fellow-students. He had the misfortune to inspire awe, not intimacy.

"I met this last week a young Mr. Sargent," Julian Alden Weir (who was studying with Gérôme and matriculated the same time as John) wrote to his mother in America (4 October 1874),

> . . . one of the most talented fellows I have ever come across; his drawings are like the old masters, and his color is equally fine. . . . He speaks as well in French, German, Italian as he does in English, has a fine ear for music, etc. Such men wake one up, and, as his principles are equal to his talents, I hope to have his friendship.[6]

James Carroll Beckwith, a student at *atelier* Duran, noted in his diary about the same time (13 October 1874): "My talented young friend Sargent has been working in my studio with me lately and his work makes me shake myself." And Will Low, another student of Carolus-Duran, assessed John later, and a bit more soberly:

> Of course we are dealing with a phenomenal nature. . . . It may be simply a further indication of an exceptional temperament to record . . . [he] had found time, even at an early age . . . to be much further advanced in his general education than most youths of his age . . . an education thus gleaned . . . may leave curious lapses – lapses calculated to make a pedagogue weep.[7]

Observers and memoirists of John's early days in Paris noted him and recalled him with strange trepidation, or caution, as if they sensed he could never be more than an acquaintance. Time after time they sounded a drum-roll of praise for his knowledge of languages, music, art. Over and over they pointed out his superiority. They were constant in their admiration. He was turned into a hero before he had a chance to be an individual. None of them could deny they were dazzled by him, and none of them would deny they felt unequal to him – but only because they believed he had benefited from a short cut they had been denied. John's acquaintances in Paris were American, and they, unlike him, sensed their foreignness, were impeded by it. But being a foreigner was not a fresh sensation for him, and he had grown accustomed to the society of displaced Americans. Throughout their travels the Sargents constantly enjoyed a false patriotism. John never doubted his nationality, but to him America was a mysterious place that housed unknown quantities such as aunts, uncles, grandparents. And, while it is fair to say this was a minor distinction that separated him from his associates, he could never be at one with them, nor could he ever merge with the local population. It was his first experience of that subtle distinction he would never be able to shake off.

Like Rome for the previous generation, Paris exerted a magnetic attraction for American artists of John's generation, and her natural pull was increased by the financial and subsequent political ructions in the mid-1870s at the National Academy of Design in New York which seriously jeopardized the future of the Academy Schools. This turmoil (which went on for years and closed down the Life School for the academic year 1876–7) naturally persuaded students and prospective students to look elsewhere for training. And by the time John was established in Paris the band of American pupils had increased noticeably.*[8] (An oblique consequence of the American influx in Paris was the sudden prestige attached to *atelier* Duran.) Still, it had not been easy for them to get to Paris; for most the journey was very expensive. They reckoned their years abroad to be some sort of basic trial, the test of ability and suitability for a career, and they knew in a few years they would have to return home. John's relations with them, as a group, were governed by a delicate admixture of their uncertainty and his seemingly effortless mastery of purpose, and resulted in a gulf between them. He knew Europe; they did not. He was completely undaunted by the novel strangeness of life abroad. He did not have to spend his evenings learning French (Carolus-Duran, in common with other masters, insisted on French in the studio). He was not cut off from his family and home; compared to them, he appeared to make no sacrifice whatsoever in order to study in Paris. The ease with which John undertook his work was utterly perplexing to them. "Sargent, according to all accounts," Evan Charteris wrote in his biography, "remained apart; not from any settled austerity of mind, but because he was absorbed in his to a point of fanaticism."[9] In truth, however, John's air of reserve, evident at such an early age, was the product of elements irreducible merely to singlemindedness. First, and most important, was the welcome novelty of formal education. He had waited a long time to be a student for anything longer than a few months. And such a status had been hard-won. Then there was the peculiarity of finding himself surrounded by so many people. He had never experienced such society. There was the unexpected release from the private hospital of his home. And all of these unique delights oscillated under the close-watched security of his family, as if to steady his behaviour amid temptation. But mostly he "remained apart" because he was unschooled in anything else, and had never sensed the omission. The surprise of Paris could never topple years of habit, a feature of his personality.

Where John's character left off assisting the mystery of his Paris years, lack of evidence took over. When Winthrop Sargent died, FitzWilliam's capacity of family secretary ended. The long-standing need for justification ceased. The European bulletin closed, and with it John's closest observer infrequently noted his activities. FitzWilliam turned his interests

* One of the happier results of these upheavals at the Academy was the foundation of the Art Students' League.

The Academy Schools Register is a telling document: between 1870 and 1875 many of John's subsequent associates in Paris attended either the Life School or the Antique School – Beckwith, George de Forest Brush, Neville Cain, Charles M. Dewey, Theodore Robinson, Abbott Thayer and Julian Alden Weir; and, of these seven, four found their way to Boulevard Mont Parnasse (Beckwith, Cain, Dewey and Robinson).

to a few old friends and to his health. He became more indolent and more introverted. He slowly withdrew into memory and total privacy. Occasionally he shook himself into action, but such effort was not sustained.

Conversely, Mary became positively buoyant. She no longer felt hampered by the myth of faulty health, and dropped the pretence – up to a point. She said goodbye to her invalid routine. This sudden burst of fine health coincided with Winthrop Sargent's death. Somehow Mary always picked up dramatically when one of her in-laws died. She rose majestically to Thanksgiving and Christmas festivities, throwing open the doors to friends from Nice and Florence, while her husband was so overcome by the gaiety and rich food he took to his bed. Mary shifted her attention to a fixed point determined to appeal to John's new friends. The Sargent apartment (their third by the autumn of 1874) at 52 rue Abbatucci was supplied with magnetic hospitality. As with Violet Paget, she was able to produce a much-needed family annexe, and she was repaid in the same ecstatic appreciation. Her Sunday dinners were warmly anticipated and fondly recalled: "I am invited to dine at Mrs. Sargent's where I enjoy spending an evening as much as any place I was ever at," Weir wrote to his mother (10 April) [1875].[10] Three weeks later he added: "These people are the most highly educated and agreeable people I have ever met."[11] Mrs Sargent, he later concluded, "is certainly the most delightful lady I have ever met. She . . . has a little round face; she talks so delightfully of the country, how she likes to ramble about and enjoy nature. . . ."[12] Weir introduced her to his friend Albert Edelfeldt, who found Mrs Sargent "very jolly, well-rounded with a red complexion, lively and witty", as he wrote to his mother (10 January 1877) in Finland. And despite the fact he could speak no English, he admired much in her character: "I have never met such a woman who can discuss painting like a professional."*[13]

---

* Albert Gustaf Edelfeldt (1854–1905) was born in Helsingfors. His education followed the customary pattern: Antwerp Academy, then Paris in 1874 where he studied under Gérôme. There he met Weir with whom he shared a studio, and Weir introduced him into the group that collected around the Sargents when they returned to Paris for the winter of 1876–7. Edelfeldt was ill-equipped for any success in their society, as he wrote to his mother (10 January 1877): "I would enjoy myself extremely well there if I weren't the only one in the party that doesn't speak English." Despite this disadvantage he, like Beckwith, fell in love with John's pretty cousin Sarah Austin (the "sort of cousin's" elder daughter), whom he cascaded with love-letters until she left Paris later in the spring.

He made his Salon début in 1877, and five months earlier John and his mother called on him at his studio to look at his work. "Sargent was here yesterday," Edelfeldt wrote to his mother (21 January 1877). "He and his mother gave me compliments in a way you know that they are of no value." He much admired John's ability, but put that very ability down to John's "profound artistic training, which has made him skilful, and opportunities of seeing much which has developed his taste".

The facts of Edelfeldt's life have been well documented. He is a hero in Finland.

Everyone who met her fell for her; she had a gift for making herself liked and a real appeal for lonely people. And after years of wandering she had learnt the art of making furnished apartments seem like home.

After his success in the *concours*, John's tuition at Boulevard Mont Parnasse was augmented first by Monsieur Yvon's instruction at the Ecole, from 4 to 6 p.m., and later by Monsieur Bonnat's lessons in drawing from the antique at the Petit Ecole from 7 to 9 p.m. John's year also adopted the order blessed by the Ecole, staying in Paris for seven months, October to April (or May), and leaving for the country or seaside during the warmer months. And this pattern extended beyond the years he was a student; for the rest of his life John adhered to a refined Ecole principle of dividing the year neatly between winter/studio and summer/ *plein air* work.

Pictures surviving from the early years of this regime tend to mis-represent the precise nature of John's industry because the outdoor pictures are more numerous. By the mere nature of academic or studio training pictures were painted, scraped, repainted, overpainted. It was exercise. The canvas and practice were precious. Once outside, however, with a chosen subject, the approach changed. The disproportion echoed in John's activity was explained by a fellow-student, R. A. M. Stevenson, who entered Carolus' studio sometime around 1876, and later became a distinguished art historian.

Robert Alan Mowbray Stevenson was nine years older than John, and the product of such a peculiar variety of preparation any talent he might have had as a painter was never fully revealed. While at Cambridge he excelled as an oarsman, gymnast and lightweight athlete. From there he moved on to the School of Art, Edinburgh, the Academy in Antwerp, and then Paris. Though he did show at the Royal Academy, his true skills were never those of a painter. Sydney Colvin had to confess he "was not a great painter; theory was his element".[14] He was a brilliant talker, immortalized by his cousin Robert Louis Stevenson. He was also an acute, perceptive critic and a marvellous writer. He died young, aged fifty-three, leaving behind masses of journalism and three books: *Velazquez* (1895), *Ruebens* (1898) and *Raeburn* (posthumous, 1900). At Boulevard Mont Parnasse he was a casual student because he was more interested in what the *patron* had to say than in the actual practice of the lessons. Stevenson has left the best account of Carolus-Duran's heretical approach to painting, and one of the rare glimpses of John as student.

> Mr. Sargent devoted himself to the routine of the studio without seeking to appear original. I do not remember that he was considered in any way other than an excellent and conscientious student for some

And he is best known for his portraits of Tsar Alexander III and the Imperial family. And, though he enjoyed considerable success at home in Finland, his work is strikingly unmemorable.

years. Only in one or two small sketches which he showed us, or in an occasional rapid portrait of a fellow-student, could other than his intimate friends foresee an especial aptitude or vision or evidence of personal feeling for Art. He made, however, a none the less rapid advance in technique, and owed to this proficiency the advantage of being especially remarked by the master.[15]

John was made of perfect student material, because he had come to education so late. He accepted every instruction like a majestic command. He hung on every one of the patron's syllables. He was not so much relearning, as Carolus had predicted, as learning for the first time. Any teacher would have been flattered by such an eager student, and Carolus, ever anxious to seize another distinction, had additional reason to prefer John. During his years with the *patron*, John amassed a collection of "official" honours that naturally reflected back to Carolus. It was as if John's brilliant début was regularly renewed. In March 1877 he was placed second in the treacherous *concours* – "the question ought to be no longer merely to get in", John had written the year before to Fanny Watts (10 March 1876), "but to get in high, which makes it more interesting".[16] Not only was such a placing "the first time that any pupil of Carolus-Duran's Atelier had been rated so high", FitzWilliam wrote to Bemis (24 March) [1877], ". . . [but] the first time that any American Art Student in Paris had ever been so ranked[?]".[17] A few months later, in May, he was awarded a Third Class Medal for ornament-drawing. The first picture he submitted to the Salon was accepted, and the following year his entry was given an Honourable Mention. John was, even from the start, Carolus' star pupil, and he was repaid with pronounced favouritism; Hinckley, who was popularly assumed to have clinched those laurels, was demoted. Even Beckwith, who was otherwise equanimity itself about studio hierarchy, was provoked to near-jealousy by the master's behaviour, especially when John was selected to accompany Carolus to Nice with Hinckley and Stephen Parker Hills in January 1875. Two years later John was again chosen, this time with Beckwith, to assist Carolus in the painting of the *plafond* for the Luxembourg (*The Apotheosis of Marie of Medici*, shown in the 1878 Salon). And the following year, in 1878, John was allowed to paint his master's portrait. As a sequence, John's progress was faultlessly assured, steady and confident, and while Carolus' own reputation travelled with his John was pushed, willingly. While the partnership lasted, it produced stunning results, and consigned John to the master's shadow. Once John began to display the threatening signs of independence, however, Carolus dropped him. But such distinction automatically encouraged remoteness, remoteness beyond John's private ration.

"I had almost decided", Mary wrote to her sister-in-law (13 December 1875), ". . . to tuck Emily and John under my (fat!) arms, and go home for a little visit, as I feel such a longing to see the old country, with its familiar faces, once more. The children talk of nothing else. . . . They have heard us speak all their lives, about people and places, wh. they have never seen; and they are full of interest to realize the pleasant visions of friends and homes, in America."[18] They discussed the plan for the best part of a year. Three months before his wife "had almost decided", FitzWilliam wrote that his wife and older children "are all very anxious to go 'home', as they say, although the only home the children have ever known has been on this side of the ocean".[19]

More than homesickness, or the lure of the Centennial Exposition in Philadelphia, played the tune of Mary's resolve to recross the Atlantic. She had had her first taste of separation from her son, and she did not like it. The Sargents had left Paris in the summer of 1875 for Maison Lefort in St Enogat on the Brittany coast. The place satisfied all their requirements – comfortable, pretty, and above all inexpensive – and they stayed on for the winter. At the end of the summer John went back to Paris, living apart from his family for the first time, at Madame Darode's boarding-house at 19 rue de l'Odéon (and working at a studio he shared with Beckwith at 73 rue Notre-Dame-des-Champs). As the winter dragged on Mary found St Enogat insufferably dull. She hatched the American scheme in an attempt to regain recent old times, and relieved her boredom with planning, anticipation and excitement. She and FitzWilliam decided early on that he would remain behind with Violet, who at six was too young to make the journey.

The festivities in Philadelphia provided Mary with the central excuse for the journey, which was hotly endorsed by FitzWilliam, who immediately foresaw the fruition of his long-frustrated ambition of introducing John and Emily to their mass of relatives. John was nearly twenty, Emily nearly nineteen, and neither of them had ever "seen such a thing as a relative before this visit to America", FitzWilliam wrote to his sister (a year later, 1 March 1877).[20]

Their tour was plotted to follow a well-packed tourist itinerary. After docking at Jersey City at the end of May (1876), they went straight to Philadelphia where they were stopped in their tracks by the heat. The heat, Emily wrote to Violet Paget (24 September 1876), "was so unheard of, that the little energy I had was expended in endeavouring to keep cool. Such a summer has not been felt for over thirty years . . . and as we were totally unaccustomed to such a high temperature, we were almost annihilated."[21] From Philadelphia they went to Newport to stay with Admiral Case, whom they had known in Nice. Then up the Hudson River, stopping at West Point Academy to visit the Weirs, and on to Montreal via Lake George and Lake Champlain. From Montreal they passed through the St Lawrence Rapids and on to Niagara Falls before returning to Philadelphia. At the end of September, John asked Emily to go with him to Chicago, but when she was told the distance and the speed needed to get there and back by the time they sailed, 4 October, she refused, and John went instead with an unidentified friend from Paris. Altogether they spent four months in America, and their reactions, like their activities, were muted by the disagreeable climate.

While in Europe the Sargents staunchly upheld the fact they were Americans, and to European observers they presented the classic image of New Englanders; to American observers, however, they were strictly European – an unexpected reversal that dogged John throughout his life. John's American cousins were totally baffled by him. Their imaginary picture of him long before he even appeared was drawn from FitzWilliam's steady accounts of his achievements and their own families' ready use of him as a model son, a model by which they were inadequate measures. At first he did little to corrupt this exaggerated reputation. His manners were correct, foreign and off-putting. Despite the 97° heat he and his mother and sister insisted on long walks directly after lunch. His knowledge and maturity were forbidding. But soon his charm undid the damage of first impressions; his high spirits warmed the frosty notion that he might really be a paragon. "His cousins remembered him that summer", Nancy Hale wrote many years later, ". . . for his delightful music . . . and a passionate Italian love song, the words composed of the names of patent medicines."[22] And he was also remembered for his constant sketching. John wrote little about his American visit and referred to it even less. Unlike his father he rarely depended on words. He used his sketchbook for his diary. His paintings and drawings were his journal, as they always had been. He was not menaced by introspection or the urge for confession. The great moment of witnessing his "home" filtered through to his work, unhelpfully. The point of travel had never been letter-writing.

His American work did show, if nothing else, excitement, and mostly the excitement of ocean travel. The dutiful accounts of the previous summer in Brittany gave way before the larger problems of perspective. Suddenly, he became bold. He made notes for future paintings. *Lifeboats on Davits*[23] records the sharp angle of the deck pitching into the sea, the distant water-line the height of the lifeboats, with written instructions for colour: "lilac blue light, greenish reflect, light and cold, warm greenish, purplish" for the hulls, and "greyish brown arriving darker than sea?" for the furled sailcloth underneath. Over and over again he returned to the single theme of distorted perspective. He rose to the novelty, in his oil portrait of his mother on deck and in his painting of a storm; in the first there was no attempt at likeness and in the latter it was all drama – he was fired by the unnatural perspective. Once on land, however, his fascination calmed. His portrait of his aunt Emily Sargent Parsons and his painting of Niagara Falls were more of the same near-reflex dutiful accounts; he made diary entries.

Once John returned to Paris he also returned to Carolus' shadow. John was excessively vulnerable to it, and Carolus meant him to be; it was cast with a magnificent awareness of effect, at once enticing students' devotion and producing the aura of worldly success. Through his painting Carolus became the prime example of "a man of the world", and he achieved this with some effort. He was a dreadful snob. He cultivated the manners and the habits of a gentleman. Every morning a carriage delivered him to his studio in Passage Stanislas. Every day he had luncheon at his club. He lived in considerable luxury. His children also followed fashion and had an English nanny. He adored titles. He rode. He hunted. He fenced. Altogether he tried to (and worse, thought he *had* to) dignify his profession by making it appear a less important feature of his life. Though his manner was loaded with pride, it was also eroded by uncertainty. His clients assumed him to be coldly professional, but his moods and tempers were vitriolic. Once, resenting a client's silence and misreading subsequent laughter unconnected with the commissioned portrait on view, Carolus slashed the canvas with a sword and roared out of the studio. For him the studio was a stage. His performance was that of a misplaced pugilist: he would leap about, hopping, brush in hand, from one end of the room to the other. His adroit footwork earned him the title during his copyist days in the Louvre of "the dancer".[24] Altogether, Carolus was fascinating, and complicated, and luckily during the 1870s while John was subject to his influence and the power of his reputation Carolus was still more interested in painting than in becoming conventionally respectable. The latter strain, like his self-doubt, was slowly corrupting his work. He was dubbed "the court painter". His exhibition of thirty-eight paintings in the autumn of 1874 (at Le Cercle Artistique) was only a qualified success to student eyes. Beckwith denounced some as "too sensational and vulgar".[25] Weir complained he was "very extravagant with his backgrounds – violent greens, reds or yellows".[26] The force of Carolus' energy was read in the startling effects, and his minor contribution to the history of painting was shown up for what it was – rotating his palette away from dull colour.

Despite all the controversy surrounding his work, despite his fame, and despite his success, Carolus added very little to the art of portraiture. He reduced an aesthetic turmoil to a banal diagnosis: the problem was one of tension between the sitter and background. No one could dare call this solution profound, or novel, or even original. What it was, however, was surprising, and only because Carolus travelled a bit further along the colour spectrum than was popularly adopted. Such a journey gave him a brilliant career. But he was not intellectual. He avoided the very conflicts of composition and perspective that were beginning to tease John's imagination. What Carolus had to teach, though valuable beyond estimate, was simple, and unchanging. Carolus was solidly rooted in the formal tradition which his originality modified but never wholly changed. His composition might have been occasionally striking, but it was rarely subtle or much removed from the mainstream. The force of Carolus' personality tended to increase the importance of what he had to teach.

John's work progressed from Carolus' lead. Where Carolus busily reinterpreted elements, John addressed himself to the fundamental problems of a painting as a whole. Where Carolus might paint brilliant passages in a sitter's dress within the safety of the orthodox conventions of pose, John looked at the pose itself. Where details alone in Carolus' work revealed his principles, John applied his master's ideas throughout. John earned his status as a favourite because he employed the teacher's language better and more fluently than Carolus himself. John was, above all else, a student of Carolus, not a mimic. He had youth on his side to help along audacity. And he was less attached to the sole discipline of portraiture than Carolus.

More often John was excited by the challenge of perspective; over and over again he returned to the problem of odd points of view. One of his most daring experiments was painted a year after he came back from America – *Rehearsal of the Pasdeloup Orchestra at the Cirque d'Hiver*. John frequently went to Jules Pasdeloup's Sunday-afternoon concerts at the Cirque d'Hiver Theatre. William Coffin* witnessed John's enthusiasm:

> Sargent, who dearly loved the music, was struck by the odd picturesqueness of the orchestra . . . seen in the middle of the amphitheater, the musicians' figures foreshortened from the high point of view on the rising benches, the necks of the bass-viols sticking up above their heads, the white sheets of music illuminated by little lamps on the racks. . . . While he listened he looked, and one day he took a canvas and painted his impression.[27]

The orchestra was a bold sweep; the focus dissolved to make the players only an arc. Any detail was brushed in abruptly so as not to detract from the single issue. The entire effect was dramatic, bold – an essay in geometry.

His experiments in perspective were carried out with brio. There was nothing tentative or hesitant. It was confident. And it contradicted the impression made by his personality. This reversal yields the strongest indication of the division of his nature. He was confident on canvas and tentative away from it. While he was prepared and anxious to take on difficulties in painting, he shirked any such vulnerability in his human relations. As a result, his progress in the studio accelerated because his purpose was wonderfully unencumbered, streamlined, certain. He found no trouble mastering the rudiments of technique.

* William Anderson Coffin (1855–1925), painter and critic. Born in Pennsylvania, educated at Yale (graduated 1874) and, finding the business career his father mapped out for him wholly unattractive, Coffin turned to art, first at Yale Art School then in Paris, where he went in 1877, and stayed for three years. He was a pupil of Bonnat. Coffin was a very distinguished art critic and wrote for several papers. He is best known as a landscape painter, though he did start his painting career as a portraitist. He sat on many committees and did much to promote American art.

But John was less enthusiastic about portraiture. His early essays were conducted with extreme caution, almost reluctance. The heroic bravery was gone. The portrait of his aunt was restrained to the point of being primitive. He could not get away from the battle for likeness. The year before (1875) he painted his two sisters: Emily in a small head-and-shoulders study, profoundly conventional but tenderly rendered, and Violet, aged about five, quicker, a little more boldly, depending more on suggestion than on close detail. None of his early work revealed a magnetic attraction to portraiture; if anything, the opposite. He preferred to be outdoors. He favoured landscapes. His sketchbooks were full of mountains, boats, seascapes, buildings, not people. He seemed to carry Carolus' lessons outdoors, under the very nose of the master who represented and encouraged their application in the studio.

Atelier Duran was synonymous with portraiture and drew nearer the discipline than the other reigning studios because Carolus himself wavered infrequently from that category of painting. Cabanel, Bonnat, Pils, Académie Julien and the other beacons of education gave more space to history and genre paintings than Carolus, not because the Ecole insisted, but because they themselves were less singleminded. Even when Carolus bowed to the Ecole's orders (as he had to after neglecting drawing) he adopted strange independence. To him all scenes, all subjects, no matter how remote or intensely felt, had to be reduced to individual activity, people reacting to events or replying to specific feelings. One of the lessons in *atelier* Duran was to portray the Flight into Egypt. Carolus-Duran conducted his students through the issues presented by the problem:

> There are two methods of understanding a subject. It may be treated heroically or intimately. In the latter case the artist enters into the life of the personages that he desires to represent, observing them as human beings. . . . The heroic manner, on the contrary, expresses but an instant of their life, when raised to an exceptional pitch. The personages presented are, as you might say, deified . . . for this very reason, they lose many sympathetic charms that we only find in beings living, thinking, and suffering like ourselves. The latter alone can move us. . . .
>
> In the subject that now occupies us . . . Picture to yourselves the incidents of this departure. See the group precipitately leaving in the night; follow them hour by hour; imagine the scenes that must have followed one another, at the morning fires, in the glimmering twilight, in the moonlight, or under the bright light of day . . . they have had in their flight a crowd of emotions such as you may have felt in your journeys. Call up your remembrances and apply them, so that the personages may be before your eyes, moving, walking, resting, forming a whole with the nature that surrounds them and of which they reflect the influence. . . . As you are very different from one another, your compositions will reflect the variety of your natures.[28]

In short, Carolus was saying, all you were dealing with was portraiture in context. The individual held the key, and the individual transmitted the complication of emotion that had developed into a set-piece, a historical metaphor.

Carolus' views of subject and portrait painting were happily in concert; the former was the logical offshoot of the latter, thus the rudiments of portraiture lay in the core of his students' mastery of their craft. Carolus' policy and activity were straightforward. But why his students and such a large number of their generation readily annexed portraiture to their career was less clear. They seemed to adopt his theory for their text with little difficulty and no discomfort. As an area of painting, portraiture was the least hospitable to experiment. It was the least accommodating to change. But the entire fabric of official French art education was manufactured to retain standards, retard adventurous expression. John's generation was aware of this fact when they left America. They did not embark to break new ground; they came abroad to learn the system and continue the tradition. Carolus represented a rewording of the tradition within the safest territory of the profession – portraiture was on the commercial edge of that profession. Carolus' students collected round him out of simple and harmless motives: they were after a trade. Portraits were a way of earning money. Portraiture was a safe means of access to the Salon, carrying with it an official recognition of skill. A portrait commanded attention and publicity, both for the sitter and for the painter. In short, the best advertisement to start a career. The student's course was plain: Carolus' lessons, tempered by Ecole refinement, bundled together and expressed in a portrait hung in the Salon supplied him with a rosette of worthiness. He was ready to go home, equipped with a skill able to earn him a living. Altogether, it was a practical approach that tore to shreds the mythology of art. John's colleagues adopted this logical reading at the very moment it was becoming unfashionable. They felt more secure blessed by official order.

John was more than Carolus-Duran's student; he was his apprentice. His first official portrait – official because it was painted for the Salon and therefore public (as opposed to family) – was painted during the first few months of 1877, when he was twenty-one years old. This portrait was important because it was his first, what his father called "his first serious work, his, as yet, 'opus magnum', a portrait of a young lady, half-length, in a sitting posture . . . to my uneducated eye it is – particularly if one considers that it is his first attempt at a serious, finished work; – a very creditable and promising one".[29] The sitter was Miss Fanny Watts (1858–1927). John had known her and her family for years. The Watts' history was similar to the Sargents', only neater. They had come to Europe from America to economize. Their life and John's friendship with Fanny followed the well-charted pattern of announced then frustrated meetings in various cities on the Continent. They met continuously, though less often than they predicted. One summer they were together in Benezal;

the following they were together in St Enogat where, like the Sargents, they stayed on for the winter, and where, in January, John did a pencil portrait of Miss Watts. In the spring of 1875 and the winter of 1877 they were in Paris. Luckily for John and Emily, the Watts family did not stay in one place to the same plan as the Sargents did not. Both John and Emily were fond of Miss Watts. She together with Violet Paget and Ben del Castillo completed the small group that passed for their collection of old friends. Though John's portrait of Miss Watts was his first non-family portrait, it was a picture of someone fairly close to him.

FitzWilliam continually referred to the portrait as "creditable". A fellow-student, Albert Edelfeldt, was less reserved: while the work was in progress he predicted (on 23 February) it would turn out well; by the end of March he pronounced it to be masterly. Carolus, for his part, entertained no doubts whatsoever about the Jury accepting it. Their confidence derived from the basic fact that the painting was a highly competent performance, a little overworked and safely undaring. The pose – seated, head inclined to the left, right arm supporting her weight on the arm of the chair, left arm fully extended – completes the suggestion he rendered in his pencil sketch of her the year before. John's choice of colouring echoes Carolus' tastes almost without distortion: black dress, muted salmon-pink drapery. This solid piece of work did more than arouse his colleagues' admiration; it satisfied his father's second-hand ambition: "He seems to be doing very satisfactorily," FitzWilliam wrote to his brother (3 April 1877), " – which is a great comfort to us – and to have chosen his vocation."*[30]

* In the Salon catalogue for 1877 the portrait was entitled "Mlle W . . .". John was described as "SARGENT (John S.) né Philadelphia (Etats-Unis d'Amérique) élève de M. Carolus Duran. – rue Notre-Dame-des-Champs, 73". The portrait is now in Philadelphia.

BOOK TWO

I must stay in Paris; it is the only place.
John to Charles Deering, 2 May 1878

Yes, I have always thought Sargent a great painter. He would be greater still if he had one or two little things he hasn't — but he will do.
Henry James to Thomas Bailey Aldrich, 5 March 1888

VI

By the time John was twenty-one the main features of his character had moved into position, leaving him unlike the people around him. His past was very much with him. His love of work was the logical extension of his mother's dictum "to complete" and the contrary acceptance of so many years of postponement. Unlike his parents he was acquiring a tangible evidence of time. But his version of domestic order had its root deeper than in mere reaction; it was protection. He was restrained by shyness. He was not altogether at ease, having discovered social life so much later than any of his contemporaries. He found himself unable to comply with the abrupt relaxation of dress and behaviour welcomed by others in the Quartier Latin. He kept his hat, cravat, waistcoat, worsted trousers and coat – the wardrobe he had become accustomed to wearing. By the late 1870s, however, his neatly trimmed beard and moustache appeared, and he never changed his mind about that addition. He carried himself with a little awkwardness, as if he still had not quite got used to his height; when his figure grew more robust, the vague tentative mannerisms of posture disappeared. He had earned a reputation as one of the few students with an assured future – a further distinction he could add to the others already in place. And still he remained modest; if he lacked spontaneity, he did at least have a rich sense of humour, which made him more human and more charming in manner than the hesitation implied by his reticence, his dress, and his keenness for work. It was plain to see John was not like the people around him.

In his social life he replaced any direct expression of emotion with mathematics. Apart from Emily, no one could claim to know the workings of his mind, but there were many round him who thought they had his friendship. He never ate a meal alone. He did not travel alone. He rarely worked alone. Numbers took over from intimacy with scant resistance. But this highly populated existence *did* have its root in reaction; his childhood had clocked all the loneliness he cared to experience. For him, life was not a transit up and down the scale of emotions; it was employment. When he was content he worked *very* hard; when he was less than content he just worked hard. Such a reordering of natural complexities made him look like a machine, with an ever-increasing production, and it was a sadly misleading impression. As a result, when he did find himself faced with some difficulty he could find no helpful terms of expression, and the consequent silence only bolstered the inhuman label.

Yet his social life was full to bursting. He was enormously popular, but his friends inevitably did more to persuade him to friendship than he found himself able to do, because there was the cold metal of reserve girding his bonhomie. And for someone who worshipped independence and work the number of people surrounding John seemed a useless irony. During his student years he moved easily in two largely unmerging spheres of acquaintance – among Americans (out of habit, and thanks to the population at Boulevard Mont Parnasse) and among the French (thanks to his mastery of the language). Paul César Helleu (1859–1927), himself from Brittany, was amazed at John's command of French when they first met shortly after John came to Paris, and throughout the many years of their long and close friendship that same reaction measured many of John's other qualities.[1]

Unlike John, Helleu found himself in Paris (studying with Gérôme and at the Académie Julien) without the benefit of his family's blessing; in fact, more as the consequence of downright undisguised opposition. At an alarmingly early age Helleu displayed the two compelling interests that would carry him through life – art and beautiful women – and neither was much to his mother's taste. She could not even decide which of them she found worse, the choice was so detestable, and she brought the full weight of her powerful character into the battle to win her son over to conventional ambition. And, while she had age, bearing and conviction on her side, her son had the equally powerful weapon of determination. When he told her he *was* going to be an artist all the unsavoury images of depravity, indulgence and extravagance loomed up before her, causing her to recoil in forbidding dread. And when she discovered he had little trouble walking over the strictest rules of etiquette to get to a pretty face her reaction was a little simpler: she blew up. That finished Helleu's patience; he had had enough, stormed out of the house, and took the train to Paris.

He had won. His mother was forced to face defeat, but she would not be crushed. At first she doled out a very meagre monthly allowance, and later, when she saw that he did possess talent, she dipped a little deeper into her purse. But throughout his early years in Paris she continued to harbour doubts, based on the thinnest evidence, cunningly discovered. She launched dawn raids, fresh from church, and was appalled to find her son not yet hard at work. None of this perverse spying and questioning did much to help his confidence, and though he was never tempted to turn back he was often very discouraged. John's friendship, he readily owned, helped to rejuvenate his bruised determination.

John effected the transition from despair to optimism with infinite, winning tact. One day he called on Helleu in his studio round the corner in rue de la Grande-Chaumière and remarked on the beauty of the pastel

Helleu had just thrown off the easel. Helleu was convinced it was "a horror", strong proof he had no future. John rounded with delicacy: " 'Because you've been looking at it too long, you've lost your eye. No one ever paints what they want to paint, but to me who can only see what you've done, not what you're aiming at, this is a charming thing I must have for my collection.' " Naturally, Helleu's spirits revived, adding that John must have it. " 'I shall accept it gladly, Helleu,' " John replied, " 'but not as a gift. I sell my own pictures, and know what they cost me . . . I should never enjoy this pastel if I hadn't paid you a fair and honest price for it.' "[2] That said, he withdrew a thousand-franc note and handed it to Helleu. It was the first money he had earned. Later Helleu was convinced it had been a premeditated act. John had changed the fortunes of his career.

Their friendship was sealed. They were constant companions, going everywhere together, having their meals together, seeing each other every day. They shared similar tastes in dress; Helleu also disliked the popular relaxed fashion of his fellow-students, and refused to wear the generous velvet trousers, tight at the ankles, the flowing silk cravats, the soft felt hats. Both Helleu and John were noted for this disdain and for their distinguished appearance; they might easily have been brothers. After John's purchase Helleu never looked back, eventually from a very elevated plane. He became one of the most successful etchers, pastellists and painters of his day. He made a brilliant passage from his friendships with Degas, Monet, Rodin, Bourget, Montesquiou, Whistler, Boldini and Proust (who used him for much of Elstir) to the highest altitude of society, sailing over to Cowes in his yachts, having acquired a terrible case of "le snobisme anglo-saxon".[3]

He never forgot his debt to John, and it later merged into real affection, on both sides. John called him "Leuleu", and Helleu always carried one of John's letters as a talisman. His devotion to John was absolute, unshaken by his vitriolic temper, and he wrote to his daughter Paulette [December 1922]: "J'ai voulu faire photographier Sargent qui a été pour moi, tout au long de ma vie, plus qu'un père."[4]

Where Helleu gave John access to the French (Rodin was one of the circle), the one person who best managed to overcome John's resistance on behalf of the Americans was James Carroll Beckwith (1852–1917), mostly because he had proximity on his side: for three years, from August 1875, they shared a studio at 73 rue Notre-Dame-des-Champs. Their friendship was a balanced ledger-sheet. John and his family provided a much-welcome domestic refuge, and Beckwith provided the introduction to the American students in Paris he had known in New York. Withal, Beckwith's affection for John was based on a combination of admiration, benign envy, and energy.

Unlike John, Beckwith's temperament was uneven. He was caught in the very same grid of financial precariousness crossed with vague optimism shared by most of the exiled American students. "I had unbounded faith in myself," he wrote in an autobiographical fragment, "and felt a queer little sense of certainty of my future . . . I was resolved to succeed or to go under in the attempt."[5] But soon this "queer little sense of certainty" gave way to self-doubt; his progress was not a straight line up the graph, but he struggled to get everything he could out of his five years abroad.

Beckwith was four years older than John. He had been born in Hannibal, Missouri, but spent his childhood in Chicago where his father owned a successful wholesale grocery business. His mother had encouraged his interest in art, and allowed him to study at the Chicago Academy of Design for three years, until 1871, when the great fire destroyed both the Academy and his father's business. Somehow the fire also relaxed his father's hatred of the idea of his son becoming an artist, and he agreed to Beckwith's long journey east to be trained, stopping first at the National Academy of Design in New York. At the Life and Antique Schools he met Weir, Dewey, Thayer, Cain and Brush, all of whom eventually beat a path to Europe. Beckwith himself arrived in Paris on 18 November 1873: "Now I think my real Art life begins. All that has gone before is but a preamble to it," he remembered. Though he spoke no French, he did have an acute homing-pigeon instinct: "I lost no time in sight seeing but hastened to search for the little American colony of students who assembled at Picot's restaurant . . . and were lodged in neighboring student Hotels." There he found his friends from New York, who welcomed him by telling him he was late, too late to gain admission to any of the great *ateliers*. Undaunted, he tried for Cabanel's, "the prime favorite with the Frenchmen. Indeed, it was rumoured that he could make a brilliant student out of the dullest possible material. . . ." He tried *atelier* Pils; he tried *atelier* Bonnat; and finally he tried *atelier* Carolus-Duran, where he joined the other, in his words, "loyal champions of his [Carolus'] talent before the clans from the other Ateliers", and where, a few months later, he met John.[6]

On the surface theirs was an unequal friendship. Beckwith's vanity was forced to withstand a good many shocks. He was quickly outdistanced by John, who was admitted to the Ecole first, who had a picture in the Salon first, and who was later awarded the commissions he had gone after. And, worst of all, John made the whole business of painting look effortless. Still, Beckwith's generosity of spirit was boundless. He awarded John (and Carolus) inviolate prominence in his highly charged romantic memories of his time in Paris. For Beckwith, Paris and John were permanently linked.

By an odd exchange, Beckwith introduced John to America, at one remove. He had arrived in Paris weighed down with the heavy luggage of his New York studentship, and with little effort he was able to keep a tight grasp on it abroad. He was by nature, he admitted in his diary, genial, companionable and expansive, all of which were accentuated by feeling displaced, foreign and temporarily settled. He moved in a pack with the others who shared these new sensations, and John was readily annexed to that pack. John's thin association with America was strengthened; he began to participate in the pack's collective interests and activities, which remained fixed on home. It was another opportunity to confuse John's nationality.

In 1877 the National Academy of Design in New York passed a rule that was aggressively inhospitable to non-Academicians who wanted to exhibit at the annual show, and was a sharp volte-face on the Hanging Committee's previous policy – only works by Academicians would be allowed. The younger painters were furious. They drew their forces together, set the full weight of bureaucracy in motion, and founded the Society of American Artists – an organization created to welcome the very painters cold-shouldered by the Academy. The Society appointed scouts to find the best work in cities along the east coast of America and abroad. Five "jurymen" were selected in Paris, and John was one of them. (The others were Augustus Saint-Gaudens* – later replaced by Edwin Blash-field – Abbott Thayer, Charles Bridgeman and Guy DuBois.) This appointment went beyond reconnaissance; it was a flagrant enticement for John to send a picture to New York for the first exhibition in March 1878. And he did. He submitted a version of the painting he was working on for the Salon and had been working on since the previous summer in Brittany: *Fishing for Oysters at Cancale*.

John had spent about ten weeks in Cancale, on the coast, from mid-June to the end of August 1877, trying to coax the peasants to pose and trying to avoid the sightseers who crowded round him. There he followed the usual academic practice of making copious sketches for a future work done in the studio. When he got back to rue Notre-Dame-des-Champs he formulated his picture – a frieze of women and children ambling down the beach, lethargically intent on harvesting oysters – which was a safe adaptation of a subject previously tried out at the Salon. He did three versions (one for the Salon, one for New York and one for Beckwith), and the inevitable errors of painting outdoor pictures indoors are evident: the angle of light varies from one figure to the next, the shadows make no sense, and the colouring is inconclusive. But none of these mattered; the pictures were a tremendous success. In the Salon it was a prudent successor to his portrait of Miss Watts, and in New York it was a brilliant début. The *Atlantic Monthly* rhapsodized:

no word less than "exquisite" describes Sargent's *Oyster Fishers at*

* Augustus Saint-Gaudens, who had a studio at 49 rue Notre-Dame-des-Champs, got to know John the following year: "a tall, rather slim, handsome fellow . . . his appearance at first sight remains in my mind distinctly" (*Reminiscences* (1913), Vol. 1, p. 250).

Founded in June 1877 as the American Art Association by Saint-Gaudens, Walter Shirlaw (1838–1909), Wyatt Eaton (1849–96) and Helena de Kay, the SAA held annual exhibitions in March until 1906 when it merged with the National Academy of Design. Dr Jennifer Bienenstock has done extensive research on the SAA: see her "The Foundation and Early Years of the Society of American Artists, 1877–1884", PhD thesis, City University of New York, 1983.

Cancale [*sic*]. We envy a mind, that can look thus at common life. . . . Where another would see but a group of rude fish-wives plodding heavily on the sand, he shows us a charming procession coming on with a movement almost rhythmical. . . . It is managed with delicious skill . . . with an airy nonchalance.[7]

DuBois called it "very luminous".[8] And it sold at once.* (So did the Salon version.)

During the winter of 1877–8, John and Beckwith were asked to help Carolus with his ceiling decoration for the Luxembourg. It was a strange, ambitious enterprise, and a fine essay in self-advertisement. John painted in a portrait of Beckwith; Beckwith painted in a portrait of John; Carolus painted in a portrait of John; Beckwith had a fight with Carolus; and John bravely painted in a portrait of Carolus. When the decoration was shown, interest automatically shifted from the decorative quality to the personalities portrayed. "Duran's plafond", Emily reported to Violet Paget (24 July 1878),

. . . looks fine, but of course the perspective is extraordinary, as the canvas could not be placed as it is intended to be looked at, for it would take the light away from the other pictures. Duran made an excellent portrait of John in it, & John made one of him which so delighted Duran, that he told John he would sit for his portrait, & John has begun it. . . .[9]

The sittings took place in Carolus' studio in Passage Stanislas while Carolus himself was churning out one of his huge dull portraits that eventually pleased no one, one of the great actress Helena Modjeska (1840–1909).† Her grace was sufficient to overcome the limitations of her

---

* Now at the Museum of Fine Arts, Boston. It was bought, in 1878, by Samuel Colman, a landscape painter. The version for the Salon, *En route pour la pêche*, or *Oyster Gatherers at Cancale*, is now at the Corcoran Gallery of Art, Washington, DC. He did an enormous number of studies for the pictures, which he finished back in Paris. The Salon version was bought by Admiral Case (1813–93), an old family friend who met the Sargents in Nice in the mid-1860s when he was fleet captain of the European Squadron of the American Navy, and to whom can be traced a long and important thread of connection throughout John's life.

Augustus Ludlow Case's daughter Annie (1848–76) married Charles Deering (1852–1927), a young naval officer who later became the Chairman of the International Harvester Company. John painted a posthumous portrait of Annie Deering in 1877 and a copy for her father. The year before, when he was in America staying with the Cases in Newport, he painted Deering's portrait; his wife's portrait was designed as a pendant to it.

(In 1917, Sargent stayed at Charles Deering's house at Brickell Point, near Miami. He also visited Deering's brother James's palace Vizcaya which was then under construction and where he did a great many watercolours. Charles Deering was a life-long friend and patron of John's.)

† Now at the Pennsylvania Academy of Art. Madame Modjeska's husband, Count Bozenta, thought Carolus' price outrageous (though in fact a friend of his

Polish accent when she played Shakespeare. Her elegance excited audiences from Warsaw to California, and was one of the many aspects Carolus failed to capture in his portrait. While she sat to Carolus, she noticed and remembered John. "One morning a tall, attractive young man came in", Madame Modjeska recalled in her autobiography, "and was introduced by Monsieur Duran as 'Mr. John Sarrrgent, of Amerrrica.' The young artist had brought with him a small canvas. . . . In an hour or so he made a sketch which looked to me like a finished portrait in its wonderful likeness. When he left the room, Carolus said, 'Il a du talent, ce garçon-la!' It was a sort of off-hand praise. . . ."[10]

John's portrait of Carolus, which was finished the following year, was an audacious rendering, braver than *Miss Watts* and just as measured. Carolus' seated posture was one he often adopted – slouched forward, one hand limply fondling his walking-stick, the other flayed out resting on his leg – and one that made his torso look enormous. The colouring was Spanish, sombre, mud hues interrupted only by his well-laundered shirt and light flesh tones. The likeness was precise – the likeness of a respectable provincial that had acquired the look of a Parisian artist. When it was shown it succeeded in capturing interest, fulfilling its purpose. People collected round it. It harvested attention because people were interested in Carolus, and even more interested in what his star pupil had made of him (for a second time). An atrocious engraving of the portrait was reproduced in the first number of *Salon illustré* accompanied by a poem of similar brilliance. Critics fell on the picture with a healthy appetite and made altogether laudatory noises. They pronounced it to be "épatant" (wonderful). FitzWilliam, up from Nice for his annual spring visit to John, proudly agreed with the general opinion: "we were very much gratified with the progress he had evidently made during the year", he wrote to his brother (15 August) [1879]. "He sent to the Salon a portrait of his teacher Carolus-Duran which was considered . . . to be one of the best portraits exposed at this Spring's Exhibition."[11]

John's portrait of Carolus launched him a little more surely than his portrait of Fanny Watts. It also heralded his independence, his departure from apprenticeship, and neatly summarized his four and a half years at Boulevard Mont Parnasse. The picture's success was considerable, furnishing him with commissions and with the heavy reputation of promise: "I think he will astonish the Paris public some day," DuBois wrote to Weir (14 May 1879).[12]

John stopped work on his studio portrait of Carolus shortly after he had begun, to go to Italy. It was the height of the summer, Paris was stifling, and like his parents he had developed a programme for dealing with the calendar in geographical terms. Unlike his parents' equation, however,

---

was paying), Carolus agreed to a rebate, and then overcharged on the frame. His wife's face had been made to look excessively commonplace.

his appeared sane, or at least less eccentric. Whereas FitzWilliam and Mary sought oppressive uneventfulness, John looked for stimuli, novelty, visual excitement. This variation was deceptively superficial, for in truth John duplicated his parents' ambition exactly, replacing their excuse for health with his need for work. John's yearning for work had its precise antecedent in FitzWilliam and Mary's monomania for health. Work did for John what illness had done for his mother.

Forty years later Emily unwittingly expressed this central impulse: "At the moment John is in his room", she wrote to a friend in 1912 (from Spain), "drawing a most intricate pattern, from an old piece of stucco, as it is not good enough light for anything. He is wonderfully patient, & as a rule, if he cannot do one thing he does another, as long as it is work. . . ."[13] John supplied himself with a stable common denominator for all his activities. In 1877 he spent the summer in Cancale, while his family went to Château d'Oex and Bex. The following year, while they went to Aix-les-Bains, he went to Italy. For John a holiday was a change of scene, a new location, not a break in activity.

Throughout the 1870s, while his contemporaries were drawn to the attractions of rural France, especially Grez, John preferred the seaside in the summer. (This independence involved more than habit, more than an urge to find an appropriate counterbalance to the staleness of Paris; the reason, however, like all the reasons for his behaviour, was never clearly stated. But even if the motive cannot be understood the result can be charted.) In 1875 he was content with pure seascape. In 1876 he was fascinated by the sea from the distorted perspective of a ship. In 1877 he was interested in the sea as a feature of composition, and by the summer of 1878 it had retired further, to a mere decorative element, abandoning exclusive importance once and for all. This progression began by accident, when he followed his parents to the Brittany coast, and continued deliberately until the subject was exhausted and taken over by other interests, when he went to Italy in 1878.

He arrived in Naples around the end of July, by the time the climate had become intolerable – an odd consideration for him to ignore. He loathed heat. All his life he rushed to find temperate weather, to avoid any severe temperature. "Of course it was very hot," he wrote about Naples to Ben del Castillo [10 August 1878], "and one generally feels used up. . . . I could not sleep at night. In the afternoon I would smoke a cigarette in an armchair or on my bed and at five o'clock wake up suddenly from a deep sleep of several hours. Then lie awake all night and quarrel with mosquitoes, fleas . . . I am frightfully bitten from head to foot."[14] In Capri, a week later, he stayed at an uncomfortable hotel. He knew no one. The place was beginning to look a great mistake, until he met Frank Hyde, who offered him a place in his studio in a nearby monastery and introduced him to a model of compelling beauty, Rosina Ferrara.*

* Evan Charteris traced the strategic value of Frank Hyde, who remains, in all

John was transfixed by her. She was about seventeen years old, lithe, wonderfully made, and an altogether perfect model, sporting a mass of unkempt jet-coloured hair. Her mellow brown skin set off lugubriously erotic features, darkly suggestive and Arabic. John could not stop painting her. He painted her doing an abandoned tarantella on a rooftop against the evening sky. He painted her walking down the stairs. He painted her draped over a frail tree in a luxurious field. He painted her in strict academic profile. She was a highly compliant subject, responsive and able to convey spontaneity, fierce energy and unselfconscious grace. She was sufficiently malleable to fit into a scene without dominating it. But, most important, Rosina was part of Capri; she belonged to the terrain. The combination of her appearance and the sharp brilliance of Capri was electric.

Rosina epitomized a "type" of beauty that had long appealed to John. His cousin Mary Austin, whom he had painted a few years before (*Resting*) and again in 1878, had the same sort of heavily hooded, languid eyes. Later he found this feature wonderfully articulated in Flora Priestley and in Sybil Sassoon (Lady Rocksavage, the Marchioness of Cholmondeley). And the model "Gitana", whom he had painted shortly after returning from America, had the same rich smoky complexion with generous brooding eyes and mouth. This affection for exaggerated physiognomy was more than a flirtation with the exotic; it was a nuance of the word "curious" which he had intoned constantly to Violet Paget in Bologna – a pull towards the mysterious, satisfying an urge to escape from the restraint of academic subjects.

John's interest first in Gitana and then in Rosina was also an indication of the great, though infinitely subtle, transmission of Carolus' influence. Carolus looked to Spain to fund his imagination; it was more than Velazquez-worship. He nurtured a devotion to folk culture, gypsies and rough picturesqueness. And, while his intoxication was not original, his ferocity was. He promoted the false belief that he was himself half-Spanish. He tortured the language with a mastery that ran close to gibberish, and was only slightly more gifted on the guitar. He moved beyond unbridled admiration for Spanish painting, which he shared with his contemporaries, to the point of extolling the virtues of all things Spanish while remaining in France. It was his version of celebrating the unsophisticated, commemorating ordinary life which supplied the trace-

---

other respects mysterious. He was living in Capri and had a studio in the old monastery of Santa Teresa – facts which are scarcely illuminating about the man or his work.

Rosina Ferrara (?1861–1928) enjoyed a life well suited to her romantic appearance. She had a bastard daughter rumoured to be the offspring of royalty. Later, Rosina married the American painter George Randolph Barse (1861–*c.*1936) and lived with him in Westchester, New York. Her sister was equally beautiful, but led a less dramatic life. (I am indebted to Mr Graham Williford for this information about Rosina.)

elements found in his students' ideas of appropriate subject-matter. Carolus simply moved the fashion for depicting French peasants south to Spain. Rosina represented the first full-blown manifestation of this religion.

John's affiliation with *atelier* Carolus-Duran ended with a paradoxical flourish. First he submitted the portrait of his master to the Salon, inscribed "à mon cher maître M. Carolus Duran, son élève affectioné John S. Sargent 1879" in writing that could easily pass for Carolus' own. Then in the autumn he expressed the virulence of the Spain-worship that had gone on in Passage Stanislas and Boulevard Mont Parnasse by going to Spain on what FitzWilliam summarized as "a sketching & studying tour".[15] He got rid of Carolus' influence by prolonging it. He left Paris in October with two friends.* Once in Madrid, where he remained about a month, he enrolled as a copyist at the Prado, going over the same ground as Velazquez, accurately and repeatedly. John's Prado work consolidated the vague invocation of Velazquez's power by transforming it into a specific field of reference. He continued to quote from it for years. Velazquez added another definite source in his library of influences, and at a crucial moment: Velazquez took over where Carolus had left off. Years later John admitted that no one equalled Velazquez in technical skills, but he had learnt more about painting from the example of Franz Hals. In the late 1890s he advised a young painter, "Begin with Franz Hals, copy and study Franz Hals, after that go to Madrid and copy Velazquez . . .".[16] But throughout the 1880s the loud, reverberating echoes in John's paintings led directly back to Velazquez. Such loyalty cumbered the reception of his work because his research was obvious. His first major pictures showed the applied tuition of both Carolus and Velazquez, and the very strength of these performances invited critics to announce his sources.

The journey in Spain was uncomfortable (made no easier by John's persistent inability to get the hang of riding a horse, which was the only means of transport in the south) and dogged by appalling weather. And if it had not been for the rain John never would have stayed in Madrid so long. He stopped in Ronda, Granada and Seville (among other towns).†

---

* Charteris mentions that John travelled "in the company of two French painters, MM. Daux and Bac" (p. 49). Research is scarcely more illuminating about these two: Benizet's dictionary reveals that Bac was Ferdinand-Sigismund Bach (1859–1952), draughtsman and lithographer, born in Stuttgart but became a naturalized Frenchman. Charles-Edmond Daux, Benizet informs, was "né a Reims au xixe siècle", and made his début at the Salon in 1878.

† Henry and Clover Adams's Spanish itinerary was very similar to John's that autumn – indeed, they met him when they were in Seville from Monday, 24 November until Tuesday, 2 December – and their impressions were breath-takingly caustic: "At best Madrid is a hole," Henry Adams wrote on 21 November 1879, "but in rainy weather it is a place fit only to drown rats in." Clover Adams was as merciless: "I never saw an uglier city," she wrote on 26 October 1879; "not

In Seville he started to amass material that formed the inventory of his huge painting on the theme of Spanish dance, *El Jaleo* (1882). The shift from Madrid to Seville was a neat parallel to the shift from Paris to Cancale: in Madrid he studied, in Seville he recorded, made notes for a later and more ambitious work. This time, however, the time-scale expanded and his purpose was unformulated. Like a good stenographer he took down elements he later enlarged and repeated in several pictures – a gitana suggestively lingering over a drink and a cigarette, a guitarist folded in concentration, a dancer reckless with excitement: taverna scenes that trapped the magnetic pull the exotic had for him. These drawings, later classified simply as preparatory to *El Jaleo*, show a turning in John's work.[17] They were more than a travel diary; they were an oblique and highly refined portion of autobiography, because they show over and over again the other ruling passion in his life – music. More than he had with the Pasdeloup Orchestra, he wanted to reproduce the dance as the best expression of that fascination.

Music was John's consuming interest, after painting. It was his chief pleasure and it became the nucleus of his social life. And such affection was, alas, about as inexplicable as the colour of his hair. He loved music and he had dark brown hair. *Why* is an impossible question.

Piano tuition had been prominent in the syllabus Mary and FitzWilliam drew up for their children's education. FitzWilliam never thought his son's or eldest daughter's ability worthy of any mention in his letters. This talent was not unusual, nor was it considered in any way extraordinary. Playing the piano, like drawing, or reading, or learning languages, was just a required skill to negotiate the time, fill the day. The fact that John and Emily had learnt to play was as unremarkable as their ability to hold a pen. But John's standard of playing was not ordinary. By the age of fourteen he knew most of the standard repertoire and was undaunted by its challenge. He managed sight-reading effortlessly. As with painting, he learnt quickly. As he grew older his technical dexterity slipped, but only by want of practice, and yet he was still capable of dazzling listeners. Charles Loeffler,* the composer and violinist, performed duets with him

---

one handsome building, no grass in its parks, a few scrubby little locust trees, and a swarming, ill-dressed, dirty populace who elbow one off the sidewalks at every step". When they moved inside to look at pictures, however, their antipathy completed melted. (See *The Letters of Henry Adams*, ed. W. C. Ford (London, 1930), p. 316, Vol. 1, and *The Letters of Mrs Henry Adams*, ed. Ward Thoron (Boston, Mass., 1936), pp. 192–3.)

* Charles Martin Loeffler (1865–1935) was born in Alsace, one of a distinguished musical family – his brother was a cellist, his sister a harpist, and his father a keen amateur musician, though by profession a scientist – who was educated in Russia, Hungary, Switzerland, Germany and France. By a strange coincidence, Loeffler might have been one of the violinists in Pasdeloup's orchestra in Paris the same season John painted his picture. In the early 1880s Loeffler went to America where he played first in Damrosch's orchestra, before joining the Boston Symphony,

and was astonished, he later recalled, by John's highly individual reading of the piano part of "Fauré's perplexingly Swift Sonata [?*Andante*, op. 75, 1897], Sargent sailed through his part. . . . Not by any means that he always played all the notes, but better than that, when cornered by a surprise difficulty, he revealed a genuine talent for music by playing all that which was and is most essential."[18] Professional musicians were frequently struck by John's *sense* of music, his understanding, his innate grasp. He was able to absorb music much the same way he absorbed painting – intellectually – and, similarly, he played in the same manner as he painted: with dash, with brio. He edited as he went along, able to create an effect and retain the essence of the piece. He was able to turn playing into a language. He used it to express himself. And this astonishing skill was modestly displayed, intensifying the standard, which was high above that of most gifted amateurs. The famous Joachim, tradition has it, claimed " 'had Sargent taken to music instead of painting he could have been as great a musician as he was a painter' ".

John's ear and eye were trained alike, both highly developed and both turned on the stimulation of the "curious". This impulse might have arisen from the sustained habit of keeping a travel diary. The *Jaleo* sketches were as much notes of what he heard as of what he saw. His memory was extraordinary. "His ear", Loeffler recalled, "was strangely sensitive for unusual harmonic progressions, in fact he had an unusually fine memory for them. I have known him to be haunted by certain ones, after one hearing he would not rest there until he had solved the harmonic riddle. Without the music, he would do this at the Piano by sheer tenacity of aural memory."[19] The allure of Spanish music was a great deal more than part of the baggage he had carried away from Boulevard Mont Parnasse; it was a subtle reinforcement of his knowledge of the scene. He pursued gitano music with analytic fervour: "You wished some Spanish songs," he wrote to Violet Paget from Paris (9 July) [1880],

> . . . The best are what one hears in Andalucia, the half African Malagueñas & Soleas, dismal, restless chants that are impossible to note. They are something between a Hungarian Czardas and the chant of the Italian peasant in the fields, and are generally composed of five strophes and end strongly *on the dominant* [,] the theme quite lost in strange fioritures and gutteral roulades. The gitano voices are marvellously supple. If you have heard something of the kind you will not consider this mere jargon.[20]

In Capri he had been satisfied with the vivid spectacle of Rosina dancing. In Seville he wanted to go further, do research, investigate, *understand*.

---

where he remained from 1882 until 1903. After retirement he dedicated himself to composing, at his farm in Medfield, Mass., where he lived as a near-recluse.

John painted an oil portrait of him in 1903 for Mrs Gardner and a portrait sketch in 1917.

This auxiliary work was not because he distrusted his eye, but because he wanted to understand his ear. Carolus' method had taught him to parse the language of the eye; his curiosity demanded equal distinction for what he heard. That interest took pictorial form in its reflection in dance. His huge painting *El Jaleo* shows the overriding stimulation of sound, relying, perforce, on the dramatic effect of lighting, long shadows, and the dancer's apparent defiance of the basic rules of anatomy – her right arm was shoved into an impossible position. Gitanos line the tavern wall playing, clapping, or waving their arms about. Altogether it was an essay about music. The very word *jaleo* literally means "noise", "uproar"; the closest synonym *juerga* means "big party". There is no specific dance called *el jaleo*.[21] The painting was John's account of one sensation by means of another. John bundled together diverse reactions and put them together in one vast canvas. Over and over again he painted dancers, culminating ten years later in his portrait of La Carmencita. After her, his musical interest subsided to listening or playing. He adored distinctly regional music, folk themes. He perfected his performance of Albeñiz's *Iberia*. He admirably executed the piano reduction of the orchestral part of Lalo's *Symphonie espagnole*. But his musical taste was more robust than the mere collection of souvenirs. It was, like his playing, intensely personal, open-minded, expansive. He never lost his love of folk music, and he always listened with the same enthusiasm as he played, and with the same prevailing urge to understand.

John was a staunch proponent of modern composers. His campaign to make Fauré's music known and appreciated in England and America was unceasing and successful. His support for Wagner was, however, less mingled with that purpose, but equally energetic. With scarcely any prompting he would play *Tristan* or *Walküre* or *Parsifal* in full. He helped young composers' work to get a hearing. He encouraged performers. He was not parsimonious with his assistance or praise; nor was he parsimonious with his judgements. Most important, John's reaction to music was a foil to his shyness, throwing into relief those aspects of his character obscured by his reticence: spontaneity, his sense of fun, and his generosity. He was an eager and willing accompanist. He could reel off jokes at the keyboard he stammered through elsewhere. His morbid fear of getting up before any number of people, even friends, evaporated when he was called on to play in a crowded drawing-room. His love of music was so great that inhibition disappeared in its favour; the two could coexist, and music, happily, was more potent. And musicianship was yet another entry on the long list of John's forbidding achievements compiled by his contemporaries to help them understand him, but serving only to increase their awe.

John and his companions crossed over to Morocco just before the New Year, 1880. The change was welcome. The weather improved, and work moved into the daylight. Suddenly, the whole purpose of this long expedition south – to extend summer's lease on outdoor work – was

generously vindicated. John's mood changed, once he returned to the excitement of being a tourist. "All that has been written and painted about these African towns", he wrote to Ben del Castillo from Tangier (4 January 1880), "does not exaggerate the interest of at any rate, a first visit." And yet he travelled rarely. After the monstrously uncomfortable journey to Tetuan – a small coastal town famous for tiles and rich decorative carving – he happily settled down in Tangier for two months.*
He and his companions rented (from the American consul) a small Moorish house indistinguishable from all the others lining the maze-like streets and ideal for their purposes. "The patio open to the sky affords a good studio light," he wrote to Ben, "and has the horseshoe arches arabesques, tiles and other traditional Moorish ornaments." Altogether, the house and Tangier unexpectedly pleased him, as if both were designed to charge his interests, his diverse jumble of interests: "certainly the aspect of the place is striking, the costume grand and the Arabs often magnificent".[22]

But, as usual, the eloquence of John's enthusiasm was not fully expressed in words. His pictures did that, yet were again more than a travel diary; they formed a sort of autobiography *in code*, because these Morocco pictures show the recurring themes that appeared throughout his work. This was not a unique achievement, only valuable for neat, tidy, concise declaration. In a series of small oils, painted on mahogany panels (measuring 10¼ inches by 13¾ inches) that fitted into his paintbox, John executed what have accurately been called "architectural vignettes":†
essays in light and shade, geometry, and scenes least likely to fascinate the traveller – doorways, walls, modest houses – highly reminiscent of Leighton's Greek and Italian studies and also unexpectedly repeated years later by Carolus. These oils were not reference notes for Paris. They were reminders of north Africa.

The summary of his visit to Tangier was completed when he returned (at the end of February) to 73 rue Notre-Dame-des-Champs: *Fumée d'ambre gris*, a large painting depicting an Arab lady lifting her headdress to welcome the thin vaporous tails rising from an incense-burner on the ground. It was a scene that utterly flummoxed scholars who were unable to pin it down with any precision or historical accuracy. The literary interest of the picture was, as in *El Jaleo*, John's flamboyant reconstruction of those details he wanted to retain, not simple documentation. *Fumée*

---

* "Tetuan", John wrote to Violet Paget eight years later when she asked for travel notes of Spain and Morocco, "is well worth going to see if you are up to a very long day's ride on horseback. We broke the journey and spent the night at an Arab caravanerie, a horrible experience against which I warn you. Don't go to Tetuan unless you have your own tent or can ride a whole day" (Miller Library, Colby College).

†In Doreen Bolger Burke, *American Paintings in the Metropolitan Museum of Art*, Vol. 3 (New York, 1980).

d'ambre gris was no recondite ceremony. Possibly it is nothing more than an elaborate version of taking an inhalation for a cold.[23]

In the eighteen months from October 1879 to March 1881, John went to Spain, Morocco, Tunisia, Venice and Holland – an itinerary unsettlingly like his parents' own. His paintings were a sort of stamp in his passport. Each journey safely carried FitzWilliam's tag "a sketching & studying tour". John could not give up studying, once free of *atelier* Duran. His travel could be measured but, more important, it was a symptom of a stronger motive than trying to sustain the habit of four years. He did not know what he wanted. During those eighteen months, only four and a half were spent in Paris, and by leaving town for so long he was making a very odd bid to establish himself as a portraitist.

The portrait of Carolus had provoked interest in John's work. "There was always a little crowd around it," FitzWilliam wrote to his brother months after seeing it at the Salon (15 August) [1879], "and one heard constantly remarks in favor of its excellence. But as the proof of the pudding is in the eating, so the best, or one of the best evidences of a portrait's success is the receiving by the artist of commissions to execute others. And John received six such evidences from French people."[24] The first on the list was Edouard Pailleron, the poet and playwright, and the son-in-law of the editor of the *Revue des deux mondes*; in short, a man in the very centre of the literary coterie which paid elaborate homage first to painters, and much later to musicians. His wife's family, the Bulozes, collected modern paintings, and painters. "Ma famille a toujours aimé, accueilli et favorisé les peintres," Pailleron's daughter wrote in her memoirs, *Le Paradis perdu*, displaying that peculiarly French gift for acquiring cultivation as if it were a commodity available in shops.

> Chez mes parents, ils se nommaient Delacroix, Louis Boulanger, Eugène Fromentin, Mme Besnard, la miniaturiste mère du grand peintre Albert Besnard, que nous avons tous connu.
>
> Chez mes parents les artistes venaient nombreux aussi: Harpignies, Meissonnier, Gustave Doré . . . Bouguereau, Munkascy, G. Jacquet, Gustave Moreau. . . .[25]

The list was intimidatingly long, and yet the addition of John's name, though in keeping with their mania, was surprising. He represented the younger generation and, like Carolus years before, John was not unpalatably radical, but just sufficiently radical to be thought modern.

He was twenty-three years old. His appearances at the Salon had been a well-planned operation. His eyes were prudently fixed on Salon etiquette, as befits a novice looking for work at the start of his career. He was confident enough to question the neat formulas predictably repeated by the giants of the Academy, and yet careful never to stage an outright attack on convention. He only wanted to shake loose from the most constricting features of formal portraiture. The pose was the tightest of these constraints. Cabanel, Meissonnier *et al.* marched their subjects on to the canvas with waxwork lifelessness. John preferred his sitters to look casual, as Carolus had, but not lackadaisical. Neither Fanny Watts nor Carolus was put into an iron-clad courtly posture; she pitches uncomfortably to one side, and he was far from relaxed, though in a stylized characteristic pose. John did not want to depict them making some bid for immortality, excessively aware of permanence. And his subjects were dressed accordingly. In this – posture and clothing – John made his basic deviation from tradition, and it was but a slight rereading of the old text. It was not unique or revolutionary; it was merely an advanced interpretation within the narrow safety of academic sanctity. Outside the Salon, such unstarched refinements had become commonplace – Manet and Degas (while conservative at the Salon) had turned their backs on the hagiography of portraiture for many years – but with the addition of John's subtle nuance of colour he gained the reputation for being modern. Compared to the Academy lions, his brushwork was less ponderous and more varied, his colour more carefully harmonized and less dependent on uniform sobriety. Altogether, his approach to portraiture was modest. It was the logical extension of Carolus' "Flight into Egypt" lesson: "an artist enters into the life of the personages that he desires to represent, observing them as human beings". Such understatement served to move portraiture beyond the narrow purpose of document, making the portraitist's job more complicated. He had to see his sitters *in situ*. But, above all else, John's greatest asset was that he was *new*, a quality more attractive than his tendency to unfasten portraiture from the prevailing attitude of monumentality. He was fresh, without sneering at convention. His two portraits at the Salon had shown either his wise caution or his sound commercial sense.

John's version of Pailleron repeated that of Carolus. The sitter wore a rumpled silk shirt, an untidy jacket, and stood leaning against the wall in a manner almost blasé: what Pailleron's daughter called "this infraction of the rules"[26] – a misdeed as great as appearing at dinner not in evening clothes. Pailleron was underdressed for the Salon. John showed him fresh from work, pensive, looking head to foot a poet. One hand grips a well-thumbed book, the other rests on his hip. He stands facing the light, his head turned showing full-face, in an attitude self-consciously unfussed. His figure was painted in sharp clarity against a background merely sketched in, a combination of styles that was modern without being experimental.

The portrait, finished in midsummer 1879, pleased the sitter, who quickly asked for a portrait of his wife. In early August, John went to stay at Madame Pailleron's family house in Ronjoux, conveniently close to Aix-les-Bains where Emily and his mother settled in to take a cure after two months in Paris. (FitzWilliam and Violet went instead to St Gervais.) John was happy at Ronjoux. He joined in family life effortlessly. His hosts liked him, but they did not quite know what to make of him. Their reaction was the recurrent one: admiration and respect laced with utter bafflement. First there was his unchallengeable deftness as a painter, complete with unselfconscious dedication. There was his near-perfect French, spoken with only the merest hint of an accent. There was his extensive knowledge of literature – "connaissant parfaitement nos meilleurs poètes, goutant nos mémorialistes du XVIIe siècle".[27] There was his easy manner, winningly modest and unclouded by any *gaucherie*. He was popular with the "literary & artistic friends",[28] Emily wrote to Violet Paget, who flocked through the house. And then there was the totally inconsonant fact of his youth: "Comment", Marie-Louise Pailleron asked, just as so many people asked throughout John's early career, "au milieu de tant de déplacements, avait-il eu le temps de s'asseoir pour étudier et lire? C'est incompréhensible."[29]

John made an indelible impression on the household. Some sixty years after his summer at Ronjoux, Marie-Louise Pailleron remembered him vividly. She was eight years old when she first met him. He was tall, very tall; his legs seemed to go on for ever. He was thin, almost lean. His face was gently coloured by the sun. His eyes were wonderfully lively, astute. His beard was neat, the colour of rich chestnuts. But, above all, his hands fascinated her – long, graceful and fine: "longues mains adroites et fines".[30] And his personality was imperturbably simple, full of winning peculiarities and spontaneity. He was ready for any excursion, any walk, of any distance. He was tireless, bounding over gates, hiking up hills, collecting butterflies,* leaping about dancing to entertain the children. He played the banjo, sang Negro spirituals. He radiated energy and high spirits. He found the atmosphere of family life altogether congenial. He even badgered Marie-Louise to pose for him, which she found unspeakably annoying. She loathed sitting still. (A year later, when her father commissioned John to paint her and her brother, she learnt real horror: she had to sit to him eighty-three times!) He painted her grandmother, who was not overjoyed by the result. And he sketched her brother.

Every clement afternoon John worked on his portrait of Madame Pailleron, who posed in the garden. If the portrait of her husband was reckoned an "infraction of the rules", hers simply ignored them. Where John was after modified realism in Edouard Pailleron, he was after *effect* in Madame Marie Buloz Pailleron. He waved aside horticultural precision – crocuses were in flower amid grass littered with dead leaves, and full-leafed trees darken the prospect of the park. He selected a black evening gown, satin with ruffles and lace, and decorated with a knot of white tulle around her neck and a corsage of red carnations on her shoulder – an odd choice for the afternoon. And the full-length pose was no less eccentric – hands crossed, while lifting her skirt. These incongruous details were employed for a purpose, in which spontaneity was not a part. He wanted to show Madame Pailleron at home and, like Rosina, part of the scene,

---

* He had an extensive collection of butterflies, carefully displayed.

using that scene as more than a backdrop. He saw portraiture not as a distinct and exclusive branch of painting but, rather, as eligible to incorporate landscape, outdoor subjects. Unlike the Academicians, and even Carolus, John did not see the need for (or value of) planting the subject in front of a wall. He did not see the need for confining visual interest to the pure technique of applying paint. He did not see the need for using Carolus' uncomfortable reliance on harsh colour to relieve dullness. And yet, despite his argument with convention, he kept attention focused on the subject. He did this by creating a network of contrasts: black against green, white against black, mauve against green; standing his subject against the deep, broad, flat reach of lawn; one carefully modelled hand against the other loosely sketched, closely outlined against suggested tulle. John's portrait of Madame Pailleron represented an advance on his initial thoughts about portraiture. He was less content to adapt or modify the rules. He looked at the problem afresh, to be treated not as an aggregate of details, but as a whole. All the elements of composition were brought in. With Madame Pailleron he produced a dramatic picture. (And it hinted at his uncanny ability to create an effect, which would eventually overtake and divest his portraits of much but straight performance.)

John chose his portrait of Madame Pailleron and *Fumée d'ambre gris* as his Salon advertisements in 1880. They were measured choices; one to stimulate portrait commissions, the other to show his grasp on the current vogue for orientalism. By submitting both pictures he was keen to tell spectators he was not exclusively a portraitist. (His Cancale picture was shown two years before.) John's eyes were steadfastly fixed on the Salon. It lay at the heart of his activities. He came back to Paris from north Africa to prepare for it. The Salon meant, above all else, employment, and employment depended on repeated proof of ability. He had to bolster his reputation as Carolus' prize student. He had to get publicity. He had to remind the public that one striking performance was not luck. And he had to inform the public that he could escape from the rule of standard portraiture without shocking or offending. He was embarking on a commercial campaign. The Salon was a great social occasion; his pictures were seen by people unconcerned by art, but concerned with fashion. The Salon was to painting what the Derby is to horses.

John was in an enviable position, compared to his colleagues. He was better placed to succeed in his business. He seemed to have the blessing of the French, which had been withheld from almost every American who had come to Paris, and he was blatantly encouraged by the expatriate American students and society. With each new picture he unveiled in his studio, they became more ardent in their praise. They talked about him in terms close to rapture and looked to him as the salvation of American art. When Americans came to Paris, John's name was the one advanced as *the* painter to commission. Recommendations inevitably led to John. In 1880, Henry St John Smith came to Paris from Boston, consulted his Harvard classmates and fellow-Bostonians and then went to John's studio to commission his portrait. "The few things I saw in his studio I did not like much," Smith wrote in his diary in late May 1880; "I go, in choosing him, chiefly on the advice of Frank [Francis Brooks] Chadwick who has been here for the past seven years and ought to know about artists here. Arthur Rotch also of Boston recommended him highly . . . R[otch] said he would rather have a portrait by Sargent than by Millais, but of course that is bosh. . . . He asked me fifteen hundred francs [$300] for a portrait of head and shoulders."[31] And as important if not more important than his standing as an artist was the fact that John was eminently presentable. He came from a good solid Philadelphian family, or so his American sitters happily believed, of respectable lineage, with safe colonial connections. He would not embarrass potential sitters. He was a gentleman. And, though none of these details mattered to John, they mattered inestimably to his sitters. They were comforted by the simple fact of being painted by an American. Smith's nine sittings during June 1880 were recorded in his diary as pleasant occasions. (Three years later John painted Smith's wife.)

During the months John spent in Paris he worked in the studio he once shared with Beckwith at 73 bis rue Notre-Dame-des-Champs: a vast room on the first floor overlooking a small patch of garden. The furnishings were spare, only a few pieces of very good furniture, odd musical instruments like a harmonium and a guitar, a ladder, an easel. Paintings lined the walls and countless drawings littered the floor. The place was remarkable for untidiness and prodigious filth. There was a film of dirt spread over the entire studio. Such a setting helped to impress prospective clients because, they concluded, John's mind was not concerned by the banal duties of housekeeping, but by painting. The place was reserved for work; John lived nearby in an hotel.[32] One client, Ramon Subercaseaux, a Chilean diplomatist and amateur painter, after seeing the portrait of Madame Pailleron at the Salon, came to see John in his studio to commission a portrait of his wife. Thereafter he discreetly arranged for sittings to take place instead at their apartment in the Avenue Bois de Boulogne.

For someone who was considered obsessed by work, John's studio routine was curiously lax. He did not race to the studio in the morning. He was never too busy to meet friends for lunch. He guided Emily, his parents, Beckwith, anyone around the Salon. He spent entire days roaming in the cast room at the Beaux-Arts with Beckwith. He readily visited Carolus at his house in Montegeron, near Fontainebleau. Not only did he seem to have time, but he also welcomed the distraction presented by visitors to Paris. People flocked in and out of the studio heedless of sittings, and occasionally to considerable purpose. One day, during the prolonged battle to make Marie-Louise Pailleron sit still, Carolus strode in, dressed in the most fantastic style, wearing a good many rings, wielding a cane. The girl stopped dead in her tracks. She had never seen anyone in such an outrageous get-up. Carolus fixed her in his gaze, exercised simple logic, telling her the sittings would take longer if she persisted in moving about, and cajoled her into helping the tormented painter. She did, and when the portrait was at last finished John danced round the studio and hurled things out of the window.

John's easygoing attitude towards commissions grew less out of their scarceness than out of his confidence.* He had been lucky in his patrons. He had the ability to make himself winningly agreeable. The Paillerons were immensely fond of him. The Subercaseaux found him altogether congenial and were delighted to meet up with him in Venice: "The months of September and October [1880] passed in their [the Sargents'] delightful company," Ramon Subercaseaux wrote in his autobiography, "occupied by art and excursions."[33] Any commission he found unpleasant he dispatched summarily and quickly. His prices, however, were the best indication of this confidence; they were very high. He sold *Fumée d'ambre gris* for 3000 francs – "only – I think it is too little", Emily wrote to Violet Paget (23 May 1880)[34] – or $600; a full-length portrait was about the same price, head and shoulders half that amount. John was content to wait for people to come to him, and when they did not he left town. He had no other choice. He had to wait, but he was not going to wait cooped up in town until he unveiled the next instalment of his advertising campaign at the Salon. And, unlike so many others, he always had the unrestrained support of his family.

* In 1879, when FitzWilliam wrote about "the proof of the pudding" commissions, John could boast of five, not six: Edouard and Madame Pailleron, Jeanne and René Keiffer, and Robert de Civrieux. In 1880 there were three: the Pailleron Children, Henry St John Smith and Madame de Subercaseaux.

VII

By the most cruel version of justice, the elaborate myth of Mary and FitzWilliam's life slowly turned into reality. For too many years Mary had exaggerated the truth about her health, and now, by the early 1880s, she knew real illness. Winter after winter she lay in bed, tortured by rheumatic pain. The only relief she found came after months enduring mudbaths and sulphur vapours at Aix-les-Bains, Marienbad, Acqui. FitzWilliam reckoned she was "well" when she returned to Nice just able to hobble about on crutches. And when rheumatism did not flatten her bronchitis did. FitzWilliam was no luckier. His many years of sacrifice were now rewarded with profound loneliness. When George Bemis died in 1878, he lost his only friend.[1] John, who had been the sole focus of FitzWilliam's ambition, now became his chief interest and solace for all that had been left undone; and, alas, John's growing success meant independence. FitzWilliam's only knowledge of his son came through letters, which were as infrequent as FitzWilliam's own to America. Mary and FitzWilliam's magnificently futile existence no longer sported the camouflage of purpose – the purpose of helping their son; their existence now materialized into the calculated distortion they had presented for decades to FitzWilliam's mother and father, brothers and sisters. Emily became her mother's nurse, and Violet was incapable, at the age of twelve, of combating the gloom. John's success, the very thing they had longed for, struggled for, spelt their decline.

For them events still remained the calendar and geography. After a couple of winters in Paris in the mid-1870s when they tried to give John something like a home, they returned to Nice, occupied themselves with accurate notations of the weather, their health, and uniform boredom. John's visits became less frequent and shorter. When he began to travel he asked his mother and Emily to join him, but they never entertained the idea seriously. They did not try to keep up with him. The Salon lured them back to Paris in the late spring, for what FitzWilliam called their "obligatory" annual visit. Thereafter Mary and Emily headed south to a spa, and FitzWilliam and Violet went to the Alps, obeying the restrictions of economy and wanting more comfort. Then, a few months later, they rejoined one another and headed back to Nice. This sequence altered little. In 1881, Mary and Emily went further, to Saratoga

Springs* for several weeks during their stay in North America. This was a flat rendering of excitement, especially for Emily. Months of being her mother's nurse were followed by months of being her maid. The strain, exhaustion and boredom told; she made herself ill trying to make her mother well. The burden somehow fell to her. FitzWilliam, quick to notice symptoms, was slow to encourage any cure. In 1882, Emily was allowed to have a holiday away from her family. It was her first taste of freedom in twenty-five years, and FitzWilliam understood it only as recuperative: "Emily left us at Nice to go to Paris to see her brother &c," FitzWilliam wrote to his sister on 12 August [1882], "she spent a month there, & then went over to Ireland where some friends had invited her to pay them a visit, and where she seems to be enjoying herself in a rational domestic sort of way."[2] Later, when she repeated the same journey, he wrote, "we hope she will renew her youth".[3]

While this uneventful routine made Mary ill and fat, FitzWilliam unobtrusively declined. By nature, he was born in a shadow. He had never been particularly lively or extrovert or sprightly; with age he became less so. Family news from America – his favourite sister's death and his brothers' declining health – slowly filtered through to him carrying a double sadness: that the nieces and nephews who had written were perfect strangers to him. He had little to console him abroad and only mystery to amplify his fading memories of home. His few interests were pursued with diminishing enthusiasm. He turned his attention to Mary's investments, which he had hitherto happily ignored, and as he could draw on complete ignorance of all financial dealings and very sparse information months out of date such an interest was unrewarding. His prime occupation was writing letters. For nearly three decades his communication depended on paper. When Mary and Emily were in America, he wrote often and at great length, sometimes as many as three letters a week. Christmas and birthdays had always provoked some salutation, far in advance of the occasion; by the late 1870s, however, Christmas came and went before he sat down to write to America. He no longer mentioned his own birthday, his keenest celebration by post. He reported his news with undisguised lacklustre, dulled reflex. And when he recorded the subject closest to his heart, John's growing list of achievements, there was an audible sigh of resignation. He replaced warm pride with dispirited verbosity: "His is a pleasant life, I fancy, is John's," FitzWilliam wrote to his brother on 16 November [1883]; "he seems to be respected, even admired, & beloved . . . for his talent & success as an artist, & for his conduct & character as a man; his work is a pleasurable occupation to him, & brings him a very handsome income; he travels about . . . he is well received every where, for his manners are good & agreeable, he is good-looking, plays well, dances well, paints

---

* Where they met, of all people, Robert C. Hinckley.

well, converses well, &c &c &c. In short he has given us, his parents, great satisfaction, so far."[4]

FitzWilliam had denied himself his profession, he had denied himself life in America, he had denied himself a host of interests; denial overwhelmed curiosity and became a way of life. It carved out the substance of his life, leaving him a fragile shell of a man. When he went to Paris to look at John's paintings, he passed on others' opinions, not his own. He grew perilously thin. John's only oil portrait of FitzWilliam shows a sad face, lowered, obscured in darkness. Shortly before his death, FitzWilliam had another very brief glimpse of the family life he had known years before in Florence, in Rome, in Nice, in Geneva, in Dresden. The Sargents were living *en famille* near Reading, in England. By day John painted, and in the evening they all dined together. Every night John helped FitzWilliam from the table, and sat alone with him. Each time, as they got up to go, FitzWilliam announced: " 'I am going to sit and smoke . . . with my son John.' "[5]

As FitzWilliam shrank, Mary grew, literally. She became no more forceful with age. She became no more active. She became no more ambitious for her children. Once John's education was over, she took no interest in Emily's or Violet's. The threat to recross the ocean ceased to influence her. She was happy abroad, but exactly what made her happy continued to elude expression. Her day-to-day life was merely a miniature account of her year-to-year, decade-to-decade life: dour eventlessness, from illness to travel and back again. She had strength to travel, but none to sit still. She had had the ingenuity to justify her version of John's education, but none to encourage Emily's or Violet's. She had infectious vitality in public among John's friends, but none at home. If, like FitzWilliam, she played out her ambitions through her children, she stopped once John left home. It was as if John's departure froze Mary and FitzWilliam, and from that moment they never went forward again.

Still, for all their forlorn passivity, the Sargents were not unique. Their style of life was not even original. The shadowy expatriate world was populated with people who were ill at ease at home, and no more comfortable abroad. They seemed unequal to the challenge of finding a place on the map and staying there. They had no stability. They had no occupation. They had no plans. They lived a sort of partial life, intimately acquainted with the superficial, enjoying long friendships built on fleeting encounters. They battled only, it seems, with time. As a result, in death, history has done much to forget them. Their lives were distilled in those fading photographs in old family albums of the passing acquaintances once loved but who no one could quite remember. Some Americans claimed to have sensitivities too refined to keep them at home, yet once away from the source of pain they could find no enjoyment. These expatriates were a band of people set in motion across a continent with no apparent motive other than never to return home. They were reassured by seeing one another again. Friendships were formed entirely on the basis of proximity, and forced to drop when apart. They depended on tourists. Both FitzWilliam and Mary welcomed with open arms people they had scarcely known twenty-five years before, and people they had never known, who arrived with family introductions. The expatriate world was also strangely and extraordinarily ignorant, closed-minded about the countries they inhabited. FitzWilliam and Mary had spent nearly thirty years abroad, raised three children in as many countries, and yet neither wanted to advance beyond the casual tourist in their knowledge of domestic life. And the fact that FitzWilliam never dropped his New England prejudices about "foreign ways" consigned him and his family to the most rarefied of communities. The effect of this international fake-life on the children, who had been denied the anchorage of memory, was incalculable, and odd. When Violet Paget unexpectedly encountered John in London after several years, her rush of impressions disagreed with FitzWilliam's quiet assessment. "John is very stiff," she wrote to her mother on 16 June 1881, "a sort of completely accentless mongrel . . . rather French, faubourg sort of manners."[6] A few days later, her picture calmed somewhat, and yet retained its sting, because she had moved on from his mannerisms to his mind, and that territory, she thought, belonged to her.

> I think John is singularly unprejudiced, almost too amiably candid in his judgements. . . . I like him now. He is just what he was, only too serious, without spirits or humour. He talked art & literature, just as formerly, and then, quite unbidden, sat down to the piano & played all sorts of bits of things . . . just as when he was a boy. . . . John is extremely serious, a great maker of theories; he goes in for art for art's own sake, says that a subject of a picture is something not always in the way. He is quite emancipated from all religious ideas. He speaks English without accent but has to help himself out with French words.[7]

A byproduct of the tangle of influences to which Mary subjected her children was that they *belonged* nowhere. What she had wanted for herself was imposed on them, for life. They could sail through the problems of languages, customs, capital cities with admirable ease, but they were supposed to be American, to have come from a country they did not know. They never lost this contradiction, common to other children of expatriates; they were hybrids, made to root in strange soil, and it became more pronounced with age.

One of the finest and most eloquent examples of the phenomenon of late nineteenth-century American expatriates was FitzWilliam's cousin, Daniel Sargent Curtis, who came abroad with his family at the very end of the 1870s.* Throughout his history like so many others' there was the

---

* He was related to FitzWilliam from some considerable distance: his maternal great-grandfather and FitzWilliam's paternal great-grandfather were brothers – Epes (1721–79) and Winthrop (1727–93) Sargent, respectively. Curtis, his wife and one of his two sons (Ralph – the other was Osborne Sargent Curtis, 1858–1918) arrived in Europe in 1879.

unsatisfied *continuo* of "why": why did he leave Boston and, more perplexingly, why did he stay abroad? He seemed willing to preserve his displeasure for both sides of the Atlantic. If he were as discontent abroad as he claimed to be on Beacon Street, he made certain no one left his acquaintance without thinking as much. By the claustrophobic intelligence of the expatriate network, Daniel Sargent Curtis's name was known to FitzWilliam as early as 1869, when he was convicted of assault and battery on the newly opened tramcar system in Boston, and was sent to gaol for two months.* George Bemis's sister was one of the horde who went to visit him, and reported at once to her brother in Europe, as in fact did another of FitzWilliam's cousins, Turner Sargent. Curtis's otherwise staid, unflorid career – Harvard-trained lawyer, agent for Brown, Shipley & Co. of Liverpool and London, and Trustee of the Boston Public Library – would never have otherwise earned him transatlantic notice. His wife, however, was made of altogether more remarkable stuff. Ariana Randolph Wormeley (1833–1922) was born to a British father (Rear-Admiral Ralph Randolph Wormeley, a great-nephew of the Attorney-General in Washington's Cabinet) and an American mother (Caroline Preeble, herself the niece of a commodore), with two equally distinguished sisters – Mary Wormeley Latimer, novelist, historian and translator of prodigious output who also found time to be a philanthropist, and Katherine Prescott Wormeley, translator of Balzac, Molière, Dumas (*fils*), Daudet, and the letters of Mademoiselle de Lespinasse, among others. As a girl, Mrs Curtis lived in London, Paris and Switzerland where she and her sisters used the courts of Europe as their playgrounds, before sailing to Boston in 1848. Thereafter they divided their winters between Washington and Boston, and spent the summer in Newport where Ariana married Curtis in 1853. Mrs Daniel Curtis was brutally intelligent, literate, and very opinionated.

The Curtises' grand achievement was the Palazzo Barbaro, on the

---

* The facts of the case are as follows: D. S. Curtis, irritated by the comments of J. M. Churchill, described by Curtis's counsel as "a man of good social position", twisted Churchill's nose and broke his spectacles. The case received considerable attention because it touched on the general safety of the public, which was why the Commonwealth was keen to make an example of Curtis, and because it touched on the deeds of prominent Bostonians. Curtis's wealth, which the judge said was not a factor, nevertheless blunted the harshness of any fine, and that is why he was sent to "the common gaol . . . to be kept at work therein in the same manner as other persons . . . after the thirtieth of July" (Ormond Family Collection). The least attractive aspect of the case was the extreme and highly vocal partisanship of Bostonians. As Bemis's sister wrote (21 September 1869), "His friends spoiled his case & the judge made him suffer for them. Churchill is very uncouth" (Massachusetts Historical Society).

Once out of gaol, Curtis bought a new house at 214 Beacon Street and, as Turner Sargent summarized, "that 9 days wonder is all over" (letter to George Bemis, 6 December 1869: Massachusetts Historical Society). If anything, Curtis's reputation was enhanced by the whole affair.

Grand Canal, which they rented in 1881 and bought in 1885 (the sumptuous larger upper apartments, that is). Once in the Barbaro, they settled back and turned into one of the chief tourist stops in Venice. The famous made a beeline for their hospitality, and the Curtises' life continued as it had begun in Back Bay. Curtis looked at the Grand Canal as if it were an extension of Beacon Street. He relentlessly babbled on about America, which he referred to as "over there", reeled off his endless supply of unthrilling anecdotes, and read – read something like nine hours a day towards the end of his life. John called him and his wife "walking libraries". While neither Daniel nor Ariana Curtis was able to inspire very deep or at least convincing affection among their friends, the Barbaro did. The Barbaro lured people to their side. The Barbaro was their entertainment. The Barbaro furnished them with importance. And the Barbaro gave them fame – in paintings and novels.* The Curtises' grand achievement was the fortuitous achievement of money.

Their eldest son, Ralph Wormeley Curtis, registered the seismographic reading of his parents' activities. After Harvard, he studied painting in Paris, and thereafter shuffled across Europe for the rest of his life. He was at home in Venice, Paris, the South of France, London and Boston. When he arrived in Paris he looked up his Harvard classmate (Francis) Brooks Chadwick, was introduced to his cousin John, and all three went off to Holland together. The chain of events was direct, the journey swift.

The map of the expatriate world was drawn on strict nationalistic lines. Once abroad, Americans stuck to Americans. In Europe they were explained by American geography. The best description FitzWilliam could produce years after his cousin had arrived was "Mr D. S. Curtis late of Boston – a relative of ours".[8] Three decades abroad had done nothing to dissuade people from calling the Sargents Philadelphians. Americans seemed unable to cross over the patriotic boundaries they had constructed for themselves.† Nor had travel relaxed American social prejudices;

---

* The Barbaro's dark, pervasive gloomy opulence, upholstered with every comfort and perfectly trained servants, had a romantic magnetism for many artists. The atmosphere was compellingly sympathetic to the arts and the location was narcotic. Browning lived across the street, so to speak, and often came to read his poetry. James was a fixture, periodically, and set his novel *The Wings of the Dove* in the Palazzo Curtis, as the house came to be known in the late nineteenth century. The Curtises' gondolas ferried painters through the canals, and to their garden, which was a rare possession in Venice. Daniel Sargent Curtis once said that he, too, would have taken up painting, were he not colour-blind!

† The Russians, alone among the expatriates in France, seemed comfortable with the French. The best example of this open-mindedness was Marie Bashkirtseff (1860–84), the painter and diarist, friend of Bastien-Lepage, Carolus-Duran, Robert-Fleury who was her teacher at Académie Julien. When her diaries and letters were published, the wide scope of her friendships was revealed – musicians, painters, writers and statesmen, all French – as well as her rare wit and intelligence. She was adored and celebrated as a tragic heroine, especially by Disraeli and Queen Victoria. The Russians' capacity to settle in Paris was unique

the unwillingness to mix with foreigners was coupled with a desire to retain the social order left behind. This whole perverse phenomenon charted John's network of acquaintance, the territory he inhabited.

Beckwith's diaries reveal the phenomenon. He renewed his habit when he got to Paris, and in the front of the 1878 volume (his final Paris year) he noted a select list of names and addresses. The only Frenchman was Carolus; the others were foreigners who also happened to be John and his family's closest friends. Miss Valerie Burckhardt was second on the list, and her family appears throughout his daily entries thereafter. The Burckhardts were a prime example of that type of expatriate who emerged from total mystery when they touched the lives of others. In Paris they were known; away from Paris they disappeared completely. It was as if they ceased to exist when observers were not looking. And, to confuse their place in the concise expatriate order, Valerie and her sister Louise were only half-American; their father, Edward Burckhardt, was Swiss, their mother, Elizabeth Tomes, American. They spent their time moving between Paris and Wiesbaden – and those few facts stand as their parents' history. From 1880 to 1885, John painted every member of the family, including Louise's mongrel "Pointie", and of the five paintings only one was a commission. Throughout the 1880s the Burckhardts cropped up in much the same manner as had the Wattses, the Castillos, the Pagets and the Bronsons – moments of brief intimacy interleaved with long absences. But, in 1881, Louise Burckhardt's name began to be coupled closely with John's, and neither party did much to deny the inevitable rumour.

Charlotte Louise Burckhardt was born in 1863, four years after her sister Valerie and seven after John. Her short life escaped much notice apart, alas, from her brief associations with two famous men. Her entire relationship with John blossomed in a cloud of rumour, and withered amid eager speculation. Throughout the timid process John spoke little, and those to whom he did speak safeguarded his trust. Emily emitted cryptic symbols to Violet Paget, and Beckwith pencilled cautious notes in his private diary. Still, even from the distance of second- and third-hand evidence, Louise was clearly pushed more by her mother at John than drawn by John's free encouragement. Mrs Burckhardt knew no reluctance. She was the famous Mrs Bennet. Her job was to see her daughters married, and she was wonderfully unconcerned about emotions. She wanted her elder daughter married, and she wanted her married to John. After Valerie married in 1880, she moved straight on to Louise, like any good shopkeeper who wanted to empty shelves. She pushed. She tugged. She engineered. Her activities were so thinly disguised that even Emily, who was otherwise incapable of saying an evil word, told Violet

---

because Russian aristocrats had tried to turn their own country into France. Americans never shared the same romantic tendency, either at home or abroad.

Paget that Mrs Burckhardt was detestable. Of all the participants Mrs Burckhardt was the least restrained, and the least involved.

John was a splendid candidate for son-in-law, one of the best. He was young. He was presentable, and almost handsome; his career was assured of fame. He was comfortably off, and would certainly soon be rich. He came from a good family, without a suggestion of lunacy in the background. He had no known defects to hinder his performance in the matrimonial stakes. His only drawback was his lack of enthusiastic co-operation. He accepted invitations to the Burckhardts' apartment in Boulevard Malesherbes, but without alacrity. He did not seem eager, though he did appear to like Louise (and her family).

Likewise, Louise showed well, if not altogether thrillingly. She was very attractive, beautifully made, but falling short of prettiness. She had rich, dark eyes and a hearty complexion. She was well proportioned, with elegant arms and hands. But her mouth, alas, was just a little bit too wide. Her chief defect was the one that often appeared in pre-matrimonial shuffles, and probably had no basis in truth – she was considered stupid, because her temperament was disastrously malleable, suited to her mother's efforts, yet leaving her poised for unhappiness. She and John were well matched for the race, and totally ill matched for the finish.

John's courtship of Louise was an unhurried progress, gently paced. It warmed in the summer, and cooled the following winter. From the start his manners were beyond reproach. His actions were born of courtesy. His restrained attentions were, however, willingly offered. It was as if the safety of etiquette had to stand until he knew some keener emotion. But Mrs Burckhardt's brisk meddling allowed little postponement. She interpreted John's reticence to mean devotion, pleading his suit when he failed to do so, without his knowledge. And she credited him with a potential for love. She was optimistic.

First she planned pleasant little excursions, obviously designed to throw the pair together, but crowded with surplus people in a vague attempt to disguise her purpose. On 5 July 1881 (scarcely a fortnight after John had returned to Paris from London) he, Louise, Mrs Burckhardt, along with Beckwith and two more ladies, piled into a hot train for Fontainebleau, where they all stayed the night. That evening, it was Beckwith, not John, who talked for a long time in the garden with the Burckhardt ladies.* A week later, John was considerably more attentive.

Whether by design or by useful coincidence, Beckwith left them the next day to go north to Andé, near Etrétat, to paint with some other friends. His plans were disturbed. Five days later he received a letter from

---

* Mrs Burckhardt's battle-plan was revealed in Beckwith's diary. His brief entries indicate that he was aware of what was going on, and yet he was cautious to avoid any conclusions. He was an essential part of the campaign. He was John's best friend, and he was able to stand in as chaperon, as well as confidant, should the need arise. Beckwith's diary, however, sketches the faintest outline of events, and remains the *only* account.

Mrs Burckhardt announcing a visit in a few days. John, Louise and Mrs Burckhardt arrived on Wednesday evening, 13 July. John's attitude, demeanour, mood had changed. His fondness for Louise was unmistakable. He was attentive. He was eager. He was positively doting. He was John as never seen before. It was obvious his bachelor status was seriously endangered. Mrs Burckhardt rose in confident victory. She had won. After dinner on Thursday she took Beckwith into her confidence and spoke openly about Louise's slim dowry: "Mrs B & I have had a talk which I fear is going to influence John's future materially," he wrote in his diary before going to bed that night.[9]

John and Louise's behaviour endorsed her certainty. They slunk off together. They sought privacy. They acted like lovers.* Beckwith caught them off-guard: "Early this morning John and Louise were under my window," he recorded the next day, "after breakfast I found them both at the mill enjoying their bath [swim]. . . ."[10] That afternoon they went sightseeing, and then took the train to Rouen. John met Beckwith again two days later, in Paris. He was on his way to the Burckhardts'.

While John's affection for Louise had altered his behaviour, it could not prompt confession. He said nothing. This unshakeable hesitation was maddening, and unhelpful. As long as John did not mention "the subject", as Beckwith carefully referred to John and Louise's relations, Beckwith was unwilling to pry or volunteer "the unpleasant information . . . I have had on my mind"[11] – Mrs Burckhardt's unimportant confidence.† John's silence was more than a strict reflex of character; it suggested caution somewhat incompatible with his actions a few days before in St Pierre. And, more important, it coincided with his return to Paris. Suddenly, Louise lost her intense appeal. Over the next few weeks John continued to show signs of fondness for her, though his behaviour ignored the episode in the country. He made no attempt to avoid her – quite the reverse – but his attentions were subdued, as they were earlier in the summer. He acted as if nothing between them had changed, but the suspicion of coolness was undeniable. He had reverted to etiquette. Louise was helpless; she could do nothing to sustain or renew the affection she enjoyed out of Paris. She was also perplexed. She had no control over his waning devotion, because she was not to blame. His

* Beckwith's hints are open to interpretation, and the degree of John and Louise's intimacy can only be guessed at. Though they "acted like lovers", this does not mean they *were* lovers. All the signs of deep affection were evident while the pair were at St Pierre-en-Port those few days in July 1881, and that alone was as significant as the activities of deep affection a century later. The fact that they were unchaperoned was sufficient proof that their engagement was inevitable. It would be stretching evidence to assume anything more.

† Unimportant because financial considerations had no influence on John's actions, though an exaggerated importance for Beckwith himself, who was very hard up. The year before he "proposed to John to invest $500 with me" as he wrote in his diary (26 June 1880), which John did. And Beckwith did pay him back.

romantic feelings for her had grown, it seemed, out of context, detached from his day-to-day working life. The two could *not* coexist. He did not *want* both to coexist. He did not want to forfeit his precious independence. Those few days at St Pierre slipped into memory, never to be regained, never to be equalled. John did not care to be vulnerable, and he never again allowed himself to be.

By September even Mrs Burckhardt sensed defeat. "I saw R", Beckwith wrote (2 September 1881), referring to Louise with an excessive degree of privacy on John's behalf, "for a moment in John's studio and there was evidence of trouble. I was very sorry."[12] Louise's moment of importance was over. Thereafter, she rejoined the ranks as a friend, where she stayed.*

The short, mysterious tale of John and Louise Burckhardt's "romance" lingered on. As a story it was full of miscellaneous, coincidental and sometimes contradictory details that teased speculation. It had all happened so quickly, yet failed to end. The brief, highly dramatic scene occurred when the constant female influence in John's life – Emily and Mary – was absent. By the time that influence returned, his fervour for Louise had tapered off, and another phase of devotion took over, superficially indistinguishable from the previous one: chaste friendship. His fondness for the Burckhardts continued; Louise's fondness for the Sargents continued. No one knew if they were getting married or not. The doubt continued for a year. By June 1882 John made a startling and totally uncharacteristic confession, undoubtedly brought on by the enormous gulf between his feelings for Louise and his behaviour which had kept rumour alive – and Mrs Burckhardt's last-ditch attempts.[13] "I have just left John in the cab," Beckwith wrote on Sunday, 25 June 1882. "We have had a long talk on the Louise affair. I am sorry for her but he does not care a straw for her, poor girl . . ."[14] Three days later, however, John, Louise, her mother, Emily and Beckwith went to Joinville where "we had a pleasant day pottering about in the rain and came back arriving in town about 11". This was an odd and painful arrangement for an extinguished "romance". And, just as the whole affair was beginning to lose interest, it was restored to prominence as a spectator sport when the Salon opened in 1882. John's enormous portrait of Louise was on show, ripe for

---

* Louise Burckhardt experienced only a few moments of happiness in her short life. In 1888 she went to London with some dim prospect of marrying a distant relation, Count James Francis de Gallin. At his house in Windsor she met his protégé, Arthur Roger Ackerley, who was the same age as she, twenty-five. They were engaged almost at once, much to Ackerley's benefactor's fury, and married in September 1889. They settled in Paris (at 64 Boulevard de Courcelles) and were given a handsome allowance by Louise's father: £2000. Louise died eighteen months later.

The year his wife died, Ackerley met the woman who was to become his second wife, who was the mother of the writer and editor J. R. Ackerley. (See J. R. Ackerley, *My Father and Myself* (1968), p. 33.)

misinterpretation. Observers concluded he was finally making the long-awaited, much-anticipated declaration. They, like Mrs Burckhardt a year before, were wrong. He was merely performing one of his rituals of friendship. Friends' portraits were his style of salutation, not some unspoken bond locked away behind shyness. He did not use painting to counterfeit his emotions. He had not loved Fanny Watts, or Carolus, or Rosina, or Mary Austin, or Ralph Curtis, or Violet Paget, or, for that matter, anyone else. Such pictures were a gesture, a kindness, a token – his version of a bouquet. But the portrait of Louise was the most elaborate greeting of them all. It was his largest canvas, seven feet high and nearly four feet wide. He came back to the studio to paint it. He loaded her pose – standing, with outstretched hand delicately but self-consciously pinching the stem of a white rose (almost past its best) – with heavy, direct and uncomfortable reference to Velazquez. Again he relied on stark contrast (on a grand scale) to make his effect: black and white. Compared to Madame Pailleron, his portrait of Louise was acutely simple, and slightly dull.[15] And, by some peculiarity, its title has never been Louise's name. It was first shown as *Portrait de Mlle* ***, which was the custom of the Salon but fooled no one, and later became known as *Lady with the Rose*. With fine, almost sardonic humour, as if to commemorate her sorry performance as Mrs Bennet, John gave Mrs Burckhardt this larger-than-life portrait of her unwed daughter. On it, he inscribed: "To my friend Mrs. Burckhardt." Louise was, of course, unequal to the task her mother had set; anyone would have been. John's short burst of affection used up his full supply. His flirtation with her had been an intellectual enterprise. He was interested in the novelty, and was carried along by curiosity. When he played the grace notes of courtesy, he did not intend to mislead Louise or, worse, her mother. When he postponed any outright declaration, he was not falsifying hope. He was unable to act otherwise. John was unacquainted with his emotions. He was surprised by them – a reaction that provided a further twist in the complicated oxymoron of his character. With the piercing accuracy people new to a language often find, Albert Edelfeldt summarized John, landing on the precise contradiction responsible for turning Louise into a victim – "s'enflammer à froid".[16] (Literally, *s'enflammer*="to flare up"; *à froid*="with cold (manner)".) Edelfeldt's mother misinterpreted her son's comment, thinking he meant John was sceptical, or tired of life. Edelfeldt's phrase was infinitely more perceptive than he realized. Even the most casual observer noticed John's electric, hearty and sympathetic reaction to what he heard, saw or read – in short, "s'enflammer". But on closer examination these responses gave off little heat because they were subjected to the filter of his intellect – "à froid". The process sidestepped the unreliability of emotions. In matters of the brain he was passionate, determined and feeling. He did not hesitate to take on Violet Paget's truculent aesthetic arguments which she was beginning to publish under her better-known name Vernon Lee. He was as fierce and cogent as she was stubborn and long-winded. He could *understand* the works of writers, painters and musicians with a graceful, full-blooded warmth that was envied. He was generous with his effort, and his compliments. No wonder people admired him, admired him to an extravagant degree – because they could get no closer, because they could not love him. Human relations were less manageable. People had the unfortunate habit of making demands, defying consistency. They strode into the territory he liked least in his day-to-day life. They rebuffed stable analysis. All these traits froze John. They threatened the safety of the mind, where he was happy. Above all, John detested even the possibility of losing control. And that was why Louise, from the outset, did not have a chance.

His portrait of Louise was not the end. John's entanglement with the Burckhardts staggered on for a few more years. Mrs Burckhardt, appropriately enough and with an adept sense of consistency, reserved that right. In the mid-1880s, when John's fortunes had declined, she staged her *coup de théâtre*: she commissioned a double portrait of Louise and herself. John's sense of gratitude could do little to soften his view of Mrs Burckhardt's appearance or conceal the brute determination that steeled her features, but it was strong enough to change his portrait of Louise. He was more tender; she was less rosebud sweet. He looked at Louise with fondness. There was a resurgence of affection, but it was the affection felt when bidding farewell to a guest who has outstayed all welcome. After the double portrait, the Burckhardts slipped out of his life. His brief shuffle with romance was over.

The great divide in John's character, the fundamental imbalance, was masked by his achievement. Had he been an accountant, he would have buried loss with outstanding profits. He was extraordinarily professional, and he never relaxed his determination. He never swerved from his grand plan of action. He set out to succeed, and by 1882 he had. He was famous. He had risen to a height unknown to foreigners working in Paris. His determination paid off, and paid off brilliantly, sending his absence of intimacy off the ledger-sheet. If his intelligence had not effected this adjustment, his energy had.

He was a towering presence in the 1882 Salon. Apart from his portrait of Louise, he showed his enormous (8 feet by 11½ feet) subject-picture, *El Jaleo*. Like *Fumée d'ambre gris* two years before, it was intended to blur his growing reputation exclusively for portraits. *El Jaleo* was not at the Salon by accident. It was not there because it shared the same unavoidable reverence for Spanish painting as his Louise. It was there to show his versatility, and show it mightily. He triumphed. Suddenly, the low rumblings of suspicion that John was on the threshold of fame erupted into deafening cheers. He had done more than fulfil his potential; he surpassed all expectation. Both pictures were widely discussed and reproduced in the newspapers and periodicals. Observers turned from one picture to the other, uncertain which was the more brilliant. "The greatest success is Sargent's Spanish Dance," Edelfeldt declared when the Salon opened, "bizarre, daring, but ingenious, hellish and smart."[17] A month later Vernon Lee granted *El Jaleo* was "very fine, striking, original; but there is a portrait of his of a girl in black which is simply superb & like an old master".[18]

The conjunction of these two pictures was deliberate. John wanted to make certain that visitors to the Salon came away knowing his name. He wanted to be an unavoidable presence. He left nothing to chance, because he was without question a very acute businessman. He knew how to advertise. Underneath John's casual, nonchalant manner, there was a shrewd talent for commerce, which was bundled together with his ambition. All his energy was syphoned into his career, with cool, practical level-headedness. John had planned his success. That spring he fixed his eye on the English market, and later enhanced his growing renown in America. He submitted a portrait to the Royal Academy.* *El Jaleo*, having been snapped up instantly by an American dealer, was exhibited in July at the Fine Arts Society in London, before being shown in New York and Boston. John had done what popularity required: he had produced a wonderful show. He was famous – at the age of twenty-six.

These two pictures also showed, despite John's reluctance to accept the fact, precisely where his true skill lay: his strength was portraiture. *El Jaleo*, for all its power to drum up excitement and spark intimidating claims, was a flawed performance. It had been conceived with a purpose. It had a job, an easy job, and the result was a shallow one. John simply wanted to get noticed. Of course his ability to apply paint, haul out theatrical devices, produce startling images were all remarkable – and none effortlessly achieved – but somehow that was all there was to the picture; John could go no further, could not go beyond an impressive surface. The awful lesson of Carolus was the convenience of superficial brilliance, and *El Jaleo* followed in the same unchallenging direction. It was the journalism of painting. If John were only responding to plain business sense in offering *El Jaleo* as a delicacy to win the public, then the limitation of the picture did not matter; but, alas, the picture was flawed by something John was powerless to overcome: he had little imagination.[19] *El Jaleo* might originally have been plotted out by his love of music and his intoxication with the "curious", yet two years later when he set to work their influence was dead and he could not conjure them back. Thus he developed the picture by accumulating parts, with several models. His memories of Spain had turned into an aggregate.

---

* Of the elusive Dr Pozzi – doubly elusive because this picture seems to have been ignored by every London critic when it was shown. Vernon Lee saw it after her tour of the Salon (with John and Emily on 2 June): "I went to the Academy," she wrote to her mother (16 June 1882), "poor stuff for the most part, but John's red picture, tho' less fine than his Paris portrait, magnificent, of an insolent kind of magnificence, more or less kicking other people's pictures to bits" (*Vernon Lee's Letters* (1937), p. 87). The portrait was painted the previous autumn, in Pozzi's apartment.

John's subject-pictures were impressive vaudeville turns. They excited cheers, loud comment, and never lingered. They were born of pure technique, and highly simple statement, wonderfully delivered. They were never deep. John's greatest ability as a painter was his endless supply of deft solutions to problems placed before him. This fact gave his portraits (and, later, landscapes) strength, and made his subject-pictures weak. His intelligence was a cool, matter-of-fact thing, scarcely ever given to fanciful leaps or absurd flights. Still, for all its lack of fantasy, it was nimble, quick, lively, acute. The chorus of praise that greeted pictures like *El Jaleo* and *Fumée d'ambre gris* hid this basic limitation. The public was heartily pleased with John's offerings, and it was a dangerous greeting. With characteristic detachment John negotiated that danger to his own advantage, by giving in *and* ignoring its temptation. He used, of all things, the comprehensive Sargent response to every issue – geography. In Paris he kept office hours; for several months leading up to the Salon and for as many after, he was available to everyone. He was generous with his time and society. All invitations were accepted. He entertained. He gave in to every ancillary demand of fame, all of which used up his energy. He gave people what they wanted, unpetulantly. But towards the end of summer he was off. He removed himself, first from commissions, then from interruption.

First he went north, "with two very nice friends", Emily wrote to Vernon Lee (25 August 1880) – Brooks Chadwick and Ralph Curtis – to Belgium and Holland in obeisance to northern masters. His tour was extended; he could not tear himself away, having "lost all count of the days" he wrote to his family in Aix-les-Bains who were eagerly awaiting his arrival before they moved on together.[20] By the middle of September he moved south, with his parents and sisters, to Venice. He stayed on alone through the winter, declining the tempting invitation to visit the Pagets in Florence: "I must do something for the Salon," he wrote to Mrs Paget (27 September) from his studio in the Palazzo Rezzonico, "and have determined to stay as late as possible . . . I am forced to consider that there may only be a few more weeks of pleasant season here and I must make the most of them."[21] Venice was another Cancale and Seville. It was preparation for the spring, study for a Venetian *Jaleo*. "There is plenty of work to be done here," he wrote to Vernon Lee (22 October), "and the only thing I fear is the ennui of living almost alone in a wet and changed Venice."[22]

For him, Venice represented more than just an escape from the professional discipline of Paris, more than an antidote to portraiture: it was a new reference library for his grand strategy. And he incorporated his notes fresh from Haarlem.

His Salon prep in Venice was a radical departure from the customary postcard reaction, so radical he seemed to make a deliberate attempt to shake off centuries of habit. He was unseduced by the panoramas. He turned away from the architecture. He was altogether nonplussed by the history. He was blind to tourist excitement. He totally ignored the usual monumentality of the town. By 1880, John was not carried away by the spectacle of Venice; he had been there at least three times before, when he was seventeen, fourteen, and less than one year old. He looked to Venice merely for a subject and, as before, he was fascinated by the common-place and, as such, surprising (even revolutionary) scenes for Venice: people talking in a narrow alley, a peasant lighting a cigarette, vacant streets *and* dark spacious interiors. Sybille Bedford once wrote that people seemed to come from nowhere in the tangle of Venetian streets, and that was the mystery John had sought to scale down in his paintings. These Venetian studies, which extended to his next visit in 1882 (when he stayed with his cousins at the Palazzo Barbaro), were more finished than his *Jaleo* notes and conclusively refute the studied absence of imagination in *El Jaleo*. They stand as a body of work independent of future develop-ment. But while he was casting around for his Salon picture he sought not drama but tranquillity – a modification in his plan of attack in Paris. It was as if he willingly lost interest in the future, lost sight of his large purpose for coming to Venice.

One observer who saw John's work during the second instalment, in October 1882, thought he was simply being perverse: "He had . . . some half-finished pictures of Venice. They are very clever, but a good deal inspired by the desire of finding what no one else has sought here – unpicturesque subjects, absence of colour, absence of sunlight. It seems hardly worth while to travel so far for these. But he had some qualities to an unusual degree – a sense of values & faculty for making his personages move."[23] John's subjects were odd enough, but his persistent reliance on black, especially in Venice, struck his fellow-painters as very strange. Luke Fildes (later RA, and famous for his royal portraits) noted in his diary after visiting John's studio in Ca' Rezzonico in January 1881: "His colour is black, but very strong painting."[24] And subsequent art historians have also remarked on John's performance in the early 1880s: they claim his perversity heralded the modern age of Venetian subject-pictures.

During his first long stay in Venice (from mid-September 1880 to the end of February 1881) John met Whistler, beginning an acquaintance that lasted twenty-three years, gave little pleasure, tested John's patience, tried Whistler's undeveloped sense of justice, and produced keen partisanship. James McNeill Whistler's early history was dogged by hardship and was overcome by fierce determination. In 1843, at the age of nine, he, his two brothers and mother left America for St Petersburg to join his father, who had been commissioned by Tsar Nicholas I to engineer the railway line to Moscow. Six years later his father died, and the family returned to America penniless. In 1851, Whistler followed family tradition and entered the United States Military Academy where he displayed no aptitude whatsoever, save for drawing, then taught by J. Alden Weir's father. He then went to Paris to study painting, first with Gleyre and then with Gérôme. He was at once accepted into the small

English-speaking circle, later immortalized by Du Maurier in *Trilby*, consisting of Leighton, Poynter and Ionides, among others. In the early 1860s he settled in London and began what was to be a volatile career. Thereafter the hardship that attended him was largely of his own making. He had a penchant for argument, disagreements, lawsuits, and sensing hostility from every direction. Though driven by the highest aesthetic ideals, he wrapped himself in controversy, determined to be a martyr, confident of self-destruction. In life Whistler had the consolation of believing he was misunderstood; in death he became merely incomprehensible. He found biographers – the Pennells – who were as enthusiastic about the maltreatment of their subject as he had been. When Whistler trod over a patron's generosity, they applauded the artist's unbending conviction and denounced the patron's shortsightedness. They produced a dire hagiography as distorted and odious as Whistler was himself.[25]

Whistler's chief defect was his inability to be alone. He had to be in a crowded room, and his arrogance insisted he be the most prominent. His desperation went far enough to accommodate infamy when he failed to gain admiration. And of course he could not avoid jealousy. When John arrived in Venice, admired, praised, Whistler, who was enduring the exact opposite reputation, could not stand it, and for the next twenty years they made no advance on a frosty sort of cordiality. Whistler could not bear John's success, deriding his painting and his fame, while at the same time respecting, with a great many qualifications, John's character: "Not that Sargent is not charming and all that," Whistler reluctantly owned (16 July 1899), " – only a sepulchre of dullness and propriety."[26] And a year later, after decrying the whole of the Royal Academy summer show, Whistler conceded: "Sargent is a good fellow, yes, but, as a painter, no better than the rest."[27]

Artistically and temperamentally they were wonderfully mismatched for conviviality. Whistler's manner was too swashbuckling for John's taste, and John's sober detachment was too refined for Whistler's taste. Whistler had enough difficulty trying to take John's work seriously, but the fact that the stupid public loved it proved that he was pandering, unashamedly. John's admiration for Whistler's work, on the other hand, was considerable, but he was too shy to express it. While Whistler was dismissing John's portraits, John was steering collectors and patrons in Whistler's direction. Both painters were stunningly unalike; friendship was an impossibility.

John stayed in Venice as long as he dared, but by the end of October the weather was turning hostile and he was forced to return to Paris, with his work unfinished. His sitters could not be put off. Such reluctance, however, had caused an uncomfortable press of time. He postponed his annual Christmas visit to his family in Nice until January (1883). He had a full order-book. And each new portrait added further confirmation of his popularity, and with good reason. He was surprising. He refused to work to a formula. He was unpredictable. The pictures he chose for the Salon in

1883 and 1884, and for the Royal Academy in 1884 – all three, curiously, of Americans – were as unexpected as they were different. These three portraits showed more than nimble versatility; they showed John's limitless capacity for originality. They were the first accounts by John at the height of his ability. He was no longer "promising", or Carolus' star pupil, or inexperienced – at the age of twenty-seven.*

The first of these paintings was a commission from Edward Darley Boit (1840–1915). Boit was an ideal patron, a man quivering on the outskirts of art who encouraged John by the sheer force of his admiration. He was, down to his toes, a Bostonian – Boston Latin School, Harvard, Secretary of Hasty Pudding, Freshman crew, tall, poetic, athletic, confident, and rich (richer still for having married a Cushing – Charlotte Louisa, known as "Iza" – the only daughter of a vastly wealthy merchant whose estate "Belmont" gave the town its name) – with a very curious difference. In 1868 he saw the work of Corot, and at that instant discovered painting in a blinding flash and spent the rest of his life in service to that revelation. " 'There are artists in France who dare to paint nature as she is,' " he said to himself at that great moment. " 'It is not essential that an artist should invent; he may copy. . . . Perhaps, after all, I too may become an artist.' "[28] He gave up his law practice, hurried abroad, studying first in Rome with Crowninshield and then in Paris with Couture. He showed at the Salon, and the Boston Museum later bought some of his watercolours. For all his seriousness, Emily considered him "a clever amateur". Nearly thirty years later John and he had a joint show in New York at Boit's invitation. "John couldn't resist this old friend," Emily wrote to Julie Heyneman (11 February 1909), "& lately sent over 84 watercolours!"[29] At this show the Brooklyn Museum made the stupendous purchase of eighty out of the eighty-six pictures John showed.[30] The Boits had a secure place on the expatriate circuit because they had very sound qualifications.[31] Henry James, who sought them out first in Rome, approved of them, and professed, at useful intervals, admiration for them, their work, and their hospitality. John liked them for somewhat more basic, straightforward reasons. They were educated. They were musical, and also ardent Wagnerians. They were agreeably uncomplicated, and Edward Boit's order for a group portrait of his four young daughters interested John a great deal.

The commission to paint Edward Boit's daughters was fraught with a jumble of basic difficulties. There were four subjects, all girls. There was their range of ages: Florence was fourteen years old, Jane twelve, Mary eight, and Julia four. The older girls had the natural superiority of size; the

---

* John was by now generally and widely known as "Sargent", and though few people were on Christian-name terms of intimacy with him the author will persist in calling him John; while his father is called FitzWilliam, John cannot be "Sargent". After FitzWilliam's death, John becomes Sargent. It is a simple matter of courtesy.

youngest had the natural advantage of appeal. Somehow John had to make them all appear equal, of similar importance. His solution was ingenious because it was brilliantly simple.

By making a deep genuflection to Velazquez's *Las Meninas* while also remembering his recent Venetian studies in perspective, he plotted out an exercise in geometry. He composed the picture as a series of horizontal and vertical planes, arranged in the Boits' spacious apartment in Avenue de Friedland. He selected a large canvas, 7¼ feet square, and he chose Jane to be his control, his theme, placing her sisters in relation to her, variations. She stood in the very centre, formally upright, facing forward. Florence was placed immediately to her right, slouching to make her a little bit shorter, in profile looking left, her hands folded in front. Mary was positioned much further away to Jane's right, closer in front, her arms clasped behind her back: a position parallel with Jane. Furthest in front (towards the bottom of the canvas) was Julia, the only one of the girls John posed sitting, with her legs out, playing with a doll, her back parallel with Florence's. Julia's posture not only enhanced her size, but unified the major planes of the floor (itself emphasized by the carpet) and the walls. The severity of this organization was broken by the patterned Savonnerie and the grand curve of a pair of enormous vases, taller than the girls. As in John's Spanish inspiration, there was a generous feeling of space and depth. The room behind Jane was cast in shadow, interrupted by a bright but obscure reflection in a looking-glass, and the red screen's hint of brilliance. John's choice of colour was dark, yet rich, offset by the girls' white pinafores. In the most elegant, assured manner, this picture married portraiture to the larger desire to create atmosphere which John had tried to convey in scenes like *Fumée d'ambre gris* and *El Jaleo*. By incorporating a sense of mystery ripe from Venice, John went far beyond the requirements of portraiture. The *Daughters of Edward Boit* was a literary picture; it could support endless interpretation, fascination. Henry James went weak at the knees over it (after recovering from his swoon over Miss Burckhardt): "The artist has done nothing more felicitous and interesting than this view of a rich, dim, rather generalized French interior," he wrote in *Harper's* in 1887,

> . . . which encloses the life and seems to form the happy play-world of a family of charming children. The treatment is eminently unconventional, and there is none of the usual symmetrical balancing of the figures in the foreground. The place is regarded as a whole; it is a scene, a comprehensive impression; yet none the less do the little figures . . . detach themselves, and live with a personal life. . . . The naturalness of the composition, the loveliness of the complete effect, the light, the free security of the execution, the sense it gives us as of assimilated secrets and instinct and knowledge of playing together – all this makes the picture . . . astonishing. . . .[32]

The *Daughters of Edward Boit* was a faultless performance, austere, restrained, and fully controlled because various elements – like receding perspective, spirited though sketchy brushwork, reliance on deep shadow – had been previously and independently explored. But the critics at the Salon were caught off-guard and they roared against such an unconventional construction. John had done it again. He had taunted tradition, simply by ignoring it. His reputation was further enhanced.

The instant he finished with the Boits, he began his portrait of Mrs Henry White, a commission from strangers that was given purely on the recommendation of what they had seen in the Salon.[33] John had the warming knowledge, for the first time, that he had earned their patronage, free of friendly influence. Mrs White went to John after seeing his portrait of Louise Burckhardt, and first sat to him at the end of February. Margaret Stuyvesant Rutherfurd White was a forceful woman. She had none of her husband's caution; he chose Bonnat for his portrait. She was also ruthlessly clever, arrestingly beautiful, having the useful gifts of height, posture, assured demeanour, together with the perfect knowledge of their advantages, and she was splendidly self-assured. She had an equally full ration of ambition, and she gave the surplus to her husband who was, until their marriage in 1879, keener on aimless pleasure than on any occupation. She prodded him into diplomacy, eventually turning him into America's "first professional . . . diplomatist". When the Whites came to England from Paris at the end of 1883, she was quickly awarded the uncertain accolade of the Souls' devotion. If society were some cloud formation, Mrs White would have been a high, fast-moving streak.

The odour of superiority had hung around her since birth. She was the eldest daughter of seven children born to Lewis Morris Rutherfurd, one of the chief pioneers in the development of the photographic telescope. Law, however, had been his first career, and he moved on to the stars when his wife became ill. The Rutherfurds were rich, and self-conscious. They lived in high style in New York and in New Jersey (on their estate called Tranquillity), when they were not travelling abroad. They were excessively aware that one of their ancestors had signed the Declaration of Independence. Mrs White was the fine result of such a background, loaded down with refined tastes and she could be little else than a frosty Puritan. During the height of her English success, in 1888, she was assessed: "very handsome, young [two years older than John], rich, splendid, admired and successful, to a degree which leaves all competitors behind. . . . She has never read a book in her life; but she is 'high up' all the same."[34] For some wholly uncharacteristic reason, Mrs White was called Daisy.

Mrs White's commission was highly fortuitous, with far-reaching, incalculable benefits. With her range of friends, her and her husband's money, her innate preference for aristocracy, her talent for getting attention, and her international sure-footedness, she outclassed the Salon as John's best advertisement. Her apartment in Avenue Hoche and her house in Grosvenor Crescent creaked under the weight of dip-lomatists, subscribers to the Blue Book, and titles – in short, the widest possible directory of John's future clients. Her commission, and her commission alone, set John's career on a different course, upward.

She was, altogether, a different class of sitter. Work on the portrait was interrupted by her suffering from the recurrent ill-effects of typhoid, and she went off to Cannes after only a few sittings. When she returned to Paris, they resumed in John's new studio. Sitters of the order of Mrs White could not be expected to brave the squalor at rue Notre-Dame-des-Champs. Madame Subercaseaux, Dr Pozzi and Edward Boit had each tactfully welcomed different settings. In June 1883, John moved across town, to a new purpose-built studio, at 41 Boulevard Berthier: "where", he wrote, "I am better off".*[35] He left the rough and tumble of the Quartier Latin. His neighbours were distinguished socialites, artists, musicians: Boldini was at number 14; Carrier-Belleuse was at 31. His old friend Ernst Duez (whom John painted in 1884) lived at 39. And the Roger-Jourdains were at 45. Madame Roger-Jourdain was a celebrated hostess and, like John's landlord, very musical. She introduced John to Gabriel Fauré, who had dedicated *Aurore* to her, and she was equally popular with writers and artists. John painted her and her daughter's portrait. One of his first visitors to the new studio was Vernon Lee, who wrote to her mother (23 June 1883):

> He has taken a whole tiny house, so extremely pretty, quite aesthetic and English, with a splendid big studio and a pretty garden with roses and all done up with Morris papers & rugs and matting. From his having invested in this house I presume Miss Burckhardt is gone off the horizon. . . . There were two very fine begun portraits in his studio.[36]

Mrs White's was the first John completed in the new studio. He saw her with uncanny precision, and wholly unlike any portrait he had painted before. He had to go back a few centuries to find the correct tradition to suit her. She was stately, implacable, cool, and forthrightly grand, filling nearly the full height of the 7¼-foot canvas. There was no hint of a smile. Her gown was bone white, a lavish, generous confection, with billowing overskirt swept round. She wore pearls and a little gold. She carried a fan in one hand, opera-glasses in the other. Mrs White was unmistakably formal, though not, she thought, quite formal enough. A few years later she asked John to alter the tilt of her head, as if to make her more imposing, if possible; he complied. And this was exactly the type of portrait Mrs White's friends would clamour to have for themselves.

---

* Rented from Paul Poirson, who inherited the studio from his brother Maurice the year before. In 1884, John painted Poirson's daughter Suzanne, and the following year his wife, Seymourina Cuthbertson, the 4th Marquess of Hertford's natural daughter. (Ormond Family Collection)

The other "begun" portrait was less straightforward. In fact, John lost his way over and over again. Essentials seemed to elude him. He had trouble finding a satisfactory pose. He had difficulty with colour. The sittings were endless. His subject lost patience. He suffered uncharacteristic doubts. He had never known so many problems. When the portrait was eventually shown he fought with the sitter's mother. John's portrait of Madame Pierre Gautreau was a lengthy ordeal. Years later when he sold the picture to the Metropolitan he wanted to obliterate her name from the title; she became known as "Madame X".

Virginie Gautreau (1859–1915, née Avegno) was born in Louisiana to Marie-Virginie de Ternant, said to be the only surviving child of the 2nd marquis de Ternant, and Major Anatole Placide Avegno, himself of Italian descent.[37] When her father died from wounds received at the battle of Shiloh, her widowed mother packed up and sailed to France, taking Virginie (aged four) and her elder sister Julie. They never returned to America. As her daughters grew older, Madame Avegno worked to place them in society, which meant marry them well. The Faubourg turned its back on these colonial hybrids; their geneaology was too flimsy, their background too mysterious, to permit them to move in the highest circles. They were, despite their thin aristocratic connection, considered *arriviste*, and were summarily dismissed. But the girls possessed such beauty – having inherited a full portion of both their mother and their father's glorious appearance – they were impossible to ignore. Their looks were a considerable social asset, and Virginie was not backward or modest about showing herself off. She was excessively proud of her features and her figure; proud to a degree that parodied such a gift. She made herself conspicuous. The Faubourg sneered at her overweening self-importance. Others were less particular. She married a wealthy banker and ship-owner, Pierre Gautreau, and found a place – not an altogether secure place – in Paris society.* She moved among the professional classes:

* Pierre Gautreau was so eclipsed by his wife that almost nothing is known about him; and this ignorance, which existed during his life-time, naturally encouraged a huge number of rumours. One of the most sensational about his marriage to Mademoiselle Avegno circulated long after both of them had died, and was probably much amplified over the years: she had a horror of the relations between man and wife, and she rebuffed Gautreau's proposals constantly. He became obsessed by her, so obsessed that he was willing to marry her without making any claim whatsoever on his rights. She would live in another part of the house. He only asked to *see* her, live under the same roof, and enjoy all the chaste pleasures of being her husband. This seemed a tolerable arrangement, and she agreed to marry him. Sometime thereafter – the story is a bit light on specific details – she started to show the unavoidable signs of pregnancy. Gautreau was furious, and naturally disbelieved her protestations that she had slept with no one. She had not deceived him. She went to her gynaecologist – presumably Dr Pozzi – was examined, and was seen to be telling the truth! Utter mystery. Pozzi operated, discovered the freakish but not unknown existence of Madame Gautreau's own unborn twin sister inside her. After that, this implausible story concluded,

financiers, doctors, politicians. She was, Julie Heyneman reported authoritatively, a close friend of Gambetta (who died in 1882). She was alleged to have had a long affair with Dr Pozzi. Gossip and mystery attended her. Great claims have been made about her social success in Paris, but contemporary diarists and memoirists never mentioned her. Even the most frivolous recollections exclude her.

Her fame was closer to notoriety, and with justification. She hardly deserved history's generous classification of her as "a beauty". Her nose was large, her chin over-prominent, her hairline strangely high on her scalp, her lips thin and mean, and her hair was an unlustrous shade of tarnished copper. Yet all these features combined, by some bizarre alchemy, to create an amazing profile. It was altogether striking, and certainly arresting. Her extreme vanity was not at all put off by the limitations of her face. She engineered to make observers forget these hindrances. Nature had given her a wonderful figure, sensuous but lithe, erotic yet forbidding. She at once set to work improving Nature's ration. She made liberal use of powder, on her arms, shoulders, breasts, neck and face. She wanted a pale complexion. (It is also possible that she adopted the slightly old-fashioned habit of taking small draughts of arsenic to help deaden the tone of her flesh.[38]) The laws of chemistry were, however, unhelpful: her skin became a ghostly white crossed with deathly mauve. Her sarcophagal colouring had the effect of flattening the contours of her face and body, making her appear two-dimensional, and accentuating the line of her profile. The whole effect was unmistakably odd. She succeeded in being noticed, because she had turned herself into a curiosity. Her make-up was a major topic of speculation. When she went bathing, she climbed into the bathing machine, wheeled out a good distance, to protect her from spectators, but the fleeting glimpse of her shoulders showed the white colour intact. She was a phenomenon that continued to excite artists. Helleu drew her on a plate when he worked for the ceramicist Deck.[39] She was painted by Courtois (in profile) and de la Gandara. John started work on his portrait of her when she was twenty-three years old. She was already acutely aware of her appeal.

The exact sequence of events that led to the portrait is uncertain. John met her in the early 1880s, and shortly thereafter he wrote to del Castillo: " 'I have a great desire to paint her portrait and have reason to think she would allow it and is waiting for someone to propose this homage to her beauty. If you are "bien avec elle" and will see her in Paris you might tell her that I am a man of *prodigious talent*.' "[40] He began work by the middle of February 1883. He wrote to Vernon Lee excitedly just before he started (10 February) [1883], "the Portrait of a Great Beauty. Do you object to

---

satisfactory marital relations between husband and wife began. They had one daughter, who died in 1914. (I am indebted to Mrs Diana Phipps for telling me this fantastic story.)

people who are 'fardées' to the extent of being a uniform lavender or blotting-paper colour all over? If so you would not care for my sitter; but she has the most beautiful lines, and if the lavender or chlorate of potash-lozenge colour be pretty in itself I should be more than pleased."[41] He gave himself three weeks, in order to submit it to the Salon. His optimism soon faded; that summer he followed her to Brittany, to continue work at her country house, Les Chênes, Paramé. There he made dismal progress. She was becoming maddeningly lazy about posing, which was only to be expected when John could not hit on a satisfactory pose for her. He sketched her seated in a contorted pose. He sketched her with her head raised, then lowered looking at a book, then playing the piano.[42] He did a watercolour of her seated in a different posture,[43] and a brisk oil study of her holding out a champagne-glass at a table.[44] In desperation he completely ignored the famous profile and drew her back as she kneeled on a sofa looking out of the window. Finally he asked her to stand beside an Empire table, twisted into a conscious profile. This was the Salon pose. That basic fact decided, he played on the graceful, undulating line that travelled along the severe profile and flowed down her arms. The pale hue of her flesh, so much an assistant in the drama of that stern fact of draughtsmanship, was maddeningly elusive. His anxiety would not let up; he wrote to Castillo:

> My portrait! it is much changed and far more advanced than when you last saw it. One day I was dissatisfied with it and dashed a tone of light rose over the gloomy background. I turned the picture upside down, retired to the other end of the studio and looked at it under my arm. Vast improvement. The *élancée* figure of the model shows to much greater advantage. The picture is framed and on a great easel, and Carolus has been to see it and said, 'Vous pouvez l'envoyer au Salon avec confiance. [You can send it to the Salon with confidence.]' Encouraging, but false. I have made up my mind to be refused.*[45]

As the opening of the Salon approached, John grew extremely agitated. He feared a hostile reception. In some ways the portrait was a retreat from the progress of his previous submissions: his colour was sombre to near-monochrome, his brushwork was more "finished", perhaps over-worked, and his simple conception of his subject as an extravagant intaglio was harshly unflattering. Her décolletage could so easily be misread as criticism. It was a very daring picture.[46]

When the Salon opened, his worst fears were exceeded. There was an alarming, universal outcry. Ralph Curtis wrote to his parents the following day (*c.* 2 May 1884):

> John . . . was very nervous about what he feared, but his fears were far

---

* As John had been awarded a medal at the Salon, he was "hors concours", which meant he did not need Jury approval for admission to the Salon.

exceeded by the facts of yesterday. There was a grande tapage before it all day. In a few minutes I found him dodging behind doors to avoid friends who looked grave. By the corridors he took me to see it. I was disappointed in the colour. She looks decomposed. All the women jeer. Ah voilà "la belle!" "Oh quel horreur!" etc. Then a painter exclaims "superbe de style", "magnifique d'audace!" "quel dessin!" . . . All the a.m. it was one series of bons mots, mauvaises plaisanteries and fierce discussions. John, poor boy, was navré. . . . In the p.m. the tide turned as I kept saying it would. It was discovered to be the knowing thing to say "étrangement épatant!"

Marie Bashkirtseff also saw the picture on opening day, and with that variety of acute perception which made her famous wrote in her diary: "It is a success of curiosity; people find it atrocious. For me it is perfect painting, masterly, true. But he has done what he saw. Beautiful Mme. —— is horrible in daylight. . . . Further, she paints her ears rose and her hair mahogany. The eyebrows are traced in dark mahogany colour, two thick lines."

After lunch, Curtis continued in his account of 1 May, "I went home with him, and remained there while he went to see the Boits. Mde. Gautreau and mère came to his studio 'bathed in tears'. I stayed them off but the mother returned and caught him and made a fearful scene saying 'Ma fille est perdue – tout Paris se moque d'elle. Mon genre sera forcé de se battre. Elle mourira de chagrin.' "[47]

John withstood Madame Avegno's tirade. He refused to withdraw the picture; it was against Salon rules. "He had painted her exactly as she was dressed, that nothing could be said of the canvas worse than had been said in print of her appearance dans le monde etc. etc. Defending his cause made him feel much better." Still, the picture had caused a scandal, starting with public indignation and continued by critical assaults. The press flatly denounced the picture; only the *Gazette des beaux-arts* printed a few balancing words of unenthusiastic praise.

The storm that swirled around the picture gathered force from a basic confusion. The fierce reaction was caused primarily by the subject, and the painting was used as evidence. People were jeering at Madame Gautreau herself. She and her mother were the first to sense this, and because their own status was slightly insecure they appealed to John to remove the offending portrait. They squirmed under the extreme publicity. The confusion was increased by the unfortunate timing. Despite his forebodings, John pinned considerable hope on the picture – hope that his portrait of a well-known Parisian figure might help to expand his portrait clientele beyond expatriate Americans. His expectations were instantly disappointed. The final and most severe side-effect of the débâcle was John's sudden acquaintance with adverse criticism. Hitherto his reputation had flourished on the encouragement of loud praise, eagerly given. He had never known the slightest obstacle, from the very moment he strode into *atelier* Carolus ten years before. His rise had been a magnificent, steady upward sweep. Now John had no other option but to overreact, distort the gravity of the whole unpleasant episode. A slow-acting poison began to work. Paris turned from "the only place" to an unwelcoming, uncomfortable one. His security was endangered. His attraction to Virginie Gautreau's "most beautiful lines" had proved to be a destructive seduction.

VIII

Henry James was like a great queen-bee; wherever he went he was utterly confident the swarm would follow. It was a strange form of arrogance, and necessity: he needed to think he was important. He had grown so used to distinction that he was incapable of dealing with anyone or anything considered insignificant. And history for the most part has smiled favourably on this amibition. Rebecca West, who admired him for more than sixty-five years, pronounced on this least likeable and most public quality: "Henry James was, it must be owned, like loud and ill-played church music in his snobbery. . . . Of him it can be said that in his youth he knew Flaubert and Turgenev, and in his middle-age he settled for Paul Bourget, a mawkish novelist and boot-licker, whom he knew to be just that."[1] In February 1884, James, aged forty, swept down on Paris again with memories of his youth still fragrant. Turgenev and Flaubert were gone, and he buzzed around looking for replacements. "The only Franco-American product of importance here", he wrote to a friend (23 February 1884), "strikes me as young John Sargent the painter, who has high talent, a charming nature, artistic and personal, and is civilized to his finger-tips. He is perhaps spoilable – though I don't think he is spoiled. But I hope not, for I like him extremely; and the best of his work seems to me to have in it something exquisite."[2] John was a fresh find. They had been introduced at the beginning of the month, through a friend of Mrs Boit's, Henrietta Reubell, and thereafter a brisk pace was assumed: John took him to Boulevard Berthier, where James saw the portrait of Virginie Gautreau, which did not arouse his enthusiasm much. But he also saw other pictures: "His talent is brilliant," James declared, "but there is a certain incompleteness in it, in his extremely attaching, interesting nature a certain want of seriousness."[3] John was foremost in his letters. James could not resist him. "I like him so much that (a rare thing for me) I don't attempt too much to judge him."[4] From that moment on he darted round John, tantalizing him with stories of London. He made himself imposs- ible to ignore, *with perfect timing*.

James was mesmerized by John, as one is mesmerized by an exotic flower. John had all the high gloss of cultural confusion that James relied on in his fiction. John was a Jamesian figure without the benefit of James, and James was determined to make up for that omission. He set out to make himself indispensable, and he did this by providing the vital link between John and the country John was unaware he had missed – England. James could smooth the path. He could render an infinite number of useful services. He could supply endless introductions. For James such activity was an aesthetic duty; for John it was an abundant display of generosity. James's siren call was only partially successful. John was coming to London at the end of March to meet Emily on her way back to Nice from Ireland, and to see the Reynolds exhibition at the Royal Academy. Before John arrived James confessed he wanted to give him "a push to the best of my ability";[5] and by the time John left it was obvious James had miscalculated his own strength – he had nearly knocked John over.

John arrived on Friday (27 March). On Saturday he and James went to the Royal Academy, dined together, and went on to the theatre. On Sunday they had lunch, then went to visit ten studios, among them those belonging to the giants of English art. (Later they called on Burne-Jones's where they saw his big Grosvenor Gallery picture *King Cophetua and the Beggar Maid* and stayed an hour. John was very impressed; Burne-Jones, James wrote, "suffers from a constitutional incapacity to enjoy Sargent's [paintings] – finding in them 'such a want of finish' ".[6]) That evening James hosted a dinner for John at the Reform Club (Burne-Jones was one of the guests). At the end of the week he took John to a large party for the actor Lawrence Barrett, given by Edwin Austin Abbey in his new studio. James's entertainment was the closest thing to courtship. Their relationship was strangely, though not clearly, chaste. James wanted to control John, and be a catalyst in his career. He wanted to help John, but such great benign generosity was suspect. And James wanted to show off his power. John was a wonderful subject for James's machinations. "His character is charmingly naïf," James asserted [2 June] (1884),

> but not his talent. But I take a great interest in him, and am desirous to witness his future. He is intelligent *en diable*. . . . I want him to come here to live and work – there being such a field in London. . . . He is afraid but he inclines, I think, this way, and will probably end by coming. He has got all, and more than all – that Paris can give him – and he can apply it here . . .[7]

Such confidence was breathtaking, and such extreme conviction prodded John just a little.

John left for Paris the first week in April, saying farewell with utterances about his return in the summer, in order to carry out a few commissions given months before: "I am to paint several portraits in the country," he wrote to Vernon Lee in February, "& three ugly young women at Sheffield, dingy hole. . . . It will take me probably from the 15th July to the 15th September."[8] These portraits had nothing to do with Henry James.

A month later the "solemn fiasco" of Madame Gautreau's portrait broke. At the time, the facts were seen as so extraordinary, gossip did not distort them, nor were they too awful to be concealed. The melodramatic confrontation with the sitter's mother was widely circulated. Everyone who knew John certainly knew the squalid story. And naturally James did not hold back from adding his own voice to this unexpected and opportune turn of events. He made no secret of his plan to lure John across the Channel. "Henry James wants to settle him here," Vernon Lee, who got her information third-hand, passed on to her mother (24 June).[9] John's future became the major topic of speculation in drawing-rooms in London and Paris. John alone seemed to be the only one to keep quiet. He tried to wait out the controversy with his customary detachment. He remained cool about the sudden dent in his reputation. His routine varied little. His life went on unaltered. The sittings continued in Boulevard Berthier. When Vernon Lee made her annual visit to the Salon, she went to see John in his studio and confessed that she had nothing unusual to report, save that she had missed John's lunch party for Paul Bourget and Mr and Mrs Oscar Wilde.* Although John might have been wounded by the ridicule heaped on his Salon portrait, he was not crushed. He told Vernon Lee that he was "prouder of it than the Jaleo".[10] The "solemn fiasco" did not send him from Paris, his home, his first home; unlike anyone else in his family, he knew what it was to be settled. He had engraved writing-paper, he had signed a lease and, while none of these things indicated absolute permanence, none could be lightly discarded. And, most important, he was unwilling to leave his family in Nice. The Salon reaction coupled with James's campaign has always been credited with sending John to England; it was not the case: there were reasons of much longer standing that had been worked at for years.

---

* When John introduced Vernon Lee to Bourget two months later, she instantly realized she had not missed much. She was appalled: "He is a flabby blond, sickly looking young man, like certain types of fat scrofulous Italians, with a glass in one eye; very slow and rather shy in manner." She suspected "that John was thoroughly bored by him. . . ." (*Vernon Lee's Letters* (1937), pp. 157–8, 172). James, who met him at the same time, was on the other hand utterly entranced by him. It was likes attracting. Paul Bourget (1852–1935), essayist, memoirist, and novelist, suffered from precisely the same sort of Anglo-snobbery that infected a number of artists at the time, among them another of John's friends, the portraitist Jacques-Emil Blanche. Bourget appealed tremendously to James's own Franco-snobbery (Leon Edel, *Henry James: The Middle Years, 1884–1894* (1963), pp. 50–2). A year later John served up another offering, when he directed Pozzi, Montesquiou and Edmond de Polignac to look up James when they came to London. James found this introduction less agreeable than the first.

John and Oscar Wilde had the most quixotic relations. When Wilde went to Paris, he made his presence known, which pleased John. In April ?1882 he inscribed a volume of Rennell Rodd's poems, *Rose Leaf and Apple Leaf* with an introduction by himself: "To my friend John S. Sargent with deep admiration of his work." Yet, by July 1883, he called "John's art vicious & meretricious" in a lecture at the Fine Art Gallery, where John's *Pailleron Children* was on view. (VLL)

PLATE IX

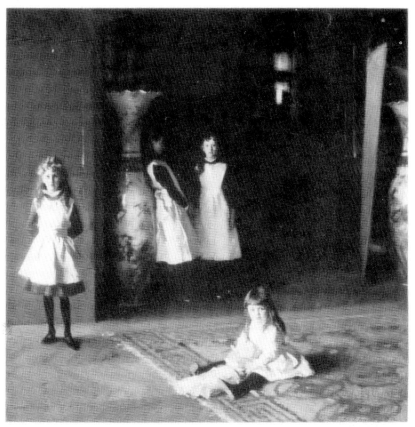

*Above: **The Boit Children**, painted in 1882 and shown at the Salon in 1883.*

*Below: **El Jaleo**, painted in 1882 – the resumé of Sargent's journey to Spain in 1879.*

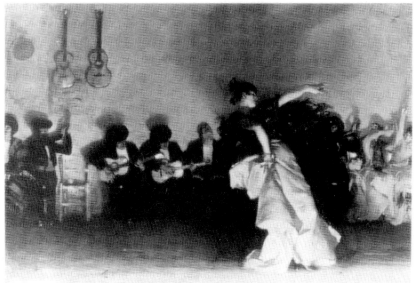

PLATE X

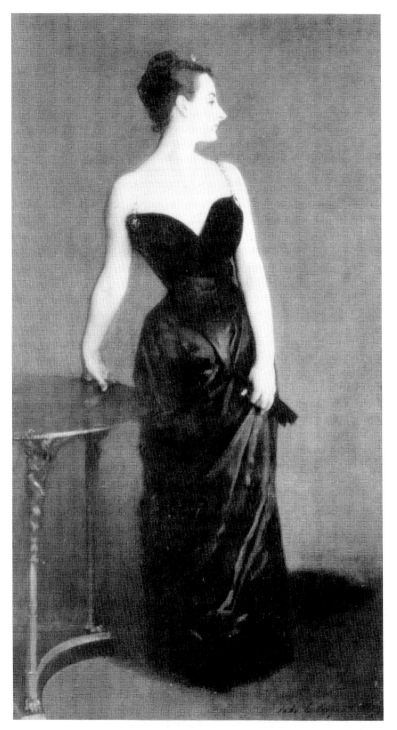

Virginie Avegno (Mme Pierre Gautreau), 1884. When the picture was sold to the Metropolitan Museum of Art after her death thirty years later, Sargent asked that the title be changed to **Madame X**.

PLATE XI

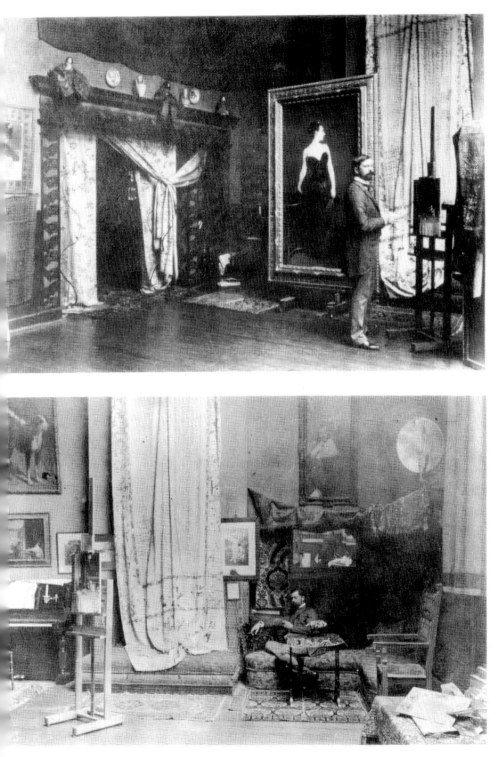

Interior of Sargent's Boulevard Berthier studio.

PLATE XII

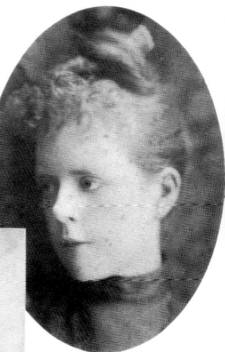

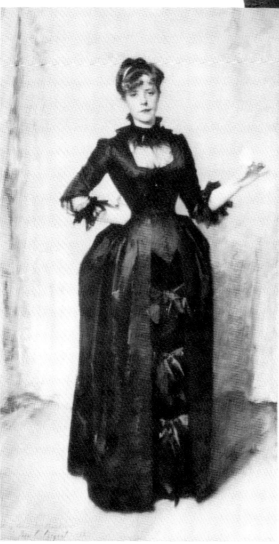

Above: *Charlotte Louise Burckhardt.*

Left: *Charlotte Louise Burckhardt, aged nineteen, 1882, in a portrait Sargent now known as* **Lady with the Rose***.*

PLATE XIII

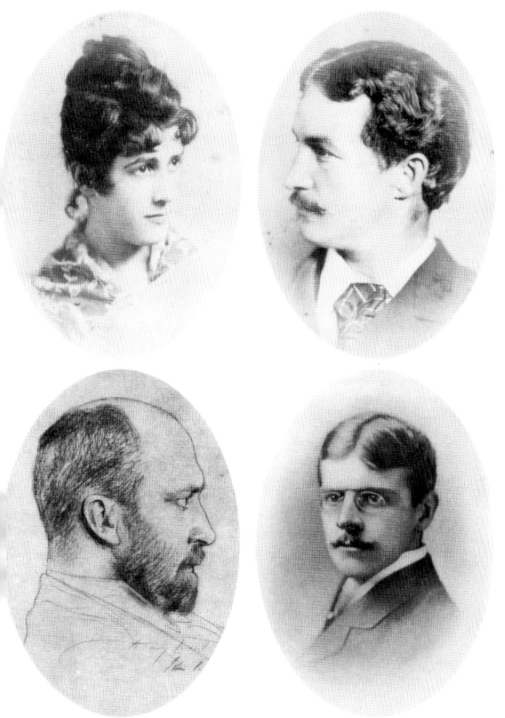

Broadway residents. **Top left:** Lily Millet; **top right:** Frank Millet; **bottom left:** Henry James (from a drawing by Sargent at Broadway, 1886); **bottom right:** Edwin Austin Abbey ('Ned').

PLATE XIV

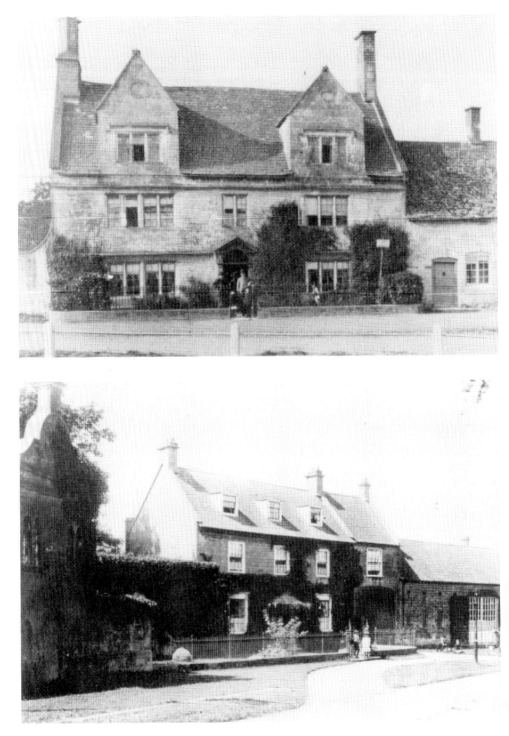

Top: Farnham House, the Millets' first Broadway home.
Below: Russell House, Broadway, leased by the Millets, Abbey and Sargent from 1886.

PLATE XV

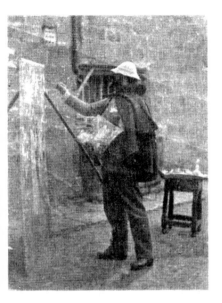

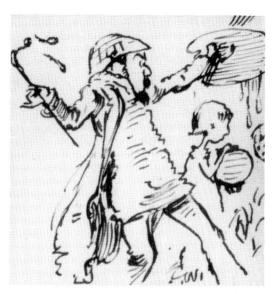

Above: Sargent painting outside Russell House.

Above right: Caricature by Millet, c.1886, of Sargent at work on Carnation, Lily, Lily, Rose.

Right: Carnation, Lily, Lily, Rose, later retitled by Sargent 'Damnation, Silly, Silly, Pose'. The painting was shown at the Royal Academy in 1887.

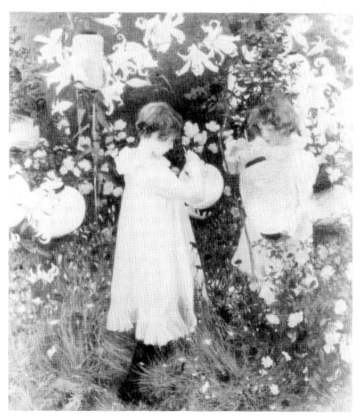

PLATE XVI

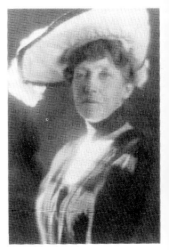

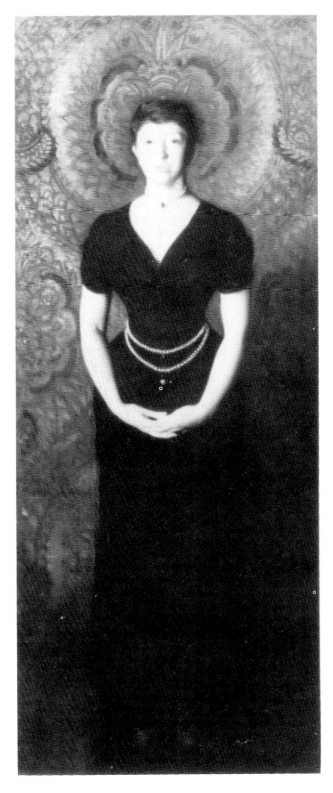

Above: *Isabella Stewart (Mrs John L. Gardner), 1906 (photographed by Alfred de Meyer).*

Left: *Mrs Gardner by Sargent 1888.*

Since 1878, John had used the Salon to broadcast his ability as a portraitist *and* a genre painter. That year he showed his Cancale scene *En route pour la pêche*, in 1880 his Moroccan *Fumée d'ambre gris*, and in 1882 his Spanish *El Jaleo*. But *Jaleo* had been revived after his failure to find a suitable Venetian scene, and in 1882 when he went back to Venice to continue the search he was no luckier. He had no subject-picture for the 1884 Salon. He had lost control of his grand strategy; his campaign had collapsed, and with it he inadvertently endorsed the portrait side of his reputation. When his Madame Gautreau failed even to acknowledge that skill, his dissatisfaction surfaced, slowly and undramatically. "It will be pleasant getting to London and especially leaving Paris," he wrote to James before his second visit (Sunday, 25) [May 1884]. "I am dreadfully tired of the people here and of my present work, a certain majestic portrait of an ugly woman. She is like a great frigate under full sail with homeward-bound streamers flying [Mrs Kate Moore]." He saw the vast treadmill of commissioned portraits stretching relentlessly before him, and it was a very disagreeable sight. The reception of Madame Gautreau's portrait sealed his fears, and James conveniently brandished hope, at least for part of the year. That summer he went to England instead of Italy.

Temporarily out of favour in Paris was one thing – he could always regroup his forces and stage another daring attack on the next Salon – but almost unknown in England was quite another. Even James could not attend to those problems. And John did not attempt to surmount them. His eyes remained fixed on Paris. He never thought of transferring his attentions to London. He sent his first English portraits not to the Royal Academy, but to the Salon, and almost as an afterthought he bolstered his slim reputation in England by sending portraits done in Paris to the Royal Academy. For someone who was desperate to leave Paris and set himself up in London (as art historians constantly assert) this was surely the most bizarre generalship.

James's perpetual banging on about the advantages of London were, however, inordinately opportune. His attentions came at a time when John was particularly vulnerable and exceedingly keen to listen. The prospect of something new was tantalizing, especially under the useful and nimble guidance of James. "I hope you are not going to leave London very soon," he wrote to James in the same letter. "I am sure you will be necessary to my happiness there. This is not a broad hint that I will allow you to put yourself out for me as you did before. jamais de la vie. But the feeling that you are there and liable to be met [?] will give a frog-eater more confidence, in that British unexplored land."[11] It took John about a year to come round, reluctantly, to the seduction of James's loud publicity: "I have been coming to England for the last two . . . summers," he wrote to a collegue from *atelier* Duran (10 September) [1885], "and I should not wonder if I some day have a studio in London. There is perhaps more chance for me there as a portrait painter, although it might be a long struggle for my painting to be accepted. It is thought beastly French."[12]

Despite James's heavy use of the loud pedal in his uninterrupted London serenade, John's future in England did seem bleak. His success had been distinctly unmemorable, though reviews of his Salon performances had been favourable. But in London his work had never had the slightest acclaim, or even well-advertised failure. *Dr Pozzi* was completely overlooked at the Royal Academy in 1882, and *El Jaleo* at the Fine Arts Gallery aroused only a mild and brief flutter of interest. A year later *The Pailleron Children* (also at the Fine Arts) fared equally unwell. By 1884 when he showed two major portraits he had managed no improvement on his negligible reputation and, if anything, did worse. While his light in Paris might have been occluded, none looked like being lit for him in London.

John's inability to find a foothold was not surprising: the atmosphere was Paris with the clock turned back. The art world was dominated by ideas worn out and long discarded in France. The "masters" of English art were caught somewhere between blinding devotion to classicism and *passé* realism. Alma-Tadema draped his figures in voluminous togas and sat them on marble loggias. Leighton (then President of the Royal Academy) scoured mythology for an unfamiliar subject. Millais went back to the eighteenth century to find an emotionally charged historic scene. And threadbare academic topics, like the "Flight from Egypt", continued to attract visitors to the crammed-full walls at Burlington House. The Royal Academy became the temple of this aesthetic indecision. Still, the public looked to the Academy as a power rivalled only by the Salon. The *Athenaeum* devoted four long notices to the annual summer exhibition. As an institution it grasped tightly to tradition, and the Hanging Committee was bellicose in its prejudice against anything modern or, worse, foreign. The Academy, like the Salon, became a parody of fuddy-duddy stuffiness and, as such, a broad target for revolt. This revolt came in 1877 and was confined round the corner, in another temple – the Grosvenor Gallery, founded by Sir Coutts and Lady Lindsay and Charles Hallé. It began as an elaborate correction to the errors habitually committed by the Royal Academy, and was determined to outshine. The doors were open wide to the aesthetes, Whistler, and all those who were thought to terrorize the established order at Burlington House. The effect was electric, and short-lived. "There were rumours", Graham Robertson remembered,

of a wonderful new picture gallery wherein pictures would be treated as pictures and not as postage stamps; that is to say, they would be hung more or less as if in a private house, thus giving them a chance to decorate instead of disfiguring the rooms. . . . The impression left upon me . . . was unforgettable. To this day [1931] old fogies speak of the first two or three exhibitions at the Grosvenor Gallery with undiminished enthusiasm: there has been no such delightful surprise in the world of pictures since.[13]

John's work found slim recognition in either place in 1884. When spectators noticed *Mrs H. White* at the Royal Academy they did not share the critics' praise: "only patriotism . . .", someone said to James, "would make me care for such a work as that".[14] *The Times* (12 May 1884) assessed that

it is hard to admit that this much-discussed picture is a completely satisfactory one, or that Mr. Sargent has this year done justice to his unquestioned talent. He has exhibited better things in Paris than he has ever yet condescended to show in London; but he has it in him to do finer work even than those, supposing him to escape the intoxication of Parisian praise.

The *Athenaeum* was equally unsubtle (21 June 1884):

Mr. J. S. Sargent has been the victim of a reputation too easily acquired. He does his powers injustice by neglecting taste in every element of his pictures except that tonality in which he excels. His *Mrs. H. White* . . . is hard, the painting is almost metallic, the carnations are raw, there is no taste in the expression, air, or modelling, but the work is able enough to deserve recasting.

That year Orchardson's *Mariage de Convenance* was justly hailed as the picture of the show, closely followed by Leighton's *Cymon and Iphigenia*, Alma-Tadema's *Hadrian in Britain* and Millais' *An Idyll, 1745*. In Gallery VII, where *Mrs H. White* (788) was hung, John was among old friends: Heath Wilson showed *Sunset from the Shore at Carrara*, Joseph Farquharson *Miss Alice Farquhar* and Luke Fildes *A Venetian Flower-Girl*. At the Grosvenor, John's portrait of Mrs Legh (later Lady Newton) was hindered by the same overcrowding and subjected to equally fierce competition: Whistler's *Arrangement in Black: Lady in Yellow Buskin, Lady Archibald Campbell*, Burne-Jones's *King Cophetua* and *Wood Nymph*, Watts's *Rain Passing Away*, portraits by Millais, Herkomer, Alma-Tadema and Hallé's *Mary Anderson* – John did not have much chance of showing well, even if that gallery had kept to its hanging policy. Mrs Legh's husband recalled in his memoirs: "When the picture eventually arrived [from Paris] it was ignominiously skied, and no one there had apparently ever heard of Sargent, or even perhaps Carolus-Duran. . . ."[15] When the picture was spotted, it was derided: "The younger French school is represented", Claude Phillips wrote in the *Academy* (17 May 1884), "by the American painter Mr J. S. Sargent, whose portrait of 'Mrs. T. W. Legh' (203) will scarcely satisfy those who bear in mind his remarkable performances in the last few years. It has passages of surprising dexterity . . . but the whole is distressingly flimsy, and bears evidence of haste and want of interest on the part of the painter in his subject. Better things may be expected from the painter. . . ." The *Athenaeum* could find no charity appraising it. The critics were mystified and a little offended by John's choice of London pictures; neither portrait gave much evidence of the reputation that had preceded him, and neither did much to help over-come their hostility to anything foreign, especially French (a fact further complicated by the tired-out confusion over John's nationality). They sensed an arrogance they had always suspected of the French: London, being no true rival of Paris, was – so they thought – unworthy of his first-class work. It was all an exaggerated reaction. They were like disap-pointed children hunting round for better reasons to support their indignation. In truth, John's choice was natural and simple. The Leghs were English and the Whites had recently been posted to London. But the reviewers would not be mollified. The result was that John's work was not ignored, and it was not liked. Only Henry James could have thought it possible to overlook such an unpromising welcome.

John's first commission in England had been given in Paris, long before the opening of the Salon, the Royal Academy and the Grosvenor Gallery, and before he had even met Henry James. John came to England to work for the Vickers family. His relations with them were much like they were with the Paillerons, and the Vickers portraits stand in much the same strategic position in the history of his painting: they mark a slight turning-point, a minor shift away from the previous nature of his work. During the summer he painted eleven members of the family, many of them uncommissioned portraits. He stayed with them, and he grew to like them. When the pictures were completed, however, he rarely saw them again.

They were, however, a new *type* of client. Hitherto his patrons had come from the social fringe of artistic circles, or were diplomatists. The Vickerses were industrialists. Their money came from the famous engineering and munitions works, and they were just the sort of person John had never met and was unlikely to meet in Paris. If they represented a new territory on the map, they were the first step in a huge stretch of terrain John would later explore. But this was just a matter of fact; more important, they supplied him with a fine excuse to try out another idea about group portraiture. Towards late summer he went to Bolsover Hill, Sheffield, to paint the three daughters of Colonel T. E. Vickers. *The Misses Vickers* was the result of a strange marriage of the exaggerated point of view adopted in his portrait of the Boit children and the technique he used for Madame Gautreau. For Madame Gautreau he used the colours of raisin and claret-soaked plum; for the Misses Vickers he used a full palette of winter fruit compote – singular hues for a picture painted in the summer. But whereas the Boit girls were themselves cast as an excuse to portray a room the Vickers girls were afforded foremost importance. He positioned them forward in the canvas, right up to the front, nearly crowded, and so acutely foreshortened he had to crop – for the first time. They sit on a straight horizontal line, which was where he made the uniformity end. Two sisters sit on a sofa vacantly leafing through a book, one staring down, the other looking off to the right without much intent. Their arms and hands were positioned to echo and contradict the graceful sweep of the sofa back. The third sister adopted a wholly implausible posture, arched over her chair with one arm laced through its back to join the thumb and forefinger of her other hand resting on her lap. Out of this contortion she alone looks directly forward. Her dress was also unlike her sisters'. It was as if John fused a double and single portrait. And, in order to counteract their placing in the canvas, John supplied small glimpses into the far recesses of the room. Because the perspective was extreme and the girls' pose peculiar and inconsistent, there is an innate tenseness. One observer cruelly assessed that the sisters looked as if they were suffering from an attack of nerves. John never tried this type of pose again. In subsequent portraits of three subjects, he employed a more languid, placid pose.

John did not want to stay in England all summer, or any part of the autumn, but when his plans to go to Spain with Ralph Curtis were abandoned (because of the reports of cholera) he gave up all hope of painting out of doors. He found himself confined indoors and, like some butler on loan to various members of the family, passed from household to household. He went to work for Colonel Vickers's brother in Sussex. And he was asked to paint Mrs Albert Vickers.

While the work was in progress James saw him, and James's passing reference to the job left more doubt than was usual in his accounts of John's enthusiasm: "I dined with the plastic John," he informed Vernon Lee (21 October), "who was in town from Petworth where he is painting the portrait of a lady whose merits as a model require all his airy manipulation to be expressed (in speech)."[16] The portrait, however, was more assured, and a pronounced warning of the emergence of that manner of portraiture he would make his own, the style of spectrum that would please clients on both sides of the Atlantic, and that would falsely credit him with deep psychological insight.

As with Madame Gautreau, he again concentrated on his subject, harshly omitting all other details for that purpose. Edith Vickers wore grey, the light in a room he allowed to disappear in shadow. Her bare arms and neck were freed of jewels, apart from a diamond ring on one hand and a vast magnolia *grande flora* in the other. Such austerity did not belie her elegance, but rather enhanced it. And while his palette took one step up in brightness from *Madame Gautreau* and *The Misses Vickers* his composition took two steps back. He painted Edith Vickers simply, without worrying about perspective, light, or trying out any neat solution to the problem of portraiture. He took no liberties. He did the job that was asked of him, that he was being paid for. Either the slow-acting poison of the *Madame X* outcry or mere disinterest made him cautious. He was unwilling to test his clients' satisfaction.

The months he planned for Spain he gave to England. He found subjects among the commonplace. He took another and different look at his hostess, Mrs Albert Vickers. This time he painted her in a less studied pose. Off duty, however, he was bold. He painted her sitting behind her well-dressed table, at the end of dinner; she and her husband are lingering over their glass of claret. And he moved outside, where he painted two of their children amid pots of towering lilies, in a sketchy picture full of the sentiment he caught from the Pre-Raphaelites. These pictures were a good distance from his commissioned work, in technique as well as in mood. He painted freely, but with the same spontaneity and brio he saved for his holiday work. He seemed to be after more than a change from office hours; he was looking around for ideas, not just for subjects – for styles of painting.

If this tourism also displayed a cautious discontent, it was one that had been with him for years (and would hang around for a good many to come) and it was expressed only in his painting. His patrons never suspected anything. The Vickerses, like the Paillerons before them, found him a charming and agreeable visitor. Subsequent generations told of the easy way in which he fitted into life at Lavington Rectory. He was more friend than servant. All his sitters agreed: he was a delightful companion. At the beginning of December, John went to Bournemouth to paint Robert Louis Stevenson;* he was the Stevensons' guest for a couple of nights. "Sargent has come and gone," Stevenson wrote [?17 December 1884]. " . . . We both lost our hearts to him: a person with a kind of exhibition manner and English accent, who proves on examination, simple, bashful, honest, enthusiastic and rude with a perfect (but quite inoffensive) English rudeness. *Pour comble*, he gives himself out to be American."[17] This quizzical conviviality that Stevenson noted was yet another, though ephemeral, part of the secret that would make John so pleasing to English and American sitters. The French, having marvelled at his social and intellectual acquisitions, regarded him as a well-adapted curiosity; the English were wholly unembarrassed by his reserve; and the Americans took the liberty of embracing him as one of their own (which they had every right to do, despite profuse evidence to the reverse). No other portraitist could exert such international dexterity, and with the fluency John innately possessed. Other painters could find the devices of flattery and employ them to better account, but none was as easy to live with in the process. John never encumbered his sitters with the jargon or behaviour of artistic high-mindedness. He called his second portrait of Stevenson, with his wife done about eight months later, "the picture of the caged animal lecturing about the foreign specimen in the corner".[18] And he never bullied his sitters, for the convenient reasons that he was

---

* It is impossible to determine when John met Stevenson; it might have been in the mid-1870s when Stevenson's cousin, R. A. M. Stevenson, was a student at *atelier* Duran. And it is equally impossible to determine how the 1884 portrait came to be painted. The third portrait of Stevenson (1887) was commissioned by Charles Fairchild, a Boston banker, as a gift for his wife, who much admired the writer. Henry James was on very close terms with the family, who, subsequent to the commission, also became life-long friends with John. Fairchild later advised John on American financial matters.

too well mannered and too shy. He tried to make the ordeal of posing tolerable. He bribed children with sweets; he asked visitors to come to the studio and amuse his sitter; or he would play the piano to lighten the mood. Years later, in 1890, he coaxed Alice Carr (Mrs J. Comyns Carr, née Strettell) to sit long past her strength, and she naturally dozed off. When she woke, he laughingly said, " 'Well, well, we won't have large, dark eyes. Anyone can have fine eyes', "[19] and the sitting resumed. He always stuck to the job at hand. He was strict about his appointments, loathed altering them, and positively dreaded the possibility of forgetting one. The language of self-importance was unknown to him. All these qualities combined to give him, at the height of his career, the cool professional bearing of a very superior Harley Street consultant, defined to inspire confidence.

Likewise, he disciplined his professional approach to keep his distance. When he was uninterested by a sitter, he calmly diagnosed the likeness, softening the procedure by applying the dressing of elegance – simply achieved by ruthless editing of other details. The small silver cream-jug and the outline of a chair back were the spare notations he allowed in the background of *The Misses Vickers* to help place them. (Later, dress alone would have this function.) When interested, however, he slipped off his consultant's demeanour, and enlarged the requirement of likeness to include the sitter's manner. Stevenson interested him. The first portrait, which Stevenson described as "a weird, very pretty, large-eyed, chicken-boned, slightly contorted poet",[20] was not much to John's taste, and not worthy of his feelings for Stevenson. "I was very much impressed by him," John wrote to Henry James (29 June) [1885] from Paris, "he seemed to me the most intense creature I had ever met".[21] He asked if he might do another, more characteristic portrait – "to do me again in several pos-tures; walking about and talking is his main notion",[22] Stevenson wrote to his parents (31 July 1885). The second portrait, finished two weeks later, was nothing like the first: "It is an open box of jewels,"[23] Mrs Stevenson described. John painted the interior of the dining-room at Skerryvole, the Stevensons' Bournemouth house – an interior with figures: Stevenson relegated to the left, astride, stroking his moustache, his wife planted on the outskirts to the right, the door open between them, showing hall and staircase beyond. "It is", Stevenson reported to Will Low (22 October 1885), " . . . too eccentric to be exhibited . . . with that witty touch of Sargent's; but, of course, it looks damn queer as a whole."[24]

John had lingered on in England for seven months, moving about, borrowing studios, living in furnished rooms. Like his parents, he did not so much act as react. He had left Paris in a state of tired boredom, but that was an insufficient reason to move to England. His eventual drift abroad was slow, hesitant and undramatic, because it had less to do with geography than with his career as a portraitist. His motives for leaving Paris for good had to be stronger than any he would try to find for coming to live in London.

He returned to Paris sometime around the New Year, 1885, to visit his parents and sisters in Nice and to prepare for the spring exhibitions in both Paris and London. When the Royal Academy and Grosvenor Gallery opened, the general response to John's submissions was dispiritingly flat. He had expected it: "neither my R.A. nor my Grosvenor [portraits] are calculated to bring me into much favor", he wrote to James (29 June) [1885] from Paris. "But this year I felt bound to collect as many good things as possible in Paris." He sent his *Misses Vickers* to the Salon where it was unfortunately hung next to Whistler's *Arrangement in Black: the Lady in the Yellow Buskin* (Lady Archibald Campbell) – "which beats John['s] into fits", Vernon Lee wrote to her mother (25 June 1885) after her annual tour of the Salon with John.[25] He had no better luck in Paris than he had had in London; his "good things" had not won over critics or public, who sensed being denied another surprise after Madame Gautreau. Though none of John's pictures created a scandal, mercifully, none regained an inch of ground he had lost. And as if this blank reception were not enough to drum off potential commissions one of his sitters got to work to complete the repulse. Mrs Mason,* "an ex-beauty", Vernon Lee wrote, "got up quite a storm against him about a portrait of her which is in the Grosvenor . . .".[26] She detested her portrait and did not keep her opinion secret. (Later she took a pen-knife to the mouth, before consigning the picture to the attic.)

Henry James, whose interest in John was as unflagging as ever, even to the point of making up stories (like broadcasting his conviction that John would, after all, marry Louise Burckhardt), told Vernon Lee, who of course passed it on instantly, that he thought "John is in a bad way. Since

---

* Mrs Alice Hooper Sumner (née Mason) (1838–1914) had an unhappy and colourful history that excited outlandish gossip. She was vilified by her fellow-Bostonians, who eagerly awaited the next instalment in her declining glory. She had the misfortune to be very beautiful. Her first husband died in the Civil War, and three years later she married Senator Charles Sumner, nearly thirty years her senior. Within a year it was common knowledge around Beacon Hill that the marriage was a disaster. For seven years her life was pure hell. Sumner died in 1874 and during the funeral procession "by accident the hearse with 4 black horses stopped 15 minutes in front of Mrs. Sumner!" Turner Sargent reported to George Bemis. Then her first father-in-law's will was read – a bizarre document that left $5 million in trust to his next of kin surviving twenty-one years after the death of his children; Mrs Sumner was specifically excluded. And rumours again flared up. She went abroad, styling herself Mrs Mason. Stories about her were legion and so divided in judgement that FitzWilliam did not know whether to cut her or not when she first appeared in the South of France. She made a better name for herself in expatriate circles than she had in Boston, and found safe lodging among people like the Storys and Henry James. She amassed a distinguished collection of art. How she came to commission John, however, remains unknown. Circumstantial evidence points to James, but he was unlikely to have kept quiet about such activity. The portrait was painted in Paris at the beginning of 1885.

Mme Gauthereau [*sic*] and one or two other portraits, women are afraid of him lest he should make them too eccentric looking."[27] John could not fool himself; his future looked unpromising. He tried to put on a brave face when writing to his friend from student days, Edward Russell (10 September) [1885]: "Since the last three or four years, I have had more or less ups and downs of prosperity. Just now I am rather out of favour as a portrait painter in Paris, although my last salon, [?and] two portraits done in England[,] rather retrieved me."[28] In conversation, however, this thin film of optimism dissolved completely. The same time he was writing to Russell, he was also talking to Edmund Gosse, who recalled:

> [John] was profoundly dissatisfied with Paris. . . . He was determined to shake the dust of it off his shoes . . . he looked in vain . . . for any genuine invitation to stay in England . . . it will perhaps be believed with difficulty that he talked of giving up art altogether. I remember his telling me this on one of our walks. . . . "But then," I cried, "whatever will you do?" "Oh," he answered, "I shall go into business." "What kind of business?" . . . "Oh, I don't know!" with a vague wave of the hand, "or go in for music, don't you know?"[29]

These were the syllables of moderate despiar, voiced with sincerity. John could find no excuse for optimism, all the signs pointed in the opposite direction, and Paris got the blame. She alone had been perfidious. After years of lulling him into the confidence that success was assured, a matter of course, she did worse than fall silent – she changed her tune, and he felt powerless to inspire any reversion. The year had been wasted. He did not know what to do. Finally, with the conviction of the downcast and much in the style of his parents, he decided to wait, to depend on postponement, and in the meantime turn his back on the studio. He gave up "office hours" for the English countryside, and yet still held on to Boulevard Berthier.

In turmoil, John maintained family tradition, and travelled, not ambitiously, not far, but travelled all the same. He came back to London towards the end of July. The discomfort of strangeness had been traded for luxurious familiarity. This transformation wore the delicate hand of James; it was one of his most generous creations. He opened the door wide on a geography John found congenial. Everyone John seemed to know in England (apart from patrons) traced an introduction back to James. His courtship of John was, in truth, the indispensable *Baedeker* of John's new social life. John returned to a welcoming sphere of acquaintance, after only two visits.

A great fan spread out from James's hinge, covering literature, drama and art. He conducted John to Blandford Square, St Marylebone, to meet the Carrs. J. Comyns Carr (1849–1916), after having found little gratification in the law, headed in a more pleasurable direction – to art and the theatre. He was an eager champion of the Pre-Raphaelites, which was rewarded in a directorship of the Grosvenor Gallery, later sacrificed for the New Gallery. But criticism and administration were not enough for his energy; he started and edited magazines, wrote plays and was at one time head of the Lyceum Theatre. His beautiful wife Alice (née Strettell) was dragged along on this wide progress, and she distinguished herself as a costume designer. She had been responsible for Ellen Terry's striking appearance as Lady Macbeth in Irving's production. When John saw "the green and blue gown like chain armour, studded with real beetle-wings" he issued a telling response: " ' I say!' "[30] His famous portrait of Ellen Terry (1889) showed Mrs Carr's handiwork. (And she and her husband were avid Wagnerians. He was responsible for the first performance of *Parsifal* in England.) Forsaking literary offices and sewing-rooms, James also showed him round the length and breadth of Kensington, conducting a deft tour not only of the Pre-Raphaelites' den, but also of the studios of expatriate Americans. He knew the ground well. Here John found rich pickings, and set in motion the long chain of events that cancelled his attachment to Paris, produced his least characteristic work (and one of his chief successes), sent him deeper into the country, retrieved him from disgrace as a portraitist, and enticed his parents from Nice. These large consequences began simply enough. John left London. He went on a short boating expedition, made shorter by an accident. He was taken to Broadway in Worcestershire. He painted *Carnation, Lily, Lily, Rose*. His companion throughout was Edwin Austin Abbey – "Ned".

John had met Abbey on his second visit to London the year before under the protective wing of James, who, suffering from that standard expatriate inconsistency of anti-American feelings at home and patriotism abroad, welcomed Abbey as a fellow-traveller in England. Abbey was four years older than John, born in Philadelphia on April Fool's Day 1852. While others of his generation succumbed to the siren-call of Paris to improve their art, Abbey heard nothing and stayed at home. But at the Centennial Exhibition that had lured John, Emily and Mary from abroad Abbey suddenly heard other notes, loud and very melodious. The English contribution to the "Art Section" – works by Leighton, Watts, Millais, Fildes *et al.* – was, in Abbey's own words, "my great eye-opener".[31] Two years later he sailed for England, where he made his home, painted his murals for Boston and Philadelphia, rendered the official record of the Coronation of Edward VII, became a Royal Academician, a keen cricketer, and where he died aged fifty-nine in 1911. Six years later Princess Louise unveiled his memorial plaque in the crypt of St Paul's. His love for England was repaid. E. V. Lucas's biography of Abbey (1921) weighs nearly a kilo.

Abbey was neither tall nor short. He had a safe appearance, with the faint air of a bank clerk: pince-nez, tidy moustache, sober but attractive features. There were no rough edges on his character, only expansive charm. If anything, he was congenial to a fault. He came alive in a crowd. He was a man born for companionship, so much so that his friends feared he might be swamped by his own popularity. It was as if he were tailored for club life. When he was sixteen he, Will Low and Palmer started a sketching club. A few years later, in New York, he was an essential member of the Tile Club along with a couple of artists fresh from Europe, a few who were about to embark, and others content to stay put – in short, the core of American art at the time. In England he was president of the Artists' Cricket Club, and listed in *Who's Who* membership of the Athenaeum, the Reform, the Arts, the Beefsteak as well as the Savile (1884: ? seconded by R. A. M. Stevenson). Throughout his life he was unacquainted with loneliness or failure – his honours piled up from Munich, Paris, Madrid, New York, Philadelphia, New Haven, and of course London. He married late, when he was nearly forty, Mary Mead of New York, who supplied him with ambition, helped to cool his friends' affection, and gave him no children. After extolling the brilliance of Abbey, John could only muster tepid praise for her, tacking on "and his wife has many virtues".[32]

There was also the air of the unflamboyant about much of his work. His career began in the illustration department of Harper & Brothers in New York, where he did those decorative devices and line drawings in *Harper's Weekly* that were meant to relieve the monotony of the close print, but not detain the reader's progress. During the eight years he was at this sort of taxing and unedifying work, always subject to the mercy of the engraver, Abbey showed himself to be able and consistent. These years were a strict tuition that stayed with him for life. He developed a copyist's mentality; he needed to stick fast to his reference. His imagination stopped once he arranged his models. He was happiest with scenes of seventeenth- and eighteenth-century England, illustrating Goldsmith, Herrick, Sheridan, Shakespeare, and he costumed his figures with a librarian's enthusiasm for detail. He never considered drawing a cuff until he saw just how the cambric flounced. He needed to sink knee-deep in historical accuracy before he sharpened his pencil. For many years he was not much tempted by colour, and only came round to painting in the late 1880s. By the time his wife had engineered his commission to fill 1440 square feet on the walls of the new Boston Public Library, he had only done two oils. Then, with the same literal turn of mind, he examined colour, studied it, and produced scenes that glowed. His vast *Richard Duke of Glouchester and the Lady Anne* might as a subject have been buried in history, but the paint still looks wet. John's admiration of him was unstinting. Several years later he wrote to a friend: "You would be interested in Abbey. He is a delightful original genius. . . ."[33]

In August, John and Abbey set off on the Thames at Oxford for Windsor. About halfway, John impetuously dived into the river. It was a mistake. "Sargent nearly killed himself at Pangbourne Weir," Abbey wrote in a letter (28 September). "He dived . . . and struck a spike with his head, cutting a big gash in the top . . . it was a nasty rap."[34] They got the wound dressed, his head bound, and then he promptly walked into something, reopening the gash. In nursing-sister fashion, Abbey suggested they remove themselves from harm's way, and they went to Broadway, safely distant from the river.

Indeed, Broadway owed much to geography. In its long history, the village sprang into importance briefly, for the simple reason that coach-horses needed to be changed often between London and Worcester. In 1860, when the railway opened nearby in Evesham, that honour was removed, and Broadway once again retired to inconsequence, which is where its attraction has stayed – wonderfully ignored by time, looking exactly as it did when the horses left. Nestled in the Vale of Evesham, in the Cotswolds, Broadway soon became a synonym for postcard illustration. Today it continues to produce a swell of high emotion in the foreigner, and a blush to any native. And the nineteenth-century American inhabitants lumbered it with fame. From the moment these painters took up residence, anonymity was lost, especially when Henry James stupidly turned his friends' home into a tourist attraction in the pages of *Harper's* with phrases like "the perfection of the old English rural tradition", "the place has so much character it rubs off", "Everything is stone except the greenness", "everything in it is convertible", and "It is delicious to be at Broadway and . . . not to have to draw".[35]

Various people have been credited with the job of transforming the sleepy place into one vast pictorial prop, but that distinction must go to Laurence Hutton (1843–1904), who never painted but was a collector, writer, literary editor of *Harper's*, of whom the *Dictionary of American Biography* could record little to introduce him to posterity: "He had no creative gift . . . left no incisive criticism. . . . His writings are all gossipy, circumstantial, and superficial." Hutton brought Frank Millet (1846–1912), who, James wrote, "appropriated" Broadway. Hutton was neither bashful nor restrained about revealing anything of the slightest importance, and he dangled the carrot of Broadway tantalizingly in front of the Millets, who had known him in New York and well enough to name their second son after him. The Millets, in turn, brought both Alfred Parsons (1847–1920) and Abbey, who brought John. Thereafter the village was flooded with great names, among them Alma-Tadema, Edmund Gosse, Henry James, Edwin Blashfield, Mary Anderson, J. Comyns Carr, Fredrick Barnard. And with Stanway nearby, one of the stops on the troop movements of the Souls, this number swelled to include Lady Elcho and Eliza Wedgwood. At the beginning of this influx, Broadway had incalculable importance as an illustrator's library, especially with Stratford so handy and useful for Shakespeare illustrations. *Harper's* and *Scribner's* magazine had an insatiable appetite for drawings, making the artists' infestation from the start more practical than romantic.

Francis Davis Millet, who really began the infestation, had covered a lot of ground before he settled down in Broadway.[36] He and Abbey responded to the same call, and while Abbey had made an undemonstrative entry into his profession Millet arrived at the same place as if hurled out of a whirlwind. He was the best sort of New Englander (born in

Mattapoisett, Massachusetts), giving himself totally to his work and to public service. He was torn between the pleasures of the mind and of rollicking action. He was modest, hearty, and if anything, beset by too many abilities. He served in the Civil War, graduated from Harvard, was the star pupil at the Antwerp Academy, assistant to John LaFarge in the decoration of Trinity Church, war correspondent for American and English newspapers during the Russo-Turkish War (where he managed to be decorated by the Tsar), an exhibitor at the Salon and the Royal Academy, translator of Tolstoy, author and illustrator of travel accounts, director of decorations at the Columbian Exhibition, war correspondent again in the Philippines, muralist in Madison, Minneapolis, Baltimore and Cleveland, and director of the American Academy in Rome. He served as chairman on the United States Committee on Niagara, on the Advisory Committee of the United States National Gallery, and was vice-chairman of the United States Commission of Fine Arts. He had a mighty career that ended, alas, when he chose to cross the Atlantic on the *Titanic*.

His achievements tended to obscure the nature of his character, which was pretty well hidden under his reticence. And with his propensity to move around in a crowd Millet's personality was subjected to too much competition to be clearly discerned. He had a straightforward, uncompli-cated, though enterprising, brain. His temperament was unboisterous. Like Abbey, he needed the specific, a clear reference before he could draw, but his touch was not as light. His work was reliable, able and accurate, but little more. W. D. Howells lamented that he had not devoted himself wholly to literature.

In 1879 he married Elizabeth Merrill, a sister of a Harvard friend, in Paris; Augustus Saint-Gaudens and Mark Twain were his witnesses. Lily Millet was strong-minded, engaging, intelligent and extremely beautiful. And while her husband had acquired a taste for Europe she soon discovered that she had developed a strong appetite for it, especially when she returned to the Millet family home in East Bridgewater. She began to accompany her husband abroad, and each year she became more reluctant to return to America. In 1885 they came to stay.

They took Farnham House on the edge of the green in Broadway. It was not a large house; it was not even a pretty house, but it was old, and in England. It had a good-sized garden, and no studio. The vast tangle of people, friendships and geography that lay behind the historical sim-plicity known as Broadway began at Farnham House. Where Millet went Abbey followed; they had been friends for years – one of the reasons London was selected for Frank and Lily's honeymoon was the presence of Abbey. They named their first son Edwin Austin (who died the year he was born, 1881). Though Millet and Abbey were inseparable com-panions, posterity has flattered them by forever coupling their names and thus confusing their work.

By the time John arrived in Broadway, the Millet–Abbey household was tightly installed. There was Frank, his wife, their children Kate (aged five) and Laurence (fourteen months), and Frank's sister Lucia, who had, since Lily's illness, shouldered the domestic responsibilities, everything from housekeeper to governess-cum-tutor to general workhorse.* Lily was not interested in domesticity; she preferred the garden. Somehow they all managed to squeeze in, leaving a little space for servants. John had to stay at the inn, a large sixteenth-century building on the opposite side of the green (the Lygon Arms, today a superior hotel), which made no difference. "I practically live with them [the Millets]," he wrote to Emily (n.d.) [Aug/Sept. 1885]. "It is in their garden that I work."[37]

Shortly thereafter, the invasion of Broadway began – it had little to do with John – at the perfect, and essential, time of the year to vacate London. Millet and Abbey were the magnets. Illustrators, it seemed, were a breed constitutionally and professionally incapable of solitude. They needed a lot of peole around them and were not distracted by their presence. Their work required period costumes, and their obsession for accuracy put a great many fingers to work. Abbey arrived with three models. They could not exist without their colleagues. In no time Broadway began to fill up. Frederick Barnard, the famous illustrator of Dickens, was quickly on hand, with his family, hotly followed by Alfred Parsons.† Parsons had grown so accustomed to sharing his London

---

* This arrangement was not as one-sided as it appeared. By attaching herself so closely to her brother's household, Lucia was able to leave home and travel, which otherwise would have only been possible with marriage. She loved children and was a good teacher – two particularly useful features visitors to Broadway did not hesitate to prevail upon. She also had an unswerving New England pride in her work that was almost defiant. In New York, on the first stop on her long journey from East Bridgewater, Oscar Wilde called on Frank; Lucia refused to go into the next room to meet him – "people are so crazy to see him they go to almost any length, which sickens me", she wrote to her parents.

Her weekly letters home from Broadway were even-minded to a fault, not only for utter indifference to posterity, but also for her preoccupation with carpets, staining floors and linen rather than the activities of the people around her. After a while, however, that changed. Lucia Millet's letters (privately owned) give the best – and only – sustained account of the early years of the Broadway settlement, and with it a host of incidental detail about the creation of *Carnation, Lily, Lily, Rose*.

† Frederick Barnard (1846–96), a Londoner, finished off his art training under Bonnat in Paris. He contributed to several magazines, including the *Illustrated London News* and *Punch*, and he became a household name when his drawings of Dickens's characters were published independently. He painted in oils infrequently. In 1870 he married Alice Faraday (1847–1918), a niece of Michael Faraday, whose younger sister Edith (1861–1952) came to live in Broadway. In 1886 Barnard began his rush of success in *Harper's* – one of the many side-effects of Henry Harper's visit to Broadway during the height of the artist-infestation the previous summer. Barnard died in a fire.

Alfred Parsons (1847–1920), born in Somerset also benefited from Henry Harper's visit and became a regular contributor to the magazine. He was an expert gardener and an avid student of horticulture. He alone among this collection of artists was as well known for his painting as for his illustrations. He collaborated

house (54 Bedford Gardens) with the Millets and his studio with Abbey that when he returned from France he hurried to be with them again, taking a house nearby in Evesham in order to continue the partnership. The reason for the arrival of other visitors was, however, somewhat more obscure. The artists came to work; the others came to watch. By the end of August, when Mary Anderson came to Stratford to play Rosalind and a party of twenty-five Americans trooped over from Broadway to see her, the village had already become the official annexe to Kensington.[38] Henry Harper and his wife came to supervise his contributors. Edmund Gosse (1849–1928) represented the competition as Scribner's English agent. And Henry James found his manipulations too tempting to miss, and played tourist for four days.

Among the hangers-on Edmund Gosse's appearance was symptomatic of the lure of the place, and fascinating. He, his wife and three children lived at Cowley House for the month of September. Gosse's early life was so eccentric (immortalized in *Father and Son*, 1907) that many people considered it odd that he could be sane. His father, with unfathomable dexterity, believed at the same time both the truth of religious dogma *and* the truth of Darwin's research. His mother, an American of fine colonial ancestry, was less perplexing only because she died when he was very young. Gosse adapted only the scientific side of his father's mind, and put it in service to literature. But Gosse's mind operated in a regular sort of way without much affection for accuracy. He was ambitious, shrewd and hard-working. He wanted success in the literary world and cleverly developed a unique expertise – in north European literature – and made his name. But he was a man in a hurry. When he branched out into the more orthodox departments of literary work he did not linger over scholastic precision, though often taking on subjects that required little else, accepting short cuts, and was of course found out: "he *has* a genius for inaccuracy", James wrote to Stevenson after yet another outcry over Gosse's appalling scholarship (18 February 1891), "which makes it difficult to dress his wounds".[39] In the end Gosse got what he wanted; industry was rewarded. He became a distinguished man of letters (a neat catch-phrase, hiding certain sins), the Librarian of the House of Lords, with a knighthood and, posthumously, the same biographer as John: Evan Charteris. In matters of painting, mercifully he was content simply to look on. He was educated in the Pre-Raphaelite academy that convened each week in Ford Madox Brown's studio in Fitzroy Square, which he valued all the more as a break from his father's influence. There he met his wife, Nellie Epps, who took a more active interest in painting, like her sisters; one was Mrs Williams, a widow, also a painter, and the other married Alma-Tadema, with whom she and Gosse lived in the early days

---

with Abbey on the Herrick illustrations (1882) and with Millet on the Danube travel-book (1893). He also supplied illustrations for James's essay on Broadway. When Millet and Abbey stayed on in Broadway, so did Parsons.

of their marriage – all three sisters were constant visitors to Broadway. Free of imaginative outbursts himself, Gosse readily admired it in others, in novelists, poets, but most of all in painters. They and their work had the appeal of an insoluble romantic mystery. Broadway was narcotic.

John's intoxication was also great. From the moment he arrived he provided a wonderful spectacle of energy unleashed. No one noticed any sign of his head injury, and the suggestion that he might be convalescing seemed implausible. Gosse of course was mesmerized, pen in hand, and recorded that John "started a new canvas every morning, painting for a couple of hours at a time with the utmost concentration. . . ." There was no nonsense about preferring one view to another, hunting out a "good" place, no debate whatsoever. He took his easel outside, walked about for a bit, stopped, then started to paint, "nowhere in particular, behind a barn, opposite a wall, in the middle of a field. . . . His daily plan was to cover the whole of his canvas with a thin coat of colour, so as to make a complete sketch which would dry so rapidly that the next morning he might paint another study over it." The others were mystified at this casual, apparently purposeless routine; John "explained it in his half-inarticulate way. His object was to acquire the habit of reproducing precisely whatever met his vision without the slightest previous 'arrangement' of detail, the painter's business being, not to pick and choose, but to render the effect before him. . . ." Such simplicity was a heresy; perhaps worse, it was foreign – "but Sargent was not moved".[40] Most of all it was straight application of Carolus' primary instructions – paint what your eye sees, not what your mind instructs what you ought to see. Gosse, not surprisingly, countered with the force of his own Pre-Raphaelite tuition. John parried with a refined version of Carolus' words, saying

> modern painters made a mistake in showing that they know too much about the substances they paint. Of course, Alma Tadema with his marble and his metal, was the eternal instance of this error . . . the artist ought to know nothing whatever about the nature of the object before him . . . but should concentrate all his powers on a representation of its appearance. The picture was to be a consistent vision, a reproduction of the area filled by the eye.

" 'Ruskin,' " John said in the heart of this lesson, " 'don't you know – rocks and clouds – silly old thing!' " Broadway was a self-imposed return to Boulevard Mont Parnasse, an advance that travelled straight back to 1874, blind to his Salon work. The continuous line of development was broken, deliberately.

While John was traipsing over Gosse's ideas of sound conventional practice, Abbey and company were on a route march back in time. Gosse and James sat, looked on, marvelled and wrote. And the ladies who were not painting sewed; all idle female hands were set to work with needles and cotton. The place was an absurdly comic hive of activity; it was also a strange pastoral idyll, free of the poison of rivalry or jealousy. After a few months working beside John, Abbey tried to work in oils; his conclusion was characteristic of his high spirits that swept aside any dark feelings: "Sargent does it better than I do and quicker, but then he's younger."[41] The domestic arrangements were equally untroubled. Everyone looked to Farnham House and to Lily Millet, whose rule was unendangered for years, until Abbey returned with a wife in 1890. The Millets had come to Broadway to stay, the others were visitors – a subtle distinction that provided some order.

A bright continuous holiday atmosphere reigned, especially throughout September, for two consecutive summers. In the afternoon there was lawn tennis, or long walks, sometimes with Gosse who eagerly extracted John's views on modern art that he usually saved only for letters to Vernon Lee: Gérôme, " 'all sugar and varnish' "; Bastien-Lepage, " 'Tricks!' "; Alma Tadema, " '*is* clever . . . but of course it's not art in any sense whatever . . .' ".[42] Gosse was dumbfounded, and hung attentively on to every syllable. Or the entire "colony", as Lucia referred to them, piled on to Alfred Parsons's steam-launch hired for a day on the river. A table was set up running the entire length of the boat, piled with a picnic lunch – goose, ham, tongue, chicken, rabbit pie, pickled walnuts, cheese-cake, tartlets, cheese. Abbey played the banjo, everyone sang, and then sat down to tea at 6 p.m. They disembarked at Pershore, walked around, and returned home in the sunset to a cold supper. The gardens and green swarmed with children – fourteen in August 1886. Adult behaviour ran them a close second. Gosse exclaimed that "everything here seems so calm and cool and lazy" they knew no restraint.[43] No birthday passed without a party. On 30 August, Mrs Blashfield's birthday party, James waltzed with Lucia Millet twice: the first go round the floor he told her he had not danced for ten years; the second time he said twenty. September 14th, Tessa Gosse's – more dancing, games and flower wreaths on the children's heads. September 18th, Lily Millet – strolling musicians, dinner for twelve, lavish presents. September 21st, Gosse's – John and Lucia dined with the Gosses in their rooms (on goose) before walking over to the inn to join the others: "We danced, played cards and nibbled cakes and biscuits till nearly midnight," Lucia wrote to her parents (22 September 1885). "The boys [Abbey and Millet] each gave him a cane. . . . Then Mr. Sargent for fun, got an immense tall hat (which is by the cockneys in London called a 'Gossamer or goss'). I helped him put a poet's wreath of bay or laurel about it and a huge bow with long ends of purplish magenta ribbon at the end. . . ."[44] The locals were completely bemused by these goings-on. "Nothing we do scandalises the villagers," Gosse wrote to Hamo Thorneycroft (7 September 1885).

Fred Barnard, with an enormous stage slouch-hat over his shoulders, chased one of the Americans down the village street, the man chased screaming all the time and trying to escape up lamp-posts and down wells. Not a villager smiled. Miss Millet, yesterday, in the middle of the village green, was reposing on a bench when the wood gave way and threw her into Fred Barnard's lap. Not a villager smiled. Whatever we do or say or hear or sing they only say, "them Americans is out again."[45]

In the evening Farnham House shook with music. Someone sang ballads and John hammered away at the piano. "Sargent is going elaborately through Wagner's trilogy," Abbey wrote to a friend (12 November 1885), "recitatives and all; there are moments when it doesn't seem as if it could be meant for music, but I daresay it is."[46] His fellow-sufferer of this Wagneritis was Mrs Carr's sister, Alma Strettell (1853–1935). They tortured the keyboard mercilessly, earning themselves the self-imposed titles of "maniac" and "co-maniac". Five years later Miss Strettell kept up the tight-knit arrangement started at Broadway by marrying the painter, L. A. "Peter" Harrison. She was a remarkable woman, gifted in literature as well as in music. She, like John, was mesmerized by folk-songs, collecting and publishing texts. John gave her six illustrations for her *Spanish and Italian Folk Songs* in 1887. He painted her four times, an indication of fondness that exceeded merely a usefulness at the piano. The following summer at Broadway, John took pity briefly on his audience and went to Bayreuth. This extreme medication did not cure him, alas, and when he got back to Broadway his Wagner repertoire had advanced to *Parsifal*.

For John, Broadway was a short, exciting burst of communal life, and a triumph over the downtrodden feelings he attached to Paris. It was an exciting change. Years later every memoirist of those two summers remembered John at work on his unexpected pastoral essay, *Carnation, Lily, Lily, Rose*. In truth his work on the picture was unforgettable because it was an eccentric development of the "musical chair" activity Gosse witnessed, the natural manifestation of his theory "to render the effect before him. . . ." About two weeks after he began to work in the garden of Farnham House he summarized the picture he had in mind: "I am trying to paint a charming thing I saw the other evening," he wrote (10 September) [1885]. "Two little girls in a garden at dusk lighting paper lanterns hung among the flowers from rose-tree to rose-tree. I shall be a long time about it if I don't give up in despair, and at any rate probably two months longer in England. . . ."[47] The picture exceeded his calculations and soon became an exercise in logistics, drawing on the full resources only Broadway could supply. Kate Millet was replaced as his figure almost at once by the two Barnard sisters (because they had light-coloured hair). Then Lucia, Mrs Barnard and her sister Miss Faraday were enlisted to sew the white dresses he wanted. When the flowers faded he replaced them, and the next year he sent fifty bulbs to Lucia to plant in pots. As he was after a fugitive light, the daily routine was streamlined to accommodate it. "Everything used to be placed in readiness," Gosse recalled, the easel, the canvas, the flowers, the demure little girls . . . before we began our daily afternoon lawn tennis, in which Sargent took his share. But at the exact moment, which of course came a minute or two earlier each evening, the game was stopped, and the painter was accompanied to the scene. . . . Instantly, he took his place at a distance from the canvas, and at a certain notation of the light ran forward over the lawn with the action of a wag-tail, planting at the same time rapid dabs of paint on the picture, and then retiring again, only with equal suddenness to repeat the wag-tail action. All this occupied but two or three minutes . . .

As the temperature dropped the girls got fatter with vests and pullovers and John "muffled up like an Arctic explorer".[48] "And all unmindful of the evening dew," John wrote in a jocular mood for Broadway entertainment, "Still to his faith in nature he was true/Till once reclining upon Nature's breast/He woke and found a cold upon his chest."[49] When the light ceased to fit his requirements, the canvas was stored away until the following summer. John's own summary of the work was not dissimilar to his style of painting: he wrote to Emily, "Fearful difficult subject. Impossible brilliant colours of flowers, and lamps and brightest green lawn background. Paints are not bright enough & then the effect only lasts ten minutes."[50]

The free and easy life at Broadway worked its spell on John; he was unwilling to tear himself away, even for London. So were the Barnards, who let their house in town in order to stay for the remainder of the year (1885). Parsons stayed. The Millets left their daughter Kate in Lucia's care while they went off to New York. Abbey stayed. Those who did leave vowed to return, and kept their promise. And people continued to come and go oblivious to the season. Social life moved indoors, going from Farnham House to the Barnards' to Parsons' house at Frome and back again. Christmas was a riotous occasion. Presents in the morning: John gave Lucia a Japanese screen, Kate Millet a doll's house, Dolly Barnard a magic lantern. Luncheon at the Barnards' and dinner at five o'clock at Farnham House – "in the end quite a large one, fourteen in all including children". When the Priory* was acquired before Christmas, Broadway

---

* Known by various names, the Abbot's Grange, the Old Priory, or the Priory as Lucia referred to it (14 December 1885), the building "is one of the oldest domestic buildings in Worcestershire, built in 1320," Dr C. C. Houghton, the historian of Broadway, wrote. "It was formerly the summer residence of the Abbots of Pershore . . . built on the lines of an Oxbridge college with a great hall, buttery and oratory." The owners, Lucia informed her parents, "Rent it to the boys for a shilling a year and this only to get over some law difficulty. Mr. Abbey fancied it would be a good thing for the coming year. . . ."

The building needed extensive restoration which was not fully complete until around 1900.

(Information from C. C. Houghton, *A Walk about Broadway* (Shepperton, 1980). I am grateful to Dr Houghton for his help.)

suddenly became possible year-round. It was a vast derelict property adjacent to Farnham House, ideal, after a considerable amount of work, as a studio. The summer idyll could be prolonged.

Early in the new year John's entrenchment in Broadway became deeper; he joined in a temporary partnership with Abbey and Millet, who took Russell House for seven years. It was next door but one to Farnham House, and with the Priory formed a triangle on the western edge of the green. Russell House was much larger than Farnham House, littered with supplementary buildings in the garden, and was house and studio combined. John and Abbey stayed on there for four years; it became his "family" home, his auxiliary establishment. The arrangement in Worcestershire, though pleasant and useful, was not sufficiently adequate to be his sole residence. He could not paint portraits in the country; commissions demanded London.

Since June 1884 he satisfied this requirement by using friends' studios, first Besnard's in Ovington Square, then Abbey's in Eldon Road, then Parsons' in Bedford Gardens, and then back to Abbey's. He had lived at Bailey's Hotel in Knightsbridge and later in rooms in Ryder Street, St James's, and throughout this bewildering confusion of addresses he asked that letters be sent to him care of the Arts Club in Hanover Square. By the early spring of 1886 when it was a foregone conclusion he decided he would stay in England. In April he went to Nice to tell his parents he was leaving Paris. FitzWilliam took the news with the sober detachment that always belied his feelings: "John has just left us after a visit of a couple of weeks," he wrote to his brother Tom (13 May 1886), ". . . [he] is about moving his traps from Paris to London, where he expects to reside instead of in Paris, and where he thinks he will find more work to do than in the latter place. He seems to have a good many friends in London, & appears to be very favourably known there." In September, John moved into Whistler's old studio in Tite Street (number 13, later renumbered 33)* near the river, in the heart of Chelsea and a good distance south from his friends in Kensington and further south from the official quarter of respectable painters in St John's Wood. On 19 September, Lucia noted he was lonely in London, and by the end of the month he was back in Broadway painting Kate Millet again and flying kites in a field with Gosse.

* Nine months later he signed the lease for "the Studio and two rooms with Dressing Room" at a rent of £140 payable quarterly for three years from 24 June 1887; in addition he agreed to pay £35 per year for "the services of the House-keeper to answer the door and take messages and use of the Kitchen fire".

IX

John stayed in Tite Street for the rest of his life. Later he also took the house next door and supplementary studios in The Avenue, which runs between Fulham Road and the south side of Onslow Square. His family gradually gathered round him, and he bought the leases on two flats for his mother and Emily in nearby Carlyle Mansions, overlooking the river. Violet and her family settled further along in Cheyne Walk. For the next thirty-nine years there was no radical change in his domestic geography. John had a permanent address, and he did not take much advantage of it for several years.

The ground-floor rooms at Tite Street were modest compared to Boulevard Berthier; if anything, they must have been somewhat cramped. The bedroom was small; there was no room at all for servants, and no garden; the living-quarters had been added to the studio as a fleeting afterthought, and were adequate only because John had the supplement of Broadway. John's ideas about studio decoration were more sober, and certainly more suitable for portrait work, than those of his predecessor, Whistler, whose taste ran to walls painted a vivid yellow. The Morris-cum-Japanese décor of Boulevard Berthier gave way, over the years, to a distinctively French scheme. He discarded the Japanese dolls Charles Deering had sent him, the north African carpets and pots, the Japanese silk, the Morris hangings, and moved in furniture that ranged from Louis XV to Empire: a table de toilette on castors, adapted to hold his painting equipment, a canapé, a fauteuil, a duchesse, a looming Coromandel screen. Another screen of curtains could be adjusted behind the platform with the sitter's chair. There was an upright piano, assorted marble busts, a gramophone on an elegant table, and on another a spectroscope (the scientific toy that projected two-dimensional photographs from glass slides). Once fine oriental rugs and Aubusson carpets covered the floor. The walls had pilasters ornamented with swags and garlands; between these he hung his student pictures, his copies after Velazquez, his portrait of Madame Gautreau, pictures by his friends, and samples from his ever-increasing collection (including, among very many others, an unfinished painting by Ford Madox Brown, watercolours by Brabazon, and oils by Monet and Annie L. Swynnerton, whose sentimentality he was surprisingly forever praising). A vast window, peering out at the trees, dominated the east wall: light was more fugitive in London than in Paris. Thick fog often settled in and stayed; in the winter he lit his lamps at two o'clock. Visitors could never quite agree on a description of his new establishment: to painters, and especially to younger painters, it had a slightly forbidding atmosphere ("that of a cultivated cosmopolitan",[1] William Rothenstein sneered in his autobiography) and to sitters it was unremarkable ("not large and very simply furnished, not the impressive studio of an amateur", one recalled[2]).

The studio was ready for sittings at the beginning of October, and was opened for a series of entertainments the following month. On Friday, 5 November he unveiled his home to Broadway – "(by invitation) and it was a great treat", Lucia Millet wrote to her parents four days later. "The rooms are large and beautifully arranged and decorated. Then too he has many wonderfully pretty things." (The American sculptor Daniel Chester French was also invited.) And less than a fortnight later he gave a lunch-party for eight, and more people came in after: "a great success", Lucia remarked.[3] The move from Paris was complete.

For many years a long portière hung over the door at 33 Tite Street and for many years John managed to get entangled in it. He had arranged the contents of the studio to line the walls, leaving the room uncluttered, which, to the unobservant, made the studio appear bare. It had to be: John's energetic approach to painting was closer to fencing. With a brush in one hand, palette gripped by the other, a cigarette or cigar smouldering in his mouth, he backed away from the sitter and canvas with slow but deliberate steps, further and further. His eyes were fixed on the sitter and canvas throughout this withdrawal. He stopped, then lunged at the canvas. Over and over again he performed this ritual dance. He once calculated he walked about four miles a day in the studio. By retreating he was able to make the model and the canvas equal before his eye,

> and was thus able to estimate the construction and values of this representation. He drew with his brush, beginning with the shadows, and gradually evolving his figure from the background by means of large, loose volumes of shadow, half-tones and light, regardless of features or refinements of form, finally bringing the masses of light and shade closer together, and thus assembling the figure. He painted with large brushes and a full palette, using oil and turpentine freely as a medium.[4]

"Always use a full brush and a larger one than necessary," John told Frederick Sumner Platt, the collector and amateur painter in August 1890. "Paint with long sweeps, avoiding spots and dots ('little dabs'). Never think of other painters' pictures . . . but follow your own choice of colors with exact fidelity to nature."[5] He painted briskly, covering a lot of ground. When the subject was more or less transferred, he stayed close to the canvas, humming or whistling, but he rarely sat down. Or sometimes he would ask the subject to supply the entertainment: Sir George

Henschel* sang passages from *Tristan und Isolde*. John's studio routine intrigued his sitters, who liked this show of eccentricity. Sir George Sitwell, for example, enjoyed the spectacle of John "rushing bull-like . . . and shouting".[6] For him such behaviour was appropriate in an artist, and he felt that he was getting his money's worth. To John, however, it was simply a matter of technique, a way of not getting bogged down by detail. Details, he was convinced, would take care of themselves. He once advised a student: "Do not concentrate so much on the features. Paint the head. The features are only like spots on an apple."

John never relied on any gimmicks or short cuts or unusual equipment. His materials were, if anything, extraordinarily usual. "The arrangements for painting", Julie Heyneman (a Californian art student who was introduced to John by Charles Deering in June 1892) observed at Tite Street, " – Mr. Sargent would probably have called them the 'instruments of torture' – were of the simplest, the most practical kind. The palettes were weighted, and a zinc fence prevented the wet paint from slipping down to the sleeve. . . ."[7] He used colours of the most ordinary variety and quality. He had no favourite paintbox – in the country he used a fruit-basket – or palette or brushes, no special tools or sacred procedures. He could paint anywhere, in almost any conditions.

In the studio John habitually wore a collar and tie, waistcoat and jacket (making no concession in his haberdashery), just as he had done since his first day in Boulevard Mont Parnasse. In the country, however, he occasionally removed his jacket, and rolled up his shirt-cuffs once or twice. Such standards of dress were maintained by his colleagues, and were not in the least unusual. Informality in dress was allowed for students and Whistler.

John's move to England was a gesture almost after the fact. The preparation of James's trumpet oblatory and Broadway's tidy settlement made the shift itself seem rather flat. His reasons for moving to London appeared to be exactly the same as those he used for not staying in Paris. His reputation as the rare American to outdistance the native competition, as Carolus' star pupil, as the portraitist of Madame Gautreau tended to frighten off potential patrons' commissions. If the French

* Sir George Henschel (1850–1934), pianist, composer, accompanist, conductor and singer (baritone), best-known, however, as the first conductor of the Boston Symphony Orchestra, London Symphony Orchestra, and the Scottish Orchestra, Glasgow. Born in Poland, naturalized British subject in 1890 and knighted in 1914, his contribution to music was so impressive as to earn him the only entry for a living musician in the early editions of *Grove's Dictionary of Music*. John first met him in the summer of 1887, through the Harrisons – John painted Mrs Robert Harrison in January 1886 – who were also very musical. They became very close friends. John gave him one of his versions of the Pasdeloup Orchestra, drew a portrait sketch of his second wife, and gave him a sketch of Eleanora Duse; but these facts can only suggest their close friendship. John wrote to Henschel more than 120 times, and these letters, sold in 1927, have disappeared. John painted him in 1889. Henschel was also painted by de Laszlo and Alma-Tadema.

admired him, the English thought, he must be dangerously modern. In 1886, John had four commissions, the smallest number for years. Somehow he sensed that prejudice could be more easily overcome in England, and he was helped to this conclusion because it was more agreeable to wait in England than in France – because of Broadway. By attaching himself to Broadway, John became better-known in America. It was an unexpected bonus.

All the laughable industry at Russell House and the Priory made the place look like an important post on the art map. The appearance was deceptive. Millet, Abbey and company were all the while really coaxing their reputations in America. They had come to England to work for New York. They dug themselves into the English landscape while being careful to retain and enhance every transatlantic attachment. They never lost an opportunity to advertise themselves. Frank and Lily Millet returned to New York every year, and Abbey's fame grew in America by leaps and bounds, while he was in England. Parsons and Boughton were carried along. And John was carried along, enthusiastically. His own campaign to establish himself in America, his showing with the Society of American Artists in New York since the late 1870s, among others, was conducted at a snail's pace compared to the hurtling progress his friends were able to make by a few artfully placed words. James, who thought he was opening up the wide possibilities of England for John, performed an even greater service when he eased his introduction to fellow-Americans. By coming to England, John laid the foundation for his fame in America.*

John's greatest asset in his career was one he had never sought, one that had nothing whatever to do with his talent, and one that was the ultimate vindication of his mother's trust in the suitability of dragging her family abroad – his cosmopolitanism. An American artist in Europe was not a unique phenomenon, but an American artist who had won prizes at the Salon, a certain, somewhat bruised reputation in France and England, was more French or English – and had a right to be – than American, was someone altogether extraordinary. Americans abroad had thought so for many years: expatriates went to him, tourists went to him, and during the last six or seven years in Paris the list of his sitters included a high proportion of Americans.[8] When James, Abbey, Millet and the stream of Broadway visitors got to work, shrieking John's praise, the travellers' tales were corroborated. It was as if John alone were free of that conscious adjustment in sensibility his colleagues sought out in Italy, Germany, France or England. From the moment he arrived in Broadway, he began

---

* Henry James himself interpreted John's departure from Paris with a housemaid's affection for neatness. On 11 March [1886] he wrote to his friend Henrietta Reubell: "I don't in the smallest degree agree with the idea that Sargent has done an unwise or an unfair thing to come to this place to live and work. He seems to me to have got from Paris all that Paris had to give him – viz. in perfect possession of his technical means. Paris taught him how to paint so well that she can't teach him better. . . ." In short, the chapter was closed. (*Letters*, Vol. 3 (1980), pp. 117 ff.)

to develop an unimaginable appeal in America. The power the resident artists and their friends exerted in New York was sufficient to draw together the nebulous influences, ambitions and impulses that were leisurely governing the course of John's progress, to strengthen them, and to catapult them on. Once John took up residence in Broadway, he was, in truth, taking his first step towards establishing himself in America. And thereafter his fame in England grew.

The Millets and Abbey shared a seven-year lease on Russell House, starting in March 1886, and John became a partner from the summer. During the four months prior to his tenancy, Russell House had undergone a transformation, making it something like a cross between a toffee-box illustration and a jumbo playroom. Abbey thought it was closer to a boys' school; one visitor believed it was nothing more than his hosts' paintings or drawings come to life, but whatever the comparison people could not stay away. At the height of the tourist season, Lucia counted twenty-two visitors (not including children) staying either at the inn or in lodgings. And there was a continuous procession of callers, like Mary Anderson, obscure European royalty – both of whom sent shudders of excitement through the locals, who assembled a brass band to celebrate – and the Souls' pin-up, Lady Elcho, one of the Wyndham sisters whom John was to paint twelve years later as the *Three Graces*, came over from Stanway with Eliza Wedgwood, herself later to become one of John and Emily's closest friends. The American Edwin Howland Blashfield (1848–1936) returned with his wife, Evangeline Wilbour, for a second tour of inspection. Blashfield had studied in Paris for fifteen years under Bonnat and Gérôme, and carried the torch of rigid academic training back to New York. He went on to paint the walls and ceilings of municipal buildings across America, which were just what the city fathers wanted and nobody else ever cared about. He advanced some hearty theories about mural painting, though he himself never put them into practice. He is better remembered for being in the right place at the right time than for any of his work. He had met John first in 1871, again in Paris five years later; but "the only period during which daily comradeship with him came to me was that of the summer of 1887 [1886]", Blashfield recalled in 1926.[9] He and his wife stayed in Broadway for most of July, August and the beginning of September. His letters to his mother during this period give one of the closest accounts of life among the artists. Blashfield's timing was once again brilliant.

Russell House was intended to be a magnet; it was got up to look wonderful. The licorice-coloured oak furniture was there to suit the house, not the comfort of the occupants. The walls were solid, befitting their age, and the floors were worn by centuries of use. The walls and chimney shelf were loaded with pewter. The rooms were dark, and smelt of woodsmoke, beeswax, oil-lamps and flowers. The ladies dressed for dinner in either cobwebby gowns or some of Abbey and Millet's period costumes so as not to disturb the spell of antiquity, while the men were strictly forbidden to wear formal dinner-clothes. Only the small sitting-rooms crossed over into the nineteenth century: in one, the walls were hung with white material figured in yellow, the furniture was painted white, and in Lily's own little drawing-room was John's unfinished portrait of her and his *Girl with a Sickle*. As another concession to modernity, the post was collected every afternoon at five o'clock. Russell House was intoxicatingly romantic, and the striking beauty of both Mrs Barnard and Lily Millet completed the deliberate image. The whole place rang with the loud clear note of dreams come true.

The garden was as remarkable (and full) as the house, littered with architectural curiosities – a small machicolated tower with greenhouse attached, a gazebo, a long brick wall trailing off into the distance, an overgrown flight of stairs rising to nowhere – a lily pond, an orchard and an admirably smooth tennis lawn. Two rams wandered in a small woodland, a peacock, which Gosse had given to John, calmly strutted across the lawn, until it caught sight of any child, who, for some reason, always had to be attacked. Lily Millet had made the garden spectacular, a wonderful show. The scent of flowers was heavy. There were long beds of pink, yellow and pale orange roses; large white marigolds; hollyhocks; a bed of outsize scarlet poppies, three to four feet tall, which all the painters found irresistible but infuriatingly unpaintable; and there were John's tall lilies. The garden was his studio. He painted Kate again, Lucia and Kate, and Gosse — " 'Oh! what lovely lilac hair,' " he said as Gosse approached, " 'no one ever saw such beautiful lilac hair!' The blue sky reflected on my sleek dun locks . . . had glazed them with colour," Gosse explained, "and Sargent, grasping another canvas, painted me as I stood laughing, while he ejaculated at intervals, 'Oh! what lovely hair!' "[10]

John's slow instalments on *Carnation, Lily, Lily, Rose* turned into the central activity in the set-piece that epitomized the *look* and atmosphere of Russell House and Broadway: Late afternoon. Gosse, wearing knicker-bockers, sits with his wife watching the tennis, when not partnering John at doubles. On the whole, the Russell House standard of tennis is high, but not intimidating. Mrs Williams plays well; Blashfield has a devilishly wicked serve; John moves like lightning across the court, playing most fiendishly at the net; Millet is swift, Abbey swifter; Alma-Tadema is comically awful, laughing constantly at his many mistakes. Closer to the house Lucia pours out tea at a table generously laden with cakes and bread and butter. Barnard hobbles about on his sprained ankle (that had threatened to keep him and his daughters, John's models, up in London). Children dash to and fro. The peacock screeches. By the gateposts Henry James is talking to Mrs Blashfield, who, being consumptive, has to stand on a small plank to keep her feet dry. Shortly after 6.30, John drops his tennis racket and strides over to the studio to retrieve his canvas and easel. He lugs them across the garden, sets them up in the same spot as he has done many times before. He calls Dorothy and Polly Barnard, who are posed among the lilies. And all three wait for the precise moment when the light is absolutely right to resume work. John bribes the girls with sweets. Then, suddenly, he begins to paint, and continues furiously for a few minutes. The tennis-players have broken off their game to watch the scene. The light fades and becomes useless. It is now just past seven o'clock. The guests disperse for dinner, some to the Lygon Arms, some to their lodgings, some to the house. John goes back to the studio, where he stays, examining what he has done, and invariably scrapes out the last addition, ready to begin all over again the following day. In a few hours, after dinner, everyone reassembles in Abbey's studio.

While the Millets were in America and Lucia carried out their detailed instructions, Abbey converted the mammoth old barn into "a studio such as one *imagines*", Blashfield wrote, " – & such as a writer would like to introduce a description of in a story".[11] He moved his furniture down from London, his inventory of props and his enormous store of costumes and wigs. In no time the place was full. (The Priory also served as a studio for his and Millet's use.)

It was his by day, but by evening he turned it over to the visitors. The gaslights were turned up and the numerous entertainments began, often all at the same time. Mrs Blashfield read palms – " 'Oh yes, a fine philistine hand,' " Henry James repeated her saying after studying his, and everyone hooted with laughter.[12] "It is not hard to give the hand", John's verse, written on a small slip of paper, began, "To one who freely gives her art/But here you'll kindly understand/I speak of Art and not of Heart."[13] One end of the long refectory table in the centre of the room was cleared for poker, the other scattered with albums of press-cuttings, Abbey's drawings for *She Stoops to Conquer*, John's drawings of Madame Gautreau, some of the day's paintings and miscellaneous sketches. Applause erupts for a tableau vivant of Raphael's cherubs. James lectured on Millais' early work. John suggested a game of "throwing silhouettes on a sheet", Mrs Carr remembered; and Abbey responded, somewhat unkindly, that " 'John had proposed a game at which he was sure of winning . . .' ".[14] Abbey pulled apart the red silk curtains in front of his costume collection to find some of his treasures to show off, like the muslin christening-gown owned by Lady Hamilton. Dressing up was encouraged, and then the company's high spirits were unleashed. There were games in which men had to wear skirts in order to be an equal match for ladies. And dancing. Abbey struck up a Virginia Reel, and Alma-Tadema swept the floor in a hooped petticoat. Millet forced a note or two out of a trombone. When Abbey had finished cutting out James's silhouette (to be added to the series of silhouettes of the habitués of the house which formed a frieze round the walls), he clowned at one of the harpsichords, then went over to sit with Mrs Carr and argue about theatrical costumes. Miss Laurence Tadema, one of Alma-Tadema's daughters, played the guitar. John sat down at the piano to play Lully, Mozart and Schubert, before he partnered Lily Millet in four-hand arrangements of Brahms's dances and *The Mikado*, singing all the parts. About midnight, the guests began to drift away.

After nearly two years, John's monument to Broadway, *Carnation, Lily, Lily, Rose* was ready for the Royal Academy, in the spring of 1887. It was a latter-day *El Jaleo*. Its effect was electric, achieving the near-impossible with an exuberant display of sentimentality *and* a command of modernity – foreign modernity. The colours glowed and the subject cloyed. Polly and Dorothy Barnard, submerged in a lush summer garden, reminded observers of pictures they had seen before, the Japanese lanterns were exotic without being totally unfamiliar, and the brushwork, which depended a lot on suggestion, was more or less comprehensible – even the roses *looked* like roses, up to a point. The picture managed to satisfy the stark requirements of the modernists without leaving the rest, and less advanced, of the population behind. John had struck the correct balance. He had won the critics' blessing. His old strategy for the Salon had gained strength when he transferred his campaign to the Royal Academy. Once again he proved the value of serving notice that he was more than a portraitist, that he did not have to be his sitters' toady to command attention. *Carnation, Lily, Lily, Rose*, which he himself later renamed *Damnation, Silly, Silly, Pose*, did for his reputation in England what *El Jaleo* had done for him in France. And, perversely, he left almost at once. Five months after his Academy success, on 17 September 1887, he sailed to America; Broadway's spell might have worn a little thin, but not its influence.

"My going to America to paint Mrs Marquand's portrait was the turning point in my fortunes," John wrote to her husband years later from Tite Street. "You have . . . been . . . a bringer of good luck."[15] John did not exaggerate the importance of the commission which lured him to America and started the dramatic reversal in his career, accelerating his progress beyond his wildest dreams. He intended to be away for two months; he stayed for eight. From the moment he arrived he was welcomed like a celebrity, and he returned to London as one. America made him famous.

The forces of Broadway were not far behind anywhere he went. Henry James got to work in the pages of their official paper, *Harper's New Monthly Magazine* (October), and introduced John to America in terms of florid adulation, unfurling a carpet impossible to ignore. Such courtesy was useful and generous, but it was also an embellishment after the fact, the usual moment when James raised his voice. Henry Gurdon Marquand (1819–1902), railway magnate, philanthropist, collector (of Vermeer, Hals, Van Dyck and other masters he later gave to the Metropolitan Museum), and from 1889 the second president of the Metropolitan, had issued the invitation to come to America, on the recommendation of John's tennis opponent at Russell House, Alma-Tadema. Marquand had recruited Alma-Tadema to take a hand in the decoration of his new music room. He accepted, and also recommended Leighton to make some contribution. When Marquand was looking around for a portraitist, Tadema pointed to John, starting a chain of events that had soaring ramifications. Tradition has it that John was understandably disinclined to leave England, a year after moving into Tite Street and fast on the heels of his success at the Academy. He therefore named a price he was confident would be refused, but when Marquand agreed John was honour-bound to sail.*

After docking in Boston, John went straight to Newport where he painted Mrs Marquand in her house, Linden Gate on Old Beach Road. John unpacked caution from his bags when he came to satisfy his first American commission. He left behind all the *esprit* of Broadway and looked back to Spain and his portrait of Edouard Pailleron for guidance. This was not the moment for risks; this was not the occasion for daring. His Mrs Marquand was sober, refined, kindly but undemonstrative. She was seated comfortably in a cushioned Chippendale chair, wearing black, with a delicate lace fichu, collar and cuffs. The colouring was sombre and restrained. He turned her into a fine piece of reproduction Hepplewhite, safe, elegant, unjarring, secure – a brilliant performance considering his raw material. And such craftsmanship suited his patron perfectly. "Sargent has done a grand thing of Mrs Marquand," her husband wrote a month after John arrived (25 October 1887). " . . . He will have plenty to do without doubt."[16] He was also not finished with the Marquands: four years later he painted their daughter Mabel, Mrs Galbraith Ward, and in 1896 the Trustees of the Metropolitan asked him to paint Henry Marquand – " 'Chicken, – chicken!' " John said to Emily when he saw the portrait on the wall of the Museum dangerously close to Marquand's Hals. " 'I can never think of anything else, when I look at this portrait, but plucked fowl in the markets!' "[17]

Marquand's commission brought John more than luck; it established the standard for future American patrons, which was approximately that of Mrs White and the Vickerses rolled into one – rich, with sufficient lineage to calm the most insistent colonial dame (a small matter

---

* That price can be guessed at, with a reasonable degree of certainty, based on the sums he got for other pictures at the time: $2000–$2500, a staggering leap on his previous earnings. In the aftermath of Madame Gautreau, Henry James told Vernon Lee that John was not asking high prices and that he doubted John had ever made more than £1000 a year. But two years later the Chantry Bequest bought *Carnation, Lily, Lily, Rose* for £700 (approximately $3000) or £19,500 by today's standards. A few months after Mrs Marquand's portrait, he asked $2000 (for Mrs Jacob Wendell) and in 1889 $3000 (for Mr Richard McCurdy). In 1890 he was paid as much as $5000 (for Mrs Dewey), which was Carolus' fee for a full-length portrait in 1896; double and group portraits were more: Carolus charged a staggering $14,000 (£3500) for mother and child, compared to John's £1500 for the Sitwell family (two adults, three children and a Pug) in 1900. Alma-Tadema charged £800 for a full-length portrait. In short, John was charging the going rate for a well-established painter before he could claim to be one. (Of course, in England, he was paid in guineas.)

Marquand negotiated by his lavish good works). With Marquand, John started more or less at the top of the social scale, and there he stayed. It was a brilliant start, much like his début in Boulevard Mont Parnasse fifteen years before: he arrived too well prepared, too well suited for it to be anything else. Over and over again he showed an unerring gift of advantage. The prices he thought excessive were in fact a considerable benefit, though they ensured he stayed among the rich. He and his work turned into an irresistible acquisition. He tried to keep his American visits brief and he rarely strayed from the East Coast, a form of modified exclusivity that also enhanced his prestige. Marquand, augmented by John's own network of expatriate connections, set in motion a long sequence of commissions that was all of a piece – and the inevitable conclusion of his mother's imposed eccentricity. John's fame in America rose quickly and smoothly, as if the obvious had been postponed long enough, as if his years abroad had been mere preparation. FitzWilliam's ambition for his son was being realized, after a very long wait.

His American tour soon turned into a triumphal progress. From Newport he went to New York where he was treated like a returning victorious hero by his old friends from Paris, who had followed his progress, disbelieving any rumour that he might not be satisfying their expectations for him. This band of acquaintance contributed the other component that governed John's sudden rise to fame in America. The Paris old boys were securely established, in the forefront of American Art. While in service to the Marquands in Newport, he again saw Stanford White, the architect. They had met in Paris in 1878 when White was playing tourist to Saint-Gaudens's Thomas Cook; nine years later White was making a very fast assault on the summit of his profession. The very fugitives who once seethed over the policies of the National Academy of Design, were themselves now installed: Beckwith served on the Jury and was an Associate Member, Alden Weir had recently been elected. Beckwith taught at the Cooper Union, Will Low was between teaching posts there and at the Academy. Saint-Gaudens was famous, and at the moment working on his portrait medallion of Robert Louis Stevenson at the Albert Hotel on 11th Street. Hinckley was married and quietly settled in Washington. New York was Paris all over again, aided and abetted by the potent influence of Abbey and Millet, who were sorely missed. John's name had been invoked for over a decade, and his reception honoured the reputation he had gained in absence. Millet wrote to White proposing John for membership of the Tile Club. "He seems to be very prosperous," Millet reported to White after receiving John's American report (1 November 1887). "I am glad he is. He deserves it."[18] White gave a dinner for him and ten other artists. Beckwith dropped everything and they searched together for a studio, and John took him and his wife (Bertha Hall, whom he had married on 1 June) to the first night of *Tristan*; as compensation John gave them a Venetian watercolour for a wedding present.[19] At the end of November, he moved on to Boston, home territory of Henry James and his cousins, the Curtises.

He was among friends, staying with them – the Boits at 65 Mount Vernon Street (who had returned to America to launch their eldest daughter in society) – and painting them: Mrs Boit, and a host of Fairchilds (at 151 Commonwealth Avenue). The Fairchilds were spectral figures in John's life, like a great many people, whose fondness was reciprocated and whose friendship cannot be pinned down to much more than cross-reference. Charles Fairchild (1838–1910), a banker, handled John's American finances. His wife Elizabeth Nelson (1845–1924) was a poet who became a literary hostess after her marriage. Her friendship with Stevenson prompted John's third portrait of him. John painted her, her youngest son Gordon, and one of her daughters, Sally, several times. They were life-long friends, and the commission to paint Fairchild's elder brother, General Lucius Fairchild (1831–96), was one of the reasons, if not *the* reason, for John coming to Boston. General Fairchild had had a distinguished career, from being first mayor of Madison, Wisconsin, to governor of the State. In between this promotion he served in the Union Army, became a colonel and finally Commander-in-Chief of the Grand Army of the Republic. When he retired, Wisconsin wanted to honour him with a portrait, and General Fairchild took the train to Boston to sit to John. The portrait was done during the first two weeks in December, bringing, or so he thought when he had left Tite Street, his American tour to an end – but that had been a prediction that excluded Mrs John Lowell Gardner, Isabella Stewart Gardner, and she was no one to be ignored, a characteristic that had required a lot of energy and money.

Mrs Gardner (1840–1924) has always been confused with her possessions; they turned her into a legend during her lifetime, and thereafter a worthy candidate for myth. She has never inspired good biography, though she has not been ignored. But it is true to say her greatest achievement was that she bought. She bought enough to pack a large building, and she bought her way through her emotions to an extent that eventually replaced them. She was selfish – in later life it was called eccentricity – and her wealth was sufficient to allow magnificent indulgence, thus permitting her to think of others. Had she stayed in New York, where she was born and where her sort of buying was a hobby shared by a few magnates, she would have never enjoyed the same powerful influence that exceeded any elected office granted her at home. Instead of conquering Europe, she had her victory in Boston.

She began her life showing every aptitude for conventionality, marrying a schoolfriend's brother and immediately enfolding herself into the standard routine of a well-connected, rich Back Bay matron, and she ended her life a monument. When her infant son died and she was told she could have no others, she began her big spree. She bought pearls, a lot of pearls, ideal specimens, with diamonds or rubies. When she had her fill of jewellery, she moved on to books, manuscripts, autographs, all of the highest calibre. Thus she could tell the Pope she owned a *Book of Hours*, set gossip alight with her association with writers like F. Marion Crawford (who John judiciously beat up in Rome when they were both very small children), have audiences with the great Norton at Harvard, and bully Henry James. And from bibliophilism she moved on to the big league – paintings. Berenson conducted great masters across the ocean to her, agents scurried, Ralph Curtis watched her swoop on luscious pickings, like the architectural ornaments he found in Venice, and in Paris Dr Pozzi's picture of Madame Gautreau (which John had given to her mother, Madame Avegno), and John alerted her to various sales, like Whistler's Peacock Room and Mrs Hunter's sale where she gathered up Brabazons and drawings by Augustus John. Aristocrats and dealers paid homage to her to get at her chequebook. Throughout this conquest of culture her army grew with writers, painters, musicians, scholars. She returned from her frequent European tours followed by crates of furniture, tapestries, carpets. When her husband died, she slowed down a little, to supervise the building of Fenway Court, her Italianate museum and home. It was her choice of immortality, not hospitals, libraries, universities or any of the more usual forms of memorial. She was hard at work on her palazzo while the Museum of Fine Arts was being established and built round the corner. Unlike the Marquands, she held out for solitary permanence, which was cool independence, considering just what she had to contribute. With characteristic conviction she believed even time could be a possession: her will left her museum to the public *for ever*.

Mrs Gardner was short and, though her face was no asset and her hair the colour of old rust, she had a most wonderful figure, beautiful arms and shoulders, which she dressed like her walls and shelves, with the highest-quality stuff arranged by Worth and Pacquin. Her skin had the perfection of a ripe Italian white peach. She cut a striking, sometimes too striking, figure in Boston.

John was introduced to Mrs Gardner the year before, by Ralph Curtis and Henry James who brought her round to Tite Street.* When he reached Boston their friendship began, lasting nearly forty years, later including Emily, Violet and her children. His letters to her were more than usually unrevealing – over the long span of time his salutation altered little, from "Dear Mrs Gardner" to "My dear Mrs Gardner" and then back again. Still, their relations, which never flourished beyond subdued fondness, were close enough to excite rumours of a deeper attachment. Her vast range of correspondents kept her posted on all of his activities, dressing up each intelligence with phrases like "your friend" and other vague endearments. When he was in Boston they were often seen together, and he was granted the rare honour of being asked to stay as well as work at Fenway Court. For years people were happy to assume,

* John met Mrs Gardner in London on 28 October 1886.

and say, that John and Mrs Gardner were lovers. (In 1951 a fictionalized account of their friendship was published, *The Lady and the Painter*, casting John as Mrs Gardner's "cavaliere servente".[20]) For John, Mrs Gardner was a generous hostess (especially useful in Boston, and a little maddening when she was abroad, renting the Barbaro from the Curtises), making free with her symphony tickets, her wide range of friends, and her interest in his work; for Mrs Gardner, John was the perfect addition to her collection, civilized, successful, and a link to people in France and England. She came to mean Boston for John by making his visits more agreeable. The whole arrangement was uncomplicated by romance and improved by careful friendship.

Prior to collecting paintings, Mrs Gardner amassed a "collection of painters" as her most recent biographer phrased it;[21] this collection began with John. A year later she also started to acquire his pictures, and by the time she died she owned twenty-two, plus nine medallion and cartouche casts from his library decorations, plus two sketchbooks. She first sat to him at her house at 152 Beacon Street. The sittings were trying; by temperament (and a desire to prolong the work) she was unable to be still. John despaired, threatened to give up, and by the ninth attempt succeeded. Portraitists, like biographers, have had a hard time with her. They could not be honest – it would have been too cruel – and yet they could not say no. Whistler got round a true likeness by studying her dress (1886), Anders Zorn by trying to capture her energy (1894), Martin Mower by casting her as a bibliophile reading through a spotted veil (1917), and only Passini went for the orthodox pose (1892). John concentrated on her figure, her pearls (which figured in most of the portraits), and her sixteenth-century red and gold brocade that formed a deifying frame. Mrs Gardner's admiration for the portrait of Madame Gautreau and her evident fondness for him, made John bolder with his characterization than he dared to be with either Mrs Marquand or General Fairchild.* She stands hands clasped in front (not unlike Madame Paul Poirson, three years before), with a black shawl tied round her black gown at the hips, her pearls with ruby pendants banded at her waist and neck, composing the portrait as a repetitive circular design, deflecting attention from her wide-set small eyes and broad ungraceful mouth. The picture was an opulent display with sensuous overtones.† When the painting was

---

* Mrs Tharp, in her biography of Mrs Gardner, relates a story about John and Mrs Gardner racing round the track in the gymnasium at Groton School; it does not have the ring of accuracy, especially as John would never have worn white duck trousers in January, or any other time during this American tour. And there are other reasons to doubt it.
† In his unpublished memoir of Sargent (in the Boston Athenaeum Archives), Thomas Fox, the architect who succeeded Stanford White on the murals, repeats a story concerning the brocade background of this portrait (without mentioning Mrs Gardner by name, that is). He said to his sitter he wanted a piece of Venetian brocade – " 'but unfortunately, it is on the wall of my studio in London'. To which

shown at the St Botolph Club in Newberry Street from 28 January to 11 February, it excited attention, laced with ribald innuendo. Again, people looked at the portrait as an excuse to comment on the sitter. Henry James judged the portrait from a photograph to be a haloed Byzantine Madonna. Her husband, who preferred Mancini for his own portrait, said: "It looks like h . . l, but it looks like you."[22] John had grown resilient to criticism – "The newspapers do not disturb me," he wrote to Mrs Gardner [January/February 1888] from New York[23] – but the Gardners never did. She refused John's requests to exhibit it again, and kept the Gothic Room where it hangs in Fenway Court locked to the public during her lifetime. John painted her two more times, both watercolours: once heavily veiled in the garden at Fenway Court (1903) and again, nineteen years later, densely robed in white cloth, her face scarcely visible.

John returned to New York at the end of January (1888) and continued along the triumphal procession he left behind two months before, living at the Clarendon Hotel and painting in a studio on the south-west side of Washington Square. He had six commissions; he was among the prominent and the unashamedly rich (Vanderbilts, bankers, etc.). He painted more freely, showing off expensive eighteenth-century French furniture, gowns by Worth, and jewels. His prices rose, and patrons did not stay away. The March number of the *Art Journal* ran R. A. M. Stevenson's shrewd and laudatory essay on John's work just in case James's admiration had been forgotten once John was in America. His fellow-painters looked on with amazement at his phenomenal rise. And on Monday, 2 April he capped his American tour with "a royal feast", Will Low remembered, at Sieghortner's in Lafayette Place – a joint Paris reunion and farewell dinner, for over thirty artists and a few select new friends: nine courses, candles, flowers, all sumptuously arranged. "The dinner started at about 7:30 p.m.," one of the non-painters recalled, Dr Gorham Bacon whose daughter John had painted in Newport, "and I am told there were still some present there at 6:00 a.m. I tried to escape at midnight but was discovered and pulled back. . . . I shall never forget, after leaving the restaurant, hearing the singing and noise for several blocks. Some of the artists were not seen for days."[24] Denis Bunker, who did not attend, but came down from Boston to visit John – and sail back with him – wrote to Mrs Gardner a week later (9 April 1888): "Il mène un existence de roi – c'est un homme étonnant."[25] By May, when John felt the weather was "hotter than parliamentary language can express" as he wrote to Mrs Gardner (9 May),[26] he was ready to return to England. He sailed on the nineteenth, having stayed six months longer than he had intended.

Paris ceased to haunt him. The American tour was a vast celebration of

---

the lady replied, 'Never mind that, Sargent, I knew exactly what would be the proper background for my portrait when I decided to have you paint it, and I have the other half of the piece upstairs . . .' " (p. 39).

success, logging superlatives in its momentum. Over thirteen hundred people flocked to his first one-man show at the St Botolph Club, comprising twenty pictures, from small informal Venetian scenes to large formal portraits and *El Jaleo*. The critics' voiced the general enthusiasm: "No American has ever displayed a collection of paintings in Boston having so much of the quality which is summed up in the word *style*. . . . There is an indefinable but palpable atmosphere of refinement, ease and – tranchons le mot – aristocracy . . .".[27] The show was seen as a compliment to Boston, Boston curtsied in gracious homage, thereafter staking a legitimate claim on John's allegiance – another unwitting step that had inestimable benefits. John sent two of his American portraits for the Royal Academy: "Mrs. M[arquand] will do him great good with the public," Henry James assessed when he had an advance look (1 April 1888) when the picture arrived in London and Abbey was using Tite Street, " – they will want to be painted like that – respectfully honourably, dignement. It is a noble portrait of an old lady." Mrs Boit, however, was less certain of success: "the philistine will find her vulgar".[28] But the American enthusiasm did follow him home. London smiled on him for the second year running. At the age of thirty-three, John had found a niche, a high-up niche in his profession; he was securely placed.

At precisely the same moment, as if with an impeccable sense of timing (which was perhaps the only talent his father had bothered to develop during his long stint abroad) FitzWilliam gave up, having lived long enough to witness John's recognition. In January he suffered a slight stroke. His wife and daughters were naturally alarmed, but they did not ask John to rush to Florence. The slow-moving wheels of convalescence were once again set in motion, this time in earnest. John, his mother and sisters hung on every nuance of his health. It was FitzWilliam's turn to be an invalid. Denis Bunker (who had crossed with John from New York and passed much of the summer with the Sargents), witnessed a sadder truth: "He seems to be quite feeble and broken."[29]

During the first few months of FitzWilliam's illness, John's plans for the summer hung fire, a characteristic state whenever he was plotting his itinerary. His friends had grown accustomed to this havering. While he did not like travelling alone, his companions never quite knew exactly where and when they had been invited. Ralph Curtis waited to accompany him to Spain for years. John was indecisive because, like his mother, he thought in large terms, countries as well as continents, and he was tempted by almost everywhere. The debate was never simple, and this year was no different, save that he was ruled by his father's health. At the beginning of spring he asked Bunker to join him in Italy; by the middle of May he wrote to Mrs Gardner that he would be going to Paris for a week before going south, and two weeks after that he was still in London receiving friends from Boston (the Boits and the Fairchilds), completely undecided where to go next. Bunker, who watched these plans unfold, collapse, and then reappear, calmly informed Mrs Gardner (25 June)

[1888]: "I don't know just how you are going to see J.S.S. He may be going to Paris but you know how hard it is to tell *where* he'll go."[30] This uncertainty loomed even after he had taken a house for his family outside Reading, Calcot Mill, on part of the Kennet, a small branch-line of the Thames, not far from Pangbourne where he had seen the Japanese lanterns that inspired *Carnation, Lily, Lily, Rose* three years before. He now had the option of real family life, rather than the counterfeit version he had attached himself to in Broadway. It was his final opportunity: FitzWilliam was dying.

Calcot was a scaled-down Broadway, quieter, simpler, with fewer people, animated under a thin veil of anxiety. All letters mentioned the varying and hopeless state of FitzWilliam's health. Calcot Mill (now called Calcot Mill House), a medium-sized, beautifully proportioned, brick house, was more conventional than Russell House, but surveyed dramatic scenery. The garden dropped to a rushing stream, fresh from turning the wheels of the mill, flanked and shaded by willows, giving way to open fields on the far side. John and Denis Bunker struggled to maintain a routine that threatened, at any moment, to dissolve into sickroom attendance, painting on the bank by day, tennis in the late afternoon, Wagner recital and poker (using beans for chips) in the evening. They enlisted Violet, aged nineteen, as their chief model: "The youngest Miss Sargent is awfully pretty," Bunker wrote to Mrs Gardner (25 June). " . . . What if I should fall in love with her? dreadful thought, but I'm sure to – I see it coming. . . ."[31] When the weather was bad they complained, and rushed up to London. Calcot, though picturesque, was an odd choice for convalescence with the steady noise of thundering water and a railway line nearby; its proximity to London was a stronger recommendation.

Dennis Miller Bunker (1861–90), who fitted into this modified Broadway system easily, got to know John well in Boston, where he himself had become one of Mrs Gardner's courtiers more out of desperation than any limitation of character. His life was too short for him to finish the battle that raged in his personality. He did not have enough time. His unsatisfactory studentship in New York (Art Students' League and the National Academy of Design) was followed by Paris (Académie Julien and *atelier* Gérôme) for too short a time for him ever to come to terms with his return. He changed the spelling of his name, depended on French for his conversation and hated Boston for replacing Paris. He managed to tolerate his job teaching painting and drawing, but longed to return to Europe. He had all and more of Abbey's famous charm and humour, plus a commanding yet unwieldy devotion to art which sparked a violent outburst at any interruption and at any of the hollow social life he thought he was forced to endure. He suffered from savage alterations of mood. Likewise his paintings were hindered by time. His portraits show his inability to soften the virulent academic tradition that had started with Chase and had continued with a strong trace of the Munich School highly favoured by the institutions in New York, and never sufficiently obliterated later by Paris. But once outside the studio, like John, he came alive. His landscapes told of his great ability. Bunker was a romantic figure, short, very handsome, lively, colourful, funny, while at the same time shadowed by unhappiness. People loved him, but few got the opportunity to know him. He and John were ideally suited as companions, but only briefly: Bunker died shortly after his marriage. Thirty years later John confessed that "he could remember no one whom he had held in greater affection".[32]

FitzWilliam's exit from life was as undramatic as the way he lived it. In the autumn he moved on to Bournemouth for the mildest winter Britain had to offer, fulfilling for the last time the chief requirement of his years of travelling. Watched over and nursed by Emily he awaited his own death with the same detachment and utter resignation that had attended the deaths of his infant children, holding on until the spring, and then, without any warning that he would not continue to convalesce throughout the summer, he died, on 27 April 1889, in Bournemouth, not far from where he had started on his long reluctant journeying. He was sixty-nine years old. In death FitzWilliam was no luckier than he had been in life; even his simple hopes were frustrated. He had come to England to be with his son, and when the end came John was in Paris. He was buried in Wimbourne Road Cemetery, Bournemouth, no closer to America than he had been for the past thirty-five years. And, though he was outlived by all of his brothers, one of his two sisters, his son, his daughters, and his wife, FitzWilliam left no will – a strange and perhaps perceptive omission.

X

"Sargent *fils* is working away at all sorts of things and making experiments without number . . .," Bunker wrote to Mrs Gardner (2 September 1888) from Calcot,¹ notifying her of what seemed to him unusual and startling; in truth it was neither of these, though a good distance from portraiture, and to Mrs Gardner, like most observers, the name Sargent did in fact mean portraiture. For the past ten years he had struggled and succeeded to be known as one, and was thereafter landed with that exclusive description. The genre pictures at the Salon and the Royal Academy were but curiosities along the way, throughout the increasing aggregate of portraits. His grand strategy had not quite operated according to *his* design. In the full expanse of his *œuvre* portraits counted for less than one-quarter of the whole. This error of accountancy, then as now, is understandable, however, because his life and work *appeared* to be swamped by the people he painted. It is fair to say they were a mighty assembly – their glamour, their rank, their money, their fame (all of which spawned the notion that they were representatives of a now-extinct species) have worked a high wall, cutting off the view, and such a construction was built on the superficial. His portraits stood as the best-known and best-liked portion of his work; and all the while he was adding to their number – at final count well over 600 – he was creating another, and much more impressive statistic: Sargent painted over 2500 other pictures. They are less manageable than the portraits because they defy neat classification, by their number, their range, their style. He executed most of these pictures for his own pleasure. They were for the most part private, rarely shown during his lifetime; and, while they were no secret, no one ever suspected the quantity during his lifetime or their importance, which was lost in his shyness. The portraits naturally won the public gaze more than this other branch of his work, and until the latter half of the 1880s there had been an untroubled partnership between the two. After that, however, his private work crept out from second place, momentarily displacing portraiture, threatened to overtake, and then retired to its former capacity. It was as if there had been a fundamental disturbance in the harmony of two voices, an unaccountable cacophony in the duet which had played on for a decade and a half. In truth, this brief revolt had been festering for as long.

The division in Sargent's work had a profounder reason than the need to earn a living; the gulf was the usual consequence of both the Ecole and Carolus' policy, which was either the result of faulty thinking or an inspired eccentricity. When the masters ordered students out into the country for the summer as an antidote to the months of close supervision cooped up in the studio, suddenly free to paint what they liked, the students discovered they were equipped with a most inadequate guide; their lessons had been insufficiently elastic to stretch to *plein air* work. The entire system of art instruction never once turned to peer out of the high dusty studio windows. The students had to look, and learn, for themselves; and Sargent, like his colleagues, had to correct the fundamental omission of his training. Unlike the others who knelt before the Brabazon school or the doctrines of Impressionism, Sargent started his self-tuition alone, resuming his old habits. He began with perspective (on his first trip to America in 1876), moved on to light (especially in north Africa, Venice and Nice), and finally took to colour (most strikingly in England). His essays carried him well away from academic limitations. By the end of the 1870s he had broken away: his two 1879 studies of the Luxembourg Gardens in twilight – promenading figures in rose half-light – was closer to the arch-heretic Whistler than to any of the directions laid down by Carolus or the traditions of the Salon. His style relaxed, his brushwork became more summary, and his palette more subtle.

But throughout this transition he was always drawn back to the studio. With his eye fixed on the Salon, he collected notes, added to his reference library ever mindful of studio polish. These essays were also referred to when he returned to portraiture; they were an assistant in his commercial development. They were easy partners in portraits like *Madame Pailleron* and *Ralph Curtis on the Beach at Scheveningen* (1880): in the first he crossed the barrier of convention by incorporating landscape; in the other, Curtis lies along the dividing line between the two large triangles of beach terrain, unhealthy parched grass on one side, uninviting sand on the other. The subject was painted merely as a feature of the landscape, trading Curtis for Rosina and Scheveningen for Capri. His subject had a geometric function; washed-up seaweed would have served just as well. Such a confident reordering of elements was a luxury granted to a portrait that had not been commissioned.

Throughout the late 1870s and early 1880s he kept faith with the Salon catechism which insisted that he produce well-developed résumés of his non-studio activities. He believed in the truth of the equation that had turned Brittany into a frieze of oyster-gatherers, north Africa into *Fumée d'ambre gris* and Spain into *El Jaleo*. This was a doctrine he interpreted in figure studies, not landscape, not still-life. But by 1883, after a series of landscapes done in Nice, his two visits to Holland, his two excursions in Venice, the solidity of the doctrine began to crumble. The accepted goal of Carolus, which had passed unchallenged on to Velazquez, began to get a bit shaky when it was handed on a third time, to Franz Hals. He risked his belief by deferring to too many pedagogues; and Venice finished it off altogether. He discarded the doctrine without becoming a heathen: his self-education had carried him away from the church. It was inevitable. His initial acceptance of his education had been too unquestioning, and the system had thrown him back on the truth of his old ways.

Venice unsettled him, forcing the first clean break with the academic influence which lay over most of his previous work. In the course of his numerous studies, he first lost sight of a Salon résumé, then abandoned that hope altogether. His notes turned into finished work; he was content to preserve souvenirs: spectral panorama in *Venice par temps gris*, austere interior in *Venetian Bead Stringers*, documents of street life in *Water Carriers, A Street in Venice, Venetian Street Scene*, and humble episodes in *Sulphur Match* and *Italian Girl with a Fan*. The entries in his travel diary now had titles. Still, he was unable to discard these explorations when he returned to Paris and the studio for commissioned portraits. The partnership could not be dissolved, though the business arrangement did enter into a new phase. His reading of the Boit sisters drew heavily, if not entirely, on his Venetian locution, as did his portrait of Madame Paul Escudier (1882). Madame Escudier stands by two tall windows, illuminating her from the side and from behind; she is framed by a sharp angle of light and the dark shadow of the room – a radical conception for a portrait and yet nothing more than a notification of the same organization of elements in his *Venetian Bead Stringers*.

Shortly after his second tour of Venice the partnership between commissions and Salon advertisement gave louder evidence of disharmony. Slowly, his *plein air* work ceased to be even a minor apprentice to portraiture, and assumed an independence completely disconnected from any studio involvement – it became a holiday from the tribulations of portraiture. Sometime in the mid-to-late 1880s he again painted one of Madame Gautreau's neighbours in Brittany, Judith Gautier, who was famous first as the daughter of the novelist and playwright, then as literary figure in her own right, and finally as Wagner's lover. In one of her three portraits, Sargent showed her at the beach, standing above some hastily sketched steps, one hand planted on her wide-brimmed hat, the other restraining her billowing robe: the picture was entitled *A Gust of Wind*. It was handled in a rudimentary manner, in basic, strong colour, unencumbered by detail – a starker version of Ralph Curtis years before. It was painted quickly, giving one of the first clues of the style he later adopted and developed in England, and a sharp volte-face on almost every feature that distinguished the portrait which had once brought him to Paremé. The partnership was at an end, leaving the studio free to accommodate patrons' whims unhindered. The "solemn fiasco" of Madame Gautreau had done much to facilitate the break. Portraiture's assistant had gone off, in the direction of "all sorts of things and . . . experiments without number . . .".

This outburst began in England and lasted until the autumn of 1889.

From the moment he started to carry his canvases across the gardens at Farnham House and Russell House, there was a distinct change of key and alteration of tempo – and neither was performed with the benefit of any secure pitch or any clear awareness of the themes he wanted to develop. He was in a strange frame of mind – a hollow state governed by the vagaries of reaction and the unwelcome awareness that he did not know quite what to do. It was the first (and, as it turned out, the only) period of his life undercut by the unmanageable sensation that he had lost his way, which indeed he had. It was a circumstance saddened by the fact that not only had ten years' work come to a blank but also he had never known anything else: his activities and emotions had never wavered from that single purpose – his work. Everything seemed wrong. He was thrown off balance. The gravity of his situation was incalculable, and a little absurd, because it was so much outside the usual sphere of human problems. He seized on Broadway as a fresh start. The pleasures of communal life helped him to disregard the scarcity of commissions and his natural temptation to flee south. And such contentment threw into relief the error of having compartmentalized his career, and helped him to see that he had been striding not in the open broad avenue he had tried to chart, but down a cul-de-sac. He found himself at a turning-point in his career.

Still, his uncharacteristic confession to Gosse, spoken in dramatic syllables of doubt and frustration, exposed the poison that had long been in his system, having only gained toxicity after the sour response to Madame Gautreau. The suspicion that he had neglected subject-pictures for portraiture could no longer be brushed aside. He had made a grave mistake to disregard his own grand strategy. And with somewhat withered confidence he started to look for a restorative that might enable him to regroup his forces, nourish his ambition and set him back on course. The success of *Carnation, Lily, Lily, Rose* quickly followed by his triumph to America gave him the courage to lock himself in a laboratory for three consecutive summers in order to find the formulae which would secure the tentatively regained partnership. He had to find the means to keep the balance between livelihood and stimulation, portraiture and *plein air* work.

He shut the once-useful and well-thumbed texts of Carolus, Velazquez and Hals, and opened another, entitled Claude Monet. This would have been a bewildering and almost unaccountable shift of allegiance were it not in keeping with an established trend – his perpetual vulnerability to the power of guidebooks. Art historians gleefully rub their hands together when they address themselves to this apparently motiveless break from all the values of his known art universe – the *atelier* system, the Ecole, the Academy, and fifteen years' previous work – and they present complicated theories which lead to the tiresome conclusion that Sargent had an abrupt revelation. They say he finally, years later than some of his contemporaries, succumbed to the truth of Impressionism. The proof, all a little strained, is paraded with an accompanying sigh of wonder that he had stayed away so long.

There are sufficient biographical cross-references to put Sargent in the way of temptation since his enrolment in Boulevard Mont Parnasse: Carolus had painted Monet in 1867, inscribed "Carolus Duran à son ami Monet"; Sargent was in Paris at the height of the Impressionists' revolution; he met Monet at the second Impressionist exhibition at Durand-Ruel in 1876 – " 'Est-ce vraiment vous, vous Claude Monet?' " he timorously enquired,[2] and that evening, with Helleu, they dined at the café du Helder – and Sargent also knew Theodore Robinson, Monet's fervent American champion. Thereafter the evidence becomes somewhat more helpful to the task of binding them together. He painted Monet in strict (and bad) portraits and also at work at the edge of a wood. He went to Giverny, the first documented time in May 1887, again the following year or the next (or both),[3] and in 1891; thereafter the evidence of Giverny visits disappears. He joined Monet's bid to buy *Olympia* for the Louvre; he bought four of Monet's paintings (between 1887 and 1891); and his admiration was boundless. One of the two pictures he bought in 1887 was *Rocher à Tréport*: "It is only with great difficulty that I am able to tear myself away from your delightful painting. . . . I have remained there before it for whole hours at a time in a state of voluptuous stupefaction, or enchantment . . ."[4] (In September 1891, Robinson went to Giverny with Beckwith, whose appreciation had hitherto been a little more restrained; but "Sargent's enthusiasm perhaps has made me more keen", he wrote in his diary (4 September 1891), ". . . I was more than ever impressed by his work".[5]) Earlier that same year Monet gave his address care of Sargent at Tite Street when he exhibited two paintings at the New English Art Club. Then the references untellingly taper off: a decade later Sargent introduced him to the new Leicester Gallery; in 1917, Sargent mentioned to a friend: "I had a very sad letter from Monet the other day – but his eyes must be much better for he is working hard at some enormous decoration [lilies] . . ."[6] And the day after Sargent's death Monet wrote to Helleu: "Nous perdons un vieil ami. C'est bien triste . . ."[7]

These facts which dot a span of fifty years are meant to bolster the much more telling visual evidence. The brief swell was said to begin with *Carnation, Lily, Lily, Rose*, painted contrary to Impressionist techniques, and end four years later, thus affording Sargent safe membership of the club. When Monet was pressed to give his own views on Sargent's eligibility, his response was unequivocal: "Il n'était pas un Impressioniste . . . il était trop sous l'influence de Carolus Duran."[8] Such words have never quieted the meaningless speculation. The simple fact that Sargent started looking around for the means to revive the old partnership to save him during the tedium of portraiture and took the fourth in his string of teachers to guide his research is too bland and uninteresting a truth for those devoted to categories.

Though the investigations really began early in the 1880s with some of his Nice landscapes, the uninterrupted flurry started in the summer of 1887, when he left Broadway for Henley, to visit Alfred Parsons and the Robert Harrisons. His fellow-guest at the Harrisons' was George (later Sir George) Henschel, who recalled:

> He had built himself a little floating studio on a punt on the river, where it was a delight to see him, a splendid specimen of manly physique, clad – it was an exceptionally hot and dry summer, I remember – in a white flannel shirt and trousers, with a silk scarf round his waist, and a small straw hat with a coloured ribbon on his large [*sic*] head, sketching away all day, and once in a while skilfully manipulating the punt to some other coign of vantage.[9]

Sargent might safely be accused of conscientiously aping both the floating studio Monet used on the Seine at Argenteuil the previous decade and producing a string of water pictures highly reminiscent of his guide's – figures asleep in punts, willows, river episodes – had he not also been reacting to the land-locked atmosphere of Broadway (*Reapers Resting in a Wheatfield*, *The Old Chair*, *Home Fields*). Sargent loved the river; it embodied that peculiar combination of elements, neatly summarized for him as "curious", that was endlessly magnetic – sharp contrasts of light, absorbed on land and reflected off water, together with the interesting scale of strange perspective. His keenness for water explained his choice of Calcot Mill the following summer as FitzWilliam's convalescent home, and there the reminders of Monet become more potent: *A Morning Walk* (Violet framed by river and parasol) was a stronger echo of *The Promenade* than Judith Gautier had been. He seemed to stride deeper into that territory called influence, adjusting it, however, for his own purposes rather than a latter-day version of Louvre copywork. He set out on the trail not just of light, but of exploring the power of strong contrast. In the summer of 1889 he contrived the same setting as Henley and Calcot, at Fladbury Rectory, Pershore, some nine miles from Broadway.

There he created his own Russell House in the vast old Rectory which stood next to the village church, on a steep bank above the Avon, towering over water marshes and willows. His mother and sisters had installed themselves there about a month after FitzWilliam's death, and the household was forcedly shaken from mourning when John arrived fresh from Paris, where he had had six paintings in the American Section of the Exposition Universelle and had been decorated Chevalier of the Légion d'Honneur. From the end of July the large house swarmed with guests, many of whom had been at Calcot, this time reappearing not in their nursing-sister uniforms but in mourning. Miss Flora Priestley was back. She was a figure as romantically made as Bunker, but infinitely more austere, whose history neatly paralleled Sargent's: born in Florence (20 January 1859), childhood in Nice, art education in Paris (at the Académie Julien) where she probably met her host. She travelled the expatriate circuit, living mostly in Florence (where she died in 1941) among Americans and her fellow-Britons. When her widowed mother married Canon Charles Childers, the Chaplain of the English Church in Nice, she became the stepsister of Erskine Childers's father and for many years she came to live near her Childers relations in London, also making her a neighbour of Emily. Like Sargent, Flora Priestley was shy, but where his shyness was broken by ferocious energy hers hardened into frightening reserve, counterfeited as distant aloofness. During her frequent visits to England she and Sargent were seen together often, a simple detail of association that reopened the flood-gates of matrimonial gossip. And if his companionship with Louise Burckhardt had been little more than a fantasy constructed on hope (which it is fair to say was his own), then his long acquaintance with Flora Priestley was everyone else's hope constructed on a fantasy: another elaborate speculation that made no advance. In truth, they looked a wonderfully matched couple. She was tall, magnificent-looking with a rare, exotic appearance – large, sultry eyes, spaciously placed dark brows, straight nose, full mouth, all loosely placed among sharp-planed cheeks and generous forehead – that was well served by her posture and her individual style of dress. She adopted unusual stances, though wholly natural to her, with her hands on her waist, her shoulders pitched back, her head high. She wore simple, carefully tailored costumes, swept over with shawls and scarves; her love of hats concealed her abundant dark hair. She was striking, with an indefinable quality all her own which was a subtle combination of haughtiness, strange unconventional beauty, originality and unself-consciousness. And she was attractively modest about her considerable intellect. At Calcot, Vernon Lee, not surprisingly, rushed to take the part of her suitor left vacant by Sargent, and she was not successful. Flora Priestley was perfectly suited, however, for the more chaste capacity of model: she was one of Sargent's much-adored types, belonging to the same genus as Rosina, gypsies, Madame Gautreau. She was painted with Violet under the willows at Calcot, and asleep in a punt; at Fladbury, again with Violet, indoors, as well as several portraits. After her first visit to the Sargents she became a friend, and as such she was awarded rare tokens of affection granted to intimates of much longer standing; by 1901, Sargent addressed his letters to her "My dear Flora".

Helleu and his wife (Alice Louis-Guérin) were back, coming over from Paris; Vernon Lee also came to Fladbury, arriving with her new protégée Clementina (who favoured the less feminine name Kit) Anstruther-Thomson; Ben del Castillo paid an unexciting visit; Alfred Parsons showed up; one of the Miss Playfairs was invited; and Abbey travelled over from Broadway for about a week at the end of September. Though there was not much room for grief, it was difficult to conjure the light-hearted spirits of previous summers. Thanks to Vernon Lee and her aesthetic-hunting companion the atmosphere was occasionally hauled up to prickly high-mindedness, before plunging back into gloom, thanks to the more than usual dependence on the weather for entertainment.

When it did not rain, some of the reservoir of guests/models were pressed into service out on the river, and the exercises of Henley and Calcot were put into operation: Violet in *Fishing, Two Girls in a Punt, Paul Helleu Sketching with his Wife* and *A Boating Party*. Sargent's Fladbury style was difficult to describe, vaguely reminiscent of Monet at times and yet tailored to fit him, and him alone. His editing process, like the one that made his piano-playing unique and impressive, suddenly assumed a sort of power and refinement. He did not load his brush with several colours to achieve, as he had the previous summer, the notion of a rose petal unifying pink and white; he isolated colour, delineating with each stroke to build to the effect he was after. The marsh grasses that engulfed Helleu, his wife and their red canoe on the bank are an inventory of shades, each blade a prismatic distinction on the scale from rose mahogany (at the edge of the river) to fading blue-green (where they are seated). He used this analysis only for the grasses, however, not for the figures. He adopted a more consistent method for *Two Girls with Parasols at Fladbury* and *A Boating Party*. His editing process took a step forward when he moved nearer his master's example. In his two studies for *Fishing* he tried his hand at a diagnosis of light, worrying more about reproducing the unmodulated colour of refracted light from the water than about the standing figure of Violet. His reference-book was wide open, and he never finished either picture.

When the weather forced him indoors he glanced back at portraiture. He borrowed Helleu's charcoals for a few quick portrait sketches, and then picked up more familiar materials and styles. He drew Vernon Lee looking stung by some fresh penetrating thought. He painted her companion in the same vein, as a strapping lass out stalking some elusive theory (exhibited, appropriately, as *Arbor Vitae* at the Royal Academy) and again with much less fascination, having dealt more attentively with the brick wall behind her. And he painted Violet and Flora Priestley.

He left the laboratory to do his portraits; they had none of the tousled fever of the work down by the river. He strode over carpet worn comfortable with habit and known results. When he left Fladbury briefly in August to start a commissioned portrait of Elsie Palmer, the daughter of American friends of Henry James and Alma Strettell (as well as her sister Mrs Carr), at Ightham Mote, Kent, he unpacked the same caution he had carried to America. He adapted the ten-year-old style and pose he first used for the Pailleron children. He took no chances. His "experiments" had yielded the desired results; the partnership was safely back on course – he had regained his command.

He had worked his way back to confidence, and it had been a strenuous effort. From Broadway to Fladbury he pushed himself with his customary near-inhuman obsession for painting. He stretched his vocabulary to manage a hitherto unknown sensation. He did not relax until he could claim mastery: "John thinks of nothing else," Abbey wrote from Fladbury

(22 September 1889), "and is always trying and trying and working at something. . . . He is absolutely sincere and earnest."[10]

Throughout this period of transition he also manipulated, which he handled with admirable dexterity, the growing tide of his reputation. In England he was more skilful, and deliberate, than he had been in France, because he had to establish himself quickly; he did not have the luxury of time. He also had the benefit of knowing where he had gone wrong before. His tactic was much the same, only faster, and that made the vital difference; while he was steadily advertising himself at the Royal Academy, he also identified himself in the tearaway groups that sneered at that official institution. He traded the Society of American Painters and his fleeting association with the Société des Vingts (Les XX) in Brussels (having contributed to the first exhibition in 1884, beside Whistler, Rodin and William Merritt Chase, among others) for the New English Art Club. In 1886 he was one of the fifty founding artists, though he did disagree with the name, having pushed for the more accurate title "The Society of Anglo-French Painters". The New English Art Club had been formed with the sole intention, like the Grosvenor Gallery and its replacement, the New Gallery, to shake English art into the modern age – in other words, recognize the undeniable and spirited lead of the French. At the first exhibition he showed his Broadway work (a portrait of Mrs Barnard and an unidentified picture, unhelpfully entitled *A Study*), at the next, portraits (the "open box of jewels" of the Stevensons and Mrs Wade), and two years later, in 1889, Calcot work (*St Martin's Summer* and *A Morning Walk*). He engineered a place in the opposing worlds, and he was identified, briefly, with both.

In a quarter of the time it had taken him in Paris, he was able to keep the critics enthralled and potential patrons enticed.

Fladbury was also a culmination, marking the most elaborate and ultimate stage in his period of reaction. Thereafter his indulgence ceased, and a different sort of music was heard, louder and far beyond his powers of mastery. In the spring of 1890 he turned to a new challenge, a far greater experiment which totally defeated any of his texts. His Monet volume was valueless when he accepted the commission to decorate the Boston Public Library. And this task, too, was another unfortunate consequence of Carolus and the Ecole's blundering. The masters had encouraged the impossible notion that a painter's real mission was not satisfied by canvases alone: he must cover walls and ceilings: abstract nouns such as "duty", "permanence", "truth" floated high around the *ateliers* inspiring the credulous and eager students to aim at some universal communication other than still-lifes, landscapes or portraits. The masters pointed to Giotto, Da Vinci, Michelangelo and others in the well-filled pantheon of Byzantine and Renaissance decorators who spent their lives perched on scaffolding. Then the masters sighed in wilted stupefaction, for these men had conquered the highest form of art. Sargent's efforts at Carolus' elbow on the Luxembourg ceiling had done nothing to inform him that he might be unsuited for the task. When he accepted the murals, he took a disastrous turning, in the idiotic belief that he was embarking on the creation of his *magnum opus*. He was listening to his teacher and ignoring his judgement; he gave way before instruction yet again. These murals swamped his powers of imagination, drained his energy, monopolized a third of his life, and never repaid this huge investment. But decoration did supply him with a new master, who took over after the Fladbury *cadenza*. While he was mismanaging his Boston work, he was content (up to a point) doing portraits, settling down to more or less predictable responses to commissions that delighted patrons for twenty-five years, and he would also turn to his other, non-portrait work with an air of calming recess. His watercolours and oils of Venice, the Alps, the Dolomites, the Rockies and other holiday sights became his version of playing patience. The great Boston commission set his other work free.

The mistake of the murals was the mistake of Sargent's personality. The drama of his life unfolded in his painting, and nowhere else, obliging it to carry a heavy burden. His emotional energy was dispersed within it, and nothing escaped from that single reservoir. He refused to recognize his strength, which was his variety of ambition, and he struggled to over-reach his talents; he was like a compass unwilling to acknowledge the magnetic north. The murals forced him to overstep the very essence of his art, and he knew it. He once explained that he could only paint objects, revealing a dismissive attitude towards his sitters: "I do not judge," he amplified, "I only chronicle."[11] Sargent could interpret what the eye saw, do elegant translations re-enforced by omission (his editing process). He was disinclined to peer below the surface because he was a born observer, and could never be anything else. The unforeseen advantages of his mother's *Baedeker* education had glossed over the truth that he had been schooled as a perpetual spectator in every aspect of his life – a perfect qualification for a portraitist and an impregnable barrier. His eye and his brush were sufficiently tuned to articulate a florid recital of appearances (which critics and patrons manoeuvred round to find some other and more interesting belief). But his account of what he saw was remarkable in terms of utter simplicity. To him this was not enough. The Boston commission opened the door to a contradictory ambition.

From start to finish his library murals were a sore miscalculation of his ability and grave omission of taste. He chose as his subject the history of religion. He drew on a fund of images and symbols. He worked on a grand scale, decorating a large part of the ceiling, walls and lunettes in a space with an overall measurement in excess of 50,000 cubic feet. Besides narrative painting, he branched out into sculpture, bas-relief and archi-tecture to enhance his conception. And before this intimidating project was complete he accepted another, for the Boston Museum of Fine Arts, and a third in 1922 (for the Widener Memorial Library at Harvard). For nearly thirty years, while he tried to master the terrifying complexities of this unknown territory, Boston cheered and praised him with ever louder salvoes. Sixty years later, however, the accolades have stopped. His library embellishments are in a sorry state: the skylights needed to supply the chief source of light have been covered over, his light fittings have been altered, bad cleaning has removed most of the original lustre, and the reliefs have lost their purpose. Today readers rarely pause to gaze up into the gloomy recesses; the murals are ignored, and his name still means portraiture.

BOOK THREE

Voilà le Van Dyke de l'époque!

Auguste Rodin, 1902

I have vowed a vow not to do any more portraits at all . . . it is to me positive bliss to think I shall soon be a free man.

Sargent to Mrs Curtis, 13 June 1907

Ask me to paint your shutters, your doors, or your walls . . . but do not ask me to paint the human form. . . .

Sargent to Helen, Dowager Countess of Radnor, 13 September 1907

XI

The doubt was over. Events crowded it out, for after FitzWilliam's death the family geometry changed: Mary, as widow, filled the centre while her children jostled to rearrange themselves in relation to her alone. Her son's otherwise narrow routine acknowledged his responsibility for her (aged sixty-two), Emily (aged thirty-two) and Violet (aged twenty). He replaced FitzWilliam. His job was to look after them, and any reluctance he might have harboured about portraiture was utterly impractical and financially naive; he embarked on a new phase in his career with an overriding sense of cold practicality.

Emily hardly budged at all. She merely took an imperceptible step over to her mother's side, charged with the profession for which she had been trained – nurse, general custodian and companion: the same imprisonment she had known since the earliest days of her father's illness, denied any diversion whatsoever, even the opportunity to spend an afternoon modelling for her brother. She did not figure in any of his Calcot or Fladbury studies. She was not at liberty to look for other jobs, and never would be. The domestic incarceration her mother dreaded was assigned to her. Her life, which had scarcely begun, was over.

Violet, however, was free. Her character had developed in open territory, uncluttered by parental worry or fears, since her birth. They had been content simply that she had survived, unlike the brother and sister who preceded her; and her untroubled youth saved her, because both FitzWilliam and Mary were worn out, their anxiety spent. Her spirit was refreshingly buoyant, unlike her sister's which had sunk under the heavy weight of years of illness and physical deformity, and whereas Emily reached adulthood without ever having known optimism Violet knew nothing else. The two sisters were opposites. Violet was not tall, and was generously made, with glowing auburn hair. She had a kindly face with unclouded features set within a soft, warm complexion. Her mouth might have been a little sharply drawn; her eyes might have been somewhat undemonstrative, and her cheeks a trifle too abundant, but the overall impression was attractive. And her personality followed suit. People liked her from the moment they met her. They did not have to wade in the complexities that had sharpened to reduce Emily, nor did they have to find some way through the shyness that distanced her brother. Violet combined the best features not readily apparent in both of them: she had a strong but unsubtle intelligence, and a powerful sensitivity. To these she added lively spontaneity, quick humour, and a capacity for intimacy. Her education had been the usual Sargent variety, but with a crucial difference of having been less forcefully applied. She was of course fluent in languages, highly literate, musical and winningly open-minded, and with the same affection for modesty that had documented her brother and sister's training; unlike them, she had not confined herself to the pleasures of the mind. Violet was more rounded, less eccentrically adapted to life.

Sargent grew fond of her at Calcot. The fourteen years between them seemed to disappear. She was a different sort of sister, and his relations with her were more easygoing than with Emily. He regarded her first as a friend, then as a brother. His fraternal emotions for her were a little less hindered by the obstacle of duty which stood between him and Emily. Violet had not been broken and she did not depend on him – two facts which tended to confuse the real nature of his love for Emily. Violet was a rewarding companion during the brief interval between their father's death and her marriage, and Violet made that interval *very brief*. After one glance at her sister's fate, she was determined to have a different future, to escape into the normal world of marriage where her emotions could spread beyond fear of illness and weary obligation. Her willingness to be courted alarmed Mary, who instructed her son to take corrective action the instant real danger loomed on the horizon. When he took Violet to America in 1889 for her first visit, he was in fact doing more than repeating family tradition; for the first time he was satisfying the unwritten, unstated responsibility he had assumed as head of the family, and from that moment on the amity they both had felt for each other was somewhat strained. Years later Violet confessed to feeling a little frightened of her brother.

They sailed to New York on 4 December, and Violet went on to Boston, a guest of the Fairchilds. In the simplest reading, in the crudest possible terms, Violet was sent to America to find a better sort of husband than she had chosen in Europe (or, failing that, to help her affection wither), while her brother went more simply – to make money. They had to face the future aggressively; they were unable to find any value in postponement.

Mary naturally was jolted most by FitzWilliam's death. At first she was able to pass the duty of superintending domestic order from her husband to her son with admirable ease. The years of habit had become a reflex. She had a real gift for delegating work, and her son, in turn, found that he had to delegate as well: faced with the problems of launching an eligible sister in the matrimonial stakes, in a country largely unknown to them both, he handed her over into the care of those better versed in the etiquette of getting to the altar. Then Mary discovered that she was alone. She had lost her accomplice in the fantastic arrangement that had passed unquestioned since 1854. She and FitzWilliam had got into a way of thinking which was a convolution linked to his pride, her selfishness and a fatally inept form of accountancy. After FitzWilliam's death Mary was denied the comfort of respecting her husband's wishes to conceal the faulty logic that allowed for capital expenditure on travel (health was the justification) but none for establishing a home (too expensive was the excuse). Now that she was alone the elaborate excuses ceased, and she tried to carry on in precisely the same manner. But the battle was over; the need to lie was at an end. Sadly, she, too, had to face the future, and the consequences of her actions. She had to accept her responsibility to Emily, her loneliness and the fact that her life was gravely disrupted: no home, no friends, no relatives, only her children – the inevitable conclusion of her dislocated life abroad. The pressure on her children was considerable, and the greatest pressure of course was on her son, for he had not had Emily's elaborate coaching in filial duty. But when Mary looked to him she was also looking on a different mode of existence. She had to consider him as the axis of her future pattern of life. She was dependent on him and, as such, much that was novel to her. Her adjustment to this new reality was made easier by his conscientiousness, and his fortunate ability to earn money in excess of her and her daughters' needs. The impediment of FitzWilliam's pride was gone and there was enough money to travel *and* settle down. Her son had gone back to portraiture to fund his devotion and generosity, to keep his family. America was the most readily assured source.

Broadway regrouped in downtown New York that winter near the National Academy of Design on 23rd Street. Abbey arrived about a fortnight after Sargent and his sister, in order to make himself available for the round of parties organized to celebrate his wedding on 22 April 1890. (Sargent was to be an usher). His studio was at the corner of 16th Street and Fifth Avenue. The Millets were some ten blocks away, on 23rd Street, close to the studio Beckwith found for Sargent, belonging to Dora Wheeler Keith, the young painter who had visited Russell House in 1887, at the top of the building at 115 East 23rd Street. Sargent returned to the Clarendon Hotel at Fourth Avenue and 20th Street, where he lived, and he was on call for commissions, for the next eleven months before the monumental intrusion of his Boston commission. By day he worked, more or less, keeping somewhat liberal office hours, especially by New York standards: "By morning I mean," he wrote a few years later, "10 o/c to 12 o/c, for by that time, being a Frenchman, I collapse and must lunch."[1] The afternoons were no more strenuous. And still the sitters flocked to him; they comprised an expanded replay of his first working visit – socialites, millionaires, and a number of actors (Booth, Barrett, Joseph Jefferson). The list was more of the same.

And by evening there were many diversions, all musical: Gilbert and Sullivan, and of course Wagner, first *The Ring* and later, in March, a highly doubtful, unauthorized performance of *Parsifal* in Brooklyn. But the most extravagant, and repetitive, diversion of all was the spectacle of

La Carmencita, the Spanish dancer, who was turning her European success into cash in New York. She danced with wild ferocity and sang with a gitana's gravelly huskiness that sent shudders of delight through her audience. Her skin had the pallor of chalk, her hair and eyes panther-black. She was an exotic novelty, precisely Sargent's type, which meant he had to paint her. La Carmencita was to prove another version of Madame Gautreau in his life, appealing and exasperating, exciting and annoying and, worst of all, expensive. She had a peasant's canny taste for money, and she neither performed nor posed for free. Ladies, mesmerized by her dancing, flung jewels at her feet, and she kept them. In truth, La Carmencita was at heart a very simple woman. Her dancing made her thrilling and famous, and in old age she bade farewell to her tempestuous youth, settling down to fat contentment, taking her pleasures knitting by the stove, at home.

Sargent and the Beckwiths went to see her at "that villainous place Kosta & Brink [Koster & Bial]", as Beckwith wrote in his diary of the music-hall on 14th Street where she performed,[2] "and heard an awful performance closed by Carmencita!!!! Such a Spanish dance I have never seen before. . . ."[3] Ten days later he arranged for her to come to his studio. Sargent engaged her for Chase's 10th Street studio – "a capital big place", he wrote to Mrs Gardner whom he wanted to lure from Boston.[4] Chase invited La Carmencita again, and Sargent had her come to 23rd Street. Dora Wheeler Keith was one of the few invited guests, and her account of the scene some forty years later spoke of its unforgettable intensity. Sargent had animated his *El Jaleo*.

A dozen kerosene-lamps were placed on the floor, with shades tilted to produce footlights. La Carmencita's accompanists, two guitarists (at Beckwith's she had had a guitarist and mandolinist), sat against the far wall, quietly strumming. The rest of the studio was black, the spectators sat on a sofa at the opposite end of the room. Suddenly, "this thing leapt out of the darkness" wrapped in a tiger-skin and started her dance, stalking from side to side, in and out of the light, gaining momentum, speed, abandon, flickering as she went. Then she stopped, crouched down, growled some notes of the music, "and all the while this rhythm was going on. It was the most wild and primitive thing I have ever seen . . . and the most artistic. Afterwards she passed out of the light and he [Sargent] put up the lights in the studio and the men vanished into a corner. . . . It might have happened in Peru in the time of the Incas."[5]

For such a show, which began around midnight, she charged $120 (and later upped it to $150). La Carmencita was vain yet unaware of her talents. Sargent had to coax her to sing because she indignantly claimed she was a dancer and singing was low. She adored make-up, though unsuitable, and when she arrived at Chase's studio covered in powder and face-paint, with hair frizzled out, Sargent took a flannel to her face and a damp brush to her hair before he would allow her to perform. She was furious.[6]

She was no better as a model, though she was painted many times. Chase and Harper Pennington showed her in full flight, arms out, head thrown back, poised for the next step, flowers at her feet; Sargent, however, saw her defiant, static and vain, a latter-day *Lola de Valence* by Manet (1862). And he had considerable difficulty achieving the static. She was petulant and insolent, impossible to control. He cajoled her to be still. He begged, he pleaded, and was forced to treat her like an infant. He painted his nose red to amuse her. When that ceased to calm her he ate his cigar to earn another few moments' peace. Then he bribed her with jewellery and money.

Though she had been more testing than Madame Gautreau, the picture was much more favourably received. When he invited Mrs Gardner to his studio to see the portrait he called it "the figure I am doing of the bewildering superb creature".[7] She wore a full, heavily encrusted gold dress, her hands poised on her hips, a shawl thrown round her shoulders comforting her neck. She was bathed in theatrical light, the embroidery emerging from the darkness shined, flashed; there was no mistaking, like his Ellen Terry the year before, she was on show, performing. His brushwork was insolent, brave and very confident. The critics on both sides of the Atlantic loved it. In New York he was offered the equivalent of £600 for it and refused: " 'I was unable to accept it as it had cost me more than that to paint,' " he later explained, adding, " 'Why, in bracelets and things' ". The picture was eventually bought for the Luxembourg, and he shrugged with regret, saying, " 'After all, it is little more than a sketch.' "*[8]

In April 1890 a more potent diversion in the shape of the Boston Public Library decorations was mooted by Stanford White (1853–1906), a remarkable man who lived life with considerable flair and died amid great drama, and his achievements have outlived the scandal of his murder (by Harry Thaw). He was a composite of several of Sargent's friends, and the most helpful: he had the loquacity and spriteliness of Abbey, the acquisitiveness of Mrs Gardner, and the generosity of spirit and deed Henry James wasted so many syllables over. He was part genie, let out of a bottle, capable of wondrous feats, and he was part dry-goods merchant,

---

* Years later, in London, she again performed for Sargent and his friends in the Tite Street studio. Somehow, the electricity of her performance was gone, and for all the dramatic show she had become only Sargent's picture – "she was industriously Spanish in the Parisian and American manner", W. Graham Robertson wrote in his autobiography (*Time Was* (1931), pp. 244–6), "she looked beautiful and tawdry, but she was not a great dancer – it was a little disappointing". But when she sang, after a good deal of persuasion, "her beauty changed, the tawdriness fell away, she became ageless . . .". She sang with a lilting, haunting beauty, that she herself despised – folk songs were for peasants, common, and not for the great La Carmencita! Yet this was the side of La Carmencita Sargent preferred. (Sally Fairchild reported that Sargent paid for the jewels she had kept.)

purveyor of all sorts of objects imported from abroad, anything from a canvas by Velazquez to a Roman bath. There has never been anyone quite like Stanford White.

He was the third member of the architectural firm McKim, Mead & White of 57 Broadway – a partnership that transformed the history of American buildings by parodying and adapting Continental styles. Their idea of modern architecture looked backwards in time and over the Atlantic, and White with good reason was the most European-minded of the three. Though the Whites had been in America as long as the Sargents, recent generations displayed some unease over this fact. White's father, Richard Grant White, detested New York, stayed there his entire life, but managed to convince himself he was in England, eventually earning that strange award the English think a compliment: "not our idea of a Yankee", the *Spectator* wrote of him.[9] Richard Grant White had too many talents to be content. He trained in medicine, qualified as a lawyer, was an accomplished musician, critic and brilliant Shakespeare scholar. White grew up in a household that frowned on the cultural backwardness of America and favoured the superiority of all things foreign, for the most part because they were not American. White went one better than his father, however, by bringing Europe to America, in wholesale quantities. And his firm's buildings were haunted by the ghosts of Venice, Rome, Athens and Paris. White began his career by wanting to be a painter, but practicality intruded (as it had for his father) and he chose a more economically secure profession, becoming apprenticed to the great architect H. H. Richardson in 1872 (about the time plans were being drawn up for the Trinity Church, Copley Square, in Boston), whose fortress-inspired edifices darkened the horizon and paid homage to the excellence of the Romanesque, and where he stayed until the late 1870s. A turning-point in White's history came in 1878 when he followed his friend Augustus Saint-Gaudens (who had helped John LaFarge to decorate Trinity Church) abroad, for a year, and Paris had the same intoxicating and lingering effect on him as on the rest of his generation who sought improvement away from home. There he moved in the same American expatriate circle as Sargent. He toured the Continent, sketched feverishly, studied buildings, and longed to stay; but the following year he returned to New York, joined forces with Charles McKim (1847–1909), whom he had met in Richardson's office, and William Rutherford Mead (1846–1928), McKim's partner since 1872. The combination of personalities was perfectly ordered. The Franco-Italian influence was strong; Mead studied in Florence, McKim trained briefly at the Ecole des Beaux-Arts (but his sympathies were "nearer to Rome than Paris", one critic wrote in 1924),[10] and White continued to adhere to his father's prejudices.

Most important, White's temperament insisted on collaboration. His first success was planning the pedestal for Saint-Gaudens's statue of Farragut, in the 1870s. He was never at his best working alone. His enthusiasm ran away with him, and he was shamelessly lax about details. He was an inspired designer who needed to be controlled. Apprentices in the office nicknamed him Benvenuto Cellini. Mead was a strict and cautious engineer, while McKim – nicknamed Bramante – was studiously precise with an inflexible nature, who "Consciously sought beauty [as] . . . the main object . . . rather than the unconscious beauty which often . . . follows a perfect plan perfectly worked out"; and without White's "bias for the picturesque", as Mead quietly phrased wild enthusiasm,[11] their buildings would have been sound echoes of that unrivalled master architect Richardson's teachings. After White's second European tour, on his honeymoon in 1884, the firm's loyalties shifted from Richardson to White's (and McKim's) affection for the Italian Rennaissance – a change that altered the fortunes of the partnership and the direction of American architecture. By the early years of the twentieth century McKim, Mead & White were responsible for churches, banks, memorials, libraries, universities, clubs, railway cars, pleasure gardens (Madison Square Gardens), tombs, renovating the White House, railway stations and an enormous number of houses, which were White's preference, "because he was, after all", his biographer wrote, "more interested in people than aesthetics . . .".[12] And he was equally, if not more, interested in what went into houses, which was where Sargent came in; the people who wanted houses by Stanford White followed his recommendation of Sargent for their portraits. White's clients commissioned Sargent; it was a neat arrangement, satisfying everyone.

Sargent and White had much in common. Both were considered modern, with the security of explicit reference to classical models. Both were unfailingly lucky in their timing: much to their advantage, they collided with that social phenomenon created by sudden (in the space of less than one generation) wealth which enabled very clever men unversed in the habits of leisure to turn away from mills, railways or mines, to devote themselves to a new profession, that of patron, collector, and with any luck that of a gentleman. These men turned to Europe, just as Sargent's colleagues in Paris had twenty years before. But this was the starkest version of the change. On a slightly less dramatic level, American finance had not only recovered after the Civil War, but had enjoyed robust health, producing sufficient money to permit men of the order of White's father to put their unhappiness with America into action by insulating themselves. They built houses, developed civic pride, and bought the surroundings they wanted. Money affected the change in temperament (as much as any generality can be explained) and money produced careers like Sargent's and White's, both of whom found themselves, by the 1890s, like servants in a big house, overseen by a mistress ignorant of domestic science. Only by exercising considerable tact were they able to inform their employers of what was wanted and needed. It was a grand moment for artists, craftsmen, builders – who had patience, and European training. The riches of America had to go through the filter of abroad, it seemed, to be wanted at home. White and Sargent were looked upon as the most presentable agents of this exchange.

The Library project began in a blaze of controversy. The Trustees had seen fit to bypass the usual procedure of competitions and open tender for the commission, handing the contract straight to McKim, Mead & White – the only eligible firm, they thought. The contract was signed 30 March 1887, and the local newspapers rose up in high indignation at this insult to civic pride. Boston firms had never even been considered. Exactly one year later the plans were submitted and approved.[13] The great Library in Copley Square was going to be a very eccentric performance and have nothing in common with its neighbours, especially Trinity Church opposite. More outrage. Today, however, the Boston Public Library is generally considered to be one of the finest examples of McKim, Mead & White's dedication to "conscious eclecticism" (and it is certainly one of their largest creations, dwarfed of course by the Pennsylvania Railway Station in New York, finished twenty years later). It was largely the work of McKim, who conducted a private tour of France and Italy. The Sainte-Geneviève Library in Paris was the façade; the Palazzo delle Cancelleria in Rome was the interior courtyard; samples of the Venetian Renaissance were on view in the Book Delivery Room and the large reading-room, and for light relief he threw in mementoes of Venice and Pompeii in two lobbies: the building evolved into a vast exploration through countries and time. His materials were also carefully chosen souvenirs – ivory grey marble from France, yellow marbles from Siena and Verona, black serpentine marble from Belgium, green serpentine marble from the Alps. Then he suddenly had a fit of patriotism; he finally acknowledged America by quarrying up some native stones: Iowa and Amherst, Ohio, sandstone, Indiana limestone and Tennessee marble.

He was, however, strikingly patriotic, up to a point, when his thoughts turned to decoration.* Here, at least, American artists (mostly trained in Europe) would shine. There was a great deal of talk, all very weak on various details, especially money. Saint-Gaudens was asked for two groups of statuary to flank the main entrance, models were made, approved, then the money was withdrawn, and two years later reinstated. The Trustees were justifiably growing nervous about money because the original estimate for the building had multiplied by four. The architects, in turn, were unable to promise adequate remuneration for the decorations to be carried out: "There isn't an awful lot of money in this – there never is in these things," Abbey wrote to his brother in May 1890.[14] Another problem was who to ask, and here Saint-Gaudens redirected

---

* Other artists represented in the Library are:
  Beta L. Pratt: *Science* before main entrance
  Augustus Saint-Gaudens: head of Minerva
  Daniel Chester French: double bronze doors (3 pairs)
  Louis Saint-Gaudens: lions
  Puris de Chavannes: 8 panels depicting important branches of literature

166

White, who was acting through his partner, McKim, to approach American artists. Saint-Gaudens sounded out Abbey's fiancée during one of the sittings for her medallion portrait wedding present, she assured him of Abbey's keenness, and McKim was immediately informed. Sargent was a less daring choice: he was too famous, especially in Boston, to ignore. Thereafter White handed him over to McKim. McKim had the precise, straightforward, conscientious sort of mind which had been built to withstand the years of haggling over measurements, alterations, adaptations that lay in front of him, and as Sargent's interest developed the questions increased. It was the collaboration of two energetic perfectionists.

The preliminary discussions moved quickly. Abbey wanted to sail home to England sometime around the middle of May. On 7 May, Sargent, Abbey, Saint-Gaudens and the architects dined in New York at the Players' Club (Booth's old house redesigned by White shortly before and hung with Sargent's portrait of Booth finished in February). After dinner the plans were unrolled and photographs laid out – "several hundreds of carbon prints from the Masters, covering the whole period of the Renaissance," McKim wrote to the President of the Trustees, Samuel Appleton Browne Abbott (9 May 1890) – and Abbey took off like a rocket, grabbing wrapping-paper to make sketches of the Shakespeare room designs. Sargent was a little more restrained, showing "interest in the direction of Spanish literature [which] was a most natural one", McKim concluded.[15] They planned to meet the Trustees within a week. Sargent was reluctant to attend, but on Wednesday, the fourteenth, they travelled to Boston (with Mrs Abbey) in a private railway car, went to a baseball game in the afternoon, walked around the library site, and dined with the Trustees. The rooms were handed out: Sargent was given the north end of the Special Libraries Hall on the top floor and Abbey the frieze (180 feet long by 8 feet high) in the Book Delivery Room on the floor below. But nothing was signed.

Both Sargent and Abbey were confident. Abbey and his wife sailed back to England in a haze of plans. He could think of nothing else but the Library, nor, as he reported, could Sargent, who remained in New York: "I wonder how John is getting on," Abbey wrote to McKim from the ship [c. end of May 1890];

and whether you have built him a model yet. I went into his studio a day or two before I sailed and saw stacks of sketches of nude people – saints, I dare say, most of them, although from my cursory observations of them they seemed a bit earthy. You will surely get a great thing from him. He can do *anything*, and don't know himself what he can do. He is latent with all manner of possibilities, and the Boston people need not be afraid that he will be eccentric or impressionistic, or anything that is not perfectly serious and non-experimental when it comes to work of this kind.[16]

It was a strange reassurance. The "Boston people" had more to worry about with the appointment of Abbey than with Sargent, but as it was they were doing nothing at all. No contract arrived, and Sargent assumed the proposal had been withdrawn.

Until the Trustees' confirmation materialized, Sargent ignored the murals and accepted commissions, dutifully enduring the summer weather only because Violet wanted to stay on in America; and while she sat to Saint-Gaudens in Windsor, Vermont (in exchange for her brother's portraits of Saint-Gaudens's wife and son), went yachting with the Fairchilds, and showed every sign that "there seems nothing to confirm the war-cry 'I won't be an old-maid' ", as he wrote to Flora Priestley (1 July),[17] he went to Narragansett, Cohassat, Manchester-on-Sea, Worcester and Nahant (for more Fairchilds) doing portraits along the way.* After Dennis Bunker's wedding, on 2 October, Sargent gave up his plans to meet his mother and Emily in Gibraltar, and booked a passage back to Liverpool, sailing on 5 November. A few days before he sailed, the long-awaited letter from the Trustees finally reached him: "I was informed by the Trustees that I might proceed with the work," he wrote to Curtis when he reached Tite Street (18 November) [1890], after nearly one year's absence, "and could not find out what had occurred to settle the matter. Did she [Mrs Gardner] intervene?"[18] (He had a much longer wait for the contract, which he signed two years later, on 18 January 1893. He was given until the end of December 1897 to complete the work and would be paid $15,000. As it turned out, these stipulations were meaningless; the original commission was extended, more money was found, by private subscription, and the deadline postponed.) His initial enthusiasm returned and he revived his previous itinerary. "The Boston thing will be (entre nous)", he added to Curtis, "Mediaeval Spanish & religious, and in my most belly achey mood – with gold, gore, and phosforescent Hellens. What a surprise [?] to the community. . . . I must go to Spain as soon as possible, and will spend all next Spring there. At first I gave up the idea of Egypt but I feel very much inclined to go there first simply to see and not to work and try not to be more than 2 or three months about it and take Sofia [in] on the way to Spain."[19] Two months later he, his mother and his sisters were steaming up the Nile, "cramming hard for my library", he explained to Charles Fairchild (1 February) [1891].[20] He was following the

---

* Bunker calculated that Sargent had "done a hundred portraits" during the summer of 1890, as he wrote to Mrs Gardner, who was in Venice (n.d., late summer 1890: Isabella Stewart Gardner Museum). For a more realistic, but no less impressive, account of part of that summer, see Susan E. Strickler, "John Singer Sargent and Worcester", *Worcester Art Museum Journal* (1981–2), pp. 19–39.

Three months after his marriage Dennis Bunker died, on 28 December 1890. News reached Sargent in Egypt, who wrote to Fairchild (1 February): "Bunker's death was a great shock to me and is an awfully sad thing all round. I am anxious to know how his wife will stand it and whether she will have a baby or not" (Boston Athenaeum).

example of Abbey, who also travelled to Italy, to do research. Portraits would cease to make any significant intrusion before 1894. Until then, the murals weighed heavily upon him and tempered almost every aspect of his life. From the very moment he began his "simply to see and not to work" style of research, his plans for the murals expanded; the more he saw, the more he needed to include, and the temptation to sightsee never waned: it proved a process exactly contradictory to everything he had ever done.

The Sargents started on their tourist circuit in Alexandria towards the end of the year, moving on to Cairo, and some weeks later embarked for Upper Egypt: Luxor, Thebes, Assouan, Philae. In March they were back in Cairo and, while his mother and Emily rested, Sargent returned to the studio he had taken in January, and finished one of his rare female nudes, of an Egyptian girl: "I have lately more or less finished one study of the girl," he wrote to Curtis (19 March), "beastly in colour but at least more or less right in form. And now I am off with a tent for a week or so in the country, the Fayoum probably."[21] By any reckoning all three of them were enterprising travellers, and Sargent himself was indefatigable. He had to endure untold discomforts in order to see the Bedouins at El Fayoum: the indignity of trying to ride, long hours in the saddle, the heat, dreadful food, and the hardships of sleeping in a tent. But nothing could dampen his curiosity or outmatch his energy. And more of the same followed. In Greece, where they went sometime around the end of March or early April, his mother and sisters stayed quietly in Athens, while he and a dragoman went to Olympia and Delphi. "Every morning he was in the saddle at 4 a.m.," Charteris reported, "only ending the day's journey when night again fell. . . . Long before his return to Athens he had filled every available corner of canvas and paper he had taken for oil and water-colour."[22] Then they went to Turkey; from Broussa (or Brussa, or Bursa, a small town famous for its two Persian-styled mosques) he wrote to Mrs Gardner [?14 April]:

> The consequence of going up the Nile is, as might have been foreseen, that I must do an Old Testament thing for the Boston Library, besides the other one [Spanish], & I saw things in Egypt that I hope will come in [to] play. While I was out here it seemed best to see Greece and Turkey, so I gave up Spain for another year. . . . In a couple of weeks I will be in Paris.[23]

They were back in Europe by the early summer of 1891, resigned to witness Violet's victory: she was to marry Francis Ormond after all, in Paris on 17 August. She had survived the great obstacle of eighteen months' separation, planted between her and her fiancé by her mother and her brother, and she would have no more of their meddling or interference. Her brother had been strangely enthusiastic about her other matrimonial prospects throughout their American tour, and her mother and Emily had subjected themselves to many months of difficult travel in order to keep her with them and away from Ormond. Violet's unconventional haste to get to the altar informed her mother that for once she was outclassed in the contest of wills. Her family was silent in defeat, keeping their displeasure dark, but they relented with quiet grace.

Louis Francis Ormond (1866–1948), from Switzerland, was scarcely their ideal candidate for Violet's husband; even his parents were in despair about him. He was a wiry, demonic little man, with a certain unusual attractiveness and great athletic strength, much given to violent flashes of charm and temper. He had never quite reconciled himself to the basic injustices of life, and his chief form of expression was to run away: he ran away to Canada when he was seventeen, only to be dragged back by Pinkerton detectives; later he ran away from his duty as the eldest son to run the family business, Ormond Cigars, leaving that job to his brother; after his marriage, he ran away from his children; and in the early 1920s he ran away from his wife, to lead a carefree existence in the South Seas (well documented in photographs). In between these dramatic flights, he was constantly on the move, which meant at least he and Violet spoke the same language most of the time. She, too, found it difficult to abandon that souvenir of her childhood. They settled for a while in Majorca; then Barcelona, where Violet gave birth to their first child (Marguerite, born in June 1892); then London, where they kept a house in Cheyne Walk; then Tunis, where they kept another house; and throughout this chronic transit they made free use of his mother's house in San Remo.

Ormond's mother, it must be said, was just the sort of woman who inspired a vocabulary of fleeing. She suffered from such an advanced form of stubbornness it could only be considered remarkable. After her husband's death, she kept a very tight grasp on business affairs, and she narrowly missed disaster. When cigars were going out of fashion, threatening the profits of Ormond Cigars, she absolutely refused to consider moving on to cigarettes, because she thought they were vulgar. (In keeping with this same sort of strong-mindedness, her grandson, Jean Louis Ormond, himself once the head of the firm, only smokes a pipe.) Madame Ormond did, however, have one agreeable quality, which took the useful form of building houses. She had five of them, and each very impressive. When she looked at her heir, her iron will was powerless. Both she and her husband could not shake off grave pessimism when they tried to predict his future. Unlike the Sargents, the Ormonds jumped at the prospect of his marriage to Violet; they sighed with a deep relief that had taken twenty-five years to materialize. Such comfort, however, was temporary.

The Sargents reckoned they had less to gain. They approached the event with half-hearted delight, behind an appearance belying their feelings. They took a sumptuous apartment on the second floor of 4 rue de Presbourg, opposite the Arc de Triomphe. Ormond was put on show to a few of their visiting friends, whose reactions varied considerably. Beckwith could not find one modifying syllable when he came to record the meeting in his diary at the end of June. Vernon Lee, ever vulnerable to any conventional reading of romance, wallowed in the emotional intensity of the event. She rushed to the rue de Presbourg scarcely twenty-four hours after arriving in town: "The fiancé M. Francis Ormond was there," she wrote to her mother (2 July), "– good looking, quite French. Much in love . . . evidently a lovematch all the same." A day later she moved into the Sargents' apartment, affording her a closer look at her goddaughter's source of bliss, which made her weak at the knees. Violet's "young man is really a delightful creature", she again wrote to her mother (4 July). "He has travelled & suffered hardships in various parts of the world, been a workman & cook in the far West, and wandered without water in the Algerian Sahara. Yet quite young and modest."[24] Vernon Lee turned him into the stuff of novels.

The wedding took place with the minimum of fanfare. Once over, Mary, whose energy had been sufficient to go up and down the Nile, across Greece and across Turkey, fell ill with exhaustion – "by all this wedding business", Sargent wrote to a friend [August 1891].[25] She spent the remainder of the summer safe in the Alps, with Emily and her son.

Once Violet had excused herself from the short-lived arrangement which had formed after FitzWilliam's death, Mary and Emily moved closer together, with eyes more urgently fixed on FitzWilliam's replacement, and all three of them operated in a new and more compact geometry. Mary's dependence on her son increased; Emily's dependence on her brother increased, obliging Sargent to slide more deeply into his father's place. But Sargent found himself unable to be as compliant as his father had been, and he gently encouraged his mother to face some basic truths. Despite her insistence that she was constitutionally sound enough to keep to her policy of perpetual motion, she would not be able to do so indefinitely. Emily could not be expected to keep to her post year in and year out. His work often took him to America, which meant he could neither follow after her nor be of much help. If she wanted to be near him, she would have to change the habits of a lifetime. These forceful considerations must have been most unwelcome, especially on the heels of Violet's desertion. By September she relented, compromising just enough to reverse a conviction she had held fast for forty years: she agreed to a fixed address. She and Emily would live at 10 Carlyle Mansions, a large, rambling flat, high up in a solid Victorian block, overlooking the Thames in Cheyne Walk, about a fifteen minutes' walk, at a very leisurely pace, from Tite Street. But no sooner had Sargent signed the lease than she was off, promptly dragging Emily behind her to Nice and Rome for the winter, Siena and Florence for much of the early spring, and then on to Barcelona to await the birth of her first grandchild. Her son was not put off by this energetic display of independence; the following year he signed a second lease, for the adjoining flat, number 9, a mirror-image of the first, and arranged for the party wall to be demolished. Like her son, who had spent months avoiding Tite Street after he had taken possession, Mary adopted a very casual attitude about implementing her compromise. She and Emily took years to move in. Vernon Lee wrote to her mother (19 July 1893) in utter amazement: "They have actually taken a top [sic] flat on Chelsea Embankment close to John's"[26] – as if two years after the fact it were a newsworthy communication.

These family shufflings, additions, rearrangements were but a minor respite from the Boston murals which hung ponderously over the landscape. There were endless consultations with McKim, all tremendously detailed thanks to the basic complication that Sargent was working in England, while in Boston the builders were making adjustments to the surface and division of the walls and ceiling. There also seemed to be an alarming distance between what McKim had suggested in their meetings – in Paris and England – and what was actually being done: "In the plan you have sent," he wrote to McKim [?December 1891], "I notice that the same moulding goes all round the room, as is duty bound, but could you not make me the concession of making it flatter as it crosses my picture? . . . The feet of my would-be colossal people above in the lunette would be hidden & there is no room to place them higher in the canvas . . . to my mind it is the *principal request* I have to make." He asked for the precise measurements of the spaces he was to decorate – "as I cannot trust to the little model", he later wrote to McKim (28 January 1892). There was a lot of talk about architectural devices, like plinths, mouldings, imposts, wainscots, and "entablature or architrave or whatever you call the stone over the door".[27]

McKim and Abbott were puppies with a new toy, capering with eager delight, exhausting themselves with pleasure; but their distraction was incomplete: they were tempted away by luscious scents. After satisfying themselves that both Sargent and Abbey were in place in June 1892, they returned to Europe six months later, in order to ensnare Whistler into their games. Sargent was pushed forward as their ambassador. "Today Abbey & I have been confabulating with McKim & Abbott," Sargent wrote to Whistler (n.d.) [December 1892],*

> . . . on the subject of the necessity of pressing you into the work if you will be coerced. They are very anxious indeed to bring it about; and

---

* A biographer's nightmare. The meeting has been dated to the summer of 1891, and even McKim's memory was hazy about the exact date, because he lumped together, quite naturally, his recruitment of Puris de Chavannes (summer 1891) and Whistler. Sargent's own surviving correspondence with Whistler is scarcely more helpful: on 13 December (n.y.) he wrote to Whistler introducing McKim, "If you are willing to hear more of the Boston Library, give audience to my friend Charles McKim, the architect thereof . . ." (Glasgow University Library). And the next letter, dated "Wednesday" is quoted above. McKim and Abbott sailed to Europe on 30 November 1892. And Sargent arranged to meet Mrs Gardner in Paris (n.d.) and see the Vermeer she bought on 5 December. He dined with her and Mr Gardner at the Whistlers' the night before the Library meeting.

during the past year they have wrought upon the minds of the people from whom the money must come and are very hopeful of getting a sum.* They feel that the room for you to do is the very holy of holies.

If you have not taken the idea en grippe I feel sure that something might result from a meeting with these two excellent fellows, so I propose that we dine together at Foyots on Saturday. . . . I am running over to Paris for a day or two only, and mainly for this . . .[28]

Whistler agreed. The dinner was arranged for Monday, and Sargent warned McKim: " 'Now,' " he said, " 'one of three things will happen. . . . Either Whistler will be as silent as the grave, or he will be outrageously vituperative, or he will be the most charming dinner companion you have ever met.' "[29] He was the last, and they dined again the following night at the same restaurant. Like Abbey, he, too, was carried away; there was juicy fragrance of money about, and he naturally succumbed. He enthusiastically sketched on the tablecloth; and that, as it turned out, was the sum total of Whistler's contribution to the Library. His commission was later withdrawn, the casualty of inadequate funds, and McKim's inability to persuade benefactors to contribute. (In 1893, when it was rumoured that Whistler's infamous Peacock Room might be for sale, Mrs Gardner preposterously suggested transporting the room to Boston, to use in various portions throughout Bates Hall; Sargent again put on the chains of office and assured Whistler that he would try to keep the room intact, for the Directors' or Librarian's Room. The Whistler space was then offered to John LaFarge, who never replied, and the large panel remained bare.)

Before Abbey returned to England with his wife, he assumed he would continue to work in Broadway, where he had been happy for the past four years, and where in fact he had met his wife, in May 1888 when she was the Millets' guest at Russell House. But once back in Broadway two years later his wife had other ideas. (Mary) Gertrude Mead Abbey had grown accustomed to opposition, and to winning. She was the only daughter in a large family of sons, and from a very early age she showed considerable aptitude for sport and scholarship. She graduated from Vassar, studied in Leipzig and Paris, and taught at the Roxbury Latin School for boys – "the only woman in the school . . . [and] 'to prove that she could earn her own living' ".[30] She was fiercely intelligent, insistent on excellence, and slightly given to frosty superiority in her manner. She held strict views about life which she, alas, did not keep to herself; when she and her husband did not take up residence in Broadway she was seen as the villainess who removed the much-loved Abbey from those who had loved him longer.

---

* The actual commissions, in the shape of contracts, were postponed on account of money until 1893. Puvis de Chavannes, unlike Sargent and Abbey, was unwilling to begin work until he had some guarantee, some two years after he was first approached.

But, if her manner was unfortunate, her motives were utterly sincere. She was devoted to her husband, admired his work without qualification, and this admiration took the happy form of encouragement. When she returned to Russell House as Mrs Abbey her loyalties were much strained, as can be imagined, and she harboured a more convenient than real belief that her husband and his work were not sufficiently respected, because she had no affection for communal life and misread the relaxed atmosphere to be some moral and intellectual laxity, knowing the danger it presented to her husband, who was easily distracted. And there was the clearer obstacle to peace: no house could have two mistresses and Mrs Abbey was not designed for partnership. She and Ned went to live in a small village about forty miles south of Broadway, in Fairford, Gloucestershire, making their own highly refined and wonderfully comfortable version of Russell House. They went there to save their marriage as much as to safeguard the murals, and Sargent followed.

The Abbeys were enchanted by Morgan Hall the moment they saw it. The place had a romantic charm (which naturally fascinated James, who more prudently did not, this time, advertise the fact) capable of reconciling the architectural discord created by the uneasy combination of Elizabethan and Georgian styles: two houses joined together, but only the purist could find any objection. The house was set in a large park with one broad open meadow perfectly suited for cricket. There was a selection of walled gardens, outlying fields, and dells wonderfully hospitable to botany. For the Abbeys Morgan Hall was ideal: large, quiet, picturesque, historic – the house was once owned by a Cromwellian (so the story goes) named Morgan, who saved the beautiful stained-glass windows in the parish church, ascribed at one time to Dürer, by removing the heads of the figures – in a generous surrounding, and close to London. They signed a twenty-one-year lease in January 1891, and set about making good the years of neglect;* the builders moved in, and the Abbeys went off to Italy, for the first session of mural prep. Abbey also ordered a studio to be built at the far end of one of the walled gardens. It was not an attractive building, made of corrugated iron sheets, and not in the least in keeping with Abbey's refined tastes, but he was in a hurry. The studio, like the very purpose for moving to Morgan Hall, was streamlined for work. (After her husband's death, Mrs Abbey dismantled the hideous studio, and the site was turned back into a kitchen garden.) What the place lacked in beauty it possessed in size: 64 feet long, 40 feet wide, 25 feet high: "où une toile de deux metres a l'air d'un timbre poste", Sargent wrote to Helleu [1891].[31] ["Where a canvas two metres square looks like a

---

* A habit Morgan Hall does not seem to have lost. After her husband's death, Mrs Abbey moved out, and thereafter the house went steadily downhill. The many decades of neglect were closer to vandalism. The present owners, among them Mr Barry Fenby, are single-handedly and with immense care and expense restoring the house to its previous/Abbey glory.

postage stamp."] This studio lured Sargent. So did the opportunity to work with Abbey, away from the distractions of London, in a place reserved and designed exclusively for the murals. It was an altogether perfect and necessary arrangement, for the murals brought strange and vexing problems which were not as easily mastered as the technical ones. The shift to narrative painting was not easy. Sargent had not had Abbey's training; he had never sat at an illustrator's easel; the years spent schooling his eye were suddenly unhelpful. He moved with caution, and the work inched forward at a snail's pace. "It is getting on very slowly as it need must," he wrote to Mrs Fairchild (6 March) [1892], " – and requires more brain work than is good for a would be impressionist."

Fairford was a considerable asset. Morgan Hall took the place held first by Russell House then by Fladbury, and while he struggled with his decorations became his auxilliary home. "We make a very good household," he added to Mrs Fairchild. Mrs Abbey and her mother Mrs Mead (who had come from New York for a six-month visit but stayed three years) managed to turn the wheels of domestic efficiency quietly and gracefully, making both house and garden parts of a well-run establishment, attentive to detail, satisfying Abbey's forbiddingly high standards, and welcoming to a constant stream of visitors, who were always reminded, however, that any disruption to the industry in the ugly factory at the bottom of the garden was *not* welcome. "This winter has been a capital one for me down here," he informed Mrs Fairchild, ". . . there is nothing outside to take one from one's work. . . ."[32] Sargent became one of the family.

His daily routine at Fairford varied little from that of Broadway, working most of the day and taking exercise when the light faded. He was too energetic to warm to Abbey's obsession for cricket;* he preferred tennis and, unfortunately, riding. Sargent's skill as a horseman was appalling, matched only by his amazing stubbornness. "Me voilà alité aussi," he wrote to Helleu (n.d.) [winter of 1891–2], who was recovering from typhoid, "d'une entorse dans le dos attrapé en tombant de cheval, ce qui m'arrive deux fois par jour. Il faut absolument que j' apprenne cet exercice." ["Here I am in bed, too, with a strained back got falling off my horse, as I do twice a day. I absolutely must learn the art of this exercise."] And he never did. He rode at every opportunity, blithely disregarding his inability: "Je continue a me flanquer par terre surtout en sautant des fossés et des murs à la chasse au renard," he merrily informed Helleu (17 February) [1892], "ce qui est l'occupation la plus gaie que je connais."[33] ["I go on flying to the ground as I fly over the ditches and walls at fox hunting, as this is the most cheerful occupation I know."] The other

---

* One very distinguished American later shared Sargent's antipathy, and pronounced a memorable verdict on the pleasures of the sport: "Well, I think it is about as interesting as watching paint dry." (Courtesy of the Duke of Devonshire)

occupants of Morgan Hall were realistically uneasy; each time Sargent left the stables they feared the worst, and their worry only made him more adamant. One evening, however, his mood changed. After yet another contest with gravity, in which Sargent did more than usually badly, Abbey overheard him mumbling " 'Horrible! horrible! most horrible!' " and noticed he was carrying a squashed riding hat. When asked to explain, Sargent said: " 'Do you know, when I fell off today, my horse put his foot through my hat, which was on the ground. It has struck me how horrible it would have been if my head had been inside!' "[34] Years later he gave in to the obvious, relented, and took lessons at the Kensington Riding School. But he was never a good rider. He told William Rothenstein he felt and looked like a sack of potatoes in the saddle, which never dampened his enthusiasm. On Sunday mornings he aired his new-found proficiency in Richmond Park with friends (among them Henschel, and his Tite Street neighbour Jacomb-Hood, whom he had met in Paris while working on *El Jaleo*). And it must be added he was no better on a bicycle and just as stubborn. In the early 1880s Albert de Belleroche (then a student at *atelier* Duran) bravely and unsuccessfully tried to teach him to balance on two wheels, but many years later Sargent's persistence was rewarded: he managed to keep upright, but it was a victory for application not for skill, which he occasionally exercised for very long distances indeed.*

His dogged affection for riding went beyond the comedy he tried to make it. His desire was too large and his ability too small not to find himself the victim of frustration, and sometimes very deep frustration. The only pleasure he could have had was the pleasure of mind over matter, the triumph of brute determination, and this was not adequate compensation for the bruises and sprains he had to endure. As a horseman Sargent discovered a frightening streak in his character, which

---

* Albert de Belleroche (1864–1944), born of a Welsh father and Belgian mother, unhelpfully assumed his stepfather's name (Milbank) until the age of thirty; Sargent always called him "Baby Milbank". They met in 1882, while Belleroche was studying at *atelier* Duran and his mother and her husband were *en poste* in Paris, living in Avenue Montaigne. The instant he began his studies, Belleroche was keen to make Sargent's acquaintance – a family trait, for his son William was just as keen to know Brangwyn.

They were life-long, if not intimate, friends. He travelled with Sargent to Holland in 1883; Sargent asked to join him in Syria and Palestine in 1905; he was invited to Broadway (where he painted his own version of *My Dining Table*); and there were a string of Milbank/Belleroche portraits done in the early to middle 1880s: the portrait of Belleroche in Spanish attire hung in Sargent's Tite Street dining-room.

Belleroche was himself a competent, though somewhat derivative, painter. His style was much like Sargent's, yet as a draughtsman he was stronger. He was responsible for Sargent's six lithographs. His real place in history was made, however, when he discovered the technique by which false watermarks could be detected.

produced the most surprising scene in his life. Late one afternoon, towards the end of 1891, he unwittingly rode across a field of winter wheat. The farmer saw him, approached, and hurled abuse at him, saying he was no gentleman. Sargent's apologies and offer of compensation were of no use. The farmer was furious, working himself up into a towering rage. Sargent rode back to Morgan Hall, and for the next two days was too distressed and worried to do any work; he milled over the episode repeatedly, driving himself to distraction: incomprehension transformed into rage – an emotion of illegitimate birth, born not out of the specific slight delivered by the farmer, but out of the unresolved issues attached to the murals. His accuser had had the grave misfortune to tap a double frustration. Sargent returned to the farmer's house and challenged him: " 'Come outside and defend yourself, I am going to thrash you.' "[35] The farmer called for witnesses and the two men fought. Sargent calmed down, dismissed the unpleasantness and went back to work; his victim, however, went after revenge, by way of the law, and demanded £600 damages. Such a sum was laughable, and Sargent's solicitors recommended lodging a much smaller amount when the summons was issued. The tactic worked: "the accursed has gobbled the £50", Sargent wrote to James [28 February 1892], who had taken a more than lively interest in the episode,* ". . . which is more than he could reasonably claim so as to be able to punish him with the law if he persisted in trying to get such an unfair sum, and to give him this option of stopping the case . . . it is worth the money to be rid of the bugbear of listening to a lot of misrepresentations at the Gloucester assizes".[36]

While his work at Fairford, in scale at least, managed to eclipse much of the absurdity that had attended the illustrators' activity at Broadway, Sargent had in fact joined the same club, where membership was based on working for America from abroad. But his sense of timing was sadly absurd: from the moment he pledged himself to Boston, from the moment the murals commanded his thoughts, dominated his interest and ruled his itinerary, his popularity in England soared – as a portraitist. *La Carmencita*, after winning the place of honour in the Society of American Artists' exhibition New York, the prize in Chicago, went on to receive thunderous acclaim at the Royal Academy in 1891. "The picture kills everything [else] on the wall," one critic reported, "and surpasses for strength almost every modern picture I have ever seen." Sargent was

* And natu·ally informed various acquaintances who also took a lively interest, especially Henry Adams. He hung on every syllable of James's account, and passed it on adding his predicted conclusion that "our artist-genius in America would certainly get some months of gaol, and may get it even here, which much distresses Henry who has a sympathetic heart. This too was confided to me, and has not yet got into the newspapers. As Sargent [sic] seems not to distress himself, I see no reason why James should do so. . . ." (*Letters of Henry Adams* (1982), Vol. 3, pp. 604–5)

now a name on both sides of the Atlantic. People wanted his portraits, at the very moment he had decided to turn his back on that branch of his profession, at the very moment he neither wanted nor needed portraits. He dismissed *La Carmencita* as "une grande figure, malheureusement très pochade" ["a big picture unfortunately very hurried"], and would not be tempted away.[37] His mind and his work would not budge from Fairford, though he had little to show for such concentration. "Je travaille beau-coup et cela va lentement," he wrote to Helleu during the winter of 1891–2. "C'est tellement une affaire de réflection, de combinaison, de recherche – Jusquà ce que tout cela soit bien arrangé. L'execution ira plus vite probablement." ["I am working hard and yet it is going slowly. It is so much a matter of reflection, of combination, of study until everything has been settled. Execution will probably go faster."][38] His first preliminary mural sketches were dated 5 January 1892.

XII

Sargent continued to be explained best by geography, especially throughout the early 1890s, but such facts were unhelpful, like so many attached to him, and unrevealing. The first three years of the decade he confined himself mostly to Fairford: the murals dominated the landscape, darkened the sky, and obscured the view, so effectively that the few sightseers who caught a glimpse of him and his Boston work and might have recorded his progress (which he, as usual, failed to do, never having valued chronicle over action) were too overwhelmed to register anything more coherent than sheer amazement. "And Sargent," McKim wrote to Mrs Abbey after his visit to Morgan Hall in the summer of 1892, ". . . what an undertaking, and what an achievement. . . . I thought I knew something about struggling till I reached Fairford . . . a *revelation* to me."[1] By the middle of the decade, the first major section of the mural complete, he returned to London, which he had previously done only for brief holidays back to portraiture, and to America, to affix his murals, and restock his finances with "another season of portraits".[2] Thereafter the murals were forced to share the terrain with portraits, which seem to have amplified their claim during the long exile: a new and merciless partnership owned him.

By the spring of 1892 the studio at Morgan Hall was full to bursting: "sometimes one is rather at a loss where to put anything", Abbey complained to a friend (June 1892).[3] Sargent had the east side, opposite Abbey; the north was taken up by three large lights and the middle was congested with Abbey's usual abundance of stuffs, props, folios, books, costumes, and Sargent's own litter of drawings, sketches, plans, rolls of paper for cartoons and the preliminary investigations into modelling and casting reliefs. Work began around 9 a.m., went on until dark, and occasionally late into the night. The prevailing atmosphere grew thick with excitement: no other emotion had the agility to clamber over the looming obstacles of the job they had eagerly but ignorantly taken on. Abbey's decorative scheme depended on stamina. The subject of his frieze was *The Quest and Achievement of the Holy Grail* and, having decided that, his prime object was to cover the eight-foot-high panel that ran for 180 feet. He relied on the techniques he had assigned to smaller works, and with his glue-like attention to detail and accuracy (a great deal of which, he himself confessed, was lost once the frieze was in place) he did not have the energy or desire to pause and consider the suitability of allowing a large narrative painting to stand as decoration.

Sargent, however, granted himself no such luxuries as either a consistent approach or a reliance on energy alone to see him through. In his mind a subtle and profound drama unfolded as his work progressed, which would have impressed the Fairford tourists far more than the wondrous curiosity of seeing him at work had they been aware of its existence, and it was only noticeable once the work was complete nearly thirty years later, in 1919: within Sargent's mind a debate raged between form and content worthy of ancient Greece. *The Triumph of Religion* (as the decoration was later called in 1895) was a loud argument, at one moment form raising its voice, at another content, only to be silenced by form once again, and so it went on back and forth throughout the Hall, in loud disagreement, and it meant that Sargent finished the saga much unlike the way he began. (See Appendix II for a partial account of the whole decoration.) The complexities increased as he went on, and many examples of his concentrated efforts, like Abbey's, were lost when elevated into position. To him the mural was a huge intellectual exercise, so huge that he quite forgot its decorative purpose. The brain had won over the eye.[4]

Just how much of the whole decoration he worked out either on paper or in his mind when he began painting in 1892 remains unknown, like many of the technical procedures he followed, but it is obvious any original plan was subjected to an organic evolution and expansion. Sections of the Hall were handed over to him only after the money was found; neither the Trustees nor the architect ever gave him any assurances about enlarging the original contract. In 1893, Sargent did ask McKim for the side walls, but two years later he signed his second contract – for the south wall. Therefore, it might be unjust to appraise the full decoration when, in truth, it was nothing more than the sum of parts.

His paintings for the north end of the Hall were determined by the architectural divisions which turned the space into three panels: barrel vaulting on the ceiling, a wide band between the wainscot and the cornice, and a lunette in the centre (measuring 12 feet by 24 feet). This lunette, the focal point of the Hebraic portion of his great narrative, was complete towards the end of 1893. It was entitled, rather lengthily, *Children of Israel, Oppressed by Pagan Neighbours, Expressing Their Dependence on the True God*, and, as the title suggests, there was a lot going on. Sargent had much to communicate; content shouted down form. The Israelites are depicted as twelve nude figures clustered about the altar, adopting various postures of despair, beseeching Jehovah above, His face screened by Cherubim wings and smoke from the altar, His arms outstretched to stay their troubling attackers who tower above him, Pharaoh on the left, the King of Assyria on the right. The great half-circle was packed with supplementary symbols and made a crowd of activity. Sargent had allowed himself to forget the very lesson he needed to remember: Carolus' single instruction for narrative painting, academic set-pieces, was to defer to the expression of human emotions involved in any scene, but here the central figures were shoved into insignificance by their three imposing neighbours. The balance was wrong.

The next instalment suffered less from this flaw, because he was dealing entirely with material already transformed and enriched by centuries of painting; his job was made easy. Above the lunette, in the vaulting, he portrayed the *Pagan Religions of the Countries Surrounding Palestine*, and on the architectural rib separating the lunette and the ceiling he inscribed a lengthy quotation from Psalm 106, running to 110 words. The Egyptian goddess Neith, mother of the universe, spans the entire width of the vaulting, twenty-four feet. Her collar, in the centre of the arch is a great gold zodiac holding on one side a gem-like sun emitting rays and on the other side a coiled serpent (for which Sargent studied in the reptile house of the zoo at the beginning of 1894). Superimposed on Neith, on the right, is Astarte, the Phoenician goddess of sensuality. She is veiled, standing on the crescent moon, in front of the tree of life, giving shelter to six priestesses. Descending the left incline of the vaulting, just below the sun, is Baal or Moloch, "the destroyer":[5] "The Assyrian god with a vulture's head," Sargent explained to Sylvester Baxter in 1895, "is simply a protecting genius, as one sees them in Assyrian bas-reliefs. Don't say much about him! or about the corresponding padding in the Egyptian corner. Those corners had to be filled."[6] Isis, Osiris and Horus nestle below Moloch, above a mummy and the symbol of the winged sun.

Beckwith visited Morgan Hall and saw the ceiling progress. "I was much impressed by the originality of John's composition," he wrote in his diary (3 May 1893). "He depicted our friend Seti [an understandable confusion because Neith is much in evidence in the tomb of Sethi II, recently seen by the Beckwiths in Egypt] and a crowd of familiar Egyptian forms. He is now deep in making casts to apply to the surface which are to be gilded. I question its propriety and also the scheme for its present color."[7] Sargent's sojourn in the realm of the plastic arts enhanced the vehemence of the growing argument between form and content. His insistence, pointing to Byzantine antecedents, that reliefs would unify as well as increase dramatic tension, spoke more for his ambition than for his judgement. Neith's serpent, busy enough playing out the competition of the seasons with Thammuz (god of vegetation), became more prominent, so did the zodiac, the sun, and various symbolic devices in the lunette, but the application of reliefs did not rescue the overweighty literary content, the layers of meaning, by restoring an emphasis to a decorative function. And, though the gilt would darken in time, the overall effect was heterogeneous.

Like Carolus, Sargent was fascinated by sculpture, but apart from his work connected directly with the murals he did very few pieces, all small save one of a turkey. He was largely self-taught, though he could call on the help of friends like Rodin, Saint-Gaudens and Gustav Natorp

(1836–1908), the German sculptor, friend of Henry James and Rodin's first pupil, who populated the indistinct circle of Sargent's acquaintance in Paris in the early 1880s (and was painted by him c.1883–4). In 1898, Sargent appealed directly to Saint-Gaudens. But the only surviving reference of Sargent seeking professional help around this time was in May 1894 when he went to Paris to consult Frederick MacMonnies (1863–1937), the American sculptor who had studied with Saint-Gaudens – whose influence helped to award MacMonnies the commission for the tremendous fountain opposite Daniel Chester French's *The Republic* on the central lagoon at the Chicago World's Fair 1893.* McKim, Mead & White were the Fair's architects, and MacMonnies was later asked to contribute to the Boston Public Library. Other than this brief tuition, Sargent solved his problems by himself, and as his confidence grew the applied reliefs became bolder and more ornate.

The third section of the Hebraic portion below the lunette was turned into a frieze. *The Hebrew Prophets, Typifying the Progress of the Jews in Religious Thought, with Final Expectation of the Messiah* – with Moses, holding the tablets from Sinai in the middle, modelled in high relief. He is flanked by sixteen prophets, the four greatest closest to him, each named in Hebrew (as are the Commandments), all in appropriately dour biblical stances, holding up a lot of drapery. *The Frieze of the Prophets*, as it was soon called, became the most famous part of the murals. Unlike the two previous instalments, it is simple, direct and honoured the purpose of the commission. It was not a breathless performance but, rather, a heroic

---

* The scale of the World's Columbian Exhibition, better known as the World's Fair, made the Boston Public Library project look amateurish. Blashfield assessed it to be "the first big general experiment in American decoration, when twenty mural painters at least tried their 'prentice hands. Only a few years later nearly the same group of men [and women], but with others added to their numbers, decorated the Library of Congress in Washington. American mural painting was now fairly launched . . ." (*Mural Painting in America* (1914), p. ix). All the familiar names in American art were drawn in; Abbey was appointed Chairman of Special Commission in England, and the ranks of the Art Students' League flocked to Chicago, under a joint conductorship of Saint-Gaudens and McKim. Sargent submitted nine pictures to the American Section, and wrote to friends in America that he intended to make a fleeting visit in September.

Sargent's views of the proceedings were less enthusiastic than Blashfield's subsequent perspective. Two years later he told Frederick Law Olmstead's son (while painting his father at Biltmore) that he was amazed and astonished by the vast undertaking by the muralists "on such short notice and without previous experience or training", Olmsted wrote to Chester Aldrich (13 June 1895). "As he [Sargent] said, nothing but the pervading and contagious enthusiasm of all who were engaged on the work of the Fair could have carried these men through with any measure of success. Millet [director of the decorations of White City] asked him by cable to paint a 30×40 (tympanum) 'or that sort of thing' in two months. He replied he couldn't possibl[y] do it. He had been at work for two years on his Boston Library work and scarcely put brush to canvas yet". (Biltmore House Archives and Library of Congress)

rendition of what Sargent could see; he was back on familiar territory.

Models came down from London to bear the weight of voluminous blankets and throw their arms up to Heaven in the prophetic postures Sargent required. They were Italian. He first employed Angelo Colarossi, famous in Paris and London, a favourite of both Gérôme and Leighton, whom Abbey had used in 1889. When Sargent had finished with him, he turned around to face Abbey once more. He then employed the d'Inverno brothers, first Luigi who was utterly indispensable for the sculpture embellishments, then his nineteen-year-old brother Nicola who followed him to Fairford towards the end of 1892: "for a lark as anything else", he later wrote. Nicola d'Inverno stayed in Sargent's employ for over twenty years. He acted as a model for about a year, and then his duties expanded to include *valet de chambre*, studio assistant, courier, and all-round manservant, as well as occasionally reverting back to model.

Their long association has often been incorrectly treated to the high gloss of homosexual love, and it is true to say that Nicola's devotion to Sargent was absolute, stopping short, however, at *complete* discretion, though his short published reminiscences of Sargent, whom he called an "aristocrat and a gentleman to his fingertips", "a good man" and "the greatest man I have ever known . . . the most eminent man, and at the same time the kindliest", were written with true affection and without the slightest suggestion that he knew more about Sargent than he was willing to publish. He was too great a snob not to try to elevate himself by hinting at some privy knowledge of a famous person. He was born in a small village not far from Rome and soon thereafter his family settled in London. He was a simple man, probably not very clever, with a head easily turned by a title. He actually believed the ennobled, the rich and the powerful were a better class of mankind, and exposure to them, no matter how brief, did improve him. He had a marvellously lithe, athletic figure and a perfectly hideous face, which his affection for boxing did nothing to improve, with elfin ears in flight away from his scalp and narrow bulging eyes. Sargent paid his subscription to the Quentin Hogg Gymnasium in order that he might keep fit, which was where he acquired his taste for boxing. When he arrived at Tite Street in the morning from his home in Clerkenwell (where he lived with his mother) with "a beautiful black eye", he recalled, ". . . I was certain to be greeted by the master . . . with 'Ah! I see we have met another man who is slightly the better' "; and after seeing Nicola lay two men out in a tournament Sargent dubbed him the "Clerkenwell Chicken".[8] His love of the turf was less rewarding, and Sargent frequently met the debts without a murmur of rebuke or threat.

Nicola spent the best part of twenty-six years in Sargent's employ; in that time he made himself indispensable. At Tite Street (and Fulham Road) he was butler, footman and studio assistant, doing the mindless, time-consuming tasks: he took letters and telegrams to the post office, delivered pictures to framers and photographers; he carried trays of tea, answered the door and telephone, and made himself useful in the studio – one of his last functions in Washington was to model President Wilson's frock-coat. He attended to the laborious machinery of travel, hauling luggage and cumbersome painting materials across Europe and America. He became a extra pair of arms and legs. The break occurred at the end of April or early May 1918 after an inglorious episode at the Hotel Vendôme in Boston, when Nicola and the hotel bartender had a drunken brawl.* Sargent went to the manager, said he would be willing to discharge his man if the Vendôme would do the same. The manager agreed and, though Nicola was given his passage money home, he elected to remain in America where he enjoyed a fairly unsatisfactory career. The parting was sufficiently amicable for Sargent to keep the legacy he had made for Nicola a few weeks before in his will: £200. And tradition has it Sargent also paid one or two of Nicola's medical expenses during the following years.

Once the "brain work" of the murals was left behind for the physical work, he turned away from Fairford to face portraiture, and it was with an eagerness that overcomes an overfed diner offered a new menu after months of the same meal: he gazed with tentative greed. The murals had been an overrich diet, and in 1892 he naturally needed a change. By the middle of the decade, he was offered the run of London restaurants. Until then, however, his rare commissions were strung along a thin thread of recommendation. In 1892 he painted a New York acquaintance Helen Dunham (who was also a friend of Vernon Lee); a year later her friend Lady Agnew; and in 1894, at the instigation of Edmund Gosse, Coventry Patmore (who also appeared in the prophet frieze for Boston, as did other friends like Bunker and Captain George Roller, a Fairford neighbour and a keen amateur artist, later turned professional, who had given him a horse), and W. Graham Robertson, after the portraits of both Robertson's mother and his friend, the American actress Ada Rehan.

The return to portraiture was slow, less on account of the demands of the murals, but because the English were still weary of him. They were resistant, unforgetful of the cruel impression of Madame Gautreau and unconvinced that he might have fully mended his ways; *La Carmencita* had not revived his reputation *enough*. The public believed, as Graham Robertson reported someone saying, " 'It is positively dangerous to sit to Sargent. It's taking your face in your hands' "[9] – the English equivalent of

* Nicola's own version of the parting, published a year after Sargent's death, strayed a good distance from the truth, which was hardly surprising: "What separated us," he wrote for the *Boston Sunday Advertiser*, "finally, was his own America. Once I saw what life over here was like I got money fever and wanted – and needed – more than my place with Mr. Sargent was worth. He would not pay the price and we parted, with a little pain on both sides, but with no ill feeling on either." This excuse concealed a much more telling and potent reason for his reluctance to sail back to England; had he returned he would have made himself eligible for the war, or at least feared that he might.

Aldrich's advice to Booth in 1890, that he had better sandpaper his soul before the sittings. But by 1893 Sargent felt confident enough to resume advertising. Both *Mrs Hugh Hammersley* (New Gallery) and *Lady Agnew* (Royal Academy) gave spectators a new thought to replace the old, fear changed to attraction, and sitters found it difficult to hold back from him. His English prices increased by approximately $1000, to reach parity with his American charges, which presented no deterrent to commissions whatsoever. The name Sargent was no longer spoken of with an inflection of doubt.

Whereas he showed Mrs Hammersley* to be lively, poised on the edge of her chair, about to get up, ready to speak, he showed Lady Agnew to be the forthright beauty she was, calm and serene; both women were well dressed, fully at home, comfortable in a bergère, among silk and fine carpet – his studio props. One was an updated Lady Newton, the other Mrs Marquand, and both postures would be repeated frequently. But his style was softer, his lighting more sympathetic; he had given greater play to subtlety than to contrast. Both portraits were given generous critical notice, and the superlatives abounded. *The Times* confidently predicted Lady Agnew would earn him election as an Associate of the Royal Academy. Such acclaim had not been a deliberate intention.

The shift in his reputation as a portraitist in England also depended on something only partially governed by the soaring expressions of praise: his portrait of Lady Agnew had turned her into a "society celebrity"[10] as Vernon Lee informed her mother (16 July 1893) after seeing the picture and hearing so much about it in London. It was another way of saying

---

* After repainting her head sixteen times – "He held that it was as impossible for a painter to try to repaint a head where the under-structure was wrong, as for a sculptor to remodel the features of a head that has not been understood in the mass," Julie Heyneman remembered from his lessons, adding her belief "that no tinkering can ever rectify an initial failure." (Charteris, pp. 184 and 137)

How and exactly when Sargent met Mrs Hammersley (née Mary Grant, c.1863–1902), the wife of a banker, remains unknown. His long correspondence with her, sold at Sotheby's in London in 1969, a sequence of sixty-four letters and cards, cannot be traced. She had a keen eye for modern art, numbered many of Sargent's close circle among her acquaintance, and was a spirited hostess at her house in Hampstead.

Sargent started his portrait in 1892, when he came up to town to see the Royal Academy exhibition. Work did not go well, provoking unhappy memories of Boulevard Berthier: "I have begun the routine of portrait painting with anxious relatives hanging on my brush," he wrote to Abbey [?May 1892]. "Mrs. Hammersley has a mother and I am handicapped by a vexatious accident (I have no luck). The other day at the Café Royal where I collapsed after seeing the R.A. and the New Gallery I was reviving over a chop and a glass of beer when I felt a frightful sting on my thigh, dropped my hands on it, struggled with hissing flames and smoke, was taken for an unsuccessful anarchist and at last extinguished a box of Swedish safety matches, that blazed in my pocket. . . . I have a Turner sunset on my thigh and certain blisters on my hands – but I go about and can work in an inferior style. . . ." (Charteris, p. 137)

future patrons had little to fear from Sargent, he would not drag them into controversy, and there was a distinct possibility their social prominence might be enhanced if they made themselves available for his canvas.

The job Sargent had been offered with much novelty in America in 1887 was now assigned to him in England. After years waiting in the dusty chambers of musicians, actors, actresses – his Ellen Terry had confirmed the suspicion he was indeed given to flamboyance – he was invited to walk into the moneyed world, where the doors opened to him silently, with a confidence that he would not interpret the terms of his employment any differently from those who were dangling the keys. But his rise in England was unlike his rise in America. The rich Americans were willing to gamble; they were also looking to the future, once money and national history had helped to make time something other than an enemy, and by commissioning portraits from a painter suspected of great things, certain to win their descendants' blessings, they were laying the foundation of ancestral tradition at home. In England where such a motive was already firmly entrenched, Sargent was being asked to lend a hand in its continuation, but only after he had cleared himself of the less respectable aspects of his reputation. And when the moneyed classes on both sides of the Atlantic had proof of the soundness of their judgement the aristocracy took him over, eager for the same reasons as their immediate predecessors – and because they were convinced Sargent would not embarrass the past. His portraits could hang in the long gallery of ancestral records furnished by Van Dyck, Kneller, Reynolds, Romney, Raeburn and Lawrence. The aristocracy had calmly waited to see how well he served his various masters before they took him into service – for his portraits were his letters of reference for such servitude. It would be as grave an error to misread the long, distinguished, titled list of his sitters for his friends or the world he moved in as it would be to think a bank clerk rich for the vast quantities of banknotes that passed through his fingers in the course of his work. Both men only did their job.

The Academy did not listen to *The Times* until January 1894, when Sargent was beckoned into the antechamber where he would wait until he was asked to go further. He was elected an Associate of the Royal Academy, and thus elevated, at the surprisingly young age of thirty-eight, to join the older generation. Lord Leighton was the President (in April, Sargent gave him an oil sketch of Astarte, which found its way into Mrs Gardner's hands after Leighton's death in 1896). Sargent received the honour with mixed pleasure. He read Academicians' congratulations to mean he "had more of an affinity with old fogies than I expected", he wrote to Ralph Curtis at the time. "Today I have called on about 20 of them, such is the tradition and it is a curious revelation to find the man whose name and work one has hated and railed at for years, is a man of the world and altogether delightful – for instance Sant, whom one considered the Antichrist."[11] And he willingly shouldered unexpected and welcome duties like "irritate one's friends with exhortations to be charitable", he wrote to Mrs Mahlon Sands (26 February)[12] (whose first portrait he had just finished after endless sittings), in his unwanted capacity of steward for the Artists' Benevolent Institution dinner. His reputation now had offical sanction, carrying with it derision from the younger generation, who, fresh from Paris, wrinkled their eyebrows at the mention of his name: somehow, by having fulfilled his promise, Sargent was a traitor to his ability, and with it became their enemy. His regular showings at the New Gallery, his membership of the New English Art Club – thought to be an Academy antidote – were themselves a different sort of irritant in their immature eyes, and further evidence that Sargent had crossed over, to the wrong side. His achievement was their ammunition.

It was the same old story, declaimed with a little more force and a lot of self-righteousness. In October 1891, Camille Pissaro's sons had called on Sargent in London, with an introduction from the author Octave Mirbeau. "What you say about Sargent doesn't surprise me," Pissaro answered his son Lucien (6 October 1891); "Monet had told me that he is very kind. As for his painting, that, of course, we can't approve of; he is not an enthusiast but rather an adroit performer, and it is not for his painting that Mirbeau wanted you to meet him."[13] The French did not care for the idea that Sargent had betrayed his student past to become a duplicate of his teacher, and when the young English painters returned home from Paris these same opinions were respectfully packed in their bags. William Rothenstein (1872–1945), who came hot from the Académie Julien to sit at Whistler's feet, unfolded Degas' contempt for Sargent the moment he reached Chelsea, and sidled up to the younger members of the New English Art Club looking for assent. Sargent was swiftly dismissed; he belonged to that group of "extremely efficient painters . . . of great executive ability" that numbered Carolus, Tissot, Bonnat, Boldini. The tiresome refrain was heard again: painting was too easy for Sargent for him to do it well; it cannot be good if it were done effortlessly. "I felt that something essential was lacking in Sargent . . . [his] unappeased appetite for work allowed him to paint everything and anything without selection, anywhere, at anytime. It was this uncritical hunger for mere painting which distinguished him from the French and English painters whom he rivalled, and often surpassed, in facility."[14]

Sargent's followers and successful friends did little to help him recoup ground lost to the younger generation. Helleu was not much liked for a start, and Charles Furse did little for himself by worshipping Sargent, whose inspiration he kept warm first by borrowing his idol's studio in 1895, and then by taking one himself in the same building. Sargent's well-broadcast affection for someone as old-fashioned and thought to be not altogether serious as Annie Swynnerton* helped to amplify Whistler's

* He wrote to Mrs Astor [13 May 1911]: "you want to know what I think of Mrs Swynnerton as a painter – further concealment is useless [his favourite phrase].

many syllables of derision. And so the munitions were piled up, though it must have been a tiresome exercise trying to remember everything Sargent had *not* done in order to keep feelings against him high: though Monet had, in Sargent's own words, "bowled me over"[15] he was never an Impressionist, and later he would not be a Post-Impressionist. Still, his success kept contrary reactions vigorously stirred. And his unerring courtesy and generosity to students and younger colleagues did not help to stem the accusations much, either. It was the same old story – new to someone, however.

Three months after his election to the Royal Academy, he asked the Council (12 March 1894) if he might be allowed to show the finished portions of his decoration which had occupied him for the past three years. The Council agreed, and the elaborate and costly frame that had been constructed to duplicate the shape of the barrel vaulting used during the painting of the pagan gods panel together with the Israelite lunette were moved from Fulham Road to Burlington House for the summer exhibition. On Varnishing Day, Sargent and Luigi d'Inverno affixed the "ornamental relief of which there is a considerable amount", as the Secretary of the Council had been warned when the request was made, before both sections were positioned in a cove best approximating the space and light of their future home.[16]

The public was baffled. Those who at least knew these decorations were not intended as a permanent addition to the rooms were defeated by the array of symbols, with no explanatory notes, shrugged their shoulders and walked away from what appeared to be a "hopeless conundrum". Lady Lewis, the wife of Sir George Lewis who had acted for Sargent in the Fairford riding case and in whose house in Portland Place he enjoyed many musical entertainments, had other ideas, and wrote to tell him so. "I was delighted to find that you", Sargent replied [?May/June 1894], "got some pleasure out of it through your eyes and were not fidgeting about the obscurity of those old symbols. What a tiresome thing a perfectly clear symbol would be."[17]

With the "alleged decorations" removed to the Academy until August, and Sargent undecided if he would take them to Boston himself when they came down, the doors of Tite Street were reopened to sitters: "For the moment I am going to do some portraits here," he wrote to Curtis, "among others Miss Rehan who is very paintable."[18] His excursions into portraiture early that year had not been encouraging. Mrs Mahlon Sands, the American beauty (the mother of Ethel Sands) who had found a comfortable place in Marlborough House entertaining the Prince of

---

I think she is a genius or words to that effect – really I am not exaggerating. . . . It is difficult to describe her style if you have never seen anything of hers, it is very powerful and rich, and sometimes rather like Watts only more intense . . ." (University of Reading Library). She was also an accomplished portraitist of children, which Sargent also admired, and recommended.

PLATE XVII

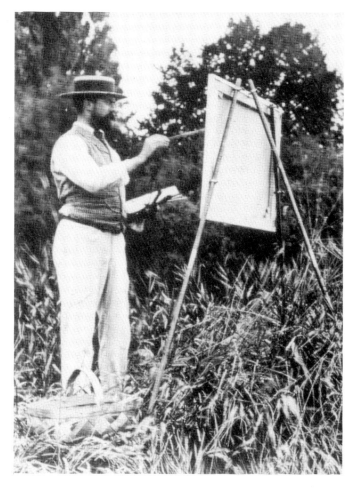

Right: Sargent painting at Fladbury, 1889.

Below: Fladbury Rectory, Pershore, in the summer of 1889.

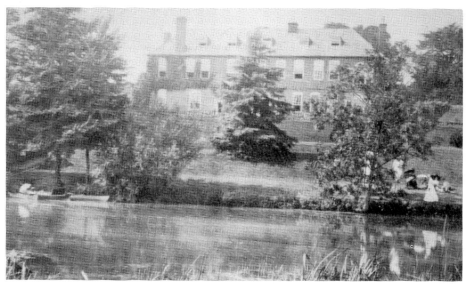

PLATE XVIII

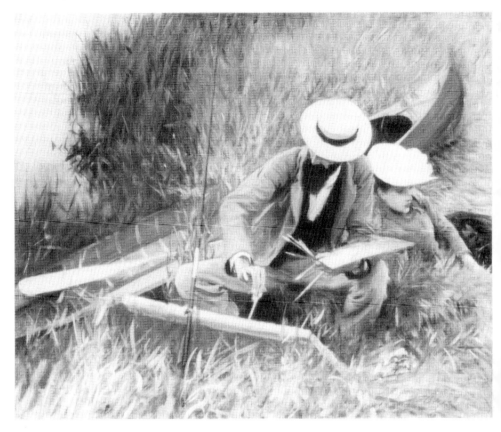

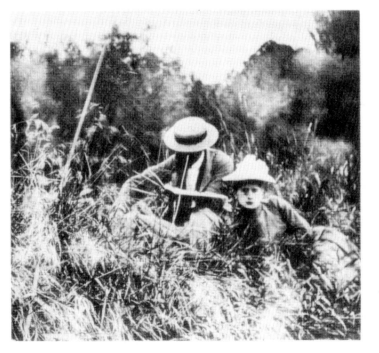

*Paul Helleu sketching with his wife, Fladbury, 1889 – painted by Sargent (**above**) and in a photograph.*

PLATE XIX

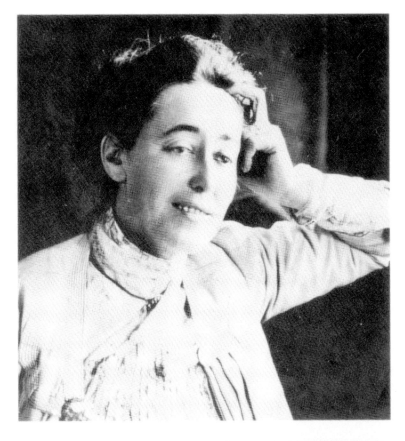

Right: Flora
Priestley.

Below: Flora
Priestley, by
Sargent, *c.*1889.

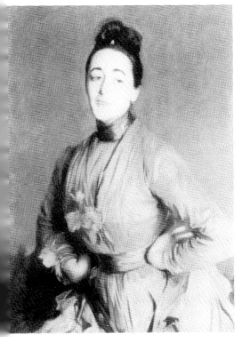

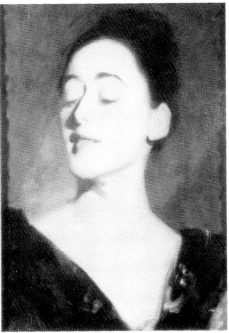

PLATE XX

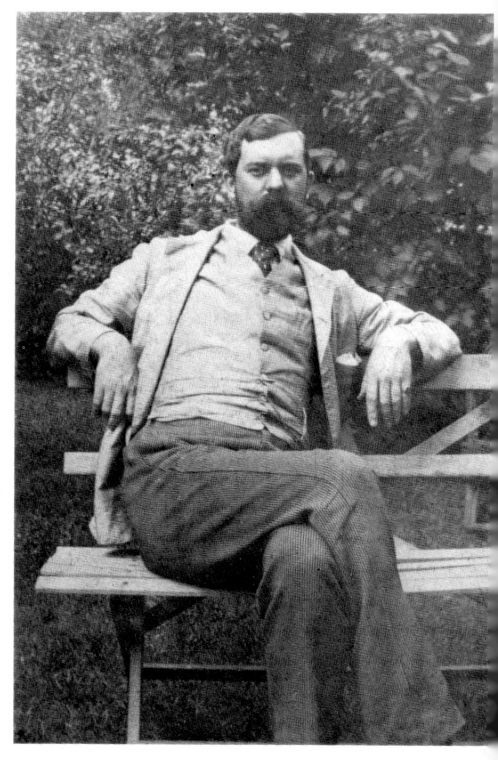

Sargent in Worcester, Massachusetts, August 1890.

PLATE XXI

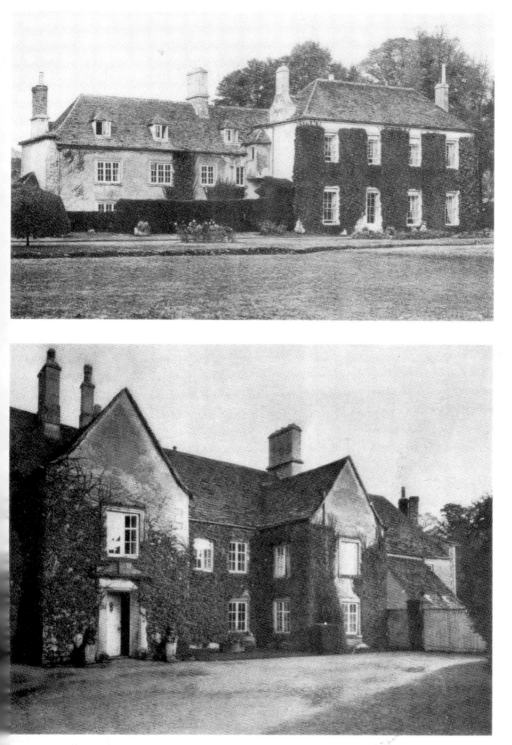

Morgan Hall, Fairford, Gloucestershire, the Abbeys' home and Sargent's from 1891, where the Boston murals were begun.

PLATE XXII

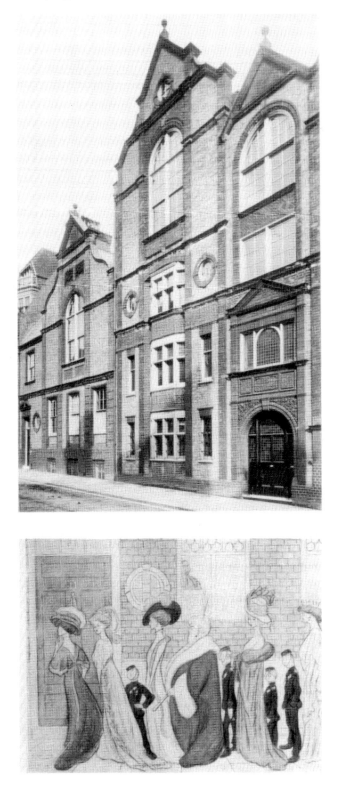

Above: *31 (left) and 33 Tite Street, two of Sargent's London studios.*

Left: 31 Tite Street, *by Max Beerbohm.*

PLATE XXIII

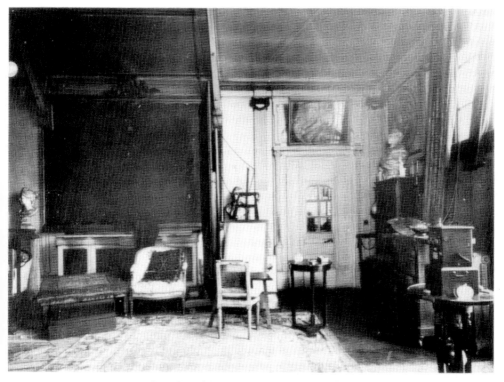

Interior of Sargent's Tite Street studio.

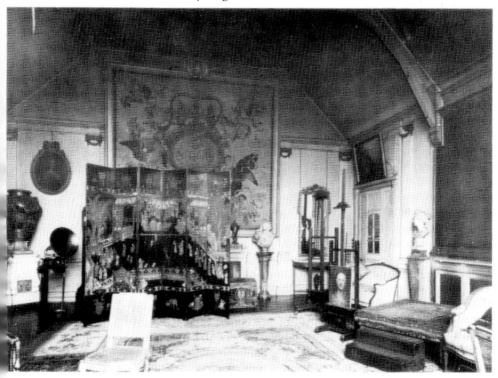

PLATE XXIV

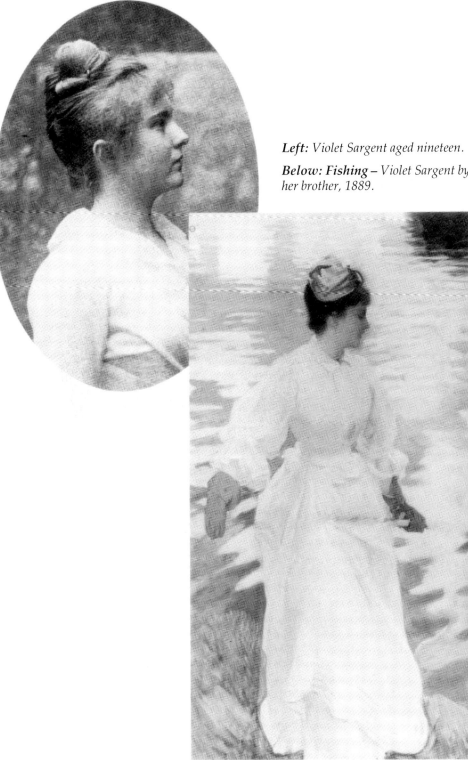

Left: Violet Sargent aged nineteen.

Below: Fishing – Violet Sargent by her brother, 1889.

Wales's eye, continued to be a particularly difficult subject because she had listened to James's instructions too well: "Cultivate indifference . . . be as difficult for him as possible; and the more difficult you are the more the artist will be condemned to worry over you, repainting, revolutionizing, till he, in a rage of ambition and admiration, arrives at the thing. . . ."[19] By the end of February, Sargent was worn out by James's meddling, though he had enough strength left to slide neatly out of Mrs Sands's recommendation to send it to the Academy. "I would rather not this year. . . . I haven't been an academician long enough to show anything so correct!"[20] he wrote to her from Morgan Hall (26 February 1894). Months later the storm clouds had not moved on and the holiday was turning very sour. Ada Rehan (1860–1916) was proving to be less than "very paintable". Though she had scored an unexpected triumph, especially for an American, playing Shakespeare in Augustin Daly's company, and was reckoned to be one of the leading actresses of the day amid very strong competition, none of her brilliance was apparent off-stage. She was beset by shyness and was otherwise unremarkable – "tall, ample . . . not conventionally beautiful but arch, piquant", *The Dictionary of American Biography* cautiously amplified – and Sargent had been asked to paint her off-stage, commissioned, to complicate matters further, by one of her admirers in America who was hard to please. When the portrait was finally done twenty months later, having survived many changes, Ada Rehan was portrayed as a comfortable matron, unworthy of a turn of the neck, well removed from the cause of her fame. But the portrait did possess many of the qualities seen in his Lady Agnew, on a larger scale: pretty, soft and by no means excessively dramatic. And Mrs Graham Robertson's portrait, done at the same time, was equally unhappy. These were uninteresting jobs, presenting but a single challenge: to finish them. Any time he sought to invest some visual interest, tried to entertain the eye, improve on the raw material, the patron objected. These commissions were enough to make him regret that he had not chosen to take his holiday with his prophets.

The next portrait, however, lifted his spirits and cleared away the gloom, putting him into a high mood, for it was not a commission and for that matter not even a portrait of a person, but of a coat. Sargent saw W. Graham Robertson (1866–1948), his coat and his aged poodle Mouton (who insisted on a ritual bite each time he saw Sargent) when they came to Tite Street to calm the frayed nerves of his mother Mrs Robertson and Ada Rehan, both of whom found posing intolerable. Robertson had trained as an artist, but it is fair to say he felt a little more at home in the front stalls sending waves of devotion over the footlights to the leading actresses of the day. He prided himself on his taste, which he educated to an advanced degree by sitting in artists' studios and bobbing between theatres; and he eventually made a name for himself as a designer and playwright. In his youth, however, he made posturing a full-time job. Sargent was too shy to ask his coat to pose and sent Ada Rehan to ask;

" 'the coat is the picture' ", Sargent later explained to him,[21] leaving Robertson's highly polished vanity with no illusions. Robertson feebly objected on account of the heat, hastily adding he would agree, in that case, to wear nothing else, "and with the sacrifice of most of my wardrobe," he wrote in his autobiography, "I became thinner and thinner, much to the satisfaction of the artist, who used to pull and drag the unfortunate coat more and more closely round me until it might have been draping a lamp-post". His enthusiasm leapt, and there were no mothers or patrons to offer any flattening commentaries. His sitter was, in truth, very pleased to help along the coat, and he posed longer than he ought at a stretch. " 'What a horrid light there is just now,' " Sargent mused one day, " 'a sort of green –' ", and then he looked more closely at Robertson's face. " 'Why, it's *you*!' "[22] he exclaimed, and rushed the coat out into the street for some air. The portrait of a coat also showed much of Robertson's effete mannerisms and was as much a stylized parody as the sitter was himself. Long, self-conscious, Huysmann-like, he sported a boyish stance of "cultivated melancholy",[23] looking as if breathing were an ordeal or as if he were convinced the world was unworthy of his carbon dioxide; one hand sighs on his hip, the other blankly grasps at a jade-top stick, and he twists his emaciated form to give a weary gaze to the spectator. Mouton lies in a blurred mass on the shiny floor, more exhausted than his master, before Sargent's Cormandel screen. The picture is an exaggeration of the vertical. The matinée-assortment palette used for Ada Rehan has turned serious. Sargent saw the portrait as a whole, and the public has since come to see the picture as an emblem of the decadence stirred up by his neighbour Oscar Wilde (who lived across the street at 16 Tite Street), *The Yellow Book* (which Sargent happened to detest, refusing permission for Gosse's portrait to be reproduced in its pages)[24] and Montesquiou (whose portrait by Whistler Sargent saw well after he had begun Robertson, but he did admit both pictures had much in common). The bout of *esprit* that carried him through Robertson's coat continued throughout his portraits of Coventry Patmore (1823–96), the poet, because Patmore *looked* sufficiently interesting, bearing a striking resemblance to a superior greyhound, designed on a beautiful stylized pattern, long, aged and distinguished. And he admired Sargent without qualification. Patmore's appearance, like Robertson's coat, possessed that element of the "curious" which excited Sargent; when a sitter could lay claim to it the portrait showed it, and when it was absent Sargent could not conjure or counterfeit it. "He is doing his work *con amore*," Patmore wrote to his wife during the sittings, "and will not leave it off until he has done his best."[25] Thereafter when his eye was not tantalized his brush moved in a routine manner. A sitter's beauty alone was not adequate excitement; some peculiarity had to be present. And it must also be said that when his eye was challenged he also reached out for his well-thumbed texts compiled in Spain and Holland, full of lectures by Velazquez and Hals.

In December, Sargent took a fresh look at his prophets standing against the wall at Fulham Road, and for many weeks thereafter had no more sittings in Tite Street. The line-up of sixteen figures seemed to him to be a little flat, lacking purpose, standing around without much meaning, and perhaps too weak especially below the frenzy of activity taking place above them. "I have suddenly determined to try to do my figure of Moses in relief," he announced to Abbott (18 January) [1895], "as I cannot manage to give him sufficient accent over the other figures without it."[26] When the murals were unveiled in Boston at the end of April, Moses was emerging from the surface of the wall, his face a little strained, grimacing from the effort.

Sargent arrived in Boston on 12 April 1895 to supervise and help with the installation of his decorations – the final exertion after the best part of four years' work. The painted canvases were affixed to the walls by a process called marouflage, whereby a thick coat of white lead was applied to the wall and a thin coat of red lead to the back of the canvas, which was then hung like wallpaper, drying with a rock-hard, permanent grip, befitting this bid for immortality. When the canvas was fixed in place small bubbles of lead came through any hole, and a great many annoying, small restorations had to be made quickly throughout the hanging. It was an ordeal. "We both suffered . . . fearfully from the heat," Abbey, who was dealing with his decorations on the floor below, wrote to Alma-Tadema (18 May 1895), "working on scaffolds under the ceiling – I in a room crowded all day with people breathing hard."[27] The Royal Academy rehearsal had been an invaluable exercise, for after seeing that "the things did not look well"[28] in the cold, hard light Sargent insisted that the lighting of the Special Libraries Hall be dimmed, softened to a pale glow. Later still, he designed the electric light fittings to produce the exact illumination he wanted.

On the evening of 25 April 1895, three months after the Library itself had opened, McKim, Mead & White gave a reception in honour of Abbey and Sargent in their usual flourish of high style for two hundred invited guests (forty of whom had been brought down from New York, among them Mrs White who had taken a lively interest in the activities at Fairford). An orchestra played at the top of the marble staircase. Sargent, Abbey, McKim received. It was a warm evening, the windows were thrown open, and there was the reassuring sound of the courtyard fountain splashing. The procession of diamonds, silk, lace, satin up and down the stairs was such as no one had ever seen before. The visitors strolled up another flight to peer at Sargent's contribution, agog, enthusiastic and wonderfully ill-informed. After the reception there was supper around the corner at the Algonquin Club (another one of McKim's creations), with speeches by Governor Russell, and uncharacteristically by Sargent, who otherwise developed an extreme case of muteness in similar circumstances. The evening was a success; McKim's bold choice of decorators was handsomely vindicated. The murals surpassed expectation. (The local newspapers, however, were more interested in revealing that a public building had been used for a private party, which was extremely offensive to the tax payer. Abbott resigned the following day.) "The Bostonians like them I am glad to say," Sargent wrote to Mrs Curtis (7 May), "to the extent of entertaining the idea of giving me a further order for more walls of the same hall. So I shall be at it for years."[29]

The pleasure earned in Boston was short-lived: three weeks after the first cheers went up, Sargent left for Vanderbilt's new Renaissance château, Biltmore, in Asheville, North Carolina, to satisfy the commissions he had managed to avoid the previous year. He had been instructed to immortalize the architect of the park, Frederick Law Olmstead (1822–1903), and the architect of the house, Richard Morris Hunt (1827–95) – two men worthy of immortality: Olmstead was responsible for much of the deliberate civic beauty ordained as some pastoral relief from all the building that was filling up Manhattan and Back Bay, and Hunt had shown himself to be the master of poaching arts he handed down to younger men like McKim. And when Sargent faced these two elderly giants he was further instructed not to believe his eyes. "My campaign here announces itself ominously," he wrote [May 1895] to his friend Mrs J. Montgomery Sears in Boston, "– both wives prove to me that I must imagine thus [that] their husbands look at all like what they look like at present – totally different really, and the backgrounds, a stately garden for one and a venerable place for the other are at present red earth stuck with specimen vegetables and scaffoldings covered with niggers. . . ."[30] Each portrait was, in truth, a double one and none of the four subjects was quite as he saw them. "Sargent arrives at his best by many substitutions," James astutely informed a previous sitter,[31] which was fine when it was a matter of subtraction, but at Biltmore he was asked to *add* as well, and both portraits suffered. It was an unfortunate reminder that portraiture was worse than enforced collaboration; it was vanity's butler. And it was also a fortunate reminder that he had got into a way of thinking about such employment as nothing more significant than a job of work, to take money.

The month he was in Biltmore his mind was still in Boston; he was loyal to what he valued most. He wrestled with the welcome problem of where *The Triumph of Religion* might go next. He eagerly plotted his next course of study. Two days after leaving Biltmore, on 18 June, he sailed to Gibraltar. There he saw his mother, who was recovering from an attack of peritonitis, and a month later, with her safe retirement in Aix-les-Bains where she felt entirely at home, he headed back to London at a measured pace – "seeing as much as I can on the way", he wrote to George Vanderbilt (21 July 1895) from Madrid.[32] In other words, he, too, returned to a much-loved comfort – researching.

At Tite Street a month later Sargent found himself in a peculiar and not altogether agreeable circumstance, the result of a miscalculation, and entirely of his own making. While he had been in America, his portraits of

Robertson and Patmore joined hands in the Academy to consolidate the gains Mrs Hammersley and Lady Agnew had won for his reputation two years earlier. He proved he had a legitimate claim (at the age of thirty-nine) to his membership' of the Academy, and the strength of these portraits affirmed that he had sailed far beyond any strenuous though unthreatening competition. Of course his timing was impeccable. Portraiture was overtaking subject/history painting in the fashion stakes. The public's taste was moving over to embrace Sargent's profession – his advertised profession. And, added to this good fortune, the old order was falling away: Millais and Leighton were nearly dead, Luke Fildes and Herkomer were novice converts to portraiture, as were Poynter and Alma-Tadema, Whistler was too dangerous (and unkind at very high prices), and the younger generation – Sickert, Steer and Tonks – were as yet too unpredictable and modern to be allowed into the Royal Academy; Orpen and Augustus John, Sargent's only real serious rivals, were waiting to come downstairs from the nursery. And his imitators – Furse, J. J. Shannon, Brough and Lavery – posed no threat. Sargent had a clear path for many years. He filled a void (and some might safely say he created a need), and he opened the shutters to some fresh air and bright light, without kicking conventional taste out of the way in the process. When each new portrait was unveiled, the language of excitement was sorely taxed; superlatives were inadequately tame. And so it went on, his wide blue *riband* fluttering in the halls of the Academy until he himself lowered the standard fifteen years later. At the end of August 1895 he began the quick march, to portraiture's unrelenting cadence – reluctantly, very reluctantly.

Before he had left London for Boston he agreed to several portrait commissions, never expecting the Library Trustees would actually present him with a second contract (which they did in December, having raised his fee by private subscription), and thereby landing him with a double claim on his time. Now he was forced to push decorative work to the side of his diary, adjust it to sittings, and leave it for leisurely consideration, to savour the challenge for many years; he was forced to give his portraits the same importance he had awarded the initial Library instalment, and for the next thirteen years the enormous, well-tuned portrait machine was set in motion, pulsing at greatest velocity around the turn of the century, churning out, in total, a staggering seventeen dozen orders, some assuming architectural dimensions: *The Daughters of the Hon. Percy Wyndham* occupies nearly seventy square feet of canvas, and *The Acheson Sisters* placed in Sargent's chosen frame weighs approximately a quarter of a ton. At the end of the first decade of the new century, the portrait works shut down completely, worn out, bored, tired, overtaxed, never to reopen again, despite countless orders. But for thirteen years Sargent manufactured the most eloquent fulfilment of the career he plotted for himself the day he announced in the Salon, when he showed his master's portrait, that he intended to overtake Carolus himself. The progress since then had been beset by fits and starts, had not always appeared to move in the correct direction, and yet there was a thin ribbon of continuity interwoven through the past twenty years. His affection for portraiture, however, never seemed to be of the same order as his affection for decoration, and seemed inadequate to transform him into the master of a production-line. But that was because it was his *stated* profession, not his true affection. During these years there were strange forces operating to renew him, to banish the staleness of consistency, and to push him to such fantastic lengths. If it were love of portraiture alone that suddenly activated him, it was a love that needed the compost of recognition to appear, and, more tellingly, it showed for the first time a weakness in his character, a weakness to be imperfectly contained. The confidence, the steadiness, the determination were not so securely fixed to his soul as they appeared; they seemed to require the extra rivets of fame. Money and fame played insignificant roles in this development, for he would never have had to work as hard as he did to maintain either. The satisfaction of work had always been adequate prompting, but the sudden increase in volume which began building up around 1893 hinted at a darker motive, as if he were making up, by some perverse, confused accountancy for his father's sad indolence or his mother's ruinous ennui. Work was for him what travel was for his mother and resignation had been for his father. His astonishing industry *could* stretch to cover two lifetimes, if that were his ambition. Such ruthless driving might have coloured-in a vacant tract, left hollow by his recoiling from intimacy of any sort, compensating for a need he suspected he missed. But the coincidence of two simple facts helps to calm these troubled waves of conjecture: his total submission to the large demands of portraiture occurred at the same time his mother and Emily finally settled nearby in Carlyle Mansions, affording him for the first time in his adult life the untasted comforts of sham domestic bliss. It was as if he had been waiting for stability before he took off. It was now portraiture's turn to command his flight, up to a point. (What Sargent himself considered to be the explanation, if ever he were asked to volunteer one, he kept to himself, joining the other unopened volumes in his vast library.) Also, about the same time his mother and sister became his neighbours in London, he no longer needed the hothouse climate abundantly supplied by Morgan Hall, for once the mental turmoil presented by the murals resolved into a plan of action the vast canvases were transferred to Fulham Road, which allowed Abbey the full run of his iron studio to complete his own decoration. Mary and Emily's presence did for him what the murals had done for his other painting: it removed the vacillating, transient quality of his life. They represented a fixed point to which he constantly and willingly returned. They brought him a sort of novel permanence, long postponed, and a comfortable stability, hitherto unknown to them all. They took the place of Broadway, Calcot, Fladbury and Fairford in his domestic arrangements. Carlyle Mansions became the warm social annexe to Tite Street; there his shyness could thaw. Other neighbours and friends gathered round. There he was happy. By the time he was nearly forty, Sargent withdrew into his second lease on family life, settling down, content. The transition was slow, but he never showed any resistance.

Carlyle Mansions had the perfect location, far enough away from Tite Street to ensure privacy and close enough to allow frequent intimacy – a happy consequence not just of Sargent's extreme tact and sensitivity, but of the fact that there were no other purpose-built flats in the neighbourhood. And after forty years of being a tenant Mary Sargent could scarcely be expected to assume the duties of mistress of a household. Still, she and Emily, with Sargent's help, managed to overcome their long-standing ignorance of settled domestic life to make their rooms very welcoming. They amassed a collection of good furniture which was set against walls hung with luxurious Venetian crimson brocade and a good selection of pictures, mostly Sargents. They entertained in a relaxed manner, insisting that guests should not dress for dinner, and usually rounding off the evenings with music or conversation or chess or draughts. Sargent considered Carlyle Mansions to be his home, where all his mannerisms of reticence disappeared – his hesitant speech, his arm-waving while searching for the accurate word, the adjustment of some trenchant opinion to undramatic courtesy. The windows opened to free his usual restraint (and let out the cigar smoke) and a few highly select people outside the family were invited into the greenhouse to see this late-flowering family plant.

Over the years the silent lift rose to number 10 on the fourth floor carrying many reminders of the past. Mary's engagement-diary had names first associated with Nice, Florence, Venice, Paris, Calcot and Fladbury: Vernon Lee, Ben del Castillo, Ralph Curtis, James Carroll Beckwith, Flora Priestley and Helleu, among others. In addition, there were numerous representatives of her son's first days in England. In many ways her guest-list was a duplicate of the ones she kept in Rome (1868–9) and Paris (1874–5), as if they had been test runs for the ultimate one she would keep. Most of her visitors enjoyed the luxury of living very near – she scarcely had to turn a page of the *Post Office Directory* to find their exact addresses and telephone numbers – as well as having earned her son's affection. His friends became hers and Emily's.

Broadway reappeared in the shape of Alma Strettell and her husband L. A. "Peter" Harrison (46 Cheyne Walk) and his brother "Jinx" (26 Cheyne Walk). The New English Art Club made a more eccentric entry with the arrival of Philip Wilson Steer (1860–1941), who moved into 106 Cheyne Walk in 1898. Steer was one of the delightful mysteries of the human condition. He had an altogether undemonstrative approach to life, hating all change, generously wrapping himself up in layers of clothing regardless of the season, on guard against draughts, scarcely budging from an ever-diminishing radius of his house. And he certainly never looked the very remarkable painter he was; when he did travel, his painting equipment was packed into a cricket bag. He did not much care for language, which brought his training in Paris to an abrupt halt before he refused to utter a word of French. And in London he was equally silent and equally unhelpful: for some reason, wholly in keeping with the oddity of every cell in his nature, he thought he could teach without speaking, and once a week he bumbled into the Slade to emit various grunts and stutters meant to guide students on to a mastery of painting. On canvas, however, he performed recitals with such grace, fluidity and heroic eloquence that he became not only one of England's finest, if not *the* finest exponent of Impressionism, but also one of her greatest painters (for which he was appropriately honoured). The man and his work seemed extraordinarily and bafflingly ill-matched. His house was crammed with china, furniture, pictures and cats; he lived as he dressed, in a well-packed defence against the outside. He inhabited a secure privacy. Like Sargent, he drew a thick silence over everything private, and nothing about the edges even hinted at what might be concealed. Steer was much like the expatriates the Sargents had known, but with one sizeable difference: while he was the master of a wonderfully vacant life, he also had a profession and was a genius at it.

Steer introduced a fellow-bachelor to Carlyle Mansions who was his idea of unthreatening conviviality and who was better made for the usual forms of companionship: Henry Tonks (1862–1937). Tonks was refreshingly less obscure, as lively and talkative as his friend was not. He even looked the opposite of Steer, tall, lean, as if he were but partially complete, with an austere, well-defined head. He had trained as a doctor, though his heart was really with art, and when he qualified he promptly switched careers, having fallen under the spell of Frederick Brown, who after succeeding Legros as Professor of Art at the Slade in 1893 invited Tonks to teach. Tonks's medical background assured him the best qualification for anatomy, and unlike Steer he was a truly gifted teacher. And thanks to Brown and Tonks the Slade nurtured a new respect for draughtsmanship, harking back to the principles laid down by Ingres. But Tonks was uninfected by the romance of France; he helped to give English art training a correct integrity beyond mere xenophobia: in 1917 he became Professor at the Slade. Sargent's fondness for him was as high as his admiration: when Sir Edward Poynter asked Sargent just who this newly appointed Professor Tonks might be, Sargent barely controlled his outrage to stutter, " 'A great teacher,' "[33] with very sharp concentration on the word "great". And Tonks's respect for Sargent's ability to draw was unbounded.

William Rothenstein infrequently drifted in, carried along in the current produced by Steer and Tonks, considering himself worthy enough to number among the Carlyle Mansions set, especially before he moved up to Hampstead. Rothenstein was a man who lived for the future. He used his not too considerable talent (though it must be said some of his paintings are really very good) to propel himself to the more interesting pools where history would be certain to shine a light. One reads his huge autobiography with a growing suspicion that he did not have sufficient patience for the day to end, for fear he might not remember everything for the page. Few have better managed the art of being at the right place at the right time, and even fewer have controlled such a high-powered social motor. Rothenstein's love of art was, however, absolutely sincere, but his love of names seems to have been greater. His autobiography is to the history of art what a film star's is to the history of cinema: his personal orbit was very closely defined, via names of the great. He was vulnerable to Sargent's fame, but not to his painting.

Around the turn of the century Fairford reappeared, along with the heady days in New York in 1890, when the von Glehns moved into 73 Cheyne Walk. Wilfred von Glehn (1870–1951), who changed his name at the outset of the war to *de* Glehn, had been imported from Paris to help Abbey with his murals at Fairford. There he enrolled in the Sargent school, worshipping Sargent with an absolute belief that he alone epitomized the grandest possible reading of the strict academic tradition von Glehn himself felt comfortable maintaining. Though he did enjoy a certain and not altogether modest success as a portraitist, and was elected an Academician in 1932, he was never quite able to throw off the heavy veil of influence he willingly adopted after meeting Sargent. His devotion to Sargent was so absolute, even history has been tricked: the rare glimpses of von Glehn which survive hint at an agreeable and delightful character, but the long shadow of Sargent obscures any sharp detail. Such image of him which can be discerned bears the involuntary handiwork of Sargent, who recommended von Glehn for the memorial stained-glass windows of both Daniel S. Curtis and the Hunters, who instantly suggested von Glehn for portraits he refused, and who nicknamed von Glehn "Premp". In 1904 von Glehn married Jane Erin Emmet, one of the three remarkable sisters from New York, who was herself a very able painter, best known for portraits of children; Sargent had known her for years – she had been one of the select audience he had invited to see La Carmencita.

Other students at the Sargent school could be found around the corner at Tite Street as well: Robert Brough and Charles Furse had studios at number 33; further along at number 26 was the illustrator, etcher and painter, G. P. Jacomb-Hood (1857–1929), who had once shared a studio with von Glehn's uncle Oswald (whom Sargent greatly respected as a teacher) when he first came to London after studying in Paris. Hood was totally captivated by Sargent; for him the sun rose and set on the ground floor of number 33.

Shortly before the von Glehns carried memories of Fairford to Cheyne Walk, the Abbeys moved into their London version of Morgan Hall, to Chelsea Lodge, at 42 Tite Street, in March 1899; here Abbey died, and a few months later, at the end of 1911, Mrs Abbey gave up Morgan Hall for good. Mary Sargent never lived to see her daughter Violet and her family move into 94 Cheyne Walk or Henry James settle into 21 Carlyle Mansions, but after her death Emily added these new and important entries to the list she had superintended for many years, and inherited entirely as her own.

At Carlyle Mansions, Emily had another job to refresh the tired monotony of being her mother's attendant, a sort of apprenticeship which would prepare her when her prime employment ceased: she became her brother's hostess, and she performed impeccably, with perfect diction, as if she had been rehearsing her lines silently for a long time, in the full knowledge she was unavailable for any other part. She accepted eagerly, without the suspicion it might be the second-best post. And soon the mechanical, domestic secretarial limitations blurred into wider, richer fulfilment, for Emily was now able to re-establish herself as her brother's closest friend – a status which had never waned, but had been at the mercy of geographic separations. She was able to furnish him with the same unthreatening feminine influence he had found so reassuring when he attached himself to older, married women; she was able to dominate the territory previously occupied by Mrs Millet, Mrs Barnard, Mrs "Peter" Harrison, and Mrs Abbey (and Mrs Mead). Emily became a constant, welcome and loving presence in his life.

Sargent's relationship with Emily was as close as he ever got to matrimonial companionship: she was his *soi-disant* wife. It was a perfect match, for both of them, uncluttered by the ferocity of sex, easily confined within the narrow limits of conventionality, and in no way peculiar, either for them or for observers. Neither partner had to adjust their own desires to make the union totally satisfying, for they were both products of the same greenhouse, fed with the same nutrients, which had also bred an identical emotional abbreviation. They knew each other's unexpressed feelings; they communicated in a perfect but spare intuition; they used the same language without speaking, and they adored each other freed of the need for reassurance – they were saved any exertion wasted on ritual, for there was not an atom of doubt between them. In time Sargent and his sister grew into one person.

Emily alone held the key to the gates which kept others at a distance. Of course some got close, but none had anything approaching Emily's liberty. Still, despite this barrier, Sargent was a compellingly engaging figure. Thirty years after meeting him in Henley in July 1887, Sir George Henschel recalled in his autobiography: "I . . . felt myself quite uncommonly attracted by his personality from the first . . . he struck me as exceedingly modest. . . ."[34] This was the uniform unflustered reaction throughout Sargent's life. He never had an enemy, though there were many people who disagreed with his painting, and disagreed profoundly, like Whistler and later Roger Fry, but all were careful to point out in their attacks they did like the man. His fame aroused jealousy, but never dislike. The personality he presented to the world was a polished surface, reflecting light, strength, easy companionability, warmth, kindness and above all courtesy. His observable personality was an open space, free of dark recesses or any hidden obstacles which might lie in wait to rebuff affection. Those rare spectators allowed to glimpse beyond the shyness which kept others uninformed saw but a magnified version of what was on show to any passing acquaintance. And this near-mastery of visible defects or near-inhuman mastery of vulnerability protected him from all speculation. During Sargent's life and after, memoirists could go no further than accumulate the features they observed and none felt the need or the urge or even the ability to shine a torch on some imagined region. In the full library of Sargent literature the harshest accusation anyone dared to record was that there might *not* be more to him than met the eye. Of course people ruminated about his sex life, but quickly gave it up as a vacant topic. Very little gossip circulated about him. Everyone knew he painted, but no one was willing to believe that was all. But it was. Vernon Lee, who pursued him with terrier-like determination throughout his life, preening herself with the idea that she knew him intimately well, could find no better understanding. Helleu was no less curious, and also could find no standard account to fit an answer to this hollow ungratifying explanation of the man. He tried to make a study of Sargent's sexual inclinations and found his efforts unrewarded at every angle of the search. Sargent housed no secrets in his soul, which was maddeningly never opened for scrutiny. He was not designed for the usual varieties of intimacy: his single brief experiment many years before with Louise Burckhardt had revealed only a willingness to try and no ability for fluency. Thereafter he was never troubled by any inkling of emotional or physical inadequacy.*

Sargent and his sister arrived at their agreeable domestic arrangement by the rights of heredity. In middle age Sargent's character spoke the distinct syllables of inheritance, for the standard family modesty that had refined itself over the generations to make his father a near-introvert worked a similar manifestation in him: emotional austerity. FitzWilliam's resignation filtered through to his son in the shape of conscious and deliberate independence – Sargent's own word. And the atmosphere which had induced him and Emily to flourish as equal specimens of the

---

* This sensitive department of his life has been, hardly surprisingly, the target for much conjecture. Students of his character have often read his obsession with work to be the evidence of some ungratified desire, the consequence of an unidentified frustration; the search for proof to support this theory has always been unrewarding in the extreme. There is not one indication anywhere in the debris of his life that this might have been a possibility: even his handwriting stayed annoyingly and illegibly the same since the early 1870s.

The concealment theory – also popular in speculation stakes – must be discounted for exactly the same reason. And, while it is of course possible he *could* have covered his tracks in life, he would never have had such power in death. No one who knew him well or slightly has ever been tempted to suggest anything whatever about his private life, which presents a major obstacle for any claim which is advanced.

same variety of plant also had encouraged hearty self-containment. It made him shy, fearful of vulnerability, and unequal to the deep friendships others wanted. He had been bred and nurtured to be alone. "He talked a good deal about you," Flora Priestley wrote to Vernon Lee during one of her long visits to London (n.d.) [1899]. "You certainly interest him more than any of his other friends. This isn't *much* compliment considering who those other friends are! The rest of the time he talked about the necessity of independence and above all self-sufficiency one shld [should] be dependent on *no* one he said, least of all on friends of any sort. It is a mania with him isn't it?"[35] And for the most part it was a well-concealed mania in the traffic of his daily life, belied by warm generosity and numerous acts of kindness which were, it must be owned, never expressions of any contradiction. He was magnificently open-handed in his contributions to everything from the subscription to purchase Manet's *Olympia* for the Louvre to the relief fund raised by the National Academy of Design after the San Francisco earthquake. The sums entered after his name were always among the highest on the list. After Jane Emmet married another friend, von Glehn, and set up housekeeping around the corner, he was intimidating in his welcome. "Sargent is too good to us," Jane von Glehn wrote to her mother (23 December 1904),[36] adding in her next letter [January 1905]; "Sargent has been so awfully nice to me and never loses an opportunity of being friendly." Over and over again his friends record instances of his ability to give pleasure and help: the sumptuous wedding, Christmas and birthday presents, the lunches, teas and musical entertainments in his studio, the recommendations, introductions and ready professional assistance – he was indefatigably liberal with both his money and his time. This was the only side of Sargent's personality available for recollection (and it was of course a less than complete picture, but by no means a distorted or dishonest one).

Though Emily supervised the domestic machinery which produced the meals for many of Sargent's friends at Carlyle Mansions, she never assumed the prerogative of mistress until after her mother's death, when she moved into the chair opposite her brother. By the mid-1890s she was fast approaching forty and the influence of genealogy had already taken a distinct hold. She, like the other Sargent children, was sturdily made, agreeing not with her father's example but with her mother's. In middle age she had a matronly figure, though of course she had never been slim, ever. Her features were firmly set, deliberate and strong, with a square-shaped face set off by a somewhat too prominent chin. She walked with a lumbering sort of self-consciousness, ever mindful of the pitch of her spine and the consequent effect on her posture. She paid careful attention to her toilette, neatly dressing her dark brown hair which was beginning to lighten with the first suggestions of grey. She wore sober, well-made costumes of the best stuffs, never breaching the fashions suitable for a spinster. Her habits were precise and regular, befitting one who knew as much about respectability as loneliness. There was little about her appearance to hint at any unacknowledged flamboyance, or to remind one she was not turning into a quieter version of her mother. But she did have a spirited, delicate intelligence, capable of profound sensitivty and very, very lively humour. She told stories well; her ear was out for jokes and comedy. Her temperament was a sturdy contradiction of the sombre wash that covered her appearance: it was brilliant sparkling colour. Emily never really believed she had been handed less than anyone else.

Sargent, too, was beginning to leave the physical similarities he had once shared with his father behind as he increasingly copied the generous proportions of his mother. He was putting on weight exercise and energy could not reduce, but with his height he was lucky enough to be large without appearing fat. His posture was erect, his step inappropriate to his size, short and quick, with an added metronome precision of an unnecessary walking-stick. His clothes, made by Henry Poole & Co. of Savile Row, were perfectly cut to cover the vast expanse. He was an unmistakable figure made for caricature neither Beerbohm nor Tonks could possibly overlook. His eyes slowly lost the clear intense blue-green of his youth and were turning a less distinct watery grey-green (and by the end of his life they turned worryingly bloodshot), and yet they still remained the most striking feature of his face, slightly bulging, topped with thick brows, and were given little competition by the effective covering offered by his trimmed dense beard, flecked by grey, discoloured by nicotine, concealing much of his pale complexion. He needed spectacles to read, avoided them in work, but never denied he suffered from a slight astigmatism.* Like his sister and his father his personal habits were methodical, framing his boundless industry, and were

* Many years later, in the summer of 1921, during lunch in Bar Harbour, Maine, his attention was drawn to an unsigned portrait in the dining-room, and he was amazed when his host told him that he, Sargent, had done it many years before in Paris. He could remember neither the sitter nor the portrait, and after examining it through the glass he carried in his pocket he mused, " 'Well . . . it *looks* like me! . . . It is me!' " and pointed to the white handkerchief as proof. " 'Do you see that green line around the white?' " he asked. " 'That settles it for me. I recognize my own style, of course, but the handkerchief is conclusive as far as I am concerned. . . . I have an astigmatism . . . that makes me see a red or green line around white objects. Often I paint it in. I have done so here. That green border obviously is not part of the handkerchief. It is a sort of penumbra. By it I can absolutely identify this portrait as mine . . .' " With that, he rolled up his sleeves, signed the painting, and added the incorrect date.

The whole issue of astigmatism and its effects on Sargent's painting opens a hornets' nest much better dealt with by art historians. Sargent of course knew that Monet suffered from astigmatism, and diagnosed its contribution to the development of Impressionism: "the whole field of vision might offer phenomena for the notation of an impressionist, but to the average vision it is only in extreme cases of light and dark that the eye is conscious of seeing something else than the object, in other words conscious of its own medium. . . ." See Arthur Train, "The portrait that Sargent Forgot", *Atlantic Monthly* (May 1929), pp. 663–4; and Charteris, pp. 123–4, 132.

described by Nicola (in his capacity of *valet de chambre*): "He kept good company, and he kept regular hours. His life was as orderly as that of a bishop." He was not keen on domestic animals, putting them in the same category as children, whom he humoured with a tolerant disdain, for they were nothing more than inevitable additions to the parents he did like. Though he claimed only to like very large dogs, in 1920 he gave Emily her second Pekinese ("Tzu") to replace the one blinded by Eliza Wedgwood's dog the year before. She loved the dog and tried to draw out the same affection from her brother: "John admits that he . . . does not bite, nor bark, but when I ask him if he does not think him very pretty John says he has not noticed it!" Emily wrote to Mrs Gardner (9 November 1921).[37] Two years later he was less detached: Tzu, Emily wrote to Mrs Gardner (13 March 1923), "is so engaging that John finds himself giving him little bits of orange at dessert. Then, suddenly, John stops these blandishments & says he does not want Tzu to expect these attentions from him!"[38]

Sargent woke every morning at seven, had breakfast at eight, then his bath (always *after* breakfast), and before going into the studio (at ten) he attended to his correspondence (and after his mother died he would speak to Emily on the telephone every morning). He never read the newspapers and though he did take both the *Daily Telegraph* and the *Daily Mirror*, he only leafed through them for photographs. He sat at his roll-top desk, and answered every letter, in his broad, assertive and illegible writing. He used black ink, always. He had three types of writing-paper which he used consistently throughout his life, ranging from small, thick, greyish blue correspondence-cards (of tumba stock) to two sizes of flysheets (neither large), engraved with his address in a small Roman typeface. His calling-card was engraved in Palace Script, and his bookplate in Engraver's Shaded Roman. Rarely, when acknowledging some honour or refusing an invitation to speak in public (which he regularly did), he would write a preliminary draft, and then copy it out, otherwise he never rehearsed his sentences, and there were very few crossing-outs or corrections, even when he wrote in French. His letters were written at great speed, getting few words to the line, draping the last few letters of a word down the far edge, covering most of the four sides of the flysheet in a crowded, uninviting hieroglyph. He knew his handwriting was impossible, and laughed at it. In 1916 he was given some writing-paper headed with his initials, followed by the phrase "so hard it seems that one must read because another needs will write". "Don't be puzzled at the above," he cautioned a friend (9 January 1917), "it is an old joke of mine that somebody has worked off on me in the shape of a Xmas present of note paper."[39] His correspondence became a heavy burden, getting larger and larger, soon turning into a stream of refusals; still, he never failed to reply, no matter how tiresome or annoying the claim on his time. He had a rubber stamp made inscribed DAMN – the only swearword he permitted himself – and when he was more than usually irritated by a letter he stamped the word all over the sheet, and thereby cleared his irritation before he composed a gentle, measured reply. He did not have the mentality of an archivist; letters were not kept, his desk was chaos, he often lost addresses, but he was never tempted to employ a secretary. By the sheer force of energy, he ploughed through the massive paperwork of his life. He attended to his engagement-diary, juggling sittings with lunch, tea, dinner and musical engagements, in addition to his travel arrangements, and from various passing references in letters he did follow some pattern of accountancy because he knew when a picture had not been paid for. And when he pressed for payment he was apologetic to a fault. In 1905 he was commissioned to paint a portrait of Sir Hugh Lane, "in recognition of his invaluable services to Irish art and in commemoration of the founding of a permanent Collection of Modern Art in Dublin"[40] in the words of Lane's biographer. The portrait was finished in 1906, and two years later, in a letter to W. B. Yeats (23 March) [1908], Sargent hedged round the issue of payment:

> There is another point on which I have more than once thought of writing to you, ever since I painted that bust of Sir Hugh Lane. The feeling is that it is rather coarse to betray such vagueness as mine in business matters has deterred me. The fact is that I have sometimes wondered whether I have ever been paid . . . as I do not find any entry to that effect in a book in which I usually keep such records. It is very possible that I was paid and that I neglected to write it down, but I am quite uncertain; as I am, for that matter, as to the price agreed upon. . . . I would be glad to have my own unbusinesslike vagueness disputed.[41]

After desk work he went to the studio. He stayed there until 1 p.m., had lunch for an hour or an hour and a half, and returned to the studio, light permitting, until five. Sargent enjoyed a prodigious appetite that he found difficult to satisfy and one which left his fellow-diners at the Hyde Park Hotel or the Chelsea Arts Club, where he occasionally went for lunch, breathless in amazement. He complained to William Rothenstein, who witnessed this untame hunger, "that he couldn't get enough to eat there", as Rothenstein wrote in his outsize and extremely helpful autobiography, *Men and Memories*.* "So he often went to the Hans Crescent Hotel, where, from the table d'hôte luncheon of several courses, he could assuage his Gargantuan appetite."[42] A friend who knew Sargent years later recalled with striking clarity that he ate an entire duck at lunch, in the middle of other substantial courses. "He was enormous," Lady Cholmondeley remembered over sixty years later, "with a huge bulging front."[43]

His style of conversation was less substantial, and he delivered his words like a miner crawling through a dark tunnel armed with a faulty

* Professor Mary Lago has beautifully taken care of the former problem in her new edition of *Men and Memories* (1981).

torch. He negotiated language tentatively, as if each syllable presented some hardship he could not quite manage. Like Henry James, he detested any help offered by a listener who was eager for him to get on as he stumbled and looked for the correct word. When he spoke to strangers his words were strung together on a rope of "er – er – er – er", and delivered with a slowness that implied an almost physical activity involved in pushing the sounds around. " 'When he can't finish a sentence' ", Evan Charteris wrote after meeting him at Mrs Henry White's house at Loseley in May 1894, " 'he waves his fingers before his face as a sort of signal for the conversation to go on without him' . . . his conversation was never fluent, but . . . it could be immensely descriptive. He wasted no words . . . he could convey a weight of meaning by a gesture or a truncated phrase . . . but his hesitation was itself often expressive . . ." There was a refinement and a precision in his talk which were, despite lugubrious delivery, neither ponderous nor sombre. No one ever found him boring or dull, because all that he did say showed the large trace-elements of considered thought and humour. To him speaking was not a spendthrift activity, not a candidate for waste, nor was it a reckless borrower. "No man had more entirely home-made opinions," Charteris wrote, "opinions so wholly the unadulterated product of his own reflection or experience."[44] Like Emily, he was drawn to the comedy of human peculiarities, spoke often of his sitters, invited people in during sittings, and delighted in repeating malapropisms he had heard from them, like Mrs Leiter, the mother of the future Lady Curzon, who "had given her daughter 'bête noir' for her trousseau".[45] And he spoke much about his reading which was wide and voluminous, ranging over poetry, history, literature, etc. Alas, no one ever succeeded in describing the sound of his voice, and it was never saved in a sound-recording.

XIII

The portrait ruled the Academy and Sargent ruled the portrait. It was an uncontested fact. Each year he brought forth another magnificent proof, carrying him higher in his vertiginous command. In England, as in America, he revealed the large vanities calling out for the sort of preservation only he could supply, and like any good butler he set to work polishing egos. His patrons were rich, well born, or professionals. He worked his way through the pages of *Who's Who*, then *Debrett* and *Burke's Peerage*, ending up with ample representation in the *Dictionary of National Biography*, but this was only a reflection of his status. There was a simplicity at work which time has distorted. His sitters were those who had a willingness to spend time and a lot of money; to Sargent, each sitter presented new but usually unexciting problems, and his solution, in keeping with his development as a painter, was the urge not to disturb convention, but to adapt it, modernize it to make his subjects a little more vital. Of course he depended on generous garments, sturdy jewellery and other stock items that assisted vanity to produce an aura of soft contentment served unwell by words. This approach gave his sitters a brilliant shine that has continued to reflect far more than he ever intended, turning his baize-apron work into sham historical document. There has always been this less than subtle complication attached to Sargent's portraits. Throughout the long parade there was heard a tempo borrowed from the murals: content battled it out with form, the individual was confused with his portrait, and the portrait was confused with the individual. Sargent had grown used to hearing this monotonous, unnecessary cadence. His technique of portraiture, so free of extraneous, non-visual judgements, aroused some observers at the time and has gone on to inspire historians. People of rank did not much care to see their inferiors portrayed in comparable terms, and the portraits have subsequently been made to line up in opposing trenches to repeat social warfare: heredity, power, order on one side; "upstarts" on the other. And none of this combat had anything whatever to do with Sargent, then or now, for he only blithely employed his eye and his brush. The quality of his work varied enormously, depending on the enthusiasm of his eye, and it is difficult to recapture his uncluttered approach. He was asked to do a job, and that job was assigned to another once it passed out of his studio.

His history of vanity's butler began badly, and continued badly for many years. He came back to London to find commissions already overdue. He was late from the very start. His plan to split the year neatly between his two London studios was sadly misjudged. In October 1895 he started his long stint as a Visitor (instructor) for one month almost every year until he died at the Royal Academy Schools, effectively removing a large slice from his calendar, and by the new year he lent his Fulham Road studio first to Helleu and then to Whistler, foreseeing no immediate need of it himself. He was at his sitters' mercy, and that mercy made his time vanish. His portrait of Mrs George Swinton (née Elizabeth "Elsie" Ebsworth) was ordered as a wedding-present before he sailed to Boston, took a long time to start, longer than necessary to paint because "we wasted a lot of time", Mrs Swinton recalled after Sargent's death, "playing the piano and singing, instead of getting on with the picture",[1] and was finished when Mrs Swinton was coming up to her second anniversary. He stayed on in London during the summer in order to carry out Marquand's portrait for the Metropolitan Museum of Art, and his sitter did not show up: "So many plans hinged upon our engagement from the 24th [July 1896]", he wrote to Marquand, who was ill in America (25 July), "that you cannot believe how opportune a cablegram received two weeks ago would have been."[2] (The non-appearance did, however, allow him to rush off two sketches of George Meredith whom he had met years before at Ightham Mote, to use in the new edition of Meredith's *Works*, despite the subject hating them.) And so it went on; portraits rarely progressed according to the most generous plans. The summer Marquand did not show up, Mrs I. N. Phelps Stokes from New York came to sit for her wedding-gift portrait, in a chair, wearing a green evening-dress. After four sittings Sargent asked for a different, less conventional pose, in the same starched white skirt, tailor-made, and blue serge jacket she wore one warm morning when she strode into Tite Street: " 'I want to paint you just as you are,' " her husband recorded Sargent saying,[3] and the canvas was scraped clean. She was to stand with her hand resting on the head of a Great Dane, who was eventually replaced by a looming presence offered by her husband. The Stokes portrait, accomplished by the collision of accidents, has been credited with a social probity melodious to modern ears. Mrs Stokes held her straw hat where the Great Dane ought to have been, at the very point in her husband's anatomy where spirited critics have been moved to assert she is de-sexing him. This sort of contention is the trap Sargent has been made to fall into, but has no place in his life. Likewise his portrait of Mrs Carl Meyer and her children has been ensnared in a web of conjecture that has nothing to do with the canvas; interpretation has constantly clogged his portraits because visual content, Sargent's only interest, has never quite seemed to be enough.

He showed the picture at the Academy in 1897, his first entry as a full Academician, two months after he learnt of his election (and the same year he was made a full Member of the National Academy of Design in New York); Mrs Swinton was sent over to the New Gallery that spring, indicating Sargent's own preference. The commission gave him the sort of challenge he adored. All the problems of group portraiture that played out the happy conclusions of the Boit and Vickers sisters were present, with added difficulties; though Mrs Meyer, like her children, was extremely pretty, she was also very short. He had to manage an unstrained link between her, her son and her daughter which got his mind working, and when his mind was excited his palette darkened, this time to licorice and fondant. He opened his geometry notebook, adopted dramatic foreshortening in perspective, counteracting that vantage by fanning out Mrs Meyer's luscious bruised-peach-coloured satin overskirt to fill the breadth of the wide canvas. Her legs raised on a low stool, she inclines slightly forward on a Louis XV sofa, one hand holding a fan, the other extending up and back to embrace her son's. He and his sister stand behind the sofa, his arms folded over the sofa back, his head exactly parallel to his mother's and perpendicular to his sister's behind him. She clasps her brother's shoulder, her eyes turned to the front. It is a composition of intricate, diminishing angles, caught in miniature by the open book that has dropped from Mrs Meyer's hand, and again counteracted by the sweep of her generous rope of pearls that curves and tumbles from round her neck, sweeping below her bosom before trailing down to her feet. The picture was opulently furnished with the stuff of money. They were wealthy Jews, comfortable amid their achievement, as comfortable as Lady Agnew or Mrs White or Mrs Gardner.

The picture created a sensation. It was Sargent at his very best, and his very best had been greatly encouraged by the wonderful spectacle of the group. James reviewed it for *Harper's Weekly* in New York:

> It is so far higher a triumph of painting than anything else in the place that, meeting it early in his course, the spectator turns from it with a grateful sense that the whole message of that art has on this occasion, so far as he is concerned, been uttered. . . . Mr. Sargent has made a picture of a knock-down insolence of talent and truth of characterization, a wonderful rendering of life, of manners, of aspects, of types, of textures, of everything. It is the old story; he expresses himself as no one else scarce begins to do in the language of the art he practices. . . . Beside him, at any rate, his competitors appear to stammer. . . .[4]

The picture was an achievement of such magnitude it silenced suspicious rumblings about the subjects, but not for long. Even Henry Adams's cut-glass mentality, chiselled counter to both Sargent and Jews, had to face the obvious: "But just now we all go to the Royal Academy to see Sargent's portrait . . . Mrs Mayer [sic] is a sprightly Jewess, who did us the favor to stand under her portrait on private opening day to show us she was as good as her picture. The art of portrait-painting Jewesses and their children may be varied but cannot be further perfected. Nothing better ever was done or can be done.''[5] And ten years later Wilfred Scawen Blunt wrote with less than accuracy in his diary (14 May 1907): "He paints nothing but Jews and Jewesses now, and says he prefers them, as they have more life and movement than our English women."[6] The long series of Wertheimer portraits, begun in 1898 and stretching over ten years, eleven canvases and a dozen subjects – " 'chronic Wertheimerism' '', he sighed to Lady Lewis early in the stint[7] – spoke more eloquently of this same temptation begun with Mrs Carl Meyer. Sargent's reason for finding pleasure in this class of sitter was uncomplicated; visually they had their place among the same attraction that had drawn him to Rosina, to Madame Gautreau, to La Carmencita, to the Bedouins, to Coventry Patmore, to Graham Robertson, and to his Prophets. These sitters joined the continuous, unbroken line – and that was the only benign prejudice Sargent could be said to possess.

Historically Sargent stood in a place that has allowed for no such tidy directness of purpose. By painting respresentatives of a class of people finding prominence and security in England, supplying a new financial and mercantile expertise, under the benediction of the Court, Sargent could be blamed for acting out a different sort of prejudice (and not an exceedingly popular one), especially as he later had the run of the aristocracy for his subjects. Sargent did for the Meyers, the Wertheimers, and later the Sassoons, what Ingres had done for Napoleon, which automatically threw into relief the unwitting precision of Rodin's comment in 1902 that he was "the Van Dyck of our times". And as such he found a role unconnected with his art. In his acutely argued essay on English art at the time, John Russell made the high claim that Sargent's Wertheimer portraits

> represent a unique contribution to the iconography of Edwardianism . . . the Wertheimer portraits could not have been carried out – could indeed, with difficulty have been conceived – at any other period. . . . One of Sargent's greatest charms, for Edwardian society, was his ability to give new money a good opinion of itself. . . . Quicker than the Home Office, he naturalized those who would otherwise have lingered in the between-world where class, nationality, money, and money's provenance, were matters not to be raised without a qualm. For the reassurance-collector there was no other painter in the country.[8]

But there was more at work than the bonus of unexpected chronological partnership: Sargent, too, was an outsider; as a born observer he could rise above the brambles that kept the social order intact. He was immune, by birth and temperament, to any of the subtle forces that found containment in the standard English reflex of xenophobia – contempt for success, money, achievement, all of which were jealously guarded as a national prerogative and strengthened by an inbred suspicion of foreigners. He was in the luxurious position to disregard the unspoken pivots of social manoeuvres, which inevitably made him and his portraits the target of so much useless speculation. He was deaf to the foul lowings of anti-Semitism. He was insulated by his emotional neutrality. And once again a basic advantage was turned into the reverse. Sargent's function as a social recorder was a happy coincidence that revealed little of his character, and was only turned to a purpose away from the studio, carried away in historians' hands.

Of more immediate importance, however, was the fact that Sargent liked the Meyers, the Wertheimers and the Sassoons. Carl Meyer (1851– 1922) came from Hamburg and enjoyed an illustrious career in England – JP, Lieutenant of the City of London, Director of the National Bank of Egypt, Chairman of the London Committee of De Beer – and eventually capped his achievement by being created a baronet in 1910: it was the sort of social mobility people liked to deride. He and his wife were energetic hosts to artists and musicians. (Meyer listed music as one of his hobbies in *Who's Who*; the other was shooting.) Sargent's affection for them was told by the seemingly insignificant fact that he stayed with them in their house in the country, Balcome Place, Haywards Heath, which for him was a rare indication of friendship. Likewise he stayed at the Wertheimers' country house, the Temple. Asher Wertheimer (1844–1918) and his wife Flora Joseph (d.1922) conducted life on a lively, individual and immense scale. Their house in Connaught Place contained ten children – four sons, six daughters – a host of dogs, and an endless stream of painters, musicians and writers, who moved about the outsize rooms loaded with impeccable furniture and *objets de vertu* assembled with Wertheimer's keen eye that had made his Bond Street shop so impressive. It was family life to a big order. The fastidious air of elegance, the great dinner-parties were all softened by the children's casual attitude, and Sargent was quickly absorbed. He painted them all, sometimes more than once, with drastically varying degrees of success, and the portraits slowly accumulated on the walls; the dining-room was called "Sargent's Mess". Of all the children, Sargent warmed most to Ena. His portrait of her and her sister Betty passing through the hall at Connaught Place, and Ena alone in a swirling cape over a borrowed tunic, holding an umbrella, were among the best of the long series. She was a dashing figure, hopelessly vague about money, engagements and any domestic routine when she set up house herself in Montagu Square. It was Connaught Place all over again, without the slightest reference to discipline. She had the same quick devotion to paintings, painters and music as her parents, and was wonderfully slapdash in its expression. Jacques-Emil Blanche, who admired her exceedingly, went into raptures about her capacity for fun, in the otherwise snobbish recital of anglo-mania he called his autobiography. The Wertheimers, who must have been remarkable, have been badly served by posterity. Only Asher Wertheimer's feeling for acquisition gave him and his family a sort of permanence through generous patronage of modern painters, especially Sargent, whose long association with the Wertheimers, sadly unilluminated by facts, was institutionalized in 1926 when Duveen gave the Sargent Gallery to the Tate to house most of the Wertheimer series, which was bequeathed to the nation. It was a high commemoration of both an artist's sustained body of work and a patron's enthusiasm for an artist.

Fame agreed with Sargent; he rose to it, welcomed it, and kept it, seizing it as a just reward and his due wage – and his reaction to fame helped him to be misunderstood. He was carried along in a fast-moving current. He became an unavoidable figure, taking up a lot of room, presenting a wide, starched expanse beyond the candles, linen, flowers, plate and silver in dining-rooms across town, to become what Max Beerbohm later called "one of the stock ornaments of dinner-tables"[9] and earning him no less than seventeen Beerbohm caricatures. In a short story by Maurice Baring, "A Luncheon-Party", an ambitious hostess enters into a pact with the devil " 'to be supplied with a guest who make all other luncheon-parties look, so to speak, like thirty cents' ". He suggests Botticelli or Bellini or Benvenuto Cellini, before being silenced with, " 'What's the use of them when I can get Sargent every day?' "[10] His name joined the guest-list parlance with James for availability. He moved about his clubs – the Arts, where he had been a member since 1885, the Reform (since 1895), the Athenaeum (from 1898) and the Chelsea Arts. The celebrity which propelled him was not enough to cover the limitations of his conversational skills to be much of an asset to the arch-puppeteers like the Marchioness of Londonderry at Londonderry House in Park Lane, Lady Desborough (who was strangely unmusical and oblivious to the charms of art) in her planetarium of Souls at Taplow Court, or the Duchess of Rutland in Arlington Street (though she herself was an enormously able artist). Yet while fame certainly set his feet in motion, it had not turned his head; he remained strikingly the same, pursuing his social entertainments among a fixed number of houses. Hostesses needed but two tugs to get a ready response, music and art, and music was the surest. Mrs Hammersley got him to Hampstead, Mrs Meyer and Lady Lewis drew him to Portland Place, Mrs Swinton to Pont Street, the Wertheimers to Connaught Place, later the Rathbones to Cadogan Gardens, Phillip Sassoon to Park Lane and Lympne and his sister to Houghton in Norfolk, and Mrs Charles Hunter pulled him over to Old Burlington Street and out to Epping.*

* Of this list, Mrs Swinton was more a musician than hostess, though art did have a considerable presence in her house; her husband studied painting with Herkomer, before distinguishing himself in the College of Heralds, and she was painted by Sickert and *en famille* in 1901 by Orpen whom she introduced to Sargent. She was a gifted musician: "the incomparable warmth of her voice cast a strange spell," Osbert Sitwell, a cousin by marriage recalled in his autobiography, *Left Hand, Right Hand!* (1944), p. 215. She began her professional career at the Aeolian Hall in 1906, introducing Russian songs as well as Fauré, whose reputation in England she did a lot to advance, with Sargent's assistance. At the same

But Sargent was an unlikely candidate for social prominence, and it was the fault of the portraits. They tyrannized him and, worse, they colonized him with an unwieldy administration that overwhelmed him. He had lost control of his routine. He was the victim of an unwelcome imperialism, denying him even the vaguest sense of balance. His despair mounted over the years, and the declension of unease grew stronger. "No more portraits after I finish the current lot," he declared in May 1896,[11] and the following spring he sighed, "from now on I am having three sittings a day and hardly an interval in between".[12] A year later it was the same when he rushed back from Venice "to plunge into five or six [portraits] some of them already begun, and I am pretty certain that I will not be able to undertake a new order this season".[13] Yet three months later, in August 1898, he groaned with the often-repeated syllables, "Several portraits are still going on and show no sign of being done . . . which means I cannot get away – for those two or three people are hanging on in London, cursing God and man, simply on account of their sittings."[14] The old formula of summer in the mountains and winter in the studio had disappeared. He was locked in town, at the height of the summer, year after year, because tourists found that moment the most suitable to pose in Tite Street. And each unfinished portrait made it harder to refuse another commission, because he would not leave work undone. Social life was his only escape; it was his only possible version of holiday. He had to steal his pleasures from under the greed of the portraits, briefly, and as a guest. It was the only possible compromise, and hostesses

---

concert Percy Grainger played. In his portrait of her shown at the New Gallery in 1897, Sargent replayed the soft harmonies of Ada Rehan, borrowed the grace of her right arm from Madame Gautreau while losing the left in cascading satin. The portrait moves in and out of pitch, explained by one critic at the time: "It is by these resources of the art of suggestion that the painter has made his canvas seem alive" (John Lomax and Richard Ormond, *John Singer Sargent and the Edwardian Age* (1979) p. 60). He also did a charcoal sketch of her at the time of her début.

Lady Lewis (née Elizabeth Eberstadt), the second wife of Sargent's solicitor Sir George Lewis, was painted in 1892 and her portrait was shown with Mrs Hammersley's at the New Gallery. She was a close friend of Henschel's, was an accomplished duet partner at the piano, and was one of the chief musical hostesses of her day. Charteris quotes Sargent's letters to her from the early 1890s to 1904.

William Gair Rathbone (1849–1919), financier and banker, was a man of exceptionally refined musical taste and ability with an ear especially tuned to modern composers; he was a champion of both Wagner and Fauré. His patronage and affection for Percy Grainger has been well-documented by Grainger's biographer, John Bird (1976; see ch. 6). And Percy Grainger was another component in the make-up of Sargent's musical life. He was introduced to both Sargent and Rathbone by Ernest Thesiger, painter-turned-actor in the early years of the century. Grainger was a regular performer at both's At Homes, as well as a frequent visitor at Tite Street, and Grainger later claimed it was mostly through the kind offices of Sargent that he was able to earn his living.

naturally sprang quickly to gain his society. Mrs Hunter moved with Olympic confidence, for she had developed a frightening stamina in the social race.

Mary Hunter (née Smyth) and her younger sister Ethel (later Dame Ethel Smyth) were a formidable pair, in opposing ways; while Ethel covered a lot of ground – from music, to bellicose feminism, to wordy autobiography – Mary gathered her troops around her, and they both arrived at their softened version of campaigning by the rights of genealogy. Their father was an artillery officer stationed in the suburbs and their mother was the product of a complicated domestic arrangement posted in France. The sisters grew up in the cross-influences of conventionality and eccentricity. And both girls were a sort of beef-cattle who lowered their eyes on the surrounding fences, taking quite different measurements. Mary was calculating how many could graze in her pasture and Ethel was kicking to get out, and their success, measured in contrary fat-stock analysis, was considerable.

In one of her many volumes (seven) of memoirs Ethel lamented the absence of any "orthodox love affair to relate".[15] In her youth she toyed with the idea of marrying a duke's son or becoming a nun; in middle age she enjoyed a spotlessly chaste romance with the American poet Harry Brewster, who wrote in French and lived in Italy; and in later life she indulged in a good deal of unsatisfied fumbling with other ladies, and throughout the long process she found true affection with her dogs. She crossed Europe for her music, meeting a lot of people, and brushing up against Vernon Lee with whom she could claim an abrasive friendship. She was an ardent mountain-climber who mastered altitudes Sargent flatly admired – 11,000 feet[16] – longing for such purity of air and light himself. He was less keen on her politicking – brick-throwing was not his line – and her unexpected talent to discard pleasure when she gave up smoking in 1899. " 'What's this nonsense about your having given up smoking?' " he blurted out. " 'Well, I never should have thought you were so weak-minded!' "[17] Her ability as a composer and a singer helped to cover over the many cracks in their unsolid friendship, as well as the discomfort of her cottage in Surrey. And when it became painfully obvious that she had lost yet another friend to her sister, Ethel Smyth searched for a higher reason than mere pique to explain her dislike of Sargent; the excuse she published in her memoirs was that he had asked her to *pretend* to like Elgar, as people might be inclined to think she was jealous! He was much fonder of her sister, who was less hard work and who made certain he would be.

Mary's amatory adventures were only slightly less unusual than her sister's. In July 1875 she married Charles Hunter who left her side immediately after the ceremony, out of respect, that is, for his new wife's dying brother, but from that day on it remained much of a one-sided marriage. Mrs Hunter tried out her ambition first on her husband – prodding him to go into the House – before moving on to bigger and more responsive game. She took little interest in his love of sport and hunting, and steadfastly refused to respect his intelligence though he did love pictures and was moderately keen on music. His chief recommendations were his unswerving devotion to her, and his prodigious wealth which came from coalmines. Still, she tended to regard him as a somewhat bothersome restraint in her " 'sacred duty' ", as she phrased it to her sister,[18] "to spend every penny she could of his money!" In this, she was too successful; the money ran out several years before she did, but while she spent, she spent with abandon, having not troubled herself to take on board the vaguest notion of the value of money: it was only meant to slip out of her hand, and to give pleasure.

Mrs Hunter was a higher calibre Mrs Gardner, generous, lively, determined, and utterly indefatigable. She was a well-tuned steam-launch, capable of fifteen knots, from which immense nets were cast, hauling in a heterogeneous crowd. She thought nothing odd in a guest-list made up of Edith Wharton, Vita Sackville-West, Chaliapin, Walter Berry and Bernard Berenson. People were the condiment of her life, and were often confused with the main course. There was the high flavour of enthusiasm about her. When she got an idea in her head, nothing would wrest it from place, she would brook no contrariness. People came for her hospitality, which she never confused, but they stayed because they liked her, and because she was clever. Everything about her was conceived on lavish lines, from her appearance to her manners, which were burnt through with a hot iron of imperiousness, because she insisted on the best, money being no obstacle. Her husband feared her adroit talent for expenditure and was helpless to restrain her. He never lived to see his discarded ambition realized, for after the war the long, ruinous coal strikes did for Mary what he never could. By 1919 she finally ceased to make free with her banknotes. But until his death in 1916, Charles Hunter's life was a series of winces brought on by his wife's unstoppable spree. For many years they had one house in Old Burlington Street, Mayfair, which was neither large enough or expensive enough to satisfy Mary, and another in Epping, Hill Hall, where she was given enough room to turn in witheringly punishing accounts. Mary Hunter felt at home in Hill Hall. It became an unavoidable stop on the social tramway (as it remained until it burnt down in 1969, for quite a different reason; it became a prison). Hill Hall was a tremendous Elizabethan house, built round a court, of considerable architectural importance, of noble pro-portions, beautifully arranged, full of lovely things. Mary Hunter had no feeling for the garden, and having once ordered a rose garden to be planted *en masse* her interest came to an end. Her pleasures were exclusively indoor, keen on crowds, keener on celebrities. Painters flocked to her table along with musicians; everyone from Monet, Rodin, Mancini, Blanche, Tonks, Rothenstein, Helleu, to Grainger, Quilter, Beecham and Delafosse. And writers had pretty active representation as well. Mrs Hunter simply moved Mayfair a good many miles to the east.

But Sargent was her principal catch. He painted her in 1898 (though they had met years before), densely cloaked, peering out from below a confection of a hat, eyes shaded but bright, quick alert smile, ready for action, and thereafter their friendship accelerated. (He decorated columns in her house.) He adored her with the brisk air of having enrolled into an establishment designed for his comfort. She considered his desires, and served them back to him fulfilled, on a silver salver. She had the fierce illumination of optimism and spread her arms wide for pleasure, extending her generosity to Emily, Mrs Sargent, Mrs Curtis and a large collection of Sargent's friends. Above all, she was considerate, giving the impression, from the few uncluttered glimpses that survive of her character, that unlike Mrs Gardner her urge for liking people was greater than her desire for collecting them. All her life she was a strong magnet for male attention, and unlike her sister she rarely gave her own sex a thought, and Sargent's customary undemonstrative response, she concluded, as so many had mistakenly before her, was a sign of some deeper affection. Their friendship instantly coupled their names in gossip's hot pursuit of some romance, and by 1910 their linked names entered common usage. People watched the non-romance unfold with nail-biting eagerness. "Sargent has started for Dalmatia leaving 'Mrs Tally ho' behind," Curtis informed Mrs Gardner (4 August) [1907].[19] Later, in 1915, people felt sufficiently bold (and confident) to ask Mrs Hunter outright "if there had been anything between her and Sargent", Cynthia Asquith recorded in her diary (29 December 1915) after hearing both the question and Mrs Hunter's reply: " 'I have *always* wanted to, but I always feel when I come into the room and see Charlie that I should have to tell him, so I haven't.' "[20] The wonderful entertainment of watching the progress of the unchased keyed up after the war, when both parties, well settled into their sixties, looked set for matrimony (Mrs Hunter having been granted the freedom of widowhood). She insisted upon going to America with him, unchaperoned, thus gathering up the obliging pressures of gossip, etiquette, chivalry and correct behaviour to force the match. His friends were appalled. Evan Charteris was begged by Lady Elcho to intercede, and he flatly refused, adding "that he wasn't convinced that the marriage would be a bad thing for Sargent", Cynthia Asquith wrote in her diary (20 February 1919).[21] Sargent sailed alone, but sent a dense volley of letters back to the defeated.

The amatory shadow-boxing was an overworked turn. From the start there had been but one participant, and yet of all his suitors Mrs Hunter was granted the clearest run of Sargent's unknown emotions, for she turned her constancy into real friendship, lasting for many years. Mrs Hunter was permitted to go where Emily had safe passage in his character. If anybody posed a threat to Emily's exclusive claim, Mrs Hunter was the one. For her, such unconsummated contact had a double benefit, because he was both a steadfast companion and the brightest medal at her dinner-table. No hostess could boast a higher consequence of her achievement. For Sargent the process was a happy one, after his initial courtesy softened into genuine, though chaste, affection. As an auxiliary Emily, Mrs Hunter had a sheltered place in his geography and became the next best thing to a confidante; next best because he had so little to confide. Hill Hall became a distant Carlyle Mansions. Their friendship strengthened over the next twenty-five years, gaining force after the death of his mother. His letters to her were long, and written in a tone of banished reluctance. He kept her informed of the facts of his life, and the worries, without ever managing to scale the protection that restrained him from intimacy. They got close, but never touched; for Sargent this presented no limitation.

Music was the accepted currency throughout his social tourism. In London, as in much the same manner begun in Broadway, music alone furnished the essence of the holiday mood. He escaped the portraits through music, and as music was primarily a domestic pastime he had no choice but to turn into a "stock ornament of dinner-tables". He was happy among musicians because he had no difficulty converting interests and activities into friends. Music was a neutral and generous channel in social intercourse, and Sargent knew no parsimony in his dealings with musicians. He used his celebrity to help Percy Grainger and Gabriel Fauré because hostesses' ears were sensitive to his recommendations, and when he suggested a performer for an evening's entertainment that performer was engaged, and paid. He turned himself into a hospitable bureau de change. His studio became a concert hall in the evenings, for string quartets, folk music, recitals. For Sargent, help and encouragement played a strong part in his pleasure.

Sargent's association with Fauré (1845–1924) has much the same uncertainty as that with Monet (and with so many of his French friends); while the evidence remains thin and widely scattered, the conclusions drawn have been significant – Fauré's biographers believe that Sargent did for Fauré what James tried to do for Sargent: establish him in England. In France, Fauré had considerable difficulty establishing himself as a composer, and his reputation only began to flourish when he was well into his forties. Hitherto he was a more notable social figure, associated closely with the Proustian galaxy, of Proust himself, la comtesse Greffulhe, le comte Robert de Montesquiou, and la princesse Edmond de Polignac, whose salon was a dense hive of musical activity: Ravel, Satie, Stravinsky, Weill, Milhaud, de Falla, Poulenc and Fauré all dedicated works to her.[22] Sargent had known Fauré since his Boulevard Berthier days, through his neighbours the Duezes and the Jourdains, and he met him again in 1889 when he was in Paris painting la princesse Edmond de Polignac (technically, then la princesse Louis de Scey-Montheliard; the marriage was anulled in 1892 and she remarried). When Fauré turned to London, as he increasingly did after 1892, he found a concentrated band of admiration for his music that put him in the way of recognition unforthcoming in Paris, contriving an atmosphere where "all is dreams and poetry" as he wrote to Mrs Swinton (October 1898) after staying with her in Wales that August: "here [Paris], alas, all is work and prose".[23] He found a willing champion in Sargent, who was not in the least daunted by his style of composition, so rich and unrelenting in harmonic pattern, neither "intoxicated",[24] as Proust claimed to be (carrying it over to his description of Vinteuil's music) nor bewildered. Fauré seemed ripe for a cause, apart from that supplied by his music (which was pushed in America by Loeffler); he was charming, modest, handsome, dedicated. And when at last he gained fame he was forced to endure a most disagreeable form of deafness that made low notes sharp, high notes flat, and the middle range indistinct. Yet he continued to compose, and when he retired from his post at the Conservatoire in 1921, he was nearly penniless. That year Sargent sent him a gift of 2000 fr., and Fauré gave him the manuscript of his Second Piano Quintet (Op. 114). It was a constant interchange of help and gratitude. Sargent got Fauré's songs, among the most beautiful ever written, into drawing-rooms and on to the concert platform. He was regarded as Fauré's prime devotee in England (perhaps unjustly, though he was the best-known admirer). Sargent opened doors; Fauré's worth took over after that: in 1908 he played for the King. Fauré referred to Sargent in a letter to Loeffler (6 April 1921) as "notre cher grand ami";[25] Sargent said the same, in his own language, painting two portraits and doing two pencil sketches. Fauré was, above all, a fortunate recipient of the strange set of circumstances that sent Sargent into society. There was an unobvious kind of mercy bound into the tyranny of the portraits.

The murals were less fortunate. His postponed loyalty to Boston assumed a criminal attitude, as if he had to steal time to devote himself to the larger, more important commission. "I am up to my ears in previous orders," he wrote to Mrs Swinton [4 July 1898], "and must keep at least six months for my decorations."[26] It was a calculation born of optimism. And though the novelty, fear and doubt that had attended the start of the project were replaced by an all too clear knowledge of what he had taken on, the second round had the unremitting challenge of the clock to hinder him. His research was conducted at a fast pace, with the urgency of theft. He rushed off to Sicily in January 1897 after nearly sixteen uninterrupted months in England, and stayed away for just over six weeks. After seeing the Cathedral in Palermo, he headed north to Rome, especially to see the Borgia Apartments in the Vatican decorated by Pinturicchio – "in view of his Boston Library work", Harry Brewster, who managed to gain them entry, wrote to Ethel Smyth after their visit, adding that Sargent "was in raptures over them".[27] And with good reason, for there he found the vital precedent he needed to smooth the eccentric marriage of iconography he was himself performing across the walls and ceiling in Boston. Sargent sighed when he saw it had been done before, long before, in the late fifteenth century when Pinturicchio painted lives of saints in lunettes and Isis, Osiris and Apis on the ceiling of the Sala dei

Santi. The necessary licence was granted; he could make free with symbols, safely.

From Rome he sped to Florence for a few days. The following year he was just as rushed, allowing himself but a month away from his post, for Venice, staying at the Barbaro, and he cut short his visit to see Ravenna. "As I foresaw," he wrote to Mrs Curtis [27 May 1898], "there were mosaics in St Apollinaire that had to be sketched & I have spent my day there."[28] By 1899 he was luckier, escaping portraits for most of the summer, three and a half years after he had signed the second contract.

Until then he was forced to perform the awful juggling act. He hurtled between Fulham Road and Tite Street, mornings with portraits and afternoons (during the winter) with the murals as natural light was less important. Towards the end of 1898 he had created the focal point of the Christian Portion – the crucifix that would have the same function as Moses holding the tablets on the opposite wall: a central image for the surrounding narrative that also held its place in historical accuracy. From each imposing symbol, executed in high relief to make the value unmistakable, his grand conception evolved. They were the two axes of the entire scheme, and they helped to move the mural beyond mere decoration to statement, and thus satisfy Carolus' dictum of an artist's high purpose. With the appearance of the crucifix his grand plan was beginning to emerge. And as with the Hebraic Portion he was excessively ambitious, but unlike Moses the crucifix was made to contain a welter of symbols. In the first model Christ's foot rests on a coiling serpent; Adam and Eve kneel below his outstretched arms, bound to the cross, raising chalices to Christ's lifeless hands; a pelican serving up its blood in a representation of the Saviour is at the base. There was nothing simple about its content or, as Sargent quickly found out, about its creation. He was beset by ignorance. "I am much in need of the head that is on your shoulders," he wrote to Augustus Saint-Gaudens in Paris (13 October) [1898],[29] who conducted Sargent through the defects in his knowledge. "But you will tell me something about patinas," Sargent wrote to him, "of which I am totally ignorant." Saint-Gaudens supervised the casting of the various models sent to him in Paris. He visited Sargent early in the new year. "I am very glad you are coming over here," Sargent wrote to Saint-Gaudens, "for I have been working at my crucifix and made very great alterations and improvements which I am very anxious to show you. I shall now start it on a large scale, and you will be able to give me some advice."[30] Bronze casts of the small version of the crucifix were given to a few friends. He sent one to Mrs Curtis in Venice as "my very belated little souvenir", he wrote to her. "It looks best, I must tell you, hung about the level of one's eye, and if possible under a vertical light – at any rate not raked by a strong side-light. Of course it is merely a cast from the rough sketch and there are lots of things that I have changed and improved upon since, for instance Adam's ridiculous hand which I deplore! He is

not at all worthy of the Barbaro.''*³¹ The large crucifix was finished
sometime around the late spring of 1900. After that, he could deal with
the frieze and lunette, which would serve largely as a frame for his
elaborate cross. The crucifix, more than Moses, provided both a unity and
such a complicated, looming device that the wall paintings could not
possibly be on the same order as the Hebraic precedent.

The juggling act went on; the portraits would not be ignored. In
February 1899 he left his work on the second rendering of the crucifix to
do portrait service in a very large house in Belgrave Square. He moved
over to *Debrett* and *Burke's Peerage* to paint the daughters of the Hon.
Percy Wyndham; he was the brother of the 2nd Baron Leconfield and
they were Lady Elcho (later the countess of Wemyss and March), Mrs
Charles Adeane and Lady Glenconner – née Mary, Madeline and Pamela
Wyndham. He was stationed in the vast drawing-room, before a canvas
that measured nearly 10 feet by 7 feet, and he dealt with the task as if it
were an extension of the murals, somewhat loose on details (knowing
how they can get lost on such an expanse) and strong on contrast. The job
was as much physical labour as art, and when Wilfrid Scawen Blunt met
Sargent on the doorstep after the morning's sitting, Blunt took him "to be
a superior mechanic".³² Sargent saw them as three unfragile aquatic
animals, lolling in the warm foam washed up on the seashore, playing in
the only shaft of sunlight. Their mother watches over them from the
shade beyond in Watt's portrait. This languid depiction owed nothing to
the geometric exercise of his other group portraits; it relied on the
elaboration of silhouette, white on a dark surface. The picture was shown
at the Royal Academy the following spring; and the critics, finding their
vocabularies more than usually strained after looking at five portraits by
Sargent there and two more at the New Gallery, managed to find the
strength to crack out a few thunderbolts of praise. D. S. MacColl showed
more reluctance than his colleagues: "one of those truces in the fight
where beauty has unquestionably slipped in. . . . This picture has the
initial persuading and welcoming appeal to the eye that springs from

* And, as such, equal to the first miscalculation he made when he offered Mrs
Curtis a souvenir of his Barbaro visit in 1898 – the group portrait of the Curtises in
their sala nobile, *Venetian Interior* as it was later called. Mrs Curtis hated the
picture and refused to accept it; James, who saw it in Sargent's studio in January,
wrote to Mrs Curtis three months later (16 March 1899): "The *Barbaro Saloon* thing
. . . I absolutely & unreservedly *adored*. I can't help thinking you have a slightly
fallacious impression of the effect of your (*your*, dear Mrs. Curtis) indicated head
& face. It is an indication so *sommaire* that I think it speaks entirely for itself – as a
simple sketchy hint – & it didn't displease me . . . I've seen few things of S's that
I've ever craved more to possess! I hope you haven't altogether let it go . . ."
(Dartmouth College Library). She did, and Sargent submitted it to the Royal
Academy as his belated Diploma Picture.

His second offering, the small bronze crucifix, measured 20 inches by 29 inches
approximately. The large version, destined for Boston, was shown at the Royal
Academy in 1901.

general design and harmony."[33] The Prince of Wales surveyed it and renamed it "The Three Graces".[34]

After the Wyndham sisters' portrait he was more firmly entrenched in the land of the Souls, joining Mrs Henry White and James as one of the token Americans welcomed into the slightly self-consious band that numbered Balfour, Curzon, the Grenfells, Cust, some Tennants and the Charterises (Lady Elcho's family by marriage). Their activities have been beautifully documented,* and Sargent owned the most fragile membership by having painted or drawn many of the list. He knew Lady Elcho from Broadway, but his only friendship was formed with Evan Charteris (1864–1940), her brother-in-law, who eventually transferred his activities from law (King's Counsel) to art, becoming Sargent's biographer. And with the Souls arrived the aristocracy. He had a new category of patron. They grew into a formidable list. Sargent joined his predecessors on the walls of Blenheim Palace, Chatsworth, Welbeck Abbey; he was chosen to continue a long tradition. His style changed, slowly, because he now had another master to add to sitters' vanity: history.

He did not give in to the weight of tradition easily or completely, for his integrity was at least absolute enough to satisfy his own standards *and* produce a canvas that could fit in. In June 1899 the Swintons accompanied him to Renishaw to meet their cousin Sir George Sitwell, and to see the Copley family group Sargent was commissioned to match. " 'I can never equal that,' " he declared,[35] and nine months later tried to do just that at Tite Street, with furniture, a huge tapestry, the Copley, five Sitwells, a nurse, a pug and a collection of toys and ornaments moved down from Renishaw for the occasion. Sir George bullied Sargent relentlessly, having previously perfected his talent of irritating artists on Tonks and Richmond. He was permitted his say in his family's clothes, and he made a most miscellaneous selection. He ordered a still-life and table scraped out. He asked that Edith's distinctive nose should be made more pronounced; Sargent straightened it and made Sir George's crooked. Sir George never let up until the picture was done, and then, when the doors of Tite Street were opened on various members of the Sitwell family who came to view, the criticism began all over again, with renewed ferocity.

The portrait works were retooled and expanded in 1900. The Sitwell tutorial had been squeezed in among the Renishaw articles, the Copley, Sargent's own portrait of them, as well as the Wyndham sisters, quite apart from several more modestly sized canvases. Aristocrats needed a lot of room. In August, with the minimum of fanfare, Sargent leased the house next door, cut through the adjoining wall, and thereafter entered through number 31 Tite Street. It was an unradical solution designed for speed and simplicity, until the builders got to work while he was in Switzerland and Italy. He rushed back to London when he learnt "news of my new house and the workmen doing the wrong thing", he wrote to

---

* By Jane Abdy and Charlotte Gere, *The Souls* (London, 1983).

Curtis. "I had hoped to find it more or less habitable instead of which hardly anything has been done, and that contrary to my instructions and the instincts of the least aesthetic brute."[36] He stayed at the Reform Club.

The two studios, connected by a short flight of wooden stairs descending from number 31 and separated by a tall door, doubled his working-space. The new studio was much like the old one, large, pilaster-lined walls, parquet floor, and a huge east window. In addition, the cramped living-quarters of number 33 were greatly increased, giving him room and need for servants; eventually his household included a cook-housekeeper, Carr, and her sister who performed the duties of house-maid, as well as Nicola's daily service.

He now had a very substantial establishment, absolutely correct for the new league of sitters trooping down Tite Street. " 'The street that on a wet and dreary morning has vouchsafed the vision of Lady Macbeth in full regalia magnificently seated in a four-wheeler' ", Oscar Wilde observed to Graham Robertson at the height of Sargent's theatrical portraits years before, " 'can never be the same as other streets: it must always be full of wonderful possibilities.' "[37] From the turn of the century, Tite Street turned into the parade-ground of titles. In 1908, Max Beerbohm cari-catured the activities at number 31. A substantial line-up of furs, jewels, hats, tiaras, gowns and toques, interspersed with bored messenger-boys holding the place for more furs, jewels, hats, tiaras, gowns and toques, patiently fill the pavement waiting for admission; Sargent scans them from the window, none too overjoyed. The employers were now flocking to the servant. And it was a stampede.

Sargent's reputation was an ibex, thriving on the thinnest air, high in the mountains. He was out of reach, difficult to track on an ever-upward climb. Triumphs came to Sargent as part of the scenery: honorary degrees, national honours from Belgium, Germany, Prussia, France. In February 1899 he was given his first comprehensive show at Copley Hall in Boston; 110 works – fifty-three oils, sixteen drawings, and forty-one sketches – an almost unknown honour for a living painter. In May 1901 he was approached by Edward VII's Equerry-in-Waiting, Lieutenant-Colonel Sir George Holford, at the suggestion of the King himself, to accept the commission to paint the coronation. "I have delayed for a day or two writing you", he wrote to Colonel Holford (28 May 1901),

> . . . in a vain hope of seeing the commission that His Majesty has graciously thought of honouring me with in another light than that of sheer impossibility. The fact of my entire dependence on nature, both for likeness and qualities of painting, make me particularly unfit for this high task. . . . The result would be a greater disappointment to His Majesty than that of learning that I am quite disqualified. It is an admission that it grieves me deeply to have to ask you to convey to His Majesty. . . .[38]

(The commission went to another American, Abbey.) Years later, when

Sargent did the portraits of the generals of the Great War, he proved the precision of his terms of disqualification for this sort of commemorative work; not only did he hate doing it, but the result was wooden in the extreme. The stampede that was clattering down Tite Street went all the way to Buckingham Palace, twice – a second time six years later, Sargent removed himself from accepting the honours his adopted country wanted to give. In June 1907, Edward VII wrote to his Prime Minister, Campbell-Bannerman, recommending Sargent for a knighthood (as well as Abbey) in the Birthday Honours, on the grounds that Sargent was "the most distinguished portrait painter in England".[39] Both Sargent and Abbey, as Americans, could not be offered the title, and the knighthoods were bestowed on Herkomer and Orchardson, the King's two other recommendations.

Some sitters, however, held back from joining the growing queue outside the studio. The Duke of Portland managed to get Sargent to Welbeck Abbey to paint his portrait with his two collies, Ben and Queen, woven about him. When Ben peed on Sargent's portrait of Queen, Sargent said: " 'Well, that is either the greatest insult or the greatest compliment an artist has ever been paid!' " Two years later he returned to paint the Duchess, staying for a month. The first attempt was slashed after nearly a fortnight's sittings, and the Duchess, on seeing a fresh canvas where an almost completed one stood the day before, broke down in tears, not unreasonably. " 'I know you so well now' ", Sargent said, " 'that if you will only let me try again, I am quite sure I can paint something "alive". . . .' "[40] And he did, quickly. After clambering across the roof and terraces of Somerset House with Lord Ribblesdale, looking for a suitable setting, they both went back to Tite Street. Sargent asked to paint Lord Ribblesdale after seeing him at an Artists' Benevolent Fund dinner, went to stay with him on his way back to London from Renishaw in the summer of 1899; and the portrait, one of Sargent's most famous, was finished in 1902. Master of the Buckhounds, Liberal Whip of the House of Lords, Lord-in-Waiting, with an aristocratic appearance more than equal to that list, Ribblesdale was taken effortlessly as the epitome of Edwardian grandeur: "ce grand diable de milord anglais"[41] was whispered as he strode through the galleries of the Salon. Sargent painted him in riding kit, white waistcoat and breeches, framed in a voluminous dark coat, shiny black boots and hat, one hand on his hip, the other gathering up his whip, casting a deep shadow across the parquet floor and on to a pilaster. To Sargent, Ribblesdale was another Graham Robertson. Ribblesdale was to aristocratic disdain what Robertson was to effete, and so, superficially, he has been taken ever since. Sargent was at work on a "type". Though the three Ladies Acheson did come to Tite Street to pose, Sargent's portrait shows them outside, at work with oranges, tied on to a tree specially for the occasion.

The dual influence of the murals and the aristocracy told in a subtle way across his canvases. His sitters, rarely denied some distinction or assurance, were given more; and they were also given more room to display it in. A substantial decorative element was rubbed into them. And the net effect made them appear to be stylized and impossibly large figures. The Ladies Acheson soar up a canvas for nearly nine feet; their skirts are too abundant to fit within the six-foot width, and they really are too sumptuously dressed to want to pick oranges. None of these incongruities was new to Sargent; his using them as a design, however, was. It was a portrait rendered for decoration, and as the picture was too large ever to be reckoned portable Sargent knew where it was meant to hang, and stay, in vast rooms, high on the wall. In such a setting it would not dominate, and once lit from below a strange alchemy occurs – the ladies descend into proportion. The murals had taught him the optical deficiencies of working to an unnatural scale, the scale of ancestral houses. And working for the aristocracy put him keenly in mind of his competition, especially from the eighteenth century.

The stock elements of the grand tradition of English portraiture were hauled into Tite Street. Sitters showed no discomfort in trading his Empire furniture for columns, balustrades, pillars in rooms constructed of drapery that fitted their ancestry but dwarfed their person. They were asked to inhabit Reynolds and Gainsborough settings. Peers and peeresses were made to prop themselves up against massive architectural elements. The ladies were asked to trade in their fashionable clothes for more classical models. After dealing with the Marquess of Londonderry in full Coronation regalia and Sir Frank Swettenham in confident mastery of the symbols of the Malay States over which he presided as Governor, Sargent was in full, rapid stride. He did not flinch when he was shown the Reynolds portrait of the 4th Duke of Marlborough he was asked to ape for the 9th Duke. "When Sargent came to Blenheim," Consuelo Balsan (née Vanderbilt, the then Duchess) wrote in her autobiography, ". . . and was told he was to paint a pendant to a picture in which there were eight persons and three dogs, he seemed in no wise daunted. . . ."[42] He had to deal with four persons and three dogs, and cover a canvas eleven feet by eight feet. The Duke wore Garter robes, the Duchess a dress Sargent had copied from a Van Dyck in the Blenheim collection, their sons were in costumes he also designed, and they were craftily posed in such a way as to disguise the Duchess's height. His treatment of the dogs was borrowed from Ruebens. His only regret, he explained to Helleu, was that the official nature of this picture meant the Duchess was not allowed to smile. "Je craine que vous n'admirerez pas beaucoup mon énorme toile des Marlborough, parce que, d'abord, la Duchesse est assez ratée; devant forcement la faire sérieuse dans cette solenelle machine, sa tête perd tout son charme."[43] ("I fear you will not like the enormous canvas of the Marlboroughs very much, because, to begin with, the Duchess is something of a failure as I was obliged to make her solemn; her face loses all its charm in this grandiose picture.") The grand tradition brought a change in the terms of his formulas; it also brought repetition and with it a souring of his attitude towards portraiture. Ingenuity and surprise were unwelcome. The inventive solution of Mrs Meyer and her children was out of place; there seemed to be more past and less Sargent crowding into his work, echoing eighteenth-century masters turned into a cul-de-sac, cutting him off from the pleasures of portraiture altogether. Sargent's move into stately homes eventually caused him to down his baize apron for good. "The Van Dyck of our times" was a label that ceased to describe an activity well before the decade was over. If Sargent had had Jacques-Emil Blanche's or Emil Fuch's head-hunting social instincts, he would have known rotund complacency. But he did not. The deeper he got into the pages of *Debrett*, the staler the job became, and portraiture had become a job with all the excitement rubbed clean, even from the edges.

The portrait factory had but one employee; Sargent alone monitored, attended to and satisfied every detail connected with the acres of canvas turned out from Tite Street. He was part-diplomatist, secretary, account-ant, joiner, as well as painter. Nicola was permitted to carry out only the most menial tasks. Each portrait demanded the mastery of numerous problems, most of which were unconnected with getting the paint on the canvas. Once a commission was agreed, itself often the culmination of months of negotiation, the paperwork began, Sargent went to see the room where the picture was meant to hang, measurements were taken, sittings arranged. And once the picture was finished the patience test was not; sitters occasionally possessed an unwelcome ability to irritate long after they had left his studio. The Portlands had a genius for it: "Every November I get (forwarded) in Italy", Sargent wrote to Evan Charteris, "an invitation for some long past weekend, to run down to Welbeck and catch that little golden shade that I unaccountably resisted years ago. You might have a chance of suggesting that old picture ought to be left in peace."[44]

In July 1898, Mrs Swinton approached him on behalf of her friends the Cazalets, who wanted to commission two very large portraits for their house in the country. Fifteen months later Sargent had the time to be able to accept and a timetable was mooted: "as to the number of sittings," he wrote to Mrs Cazalet (18 October) [1899]. "That is a very difficult question and depends on many things – as a rule a lady's portrait requires more sittings than a man's, and I think I should require at least ten sittings for this one and at least eight for the other [her husband's] and unless I should be extremely favoured by circumstances, this is probably the minimum." Dress was always a matter of a certain delicacy, and was not decided until the sittings began: "I often prefer," he wrote to her earlier in March [25 March 1899], "to choose among dresses already in existence to ordering something which after all may not [?suit]. . . . I should much prefer white silk with rather an ample skirt and some opportunity for folds and arrangements."[45]

Then the sittings began, putting the "favour of circumstances" to the test. They failed him with Mrs Lionel Sackville-West (later Lady Sackville) in January 1905. "I am done in a simple black dress and a lovely scarf," she wrote in her diary (21 January 1905), "and I wear some of my fine emeralds. I go 4 times a week and sit over 2 hours." A week later she admitted it was going badly, and she was back in London the following week. "Sargent had painted a lovely head of me but", her diary entry for 11 February reads, "has scratched it all out again. He said the painting was not good enough for him to sign. He began again and made a horrid face and he was not pleased when I told him I did not like it at all!"[46] She sat four more times in the middle of the month, again at the beginning of March, and then the portrait was abandoned.

Group portraits had the added complication of arrangement first, individuals second. In 1905 he painted Drs Welsh, Halstead, Kelly and Sir William Osler for Johns Hopkins University. "Dr Welsh described Sargent as grouping his four sitters, over and over again, before he was satisfied," Royal Cortissoz said at the time of the picture's unveiling. "Sometimes he requested two of the doctors to stand, and then only one of them. He changed their positions, again and again." Dr Welsh was painted in one sitting, and the sitter "was struck by Sargent's unobtrusive way of studying him. . . . Sargent talked constantly while he was at work, smoked . . . and was always walking to and fro . . . he said laughingly that he had once estimated that he walked about four miles a day in his studio." Osler had a less easy time. Sargent refused to allow him to wear his Oxford robe, adding humorously:

'No, I can't paint you in that. It won't do. I know all about that red. You know they gave me a degree down there [the year before], and I've got one of those robes. . . . I've left it on the roof in the rain. I've buried it in the garden. It's no use. The red is as red as ever. The stuff is too good. It won't fade. Now, if you could get a Dublin degree? . . . they come down to a beautiful pink.

Just as the picture looked near completion, "Sargent himself suddenly grew discouraged. He paused . . . knitting his brow, and lifting his hand with a gesture of bewilderment, he said: 'It won't do. It isn't a picture. I cannot see just what to do, but it isn't a picture.' "[47] Shortly thereafter he asked the doctors to regroup around a vast Venetian globe* he had moved into Tite Street from Fulham Road, chopping the frame of the door to get it in. He sketched it into the background, and declared: " 'We have got our picture.' "

He prepared his own canvases, often very badly, and his habit of scratching out did little to help or preserve the surface. He varnished them, found antique frames or gave detailed orders for new ones, arranged for photography, packing, shipping and, if necessary, consular

---

* The globe he had used for Sir Frank Swettenham.

documents. (All paintings and other works of art entering America were subject to duty.*)

"I have come to this tuberculous place," Sargent wrote to Saint-Gaudens from Palermo (2 November) [1901], "to avoid portraits. The plague in Naples answers very well too."[48] His other purpose was to expose himself, and his decorations, to the Byzantine – and Christian – influence of Sicily and Italy, again. He depended on Italy, as he had depended on Egypt. He went in 1900 as a supplement to Switzerland; he went in 1901 as a supplement to Norway, and he went in 1902. His visits might have been brief, but they were frequent, as well as being a necessary recess from the other tyranny. By the end of 1902 he was ready for "several weeks in shirt sleeves" in the Library: the lunette and frieze were ready, with the crucifix, to go up. He sailed for Boston in January 1903.

The south wall was handed over to the *Doctrine of Redemption* (frieze and crucifix) and the *Doctrine of the Trinity* (lunette). Both are separated by a cornice on which is inscribed a legend taken from the cathedral in Palermo: "Factus Homo, Factor Hominis, Factique Redemptor.

---

* This fact, which slowed down Mrs Gardner's activities to a near-halt, was a source of unending irritation to painters and purchasers alike. In 1909, Sargent wrote to Julie Heyneman an eloquent account of the turmoil he endured. "My little brain has a real talent for seeing difficulties ahead," he wrote to her (9 March 1909),

> and none for overcoming them, so this matter of my two watercolours has seemed to me too complicated to unravel – but here goes.
> There is a lawyer in Philadelphia, Johnson or Johnston and his partner, who has or have behaved very politely . . . and is refusing to make any charges. So I promised them each a watercolour, and I cabled to you [in San Francisco] not to return the two you took over – and meant to write you at once to ask you to be so good as to send them to Philadelphia. Then I fussed in my mind [?] at the thought that they have probably been smuggled in and that that might be found out and cause trouble to Mr Johnson, as he is a celebrated collector of pictures – also that one of these water colours has, I believe, a dedication in ink to my sister.
> Months went by and I had not mastered these problems, and then came a letter from E. D. Boit which determined me to have a show of water colours in New York & Boston, & I thought I should ask you to forward them to New York so as to add them to the lot I was sending over from here – and the same custom house scare paralysed me about that – as all the others went over in bond to be returned here. . . .
> Well now I have made up my mind (unworthy of the name) to risk being a source of infinite bother to Mr Johnson & yourself, and ask you to send the two water colours to him. . . .
> This means that you will be an angel. . . . You will acquire still greater merit if you would take the one with the oxes out of its frame first and either scratch out the words "to Emily" or whatever they are, leaving the signature, or blot them out with body colour. Emily agrees to this as you need not fear the arm of the law, & I should be very much obliged. (Julie H. Heyneman Papers)

Corporeus Redimo Corpora Cordi Deus"; the original read "Judico" for "Redimo". "Some wiseacre has discovered a fault in prosody in my latin inscription," he wrote to Thomas Fox from Fenway Court, "– it ought to be corporeus redimo instead of redimo corporeus – Do you think it would be easy to make that alteration without it showing? If so I suppose it would be worth while."[49] The crucifix rises from the frieze of angels, who have their hands full with the instruments of the Passion, and Christ's outstretched arms are planted across the Persons of the Trinity, three massive crowned figures, each with the same face, bundled into a scarlet cope with a gold orphrey reciting the Sanctus on its journey round the enthroned figures. Sargent made lavish use of red and gold, in his ornate setting for the crucifix, for the lunette and frieze were more of a backdrop than a lexicon of religious-historical information. The installation was complete by the first week in February, when Sargent circumspectly applied to the Trustees for a private viewing for Stanford White, Saint-Gaudens, Daniel Chester French and Mrs Gardner among others.

With the second instalment it became apparent that the eclecticism of the building had seeped deeper into his decorative scheme. The north and south walls were pendants only in the widest possible sense; they defied comparison, because he had also absorbed decorative styles from different centuries in the course of his research. *The Triumph of Religion* was a two-tiered pastiche, enjoying a historical consistency that did not reward the eye in similar terms.[50] On the south wall, content had made way for technique, or style. And the vaulting and niches added to the lunette and frieze thirteen years later made an even louder declaration of this fact. Boston, of course, loved the second instalment. It was more accessible than the previous one. Superlatives were directed at the wall and the decorator with ardent gusto. Sargent had yet another triumph, and he turned around to adjust the background to his Frieze of Prophets, which he felt necessary once the competition was in place.

Echoes of the triumphal march played in England for the past years reached America, where no encouragement was needed. A red carpet was unfurled for Sargent all the way from Boston to Washington. Accolades were tossed before his stride. Receptions, dinners, exhibitions interrupted his gait in New York and Philadelphia as well. He was a towering presence, a returning hero too long abroad. His few words were hung on, saved for posterity, and yet they were syllables utterly unchanged. No honour was too great. In short, it was more of the same.

Sargent had also come to put in portrait service, and America offered up her best candidates, from the classes he was accustomed to visit – business (Cassatt and two Wideners), the arts (Loeffler, his fellow Fauré champion), society (Mrs Arthur Rotch, the wife of one of his earliest subjects, Mrs Endicott, Mrs Hammond, Colonel Higginson, Mrs Fiske Warren) and politics (John Hay and President Roosevelt). He went to Washington in February. There he ran into his chief detractor, Henry Adams, who found him (1 March 1903) "as unresponsive as ever", and

(8 March) his Roosevelt excellent, volunteering, with his usual extra sting, "Indeed it offers nothing to criticize but Sargent".[51] In March he went to New York, where he painted Edward Robinson, later the Director of the Metropolitan Museum of Art, who, more important, was responsible for the $15,000 needed for the contract for the second instalment of the Special Libraries Hall eight years before. He went to see the American première of Ethel Smyth's *Der Wald*; its composer had crossed the Atlantic with her sister who used the occasion as an excuse to see Sargent.

Back in Boston, Mrs Gardner was determined not to be outdone in the award-giving. She had two mighty ribbons to affix to his chest. Her great art-stuffed palace had opened on New Year's Eve to an invited audience who were laboriously received by the châtelaine on her throne. Two months later the public was given the first glimpse, and neither category of visitor was allowed even a sight of her Gothic Room (or the Chapel). To Sargent she granted not only access and the use of it as his studio, but also the unheard of privilege of coming to Fenway Court as a guest; he was invited to stay within the walls and sleep under its roof. There he painted Mrs Fiske Warren and her daughter in the Gothic Room, and both were shown as if they were incapable of rising to the distinction they knew only Sargent had a right to claim. Towards the end of March he arranged a private audience with Mrs Gardner for Mrs Hunter, Miss Smyth and von Glehn and a tour of Palazzo Gardner. He had been appointed her knight.

Sargent swept over America in a cloud of glory, and the dust never settled; if anything, it was stirred up even more, eagerly anticipating his return when he left for Spain. He wrote to Mrs Gardner from Madrid (16 June): "I am leaving Madrid for Portugal and out of the way places and am not likely to be back for 3 weeks or a month."[52] He permitted himself five months' recovery after his four months in America, stopping in Venice again before braving Tite Street in November. He could stay away no longer. After ten months, he caught his breath, braced himself, threw open the studio door, and faced the queue of duchesses, marchionesses, countesses, and their lesser-titled companions regrouping outside number 31. He stepped back on to the treadmill, reopening the portrait works in England, resuming manufacture for four more years. Even his holidays got confused with orders. In October 1904 he left the Barbaro for Palazzo Giustiniani to paint Lady Helen Vincent, a terrific beauty (and later Viscountess d'Abernon, whose husband eventually steered the Wertheimer portraits into the national collection).

By 1907 he had had enough. At the age of fifty-one he shut his ledgers and hung a "closed" sign on the door. It had been coming for a long time: "Painting a portrait would be quite amusing if one were not forced to talk while working," he said to Jacques-Emil Blanche. "What a nuisance having to entertain the sitter and to look happy when one feels wretched."[53] He could not go on with the lie any more. "I have vowed a vow", he wrote to Mrs Curtis, "not to do any more portraits . . . it is to me positive bliss to think that I shall soon be a free man."[54] "No more paughtraits," he repeated to her son, using his individual spelling of the dreaded word, ". . . I abhor and abjure them and hope never to do another especially of the Upper Classes."[55] To Lady Radnor he was as emphatic: "Ask me to paint your gates, your fences, your barns, which I should gladly do, *but not the human face.*" His disenchantment reached its most cogent form with the terse declaration, "No more mugs!", and later settled down in the definition he inscribed on the flyleaf of the French edition of reproductions of his work: "A portrait is a picture in which there is just a tiny little something not quite right about the mouth."[56]

And thus resolved "to devote my life to something more satisfying"[57] he submitted four portraits to the Academy in 1908: an ex-prime minister (Balfour), a royal duke (HRH The Duke of Connaught) and his Duchess, and one other (Mrs Huth Jackson); the following year two more – Mrs William Waldorf Astor* and the Earl of Wemyss – and a landscape. In 1910 he sent only landscapes. The great wheels of the portrait works had come to a halt.

* Nancy Astor (later Viscountess Astor, and later still the first woman Member of Parliament) entered the hostess race almost at the exact moment Sargent made himself ineligible for all such attentions. At the start, however, he did agree to go to Cliveden for Easter in 1908, but only on the condition the von Glehns were also asked. Thereafter, he avoided the sport altogether: "Cliveden is not for me," he informed her [March 1910]. "Together with paughtrut painting I have renounced the polished circles into which it led me for a brief and anxious time." But, having once had the taste of victory, she continued to give spirited and stubborn chase. She even added another inducement to the stream of invitations she sent to Tite Street – with some considerable dexterity she managed to strain genealogy enough to make them cousins; from July 1909 his refusals began "Dear coz" instead of "Dear Mrs Astor". And practice made his rejections very lively: "I cannot possibly come to lunch tomorrow," he wrote [5 February 1913], ". . . I *never* can lunch, even on a 13th – What is this mawbid wish to civilize a horny-handed son of toil? Who can't even spell." "I shall be in Paris on May 11th," he wrote another time (28 April), "deprived of the pleasure of accepting your kind and reckless invitation – reckless because I always do and say the wrong thing to Royalty. This time it seems as if Providence, in its wisdom, had interfered – on your behalf no doubt, for it never has on mine" (University of Reading Library).

XIV

Sargent's victory over the tyranny of the portraits was slowly won and never total; it was achieved not by the strength of the murals alone, but by his determination to escape from London for stretches longer than a few weeks or a month, for more than research – for a real holiday from the studio. Once the second portion of the mural was in place, he left sitters behind in the late summer and autumn every year. He was after the refreshment of brilliantly clear light; he wanted what London refused to offer. And during the next few years he was also on a different sort of journey, moving slowly along an arc which in time traced a complete circle. There was a transition in his life that depended not at all on geography, and he was taking Emily with him – he was recapturing the lost safety of his childhood.

In September 1905 he went to Switzerland with the Harrisons and then on alone (with Nicola) to the Middle East by the new year. This long absence from Carlyle Mansions made him anxious, but while his mother and sister were in Spain and the posts were reliable he was not too concerned, but when he learnt that his mother was suffering from an abscess of the ear he wrote saying he was coming home at once. He had developed FitzWilliam's anxiety about health. His mind could not resist jumping to fatal conclusions, and it was an acrobatic exercise helped by the knowledge his mother was seventy-nine years old and had never lived, or so she thought, far removed from death's path. She wrote back insisting there was no danger, that she had not only recovered but was going out, seeing friends; there was no reason to worry and even less for any interruption in his plans. Reassured, he stayed away, going on from Syria to Palestine, where a telegram reached him "far in the interior" "on the East side of the Jordan" on Monday, 22 January 1906: Mary Sargent was dead; she had died on Sunday.

He was shocked. He wired his sisters, asking them not to have the funeral until he returned, and the soonest that could be was nearly a fortnight off. He was sentenced to six "grievous days that I must still spend here waiting for a steamer" as he wrote to Mrs Curtis from Jerusalem (25 January),[1] before he could even start. During that time the mystery of his mother's death was cruelly solved, in her own words: "With the telegram came 6 charming letters from my mother," he wrote to Mrs Hunter (24 January).[2] ". . . And I shall get other letters from her affectionate and cheerful and telling me she is getting better. . . ." He read and reread her account of the sequence of events which had preceded her death, answering his questions and amplifying his grief. After the abscess had cleared, she had begun treatment to ward off bronchitis with some sort of fomentation of steam, and in the process boiling water splashed on to her chest. From these spare facts Sargent worked out just how she came to have the heart attack which killed her: "it must have been the shock from this coming after the other illness that weakened her," he wrote to Mrs Curtis, "for several weeks after this, and again being able to go out, the end came suddenly and unexpectedly. She did not know it, I am glad to say."[3] He found the waiting to be absolute torture; he longed to know what was happening in London: "what may be being done to her in Cheyne Walk today – " he asked Mrs Hunter. "What may Emily and Violet be hearing and saying. It is dreadful to be away. I regret deeply not having returned long ago. I had no idea. . . ."[4]

He arrived in London on 2 February. "Just now I seem to feel nothing at all," he admitted to Mrs Hunter [3 February] " – but I have had bad spells."[5] He shut himself up with his sisters, seeing no one unless they called at Carlyle Mansions. On Monday, 5 February he and his sisters took Mary Sargent's body to Bournemouth where she was buried next to FitzWilliam at the Wimbourne Road Cemetery; at exactly the same time a memorial service was held at St Paul's Westminster, in London. Mary Sargent's life, buoyed constantly by illness, passed on to its logical conclusion, rather later than anyone would have foreseen. She had spent her seventeen years of widowhood much as she had lived her marriage, only slowed down by age, and with the added novelty of a home. Her travels continued to encompass spas, but only on the direct line that connected her to the members of her family, enlarged by the addition of Violet's children, her six grandchildren (three girls and three boys, born between 1892 and 1898: see Appendix I). She and Emily followed in the wake of the Ormonds, to France, Italy, Spain, Tunis and Egypt. Mary Sargent had plotted a strange course for herself, her husband and her children. She stuck to it, and never wavered with regret. She never returned to America after FitzWilliam's death, as if to confirm she had made no error to leave more than half a century before. And, though she held the compass that had directed four lives with a merciless tenacity, she had also lifted a very brilliant light to shine down on them. Her interests were encyclopaedic. Her feelings for art, literature and music were ardent and enthusiastic. She loved conversation, and emotionally, if nothing else, she knew no meanness. The narrow circle that collected round her high up in the Carlyle Mansions rooms admired her and liked her to an equal degree. She cared nothing for posterity, and her eccentric life ended leaving very little of the material that accumulates to remind mourners of the past. And she left very little money, but entirely to Emily, in the full knowledge that no sum would ever gain Emily independence. In her will she looked to her son to assume that guardianship. Again the geometry of the Sargent family changed. Emily was alone; she had lost the only job she had known all her life. Her brother steered her into another, and he never left her side for nineteen years.

After their mother's death Sargent generously suggested to Emily they set up house together. It was her dearest wish. Nothing could have given her greater happiness, and she was profoundly moved. But she refused, feeling she might be trading too heavily on the grief of the moment, taking advantage of his sadness, "& was afraid [after] many years of life as a bachelor, he would find it irksome", one of their closest friends, Eliza Wedgwood, recalled after Sargent's death. They were trapped by the stalemate of extreme consideration. Emily never revived the plan because she was haunted by an idea that never left her: that pity had intruded on his love for her. Her temperament, otherwise so well arranged, so lightened by a high sense of humour, was jolted into severe depression when she dwelt overmuch on her deformity, thus allowing herself to misread genuine love for some lower attraction. "I found Emily once sobbing," Miss Wedgwood remembered. "She told me it came over her overwhelming[ly]."[6] In truth she and her brother lived apart only as a fact of domestic reality; in every other sense they set up house together. After 1906 the *Post Office Directory* recognized Emily as an occupant of Carlyle Mansions. Hitherto Mrs Sargent alone had been granted that place. Emily crept out from under the shadow of her mother, and slipped into the long shadows cast by her brother and her sister.

She began to paint more conscientiously. She started to work from a live model. Her brother praised and encouraged her unstintingly, but she rarely showed her watercolours beyond the safe range of her family and a few very close friends. Her style was much like her brother's, yet without his brio. She had considerable ability, and tradition attributes her reluctance to show to her fear of trading on her brother's reputation, though she had exhibited at the New English Art Club. She did not want to open the door any wider on pity. And her letters became notations of her brother's activities. He now occupied the place in her life he had always held in her emotions. And the feeling was mutual. After Mrs Sargent's death, his social life in London declined, replaced by at least three evenings a week at Carlyle Mansions, dining quietly with Emily and playing chess. These were the entertainments he came to value most. He planned their annual holidays carefully. In 1913 he toured the Alps above Botzen alone; "to find a moderately high place for next summer", he wrote to Mrs Curtis, "not too high for Emily & paintable enough for me".[7] Over and over again he adjusted his itinerary to Emily's welfare. She became the dominant variable in his calculations.

Mary Sargent's death worked a result contrary to her husband's, erasing the very instructions her son had followed for the past seventeen years. In that long interval it was as if he had acted out yet another of his mother's ambitions, as if he had made great advances in areas he cared little about, as if he had performed according to rules he never found comfortable. Once his mother died, however, it was safe to return. The long expedition could end. And whereas Emily became her mother he became his father – the children slipped back to the older generation. The circle was nearing completion.

And as a frequent Visitor at the Royal Academy Schools he also rotated back to the spectre of Carolus-Duran. Since his election in 1894 he taught one month in the winter. He took his job extremely seriously. In one of his two surviving Visitor's Reports, for the Drawing School from 28 October to 23 November 1907, he again lamented the appalling attendance in the evening class and suggested a change

> in the lighting of two of the life schools. Firstly [.] The arrangement of the lamps for lighting the model in the men's life school. It now consists of a level row of 8 lights about 8 inches apart, each of which throws a distinct shadow. I suggest that they should be grouped in a mass closer together.
>
> Secondly. In the smaller life school for women the row of lamps round the room is so low that it almost touches the drawings that are on the easels, throwing them into a dazzling light, whereas the model looks consumptive, in the shade. I found this not only very trying to the eyes, but also a great disadvantage for study. It also tends to making very black drawings.[8]

Like Carolus, Sargent laid great stress on fundamentals, on the arrangement of masses. " 'When drawing from the model,' " he instructed, " 'never be without a plumb line . . .' ", which corrected one's natural bias either to the left or to the right and developed a sense of the vertical. "On one occasion in the evening life school I well remember", one of his students wrote to Evan Charteris, "Sargent complaining that no one seemed concerned about anything more than the *approximate* articulation of the head upon the neck and shoulders. The procedure was, to register carefully the whole pose at the evening's sitting of two hours."[9] The details, confined to this preliminary outline, came later. For painting he was as strenuous as Carolus had been on the acute dissection of tones and values of colour. "He believed . . . that painting was a science," another student, Julie Heyneman, recalled. His teachings also revealed the clearest analysis of his own work. A painting was a construction built on the foundation of middle tones; large planes formed a blueprint. The brush did the drawing. Features and likeness emerged only as a refinement, supplied by the most economical terms. "To watch the head develop from the start was like the sudden lifting of a blind in a dark room. . . . Every stage was a revelation." With a few strokes of charcoal on the canvas he indicated the head, and then rubbed them out, leaving a hint of where he had been. With turpentine he mapped out the background and outlined the head – "the real outline where the light and shadow meet, not the place where the head meets the background". This all occurred in seconds. Next came the application of colour, spared the benefit of "a medium of any kind, neither oil, turpentine or any admixture. 'The thicker you paint, the more your colour flows' he explained." Smudges, nothing more, were seen to augment the outline, and now he began

> really to paint . . . with a kind of concentrated deliberation, a slow haste. . . . He aimed at once for the true general tone of the background, of the hair and for the transition tone between the two. He showed me how the light flowed over the surface of the cheek into the background itself. . . . As he painted it, the mouth bloomed out of the face, an integral part of it, not . . . painted on it. . . . In fact, it seemed to me the mouth and nose just *happened* with the modelling of the cheeks, and one eye, very luminous, had been placed in the socket so carefully for it (like a poached egg dropped on a plate, he described the process . . .).[10]

In short, the elements of a painting massed in a general harmony governed by a key found in the play of light off the surfaces. The high notes and the low notes were confined to the same scale. Such musicianship was achieved by rigorous schooling; the result of interpretation, not of tricks. " 'If you see a thing transparent, paint it transparent,' " he advised; " 'don't get the effect by a thin stain showing the canvas through. . . . *The more delicate the transition the more you must study it for the exact tone.*' "[11]

These were difficult lessons for students to absorb, and not readily apparent. His approach, even thirty years after he had acquired it at Carolus' elbow, was still unorthodox. He spoke in abstracts – " 'cultivate an ever continuous power of observation . . . make slight notes of postures, groups, incidents. . . . Store up in the mind without ceasing a continuous stream of observations . . . test what you remember . . . mental notes, make them again and again . . . the power of selection will follow. . . . Above all things get abroad, see the sunlight, and everything that is to be seen. . . .' "[12] Once the eye had the firm discipline of the brain, the student had acquired the basic principle of his teaching, and of Carolus' teaching.

"Sargent is teaching most extraordinarily well at the RA," Vanessa Stephen, later Vanessa Bell, wrote to a friend (4 January) [1904] towards the end of his four-week Schools duty. "He gave lessons . . . that would apply to any paintings. They're chiefly about tone. . . . The one thing he is down upon is when he thinks anyone is trying for an effect regardless of truth."[13] Such admiration was later, after having been passed through the Bloomsbury mill, reckoned to be instruction from the hands not of an artist, but of "a devastatingly brilliant technician".[14] And yet, if his lessons were not considered to be of lasting value, the spectacle of him giving them was memorable. His stuttering and irritating hesitation was gone.

His movements were braced with confidence, and with conviction. He was Blunt's "mechanic" given over to the service of art. He stood at the easel, charcoal in hand, arm fully outstretched, head thrown back in a fever of concentration, and then his hand danced across the paper after a slow start. He presented a wonderful sight, his eyes aglow, his certainty intense, and with his size and the aura of his fame the performance was forever caught in students' minds.

But not for long. There were forces at work intent on eroding Sargent's position, and with it his teaching, as well as aimed at the power of the Academy. These were the same forces that had inspired the Grosvenor Gallery, the New Gallery, the New English Art Club, but these achievements were nothing more than rehearsals for the opening of "Manet and the Post-Impressionists" at the Grafton Gallery on 8 November 1910, which has subsequently been taken as the watershed, separating the new from the old – a marker historians love to plant for guidance; at the time the appearance of Manet, Cézanne, Gauguin, Picasso, Signac, Derain and Friesz was taken as a bad joke and, worse, an obscenity. Sir William Richmond said that the show's organizer, Roger Fry, ought to be banned from decent society. Sargent was dragged into the controversy, and forced to state his position, and with the benefit of hindsight was seen to be on the wrong side. Fry had invoked his name as a supporter of the exhibition in the pages of the *Nation* on Christmas Eve 1910 and two weeks later Sargent's letter to the editor was published:

> Mr. Fry has been entirely misinformed, and if I had been inclined to join in the controversy, he would have known that my sympathies were in the exactly opposite direction as far as the novelties are concerned. . . . I had declined Mr. Fry's request to place my name on the initial list of promoters of the Exhibition on the ground of not knowing the work of the painters. . . . Mr. Fry may have been told – and have believed – that the sight of those paintings had made me a convert to his faith. . . .
>
> The fact is that I am absolutely sceptical as to their having any claim whatever to being works of art. . . ."*[15]

He made Gauguin an exception, "admirable in color, and in color only".[16] It was a statement he did not welcome making, he would have preferred to keep his views private, but it is fair to say his conviction would have

---

* The phrase Sargent objected to in Fry's "A postscript on Post-Impressionism" (*Nation*, 24 December 1910, p. 536) was as follows: "Mr. Robert Morley says that all the abuse of the Post-Impressionists which has come from certain quarters is more than justified. Having thus thrown the great weight of his name into the scale against these unfortunate artists, all that I can do is to pile on to the other scale such names as Degas (who owns several Gauguins), Dr. von Tschudi, Mr. John S. Sargent, and Mr. Claude Phillips (at least as regards Cézanne). . . ."

been as strong. And his views were the ones generally accepted, shared by Tonks, MacColl, Comyns Carr, Sickert, Ricketts and a great many others – a list dismissed as the "old guard". Two years later, after the second Post-Impressionist exhibition, he endorsed his original opinion, adding that Van Gogh's "things look to me like imitations made in corals or glass of objects in a vacuum", as he wrote to D. S. MacColl.[17]

Sargent's reaction to the Post-Impressionists was predictable. His insistence on schooling the eye, dissecting gradations of tone – in short, very strict discipline – demanded that the sloppiness on show at the Grafton Gallery was a violent contradiction of everything he believed. More important, however, a fissure was opening up, getting wider and deeper, cutting him and the adherents of representational art off from Fry and his new religion. And Fry's persuasive discourses did require faith. Tonks's cartoon of Fry at work winning converts was entitled *The Unknown God*, showing Sickert, MacColl, George Moore, Steer and Sargent (among others) remarkably resistant in the front row, while Clive Bell intones "Cezannah Cezannah", shaking his handbell. Sargent was not vulnerable to the intoxication of any faith whatsoever, but as one of the bulwarks of the Royal Academy he epitomized the heretical point of view, the enemy, and all those Fry wanted to win over. In Sargent, Fry found all the values he was struggling to dismantle, and though he was convinced he was successfully placing Sargent's reputation in grave jeopardy his doctrines were inconsequential threats to something so solidly established. Fry was trying to bring Sargent down yet again for what he was *not*. After the brief skirmish scarcely anyone noticed the slightest dent in Sargent's fame.[18]

Fry seemed an unlikely opponent in 1910. He had picked up the banner to lead his crusade fresh from a directorship of the Metropolitan Museum of Art in New York, where the religion of Sargent brooked no heresy. Hitherto he had displayed an eloquent grasp of the Italian Renaissance and adroit critical faculties, especially in his edition of Reynolds's *Discourses*. And, though he had fired his first warning shot at Sargent in 1900 when he separated his voice from the adulatory chorus rising from the Wyndham sisters, Colonel Ian Hamilton and the rest of Sargent's portraits, and a second shot in 1903 when he admitted (anonymously) that after seeing Sargent's landscapes at the Carfax Gallery he would do better to stick with portraits after all, a year later he neutralized both

---

Fry replied to Sargent's letter on 10 January, and it was published in the *Nation* (14 January 1911, p. 646). He tried to weasel out of the charge of inaccuracy in a somewhat laughable assault on credulity: "What I did was this: In answering Mr. Robert Morley's *ipse-dixit*, I mentioned as supporters such names. . . . By coupling Mr. Sargent's and Mr. Claude Phillips's name in this way, I thought that I had made it clear that the qualifying clause '(at least as regards Cézanne)' applied to both, and this statement was based upon a letter of Mr. Sargent's to me, in which he expressed admiration for Cézanne."

attacks with carefully worded praise.* After the carnival of the Post-Impressionists, however, there was no mistaking Fry's position, and thereafter he had all the ferocity of an outcast. In 1926, on the occasion of Sargent's memorial exhibition at Burlington House, Fry finally published his articles of war. It was not a personal attack, he was mindful to point out; he was pursuing the battle of aesthetics, generations and fashion. He had the bravery of an evangelist, protected by his faith to give him safety, because popular opinion was still against him.†

The Post-Impressionists, Fry and his followers were an annoying swarm of mosquitoes with their infernal drone of abstract nouns. The public did not care for the irritating distraction, which was best ignored. Sargent and his fellow-inhabitants of the Academy put on a strong wash of repellent and went unhindered about their business. The critical brickbats were an amusing diversion, but Sargent's reputation had not altered one inch. If anything, it inclined upwards. To those who warmed themselves before the well-stoked fire at Burlington House, he was perhaps the greatest living painter. Apart from teaching, he busied himself with the affairs of the Academy, sitting on selection committees, the Council, and holding various secretaryships. "Where were my wits the other day", he wrote to D. S. MacColl (n.d.) [pre-1900], "that I didn't tackle you for a guinea for the Artist General Benevolent Institution. I am steward for the dinner . . . and no one is sacred, not even the revengeful critic."[19] He was a very prominent figure, a model Academician. And when the presidency fell vacant in December 1918 he was Poynter's obvious successor. There Sargent drew the line: "I would do *anything* for the Royal Academy but that," he said to Sir Arthur Cope, "and if you press me any more, I shall flee the country."[20] His activities were more

---

* In his review, "Mr. Sargent at the Carfax Gallery" (*Athenaeum*, 23 May 1903, p. 665), Fry wrote: "Frankly, we like Mr. Sargent better on parade at the Academy than in undress at the Carfax Gallery. Put before him a definite problem in portraiture . . . and he will find an acceptable solution with unequalled readiness and precision, and without any bungling or hesitation. He is, in fact, our best practitioner in paint, a man whom it is always safe to call in. He will never perform miracles, but he will always be up to the mark."

† Fry's charges were fired off with unremitting zeal. "That Sargent was taken for an artist will perhaps seem incredible to the rising generation," the litany begins, with scarcely a respite thereafter. "We must abandon, then, this futile search for aesthetic values in Sargent's work – a search into which the misleading use of the word 'artist' has led us. . . . We must look at these pictures not as works of art . . . but as illustrations or reports about other things . . . for Royalty or the genuine aristocrat he seems to have felt the same glamour as the great mass of the English middle classes . . . on his holiday travels . . . those rapid and accomplished diaries in water-colour which he used to bring home . . . what he saw was exactly what the average upper-class tourist sees. . . . What surprises is the uniform superficiality of the observation . . ." (*Transformations* (1926), pp. 125, 127–9).

If nothing else, Fry could at least boast about being among Sargent's earliest detractors.

than a statement of his dug-in status, they were his *duty*, which he willingly assumed. And the medals, awards and rolls of vellum continued to pile up at Tite Street. By the end of his life he had amassed five honorary degrees from American and English universities, sixteen exhibition prizes, membership or honorary memberships of sixteen institutions in America, England, Italy, France and Germany, and official decorations from the French, Belgian and Prussian governments. Fry had taken on a near-monument.

Sargent made certain his "duty" stopped short of making speeches. Stories of his inability to make even the most casual toast abound; tales of his slumping into his chair, terror-struck, after a futile attempt to deliver a few syllables are legion. It became a recognized fact that Sargent could not be called upon to make a speech. When the Phi Beta Kappa Society of Harvard chose him as the orator at their annual meeting, he replied, after many words of humble gratitude, "I should be proud to accept if I had the least right to hope that a miracle would happen in my favour. The miracle of overcoming something like panic when asked to speak has never happened to me yet, and the spectacle of panic instead of a speech is the entertainment I have afforded and long since resolved not to afford again."[21] He made one notable exception, provoked by his loyalty to the Academy: a short address on 16 July 1923 to mark the bicentenary of Sir Joshua Reynolds's birth, and the audience was as nervous as he.

For all the worldly achievement, fame and admiration which stapled a dense upholstery on the name of Sargent, the man himself remained essentially simple, living a simple life which got simpler once he gave up portraiture. His energy, like his celebrity, got in the way of this fact. He seemed to be able to do more than most people. And while it is true to say his life was his work, the converse, by some sinister treachery of logic, was not fully correct because Sargent's humanity was not shaved away by the monomania of the first statement. He was never trapped within any of the well-sealed compartments of his life; he gave to his friendships the same boundless loyalty he gave to his work. (But it must be owned it was loyalty born of demand.) When his neighbour, the portraitist Robert Brough (1872–1905), was fatally wounded in a train accident, Sargent took the 6 a.m. express to Sheffield to be with him before he died. When Harry Brewster died at Ethel Smyth's cottage in 1908 he rushed to make a deathbed portrait for his friend. And when Mrs Abbey asked him to return to London from Munich (where he was savouring the luscious rococo ornamentation) at the end of June 1911 he did not hesitate; Abbey was dying, and only Sargent could attend to the necessary alterations to his Harrisburg (Pennsylvania) decorations which had gone on show at White City as part of the Coronation Exhibition. Throughout July, Sargent carried out Abbey's instructions successfully, he informed Abbey before heading back to the Tyrol and Simplon. His generosity was of the same order. The stories abound, the record of his philanthropy was long. He was literally open-handed, foremost to his family. He assumed

Emily's expenses. He sent cheques for huge amounts to Violet for Christmas and birthdays, cheques for medical expenses, travel, holidays – all willingly volunteered, unasked. He gave his nephew Guillaume (1896–1971), a gifted musician, a new Bechstein for his rooms at Oxford. When 92 Cheyne Walk, the house next door to Violet's, came on the market he offered to buy it for Emily. He looked at his money as freedom, a leverage his parents never allowed. During his long visits to Boston he stayed in hotels, first at the Vendôme on Commonwealth Avenue, and later at the new Copley-Plaza across from the Library, and neither was cheap. And as he stayed away for many months at a time none of this was inexpensive; his suite at the Copley-Plaza was something like $30 a night.

After his mother's death he became restless to a pattern; between 1906 and 1914 he left London for about two months in the late summer for Majorca, or Corfu, or the Alps, the Dolomites, the Tyrol, Simplon and most frequently Italy, especially Venice. These journeys became a sort of Continental Broadway, complete with high-spirited children, days crammed with bathing, games, walks, picnics and work – it was outdoor life with a vengeance. He and his guests stayed in one place for a long time, where the housekeeping fell to Emily. Many of the same people were asked to join him year after year: his nieces and nephews, the Barnards, the von Glehns, Tonks and Eliza Wedgwood.

Miss Wedgwood (1859–1947) found herself, after the death of her mother, in the same department as Emily (and Flora Priestley) – a spinster landed with freedom for the first time in advanced middle age. During her long wait she had developed a very strong character but, apart from that, very little was allowed to crowd into her history. From Sargent's portraits of her, she seems to have had a perfectly agreeable face, and a sweet, unprepossessing demeanour. She did receive the light thrown off the Souls, living near to Stanway, and she came to be regarded as an honorary Charteris. She had first met Sargent through the Broadway network, asking Alfred Parsons to arrange Sargent's portrait of her mother in 1896, and also through her friends the Curtises. In 1906 she was invited to the Barbaro, and there established her close friendship with Emily and her brother; "those 5 days [in October 1906] would lay the foundation of one of the greatest friendships in my life", she wrote to Evan Charteris (22 November 1925). Thereafter she became an honorary Sargent as well. She kept the memories of her four Sargent holidays very warm. She saw them briefly again in Rome after meeting them in Venice and then quickly lost sight of them. "Mrs Hunter has caught us up in her whirl," Sargent wrote to Mrs Curtis from Rome [29 October 1906], and we have been motoring violently all day & every day. . . . We are living at 40 horse power – we travel like meteoric stones." In September the following year Miss Wedgwood again joined them at the Barbaro, before setting off for Perugia, Frascati and Rome, where the three of them rejoined the von Glehns; in 1908 they took a house in Majorca; in 1909 in Corfu; in 1910 in

Florence; and in 1913 at Lake Garda. Every year the cast of characters increased, and Miss Wedgwood wrote to Evan Charteris: "Every autumn we spent together the routine was the same – breakfast generally 7.30, afterwards work literally all day till the light failed. At rare intervals an excursion – if very hot a siesta after the midday meal, but work was the order of the day. . . . After dinner [piano] duets and chess & early to bed." Though Miss Wedgwood could play the piano, if not so well as Jane von Glehn, she did not paint, and Sargent either allowed her to watch him at work or made her pose. He painted her sitting beside Emily, who was painting (in Majorca), and again reading, protected by Emily's strange contraption designed to ward off mosquitoes – "in what John called 'Garde Mangers' " – and several times alone, or as each of the three figures in a group. When she was taken by the colour of blue painted on the doors and rafters at the old inn in Palma, and said she would paint her dining-room at Stanton the same shade, Sargent arrived one Sunday and set to work in a red and white check apron round his waist. And she never forgot how ill-made Sargent was for the job; he was too large for her tiny cottage, found it a very tight fit whenever he visited her and, if she had other guests, exited more easily through a window.

Everyone packed books in his luggage, but no one travelled with more than Sargent; reading was one of the most important features in the pattern of his days, abroad or at home. He read with tremendous speed and very quick understanding, moving easily from history to memoirs, biography to fiction, verse to philosophy. His holiday library was well chosen because he preferred to "read in a wedge – or period", Eliza Wedgwood explained. During the weeks he was abroad he would stick to one subject or all the works by a single author. But he was always most comfortable with French literature. "He cared little for English literature," Eliza Wedgwood recalled, "and explained this to me as having been brought up to care for . . . the French style."[22] His Tite Street library was enormous and reflected his affection: Voltaire, Diderot, Leclos, Molière, Balzac, Madame de Sévigné, Montaigne, Musset, Prévost, Saint-Simon, Flaubert, Dumas, Stendhal, and French translations of Plutarch and Tolstoy, all in sets of complete works and all well thumbed.

During the day, however, Sargent busily recorded the time, place and people of these travels in his paintings. His activities always paid generous service to that single purpose. He only turned to reading or writing letters when the weather was too bad for outdoor work. He was following an order established in childhood, strengthened in Paris, Broadway, and Fladbury, and suspended somewhat during the worst days of the murals and portraits. He fell back on the habit with renewed gusto. He could think of little else. Once, in Italy (1906 or 1907), after some administrative eccentricity at a rural railway station, the entire party watched their train leave without them. They had a two-hour wait for the next in excruciating heat. "We sat very cross all round the waiting-room,"

Miss Wedgwood remembered, "but John, true philosopher that he was, sat down outside and painted one of the loveliest of all his great white oxen with blue shadows."

"Above all things get abroad, see the sunlight, and everything that is to be seen," he instructed his students at the Academy Schools, and that is precisely what he was doing himself, with the added energy of reacting against the portraits. From the early part of the century he expressed himself in an ever-increasing torrent of pictures – of doorways, cattle, brilliant skies, the von Glehns painting, his nieces turning into rock formations lying on the grass or by a brook in Purtud, Padre Sebastiano who was keener on botany than God studying wild flowers in his room, a hermit in the Val d'Aosta who took on the camouflage of the dense undergrowth, his hotel room with his luggage littering the floor, stone-masons dragging marble from the quarries at Carrara, Venetian scenes from his floating studio. The investigations into perspective, technique and light were gone. The specific research for the murals was gone. He was amassing a library of souvenirs, postcards, which were augmented by photography.* He worked at terrific speed, both in oils and in watercolour, his dates imprecise, often because they were added later. He was after quick impressions.

Watercolour was ideal for his purposes, depending on speed and conveniently portable, and though he was not new to the medium he began to use it increasingly from around the turn of the century. For Sargent, watercolour suited his shorthand. In 1892 he contributed a preface to the catalogue of works by Hercules Brabazon Brabazon (1821–1905), whose " 'amateur efforts' " – Brabazon's words – Sargent found " 'wonderful. . . original and finished works of art which the world ought to know about' "[23] and arranged an exhibition shortly after first seeing the paintings. His words about Brabazon speak of his own attraction:

> The gift of colour together with an exquisite sensitiveness to impressions of nature has here been the constant incentive, and the immunity from "picture" making has gone far to keep perception delicate and execution convincing. . . . Immediate sensations flower again in Mr Brabazon's drawings, with a swiftness that make one for a time forget that there has been a medium. Those who look principally for suggestions of nature in pictures will be grateful. . . .[24]

Watercolour afforded Sargent the means to refine and simplify his

---

* Exactly when he took up the camera is not known. In 1913, at San Vigilio at Lake Garda, Miss Wedgwood recalled "Jane de Glehn [then von Glehn] and I were so amused one day on hearing strange noises, to see John, camera in hand, squatting and gobbling, till he was red in the face, trying to attract the turkey-cock, who he afterwards reproduced in plaster [and bronze]" (Ormond Family Collection). His stereoscopic viewer at Tite Street was one of the features of the studio often used to keep children quiet.

vocabulary. He was able to explore immediate responses, free of detailed analysis. Watercolour gave him a splendid modification of his technique, thus enabling him to capture white oxen in the blazing Italian sun while waiting for a train. And watercolours also became his favourite gifts. He doled them out for wedding presents, birthdays, Christmas and a general expression of greeting. They were, in many ways, his style of postcard.

Likewise, he turned to a shorthand in portraiture that saved potential sitters disappointment, got the ordeal speedily dispensed with and added so many portraits to his catalogue which made this uncomplicated explanation ring *too* simple: the charcoal sketch. Those who arrived too late to find permanence in a Sargent oil contented themselves with what he had to offer. For them it meant far fewer sittings, less money; for Sargent it meant braving a modified version of the old tyranny, but only for the mornings. "Sargent", Ralph Curtis wrote to Mrs Gardner after a brief visit to London, ". . . between meals does too many excellent charcoal portrait heads, at £50 a mug. . . . He would better do but a dozen at 300 each."[25] Like the watercolours, his use of charcoal was not new, but only remarkable for its sudden and frequent appearance, especially around 1910 and after. He did around a dozen in 1908 – at 21 guineas – and over forty in 1910; by the early 1920s he raised his fee to 100 guineas, which did nothing to deter the demand. His charcoal portraits eventually entered safe dinner-table parlance, equal to the weather as a respectable topic of conversation, certain to entice some response. He stuck exclusively to head and shoulders, moved the charcoal with brave, quick decisiveness across thick Whatman paper, allowing the likeness to emerge as he did in painting, often blacking in the background for maximum contrast and concentration on the subject. His studio technique remained unchanged while drawing: pacing, spluttering his toned-down expletives – "Pish-tash!", "Demons!"[26] – and occasional retreats to the piano. On the whole, the drawings were accomplished in one sitting of approximately two hours. Sargent had moved the production of likenesses into the realm of an hourly wage. By 1921 he felt about the shorthand solution exactly as he did about its predecessor: "I hate most of these portraits," he wrote to his cousin Nancy Potter, "and really hate to see them come out in the papers. I see an advantage in having yours done: it falls so far short of the impression that you yourself make that it will act as a deterrant to future candidates. . . ."[27]

The charcoals ran an effective defence against the threat of oil commissions because they supplied him with a freedom to transgress his "no more mugs!" rule for oils as a matter of choice, which he infrequently did in extraordinary circumstances (and under the veil of secrecy). In 1913, after three years of near-total retirement, he emerged, to make his contribution to Henry James's seventieth-birthday celebrations. The occasion was fraught with administrative complications, and got off to a bad start. At the beginning of the year (or shortly before) Edith Wharton, James's own Mrs Hunter, hatched a hare-brained scheme to raise a

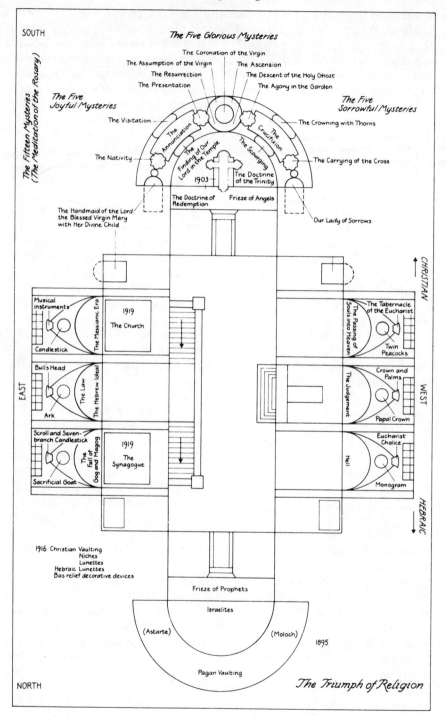

SOUTH

The Five Glorious Mysteries

The Coronation of the Virgin

The Assumption of the Virgin — The Ascension

The Resurrection — The Descent of the Holy Ghost

The Presentation — The Agony in the Garden

The Five Joyful Mysteries

The Fifteen Mysteries (The Meditation of the Rosary)

The Five Sorrowful Mysteries

The Visitation — The Crowning with Thorns

The Annunciation

The Crucifixion

The Finding of Our Lord in the Temple

The Scourging

The Nativity — The Carrying of the Cross

1903

The Doctrine of the Trinity

The Doctrine of Redemption   Frieze of Angels

The Handmaid of the Lord; the Blessed Virgin Mary with Her Divine Child

Our Lady of Sorrows

CHRISTIAN

Musical instruments

1919 The Church

The Messianic Era

The Tabernacle of the Eucharist

The Passing of Souls into Heaven

Candlestick

Twin Peacocks

EAST

Bull's Head

The Law   The Hebrew Ideal

Crown and Palms

The Judgement

WEST

Ark

Papal Crown

Scroll and Seven-branch Candlestick

1919 The Synagogue

The Fall of Gog and Magog

Eucharist Chalice

Hell

Sacrificial Goat

Monogram

HEBRAIC

1916 Christian Vaulting
      Niches
      Lunettes
Hebraic Lunettes
Bas relief decorative devices

Frieze of Prophets

Israelites

(Astarte)   (Moloch)   1895

Pagan Vaulting

NORTH

The Triumph of Religion

substantial sum of money by subscription from his American admirers. James was horrified, insisted it be stopped, and the money was returned. His English admirers embarked with more probity. A small committee was formed, with Percy Lubbock as secretary, and a long list of people were petitioned to subscribe, to a maximum of £5, and it was hoped £500 would be raised. The letters went out, under the names of the organizing committee, informing potential birthday signatories that the sum would " 'take the form of a painting of Henry James himself by Mr John Sargent' ", Max Beerbohm wrote to Reggie Turner [11 March 1913], quoting from the appeal. Sargent's name was on the letter. "Poor Sargent," Beerbohm concluded from appearances, "most sensitive and most correct of men, can't have known his name was going to be included . . . as he is such a devoted old friend of H.J., I think he might have done the thing gratis – else better not do it at all. However, I hope he will buy himself something nice with my two guineas."[28] There had been much discussion about this very point. James wrote to his sister-in-law the day after his birthday (16 April 1913):

> Sargent, most beautifully, as a member of the Committee, tried to insist on doing it for nothing, but had to yield to the representation, of course, that if this were allowed the work would become practically *his* present altogether, and not that of the Friends. . . . So he agreed, with the one condition, that, when I should have sat, he was to be free to tear the canvas straight up if he himself doesn't like the result.[29]

In the end, however, he waived his fee absolutely, handing it on to the sculptor, Derwent Wood, whom he recommended for a portrait bust of James. James also insisted on certain conditions. The portrait, when and if complete, would be on loan to him for his lifetime, and thereafter the property of the nation; it belonged to his admirers. On his birthday he received the first of the honours provided by the appeal – a silver-gilt, eared basin with lid, a golden bowl, inscribed " 'To Henry James from some of his friends' ";[30] 269 to be exact. The portrait would be their second gesture of admiration.

The first of nine sittings began in May. James was patient, and Sargent highly dubious – scared in fact. The year before Edith Wharton had commissioned one of his charcoal sketches of James; "the photograph [of the drawing] that has reached me", he wrote to Edith Wharton (28 March [1912], "proves that I am right in considering H.J. drawing a failure . . .".[31] His confidence was no greater a year later. In that time James had become a neighbour, taking 21 Carlyle Mansions, and his interest in Sargent's work had not wavered in the slightest; if anything, as a subject himself, was even more intent. Sargent had taken the precaution to ask James to invite a companion to the sittings to occupy the sitter and deflect some of his frightening curiosity. After the first sitting James wrote to his nephew: "It struck me that he could say to me – even *he* – after all his record – that in consequence of his having now stopped portraiture for these last three or four years, he had quite 'lost his nerve' about it. . . ."[32]

The portrait was finished by the late spring; it was one of Sargent's best, showing an unusual – and almost unique – capacity for insight into his sitter's character. But, then again this had been no usual commission. It drew on thirty years' intimacy, occasionally lost, but regained in full for the occasion. Sargent was overmodest, even by his own high standards, which James quickly took to be a true indication of his greatness, and Sargent's admiration for James was of the same order. Sargent had nearly 300 patrons to satisfy, and James was sitting first for his friends and then for posterity. It was a portrait overburdened with a complication of purposes, and an unqualified success, as the subscribers found out by the end of the year. Each was sent a photograph signed by artist and sitter (Sargent's, not James's has faded in time) and all were invited on three consecutive days to 31 Tite Street to examine both subject and portrait. "I do really rejoice so that I have been able to be the occasion of such a supreme manifestation of Sargent's genius," James wrote to the Ranee of Sarawak (8 December).[33]

Sargent's modesty never wavered amid these superlatives. When the public was given a glimpse of the picture that would eventually belong to them, at the Academy, a suffragette made it manifestly clear she did not want it or, rather, wanted the vote more than she wanted Henry James: the picture was slashed on 4 May 1914. Sargent, like other members of the Council, was called to the Academy. When he got there his first thought was to comfort the Secretary, Walter Lamb, on whom it fell to conduct the attacker to the police station. "And it was only when I led him to the picture," Lamb later recalled, "that he thought of examining the real disaster. I have no doubt that other friends can quote similar instances of his quick self-forgetting sympathy."[34] The portrait was restored, and now hangs at the National Portrait Gallery, under glass.

Since his mother's death and until the war, Sargent's routine was wonderfully unvaried: the winter, spring and early summer months were handed over to London – charcoals, Academy Visitor and tinkering with his Boston decorations – while the late summer and autumn were devoted to abroad – landscapes, figures and landscapes; in short, private work. It was the old divide of Paris versus Broadway, Calcot and Fladbury. When the geography changed, he merely altered the nature of his work. His life was a catalogue of where pictures were painted: there was never an alteration in the nature or substance of his life. There was no winding down of his energy, no seeking comfort in complacency, no retiring. Yet whereas Vernon Lee was correct to say "his life was absorbed in his painting" with staggering consistency he was as indefatigable in looking. He frequently went to Paris expressly for exhibitions, the Salon and, in 1914, the Ingres Exhibition. His pantheon of heroes admitted new names, as he drifted over to an increasing fascination with technique. With age – he was fifty-eight in 1914 – he started to walk away from the science of Carolus, the precision of subtlety, the accuracy of interpreting the eye's job. "Ingres, Raphael and El Greco," he wrote to Helleu in 1914, "these are now my admirations, these are what I like." In the autumn of 1912 he sought out little-known El Grecos in Toledo and Madrid and concluded "he is certainly one of the very most magnificent old masters".[35] The gulf between him and the Post-Impressionists was becoming unbridgeably wide. This small modification in values was, however, more significant as an index of his total obsession with his work, an obsession that isolated him increasingly, causing a near-total withdrawal. He had propelled himself into a state of complete oblivion. Nothing else mattered or existed, apart from categories that directed his brush and pencil. If such monomania had begun first as a defence, it had now ceased to have that extra function.

His powers of oblivion were put to their gravest test in the summer of 1914, and he acquitted himself brilliantly; he could do no other. He painted when the war began and continued to do so until it was over, while Emily busied herself making bandages in the Hill Hall smoking-room and Mrs Hunter occupied herself in two additional roles – hotelier and hospital matron. Sargent continued to do the only thing he ever knew how to do, and in 1918 made that knowledge available to the Ministry of Information. He never ignored the war; he merely made very few compromises to it.

Despite warnings, he left London in July 1914 as he had done for the last nine years. He went to the high altitudes of the southern Tyrol to revisit a location in the Seisser Alps fondly remembered from childhood – a memory of distant years he could not confirm, and he and his party quickly moved on. They were travelling with their customary visual Baedeker, sightseeing for work. With him were Nicola (in his capacity of pack-mule/courier, burdened with his master's three enormous sketching umbrellas, stool, canvases, paper, paint, luggage, camera, as well as his own luggage), Dr Ernest A. Armstrong (who was also a lieutenant-colonel and an amateur painter), Adrian Stokes (1852–1935, painter and a fellow-Visitor at the Royal Academy), his wife Marianne (an Austrian, and like her husband a keen watercolourist) and her maid. The Stokes had been well schooled in Sargent holidays, having been with him in the Simplon in 1911 after the flight from Munich to Abbey. For all of them it was just another holiday, but very shortly after it began events caught them up and made it seem, in retrospect, much different. When Austria declared war on Serbia, on July 28, a few slight difficulties crossed their path: mules, horses and traps were requisitioned for the army, other tourists cleared out, everything became much quieter, and the painters found themselves somewhat more isolated. Then their letters were returned and none reached them for two months. Passports were required for travel within Austria, and they had none. When England declared war Armstrong and Stokes instantly became aliens; Armstrong, eager to get back to England, was arrested and interned, first by the police, then in an hotel before being allowed to leave the country.

Sargent's paintings were confiscated, sent to Innsbruck for inspection, as well as his painting equipment, which did not seem to bother him much. Weeks went by before he could get letters out (via the American embassy in Vienna or through Switzerland) or receive news of his sisters and friends by way of Italy. He was anxious about Emily, and more anxious she should not worry about him. After all, his routine had scarcely altered, painting in lower altitudes as the weather turned cold: in Colfuschg for most of September and St Lorenzen in the Pusterthal throughout October and much of November. He never hinted at the slightest inconvenience, because he had FitzWilliam's tact and delicacy to tell the recipient what he thought they wanted to hear. "The Stokes & I are very comfortable & happy at the house of an old Austrian friend of mine," he wrote to Mrs Hunter (18 October), "and we are painting away while Rome is burning."[36] His sisters could not respond in kind, alas. Violet's daughter, Rose-Marie, who had assumed her mother's old post as one of Sargent's favourite models, had become a widow after only fourteen months of marriage. Her husband, Robert-André Michel, was killed on 12 October, and her mother and aunt were powerless, in London, to help her or go to her in Paris; nor could her uncle. The forces of isolation were slowly gathering against him. His confidence about getting back in November was slipping away. He asked Emily to write to Poynter to warn that both he and Stokes might not be able to take up their duties as Visitors. He asked her to make certain the Fulham Road studios were insured against war damage and fire, for £10,000. He instructed her to pay his bills and his servants' wages – Nicola's salary was to be paid direct to his mother in Clerkenwell (30s a week or £6 a month, in advance) – and begged her to take whatever money she needed herself from his bankers, Morgan, Grenfell. He gave way to despair; the prospect of getting all of his luggage and paintings home was going to be very risky as travel had become "hopeless" and his passport was very slow to materialize. Somehow, almost miraculously, he did manage to get back to London by the end of November, only about a week later than he had originally calculated.

In truth, he had only suffered the most minor inconvenience by the sudden disruptions of the outbreak of the war; he was able to keep to his "holiday as usual" plan, more or less, and the paintings he brought back comprised his customary reflex summary of those weeks abroad – *The Master and His Pupils* (Stokes and several versions of his wife's maid painting outdoors), *Tyrolean Interior* and crucifixes in the fog, among others. But these souvenirs were unlike all others he had unrolled over the years in Tite Street: they gave a lie to his powers of oblivion. The war *had* intruded. His colours were more sombre, the sun did not appear, the *esprit* of Norway, Italy, Corfu, Majorca, Simplon was lost, forever. The war accelerated the pace at which he was withdrawing into himself. He was bringing down the safety curtain separating himself and the outside world, and for the next ten years he was content to occupy an ever-narrowing territory. The war *did* affect him, though he expressed it silently, in the mastery of oblique terms, with that gift the Sargents had for being indirect.

The spirit of London had also changed during his absence. Everyone was making adjustments to accommodate the war. Mrs Hunter abandoned her policy of exclusive pleasure, turning Hill Hall into part boarding-house for Belgian refugees, the Rodins and other select exiles (like Mrs Curtis, who was waiting for a passport to return to America) and part convalescent home for officers. Emily toiled away with lint while waiting for the erratic news from Violet (and her children), who had got back to France. Sitters came to Tite Street for their charcoal portraits, but spoke of the disintegration of family life, the loss of brothers, sons, husbands. Christmas was a dour occasion at Carlyle Mansions that year, attended by James and "3 or 4 waifs & strays", as he wrote to Jessie Allen (27 December 1914).[37] Altogether London seemed a darker place than usual. And in January Sargent returned his Prussian Ordre pour le Mérité.

Eight months later James took a bolder step; on 28 July 1915 he became a British subject. Like Sargent, he was technically an alien, obliged to register and report to the police; unlike Sargent, James found it an odious status, unharmonious after forty years. To him, England was *home*, and only a declaration and paperwork stood between him and that fact. "I also was shocked, at the moment, on hearing of James' apostasy," Sargent wrote to Edith Wharton (6 August) [1915] when she petitioned him for a contribution to her charity volume, *The Book of the Homeless*, " – but I soon admired the action as a protest against the apathy under kicks of the American Government. I think of him with awe, as being like the Chinese Censor Wu Ko Tu who protested and committed suicide to make his protest final."[38] Sargent's feelings and irritation ran differently from James's. He never contemplated changing his citizenship, despite confusion, despite the commonly held notion he was a British subject. Twenty years earlier he made his position manifestly clear to Whistler: "As for the question of nationality I have not been invited to retouch it and I keep my twang. If you should hear anything to the contrary, please state that there was no such transaction and that I am an American."[39] Sargent held fast to his nationality. It had always been endangered and never altogether clear, but he was accustomed to the inconvenience. He had known nothing else. Being an American was his father's proudest and only possession in exile – a legacy he passed to his son. Had Sargent refused it, he also would have refused his father. His nationality was part of the tightly bound parcel labelled "family".

Though he did not clutch his breast in despair or issue profound statements about the sadness of the war, he was not contained by ignorance as he had been during the Boer war. He bypassed gloomy meditation in favour of action. He ransacked his store of saleable pictures for charity. He designed stationery for the Red Cross. There were concerts for benevolent funds. And, though the tenor of his life was much the same as before, his music and work veered off in another direction. In the autumn 1915 he took still longer strides, all the way to the War Office, when Abbott Thayer, the American artist he had known in Paris forty years before, asked him to make representations on behalf of his researches into camouflage. Thayer had made a detailed study of the protective colorations found in nature, and was shocked by the military's persistent use of white, so dangerous with the advent of aerial reconnaissance. In September he sent to Sargent various stencils and sample uniform designs to demonstrate his case and act as an introduction before he arrived in Europe himself. Sargent did what he could, but made little headway against the opposition: "I have just come back from the War Office," he wrote to Thayer (12 November 1915),

> . . . I talked for an hour about parti-colour versus monochrome, and demonstrated with sheets of white paper held at different angles to each other that white [was?] necessarily white. . . . I have come away with the feeling that, although they admitted that your observations of nature and efforts were "gospel truth" as they said, there is little likelihood of their ordering in large quantities anything resembling your uniforms. They seem to think protection against rain is the main thing, & that is that.

He introduced him to H. G. Wells, whom he scarcely knew, suspecting a sympathetic hearing and a useful proponent. He supplied an introduction to Bonnat "whom I know very slightly but who is certainly the most influential artist in Paris, and probably in touch with many generals".[40]

The results were negligible. The War Office debated for the best part of two months, and decided to take their preliminary investigations a stage further, Thayer was written to, more than once, and the letters were returned. Sargent was again consulted, and was reluctantly forced to confess he could be of no further service. To Thayer, however, he wrote in white-hot indignation (31 January 1916):

> In case you again imagine that your efforts have met with no response, please consider that your habit of changing your address without letting anyone know has made any action on other people's part absolutely useless and has kept you quite in the dark. . . . Anybody else would have let the War Office, and the people who were busy about your affair, know.
>
> I am going to Boston soon, and shall be curious to learn what made you vamoose.[41]

Sargent, whose generosity was offered liberally without conditions, had never put himself in the service of someone so remarkably vague, and he was angry; it was an almost unique demonstration of temper, more from disbelief than from a sense of wasted effort. (The value of deception as a military strategy was eventually adopted in 1918 after much work by Solomon J. Solomon, though the Americans appreciated its value somewhat before the British. Thayer's actual contribution, while incontestably significant and fundamental, has been debated by historians.)

Otherwise it was business as usual, at the same unrelenting, withering pace. He took his place on the Committee of the Royal Academy Winter Exhibition, the Chairmanship of the London Committee of the Panama-Pacific Exposition (to which he contributed thirteen pictures, among them Madame Gautreau, which he offered to the Metropolitan to save it the return journey), and he arranged an exhibition of his portrait sketches at the Grafton Gallery. And his studio work was given over to the Boston murals: the Christian vaulting and niches were ready, some thirteen years after the angels, Trinity and crucifix were placed on the south wall, as well as the six lunettes that linked both ends of the Hall. After twenty-six years the grandiose scheme was nearing completion. At the beginning of 1916 packers moved into the Fulham Road studio; Sargent supervised the work, distinguishing himself first by smashing his finger with a hammer, and then as the "big cases were being loaded on vans at Fulham Road . . . one of them toppled over, knocked me down and squashed my foot. Most vexing," he wrote to Evan Charteris, and he took to his bed for a few days while the crates were *en route* to Boston. "Don't make much of this to friends . . . I don't want to be kodaked landing in America in splints & crutches. . . ."[42] His ship, *New Amsterdam*, was scheduled to leave on 20 March; he and Nicola packed their own cases, locked up the studio and prepared to leave for Falmouth when the sailing was postponed. As they did not know from one day to the next when they would be allowed to sail they waited in Falmouth: "I dreaded the extra day in London with everything locked," he wrote to Mrs Hunter, "and good-byes spreading overboard. I am afraid Emily will be in a great state of anxiety for several days. . . . There won't be any telling until tomorrow morning whether this blessed ship will get here, and leave – it appears they are sometimes detained here for 9 days. The town is packed with Americans waiting."[43] Every aspect of the journey was disagreeable, from the wait to the crossing. Sargent loathed sailing in any case. He was bored and uncomfortable, always suffering from seasickness. It was a necessary ordeal, lightened partially by Mrs Hunter's gift of several books, including two souvenirs of Henry James, who had died a month before – his first posthumous volume and *The Wings of the Dove*. His anxiety about Emily started at once and never deserted him: Marconi-grams went back and forth when he heard the vague reports of zeppelin raids. "They keep the news very secret on board ship," he wrote to Mrs Hunter the day before landing, "for fear of rows between the German & English passengers."[44] The reporters were waiting for him when the ship docked, and when he displayed all his usual unforthcomingness in reply to their questions they promptly invented interesting stories.

He stayed at the Vendôme, the scaffolding went up in the Library, and the paintings stayed in rolls in the lecture-room until the builders finished the ceiling. While waiting for the paintings to be installed, he toiled away at the bas-reliefs. "I am terribly busy here with the carrying out of the plaster work of my ceiling," he wrote to Charteris. "It is progressing well but it will be a long job, and I have to work like a nigger at modelling things that the workmen want to carry off and cast. I doubt if all this is accomplished so that I can put up my paintings before the midsummer heat sets in. . . . So I shall be over here a long time."[45] He stayed in America for twenty-six months. Tite Street was replaced by the Vendôme, and Fulham Road first by a studio in Newberry Street and then by an enormous "skyscraper studio" in the Pope Building at 221 Columbus Avenue. The country had changed, but the routine was unvaried. America had waited a long time for him to return. Both Yale (on the fiftieth anniversary of its art school) and Harvard bestowed honorary degrees on him within months of his arrival. Everything he did was copiously documented, and he found his celebrity a cumbrous thing. His letters to England were sent with a frequency that showed his sense of being cut off. Though he had come to America for a job, he had also removed himself from the dangers at home, and he was alarmed by the distance separating him from his sisters.

During the summer, while the various changes were being made to the ceiling preparatory to receiving his canvases, Sargent headed west to sample what North America had to offer as a replacement for the Dolomites – the Rockies.

After stopping at Glacier National Park in Montana (for about a fortnight with friends from Boston) he and Nicola headed north to British Columbia and "the simple life (ach pfui) in tents", as he wrote to his cousin Mary Hale (30 August).[46] "I have been camping," he wrote to Mrs Hunter after three weeks in Yoho Park, Field, British Columbia (31 August), " – one has to do that here, there is nothing to paint near these enormous hotels along the C[anadian] P[acific] railway. I am off . . . again in search of some alpine nightmare."[47] He made no secret of his discomfort: "Two things have got on my nerves," he wrote to the architect Thomas Fox, who was helping him with the Library ceiling (28 August), " – one the roar and hissing and pounding all night long of a tremendous waterfall that I am near, the other the alighting of snowflakes on my bottom when it is bared once a day. Perhaps this is the poetry of camping out."[48] His three-month escape from the heat and scaffolding of Boston was merely an exchange of discomforts: monotony, canned food, porcupine-gnawed boots, mules, ponies, cold and damp. He returned to Boston in October, loaded with watercolours of tents and camp-sites, and oils of Lake O'Hara and Yoho Falls, which went on sale at the Copley Society Show in November, and were all quickly snapped up.

The third and final (or so he thought) installation for the Special Libraries Hall stretched through the autumn. By the middle of November, shortly after the Trustees had expressed their impatience, the work was unveiled. "The whole architectural and ornamental scheme seems to work out on the large scale," he wrote to Charteris after a preliminary glimpse before he embarked on his rustic idyll (25 July), "and it has been a great satisfaction not to have to make any changes. Whether or not it is another of the palpable signs that I am getting old, I am rather revelling in the appearance this white elephant of mine is taking on of amounting to something, after all these years."[49] "The total effect is better than I hoped," he wrote to Mrs Hunter (9 January 1917), "and it doesn't matter if the individual paintings are good or bad."[50]

In 1903 he had served notice that he was beginning to favour the ornate, having moved on from the vast narrative scale conferred on the Hebraic walls. He had sunk in knee-deep homage to his Renaissance models, and went one better than Raphael's fictive bas-reliefs and adapted Tintoretto's linking narrative across the ceiling of San Rocco. It was the same dialectic as his portraiture – transforming historical antecedents sufficiently to make them palatable to modern tastes, without discarding much of the essence. He simply went to the edge of an established tradition. And it suited the scaling-down process that had embraced charcoals and water-colour. The 1916 additions were an aggregate, a collection of manageable scenes. He wanted to get through a lot of material, wholly unsuited to any other form. It was a large installation.

On the left (east) of the angel frieze, the *Handmaid of the Lord, the Blessed Virgin Mary with Her Divine Child* stands in an arched niche, angels flap above her with arms clasped upholding a crown with a Dove. In case the profuse symbolism is inarticulate, a ribbon inscribed with Latin threads the angels aloft. Opposite the Handmaid, in the niche on the west wall, *Our Lady of Sorrows* bedecked in a silver crown and halo, a thickly embroidered cope, clutches seven swords (the sorrows) piercing her heart. She is protected on her altar by a screen of candles in relief. The two niches serve as introductions to the story that rises above in the vaulting: chapters from Christ and the Virgin's biography; a visual account of the Meditation of the Rosary – the fifteen Mysteries. Each section of the narrative was assigned a round, oval or large square bead, set in a gilded mount. The five Joyful Mysteries incline up from the east, the five Sorrowful Mysteries from the west, and both connect on to a huge filigreed lozenge in the centre of a modelled rendering of the five Glorious Mysteries. The vaulting is an elaborate brooch, housing an important gem, resting on a background dense with supplementary symbols. The Joyful clasp is arranged about *The Annunciation*, flanked by *The Visitation* (Mary and her cousin Elizabeth) and *The Finding of Our Lord in the Temple* with *The Nativity* below, and above *The Presentation* (Simeon clutching the Child). The Sorrowful clasp is ordered about *The Crucifixion*, occupying like *The Annunciation* the large rectangular panel; *The Agony in the Garden* is above, *The Carrying of the Cross* below, *The Scourging* and *The Crowning with Thorns* at each side. The two clasps are the beginning and the end of the story. The jewel of the Glorious Mysteries, *The Coronation of the Virgin*, is ringed by *The Resurrection, The Ascension, The Descent of the Holy Ghost* and *The Assumption of the Virgin*.

Each end of the Hall was now complete, and to complete the decorative sweep of the compass Sargent added six more lunettes, three on the east wall, three on the west. He had insisted on architectural adjustments to the ceiling to achieve at least a strained link between the Hebraic and Christian instalments. The staircase wall or the east wall was handed over to Hebraic mythology. Perpendicular to the Israelite lunette *The Fall of Gog and Magog* portrays the destruction of the universe, the suggestion of Mars and Mercury falling through space; the end of order has arrived. Next is *The Law*, the central lunette, showing Jehovah concentrating on divine law. (When a lady asked Sargent why Jehovah's face was indistinguishable, he reminded her that he had given up portraiture.) The third lunette, perpendicular to the Trinity is *The Messianic Era*, illustrating and repeating (in Hebrew) the prophecies of Isaiah, as a child is being showed into paradise.

On the west wall there are the three Christian lunettes. *The Passing of Souls into Heaven* faces the Messianic scene, with angels strumming on harps, leading the way upwards. In the centre *The Judgement*, with haloed angels and an immense scale, equivalent to *The Law*. The third, at right angles to the Israelites, is *Hell* volunteering the same chaos endured by Gog and Magog.

And, after having gone the distance of eight lunettes, each twenty-four feet wide, two friezes of the same width and about ten feet high, and two vaultings larger than any of the other sections, Sargent still did not consider the work at an end. He added twelve ornamental devices, within the conjunctions of the ribbings that rose from the side lunettes, plus dolphins above the Music Library door, plus electrical light fittings, bookcase frames of his design, as well as all the ribbing decorations, which were enhanced by the application of gold, like the Hebrew inscriptions.

The Triumph of Religion was a long journey, covering a lot of ground, and when it was over Sargent was reluctant to let it go. The murals had become a habit of some long standing. He had got the precision of symmetry into his blood, took another look at the decorated Hall, and decided that two large panels on the staircase wall were needed to correspond with the square bookcases on the opposite wall: *The Synagogue* and *The Church*, added in 1919. The former created an outrage. "I am in hot water here with the Jews," he wrote to Charteris (24 October [1919], "who resent my 'Synagogue' and want to have it removed – and tomorrow a 'prominent' member of the Jewish colony is coming to bully me about it and ask me to explain myself. I can only refer him to Rheims, Notre Dame, Strasburg and other cathedrals and dwell at length about the good old times. Fortunately the Library Trustees do not object and propose to allow this painful work to stay."[51] (See Appendix II.)

The public elected to be impressed by Sargent's colossal endeavour, leaving comprehension behind; he had spread himself too wide to be readily understood. The scope of the enterprise was overpowering,

PLATE XXV

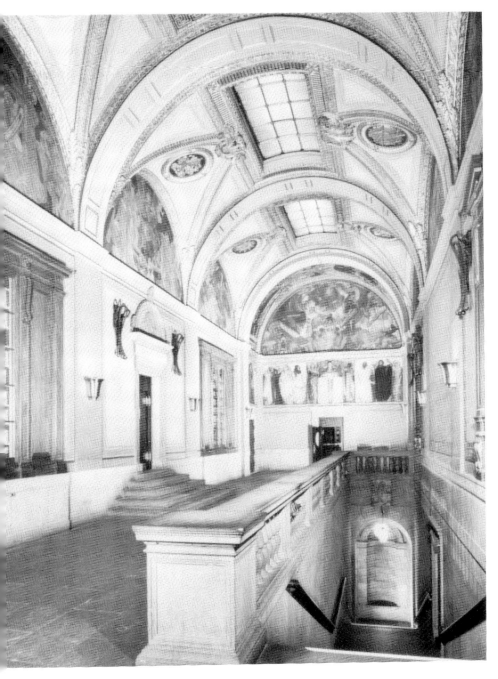

The Special Libraries Hall (later known as the Sargent Hall), the Boston Public Library. This shows the north end (Hebraic portion) with frieze, vaulting and lunettes, as well as the decorative bas-reliefs devised for **The Triumph of Religion**, 1890-1919.

PLATE XXVI

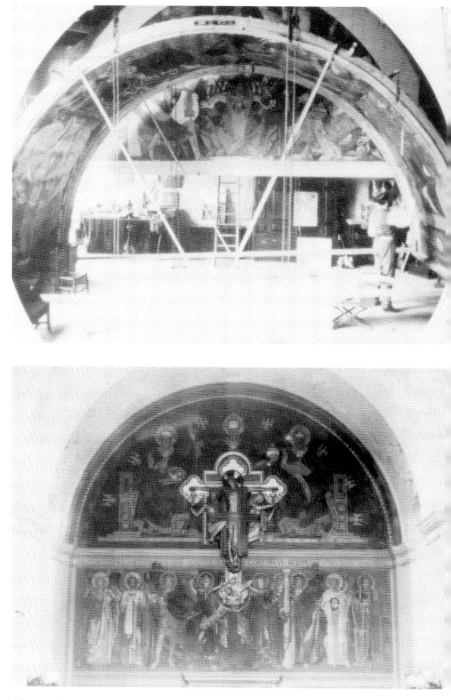

Above: Sargent painting the Pagan vaulting in his Fulham Road studio.

Below: The Christian frieze and lunette, 1903, from a contemporary photograph. It was taken shortly after they were affixed to the wall and shows them without the Mysteries vaulting and without Sargent's specially devised lighting.

PLATE XXVII

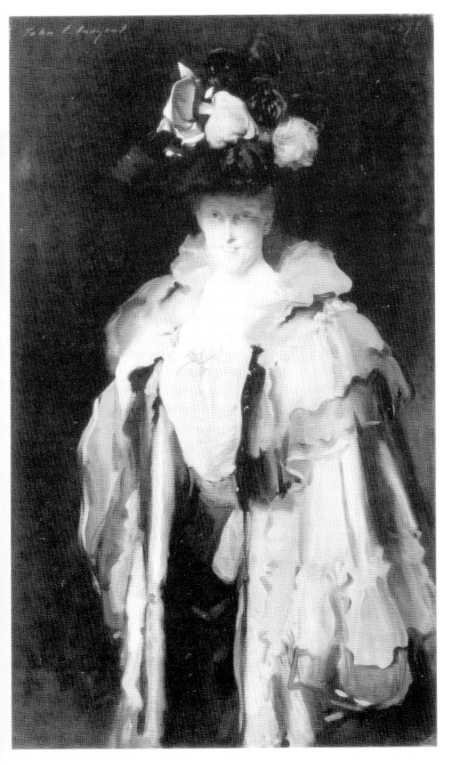

Mary Smyth (Mrs Charles Hunter), by Sargent, 1898.

PLATE XXVIII

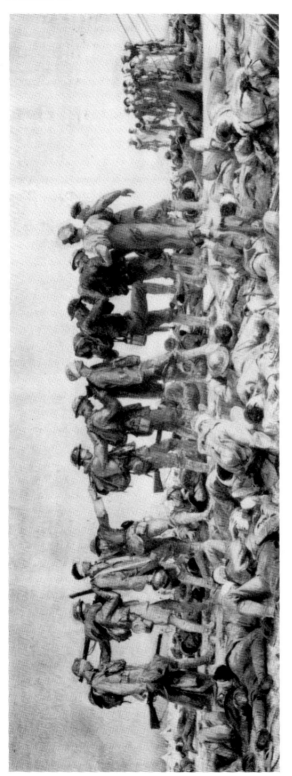

Above: Gassed [1919].

Opposite: Rotunda, the Museum of Fine Arts, Boston. The decoration was unveiled in 1921.

PLATE XXIX

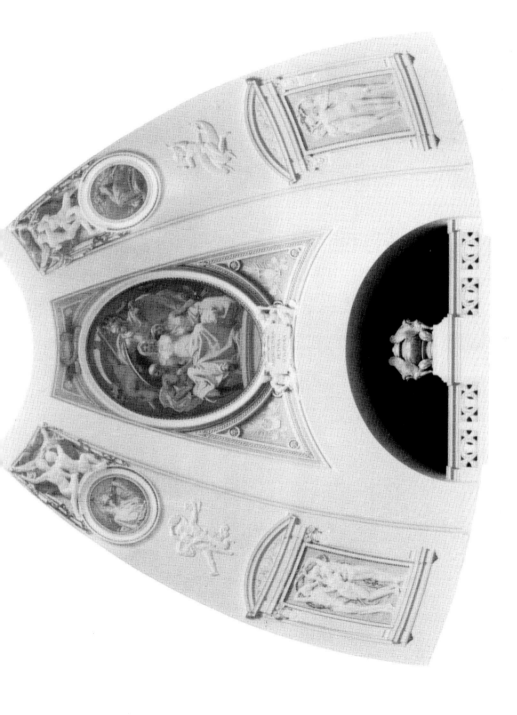

PLATE XXX

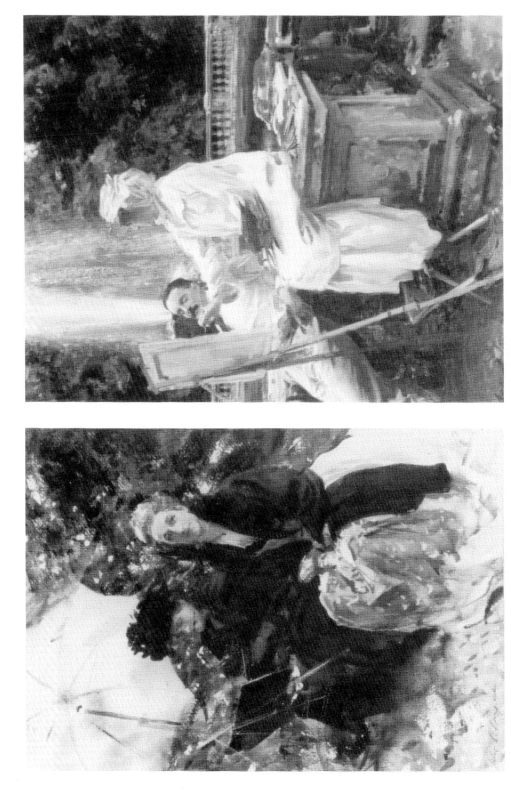

PLATE XXXI

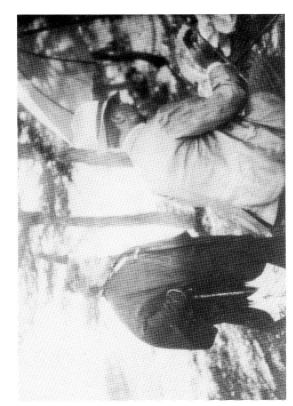

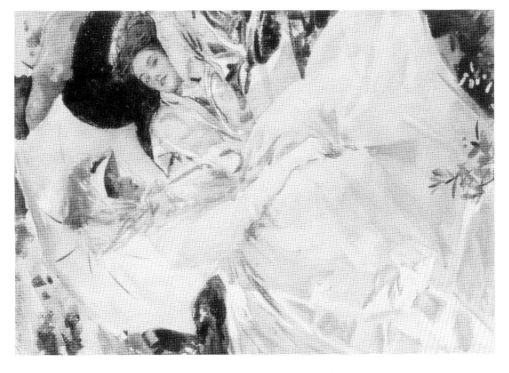

Opposite left: Emily Sargent and Eliza Wedgwood in Majorca, by Sargent, 1908.

*Opposite right: **The Fountain, Villa Torlonia, Frascati** – Wilfred and Jane von Glehn in Frascati, by Sargent, 1907.*

Below: Emily and John Sargent, Simplon Pass, 1911.

*Left: **Reading** – Sargent's painting of the scene.*

PLATE XXXII

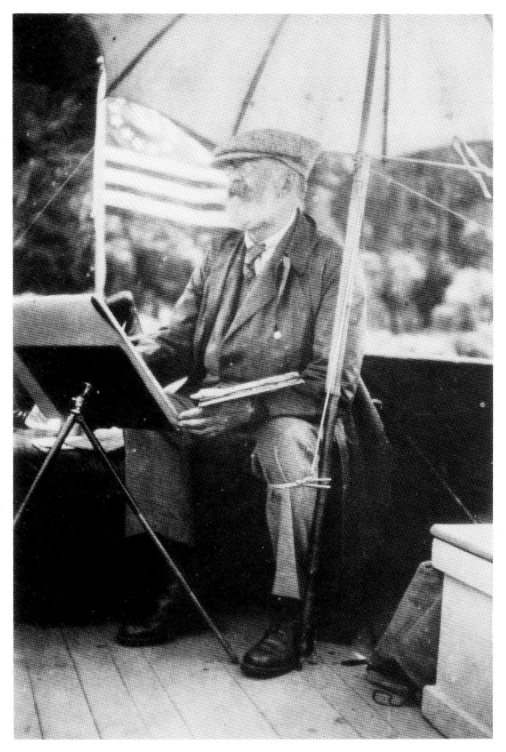

Sargent sketching in Ironbound, Maine, 1922.

embracing every detail of the decoration from lighting, skylight frames, mouldings on the architraves and archivolts, ceiling ribs, to the panels themselves. No detail escaped Sargent's attention, and adjustment. "In matters of detail," he wrote to Thomas Fox, one of the architects delegated by the Trustees to see the scheme through (22 November 1915), from Tite Street,

> I think the acanthus leaves with which I have covered the mitreing are clumsy and start too far from the cornice – I don't know whether there ought to be rosettes on the squares of the continuation of the pilasters [from the niches] across the ceiling – nor how such panelling should be treated on the half continuations that abut against the wider ones at each end of the hall. Also I think that there ought to be another inner line of moulding on the little shallow triangular panels – also I don't know what would be the best way to treat the perpendicular surfaces of the walls of the skylights.

Sargent seemed to have achieved an almost impossible mental dexterity by the time the decoration was complete: he was able to conceive an idea of the whole through a long process of dealing with parts. The hardest, and most important, feat was saved until the end: sewing the instalments together. And he himself confessed the ignorance his energy managed to overcome: "I don't know much about architecture or much about archi-tectural decoration, and in carrying out this scheme I have tried one thing after another until it seemed to me to do."[52] The public, however, assured him he had exceeded such a modest calculation. The cheering squashed incomprehension; the Special Libraries Hall was renamed the Sargent Hall.

Shortly before the "completed" Hall was unveiled, he accepted the commission to decorate the new rotunda in the Museum of Fine Arts on Huntington Avenue – an acceptance that greatly expanded the original suggestion. The Trustees asked him to supply three lunettes to fill the recessed arches at the base of the dome. Sargent considered them too dark, refused to allow artificial lighting, and asked to transfer his work up into the dome itself, thus giving himself a much larger surface to cover. He insisted on architectural changes as well. A one-eighth scale model was made for his studio, preliminary sketches began (eventually number-ing more than 200), the bas-reliefs were plotted, and models came to pose. His loyalty to the enrichment of Boston civic buildings began again, tying him to decoration for the rest of his life – and keeping him from London.

He postponed his return to London. He could not leave before the Museum details were worked out to everyone's satisfaction and, in any case, Emily planned to come to see him. In the interval he suffered from "a temporary relapse into paughtraiture", as he wrote to Charteris.[53] Rockefeller insisted Sargent paint his portrait, and insisted again: he could not hear the word "no", dismissing Sargent's "no more portraits" rule. He laid a formidable siege on Sargent's resolve, and Sargent gave way. Towards the end of February 1917, he went south to Ormond Beach, Florida. "Here I am in a temperature like a Turkish bath," he wrote to Curtis (26 February [1917], "about to begin work on the Old Gentleman who looks like a mediaeval saint."[54] From there, about three weeks later, he went to stay with his old friend Charles Deering at Brickell Point, and was given the run of James Deering's unfinished estate, Vizcaya: "It is hard to leave this place," he wrote to his cousin Mary Hale. "There is so much to paint, not here, but at my host's brother's villa. It combines Venice and Frascati and Aranjuez, and all that one is likely never to see again. Hence this linger-longing."[55]

America entered the war on 6 April; in December, as a sort of delayed reaction, he tendered his resignation from the Berlin Academy. And now he could not leave; and Emily could not, with any safety, come to America. It was the Tyrol all over again. "I only hope Emily won't suffer from this isolation," he wrote to Mrs Hunter from Deering's houseboat *Nepenthe* off-shore from Miami (21 April 1917).

> I do myself a good deal, and think that I ought not to have allowed myself to be caught in this impasse. . . . With all this preoccupation [?] it has seemed absurd to be lazily cruising about for ten days in these tropical waters with very little chance of sketching – and a strong moral pressure put upon one to fish. . . . By the way [he wrote earlier in the letter], I am extremely proud of having landed one weighing 140 pounds & 6' 10 inches long.[56]

"I am only fit to fiddle while Rome is burning," he wrote to Charteris (14 September), "and am doing it with a vengeance. My new big job absorbs me to a degree that is probably discreditable, or it is probably discreditable to put one's energy into anything so remote from the only big job. A curious case for my New England Conscience."[57]

His "temporary relapse" was difficult to shake off. Rockefeller wanted a second portrait, and in June, a month after coming back north, sittings began again in the garage of his Pocantico Hills estate, New York. This portrait was, Sargent wrote to Charteris, "for my own pocket",[58] and both Rockefeller portraits helped a number of other pockets: Beckwith and James's nephew were authorized to make copies of both. (Sargent got Beckwith the commission.) The Ormond Beach version was stored in Beckwith's New York studio, and while it was there the Paris rebels of the 1870s turned potentates of American art processed round the canvas, nodding sagely. Sargent had done it again; nothing had changed since rue Notre-Dame-des-Champs; he still dwarfed them.

The relapse took another bad turning in the autumn: Sir Hugh Lane's Red Cross portrait could be dodged no longer. Sargent had to keep his word, given at the beginning of 1915, when the plot was hatched. Sargent simplified the confusion of the scheme in a letter to Mrs Gardner (n.d.) [1917]:

All I know is that Hugh Lane took up an idea started by another man (who repented) that he would give £10000 to the Red Cross if I would paint his portrait (the first man's). Hugh Lane of course had some other idea about whose portrait it was to be. Then Hugh Lane was drowned [in the *Lusitania*]. He had left his estate to the Nat. Gallery of Ireland, who handed over the £10000 to the Red Cross in 1916, and have lately decided the portrait should be that of President Wilson.[59]

And Sargent waited around until Wilson was able to sit to him, in October 1917.

The old fears that prefaced the James portrait returned. He was back in the realm of official portraits. His memories of politicians were not pleasant. Roosevelt had been particularly disagreeable, adopting the most imperial manner towards his court recorder. The portrait of Speaker Reed was not generally appreciated as an example of quality. And Balfour had proved to be the sort of nightmare which Sargent did not care much to endure ever again. After the sittings began, his worries proved groundless: "I am still here," he informed Mrs Gardner from the New Willard Hotel in Washington (Sunday, 28) [October 1917].

. . . It takes a man a long time to look like his portrait, as Whistler used to say – but he is doing his best, and has been very obliging about finding time for sittings. He is interesting to do, very agreeable to be with, and the conditions are perfect as he allows no interruptions and does not hold levees as Roosevelt used to do – and his wife approves and does not even think there is "just a little something not quite right about the mouth".[60]

None of this managed to shake him from his growing fear. Throughout the winter he was menaced by "the thought of not being with you and Em[ily] while all these disagreeables are going on", he wrote to Violet (31 March 1918), "and I mean to come over before long, say towards the end of May, if sailings are handy". A further inducement to leave his museum was supplied by another Red Cross portrait, and he instructed Violet not to say anything to Emily who would of course worry "for she takes everything so tremendously to heart that I can't bear the idea of her worrying for weeks before hand".[61] Three days later he received a telegram on Good Friday informing him of the death of his niece, Madame Rose Marie Michel, killed in the German bombardment of the church of St Gervais, in Place Lobau. The war was creeping deeper into Sargent's isolation. "I can't tell you", he wrote to her mother (3 April) [1918], ". . . how I feel the loss of the most charming girl who ever lived. And what a death – I hope it was instantaneous."[62] Her short life – she was twenty-four years old – had been immortalized in a long series of memento moris, a sort of Fladbury for the next generation, during family holidays in the Val d'Aosta and the Simplon. Sargent had painted her in *The Cashmere Shawl, The Brook, The Black Brook, The Pink Dress*, and several times in one picture, *Cashmere*. Like her mother, he found her a wonderful model, and tradition has it she was his favourite. "I ought to be with you instead of over here," he again said to Violet,[63] who was herself unable to get from London to Paris.

He sailed about a month later (without Nicola), having taken the precaution to make his will, eager to be with his sisters, and as eager to return to his Museum decorations. He hoped to get back to Boston in about three months.

XV

Sargent's motives rarely enjoyed the logic of directness; they were defended by his bewildering energy – sufficient to take him from one ceiling to the next without pausing to draw breath – and obscured by his blind loyalty to work, which activated him quicker than any other impulse. But the war troubled his conscience; if he stayed in Boston he fretted about his family, and if he stayed in London he could not get on with his decorations. He concocted a compromise wholly suitable to himself and was undone by his selfishness. "I feel very homesick for Boston," he wrote to Mrs Gardner (31 May 1918) from Tite Street,

> and at loose ends for lack of work. Two or three hours a day of a dull Red Cross paughtret are a sad come down from the routine of the Pope Building – and the prospect that I cherished of getting back soon with my sisters is vanishing fast. The married one won't leave because her boys are enlisting and the other one does not feel that she can leave her – and my New England conscience dictates that I must chance at least a dozen raids with them.[1]

Once back in London, however, he was lured deeper into the war by the Ministry of Information's invitation to become a war artist. Negotiations continued throughout May, he jumped at the scheme, and accepted on 10 June. It was the old siren's wail of the curious, not patriotism or the notion he might be missing something. He had long been tempted. To him the spectre of the war loomed as an irresistible visual oddity. "If the accursed is still going on," he wrote to Charteris eighteen months before (19 October 1916), ". . . I shall feel tempted to go and have a look at it. . . . But would I have the nerve to look, not to speak of painting? I have never seen anything in the least horrible – outside of my studio."[2] "I hope to have the chance of being well scared," he wrote to Mrs Gardner once he had accepted the offer.[3] His homesickness for Boston was cured.

Lord Beaverbrook ran his Ministry of Information with determined gusto. He would have no nonsense. He set up the British War Memorials Committee and thus shifted the purpose for unloading artists on to battlefields from propaganda to posterity. Artists would now be dispatched to fill the walls of the future Hall of Remembrance, which was eventually lost in all the planning and was replaced by the Imperial War Museum. The Memorials Committee, under the secretaryship of Alfred Yockney, moved into action, drew up lists, kept copious files, in the campaign to get every aspect of the war immortalized on canvas. Pictures were classified by size and subject, then doled out to the artists, who were given ungenerous fees, plus expenses. Sargent was assigned "the key-stone of the collection", as Yockney later wrote to Sargent (24 October 1918): "The subject the committee have in mind", he wrote earlier (26 April 1918), "is one which would suggest the fusion of British and American forces", occupying a canvas twenty by eleven feet.[4] Lloyd George endorsed the Committee's proposal (three weeks later), giving a subtle reminder that there was no room for negotiation; Sargent was an employee of the government. His protests about the size and subject were acknowledged, and then dismissed. In the end, however, the Ministry got neither, in the strictest reading of the original instruction.

From the moment Sargent started for the front with Tonks, on 2 July, the whole enterprise was glazed with comedy. He rolled up at Charing Cross for the 11.50 to Boulogne decked out in a get-up that could only be called civilian with military additions, succeeding in neither mission, weighed down with his sketching umbrella, books, camp-stool, easel, painting equipment and a good many clothes – the memory of camping out in the Rockies was still fresh. He did not look like someone ready to set out to make a contribution to posterity, but his excitement was intense.

From the outset he was given very special treatment, a distinction put to the test by his desire and the Ministry's chosen subject. He had made it clear to Beaverbrook he wanted to see "the more rugged side of the war . . . the real thing in regard to warfare".[5] And in order to satisfy the commission he needed to follow the progress of American troops new to the war. In a supplement to one of the many minute papers dealing with Sargent (11 June 1918), Yockney was forced to admit that his plan of action was indeed a problem, but reminded his colleagues: "The point is that Mr Sargent is a very distinguished man and everything possible should be done for him."[6] It was. He was treated like a tender parcel, passed from one protectorate to another, and all the while was never quite able to grasp the idea of his own fragility. He knew absolutely nothing about the workings of the Army. Tonks found it impossible to drill the most rudimentary account of military ranks into Sargent's head, and he gave up after the third attempt. Once a guardsman levelled his rifle at Sargent, who was busy sketching, and asked who he was; Sargent looked up from his work and calmly gave his name "'The hell you are! I know the ser-geant. Come along.'"[7] The grave seriousness of the war never got through to him, having stopped well short of any profound reading as a spectacle. He assumed his exclusively spectatorial capacity with admirable applic-ation. He once asked in all seriousness if the war stopped on Sundays.

On landing in France he and Tonks were placed in the care of Major Sir Philip Sassoon, Bt (1888–1939), Private Secretary to Field-Marshal Sir

Douglas Haig, Commander-in-Chief of the British armies in France; in such custody Sargent not only started at the top but, more important, caught up with an old friend – he had known Sassoon for years.

On the surface he was as unlikely a character to meet in the circumstances as Sargent. Sassoon had had too many of life's good fortunes handed to him – and in such abundance – to escape a legion of enemies, and his reputation was not helped by the fact that his skills were too subtle to be generally recognized. More than the immense Sassoon legacy of houses – 25 Park Lane, Trent Park, Sandgate and a shooting-lodge – pictures, china, furniture, investments and capital fell into his lap at the age of twenty-three; his mother (née Rothschild) made certain her highly placed friends were also part of her children's inheritance, and these friends started with the King, the Prime Minister, and only worked down this elevated scale slightly. Sassoon lived with an eye keenly fixed on pleasure. He was an avid collector and was sufficiently clever to have acquired impeccable, though expensive, taste. He entertained with an adroitness and generosity that put Mrs Hunter to shame and dumbfounded his guests. But he was a little too effete for some people's tastes, especially in political circles, where his ability showed more impressive than his lapis boxes, French furniture and marble floors. He was an extremely gifted diplomatist, so well versed in the silences and hints and invisible machinations of society that the art of manipulating politicians came to him effortlessly. As an MP he knew the workings of the House; as a friend of royalty and Ministers he had the easiest channel of communication. He performed an immeasurable service for Haig, doing the legwork between Downing Street and the war as well as between the Allies and the British.

He and his sister Sybil had no difficulty in taking on their parents' affection for Sargent. They admired him and his work enormously; they were generous with their praise and hospitality. And it was never a one-sided friendship. His affection for them was based on something more than a pleasing echo from the past; their personalities were too strong to stick to the narrow category defined as loyalty to a memory. For them he broke his "no more mugs" rule, many times. In 1913, fresh from the James birthday portrait, he spent three months painting Sybil, in a dress he had ordered for her from Worth, on the occasion of her marriage to the Earl of Rocksavage, heir to the marquessate of Cholmondeley, Joint Heredity Lord Great Chamberlain (on 6 August 1913). He used her hands for *Our Lady of Sorrows*; he gave her the cashmere shawl often modelled by his niece Rose Marie. He drew her husband, painted her brother, and drew her son, which was the last thing he ever did. He was sidetracked from his retirement by their elegance and their beauty, flavoured so attractively by the slight wash of their Persian ancestry. But above all their liveliness was refreshing after the steady decline among his ageing friends.

Sassoon took on the task of educating the new boy (Tonks was sent off to Ypres on landing) to the ways of the war and army life – an unstrenuous tuition much softened by his affection for luxury he somehow was able to keep intact throughout the war, though by necessity somewhat scaled down. Sargent was then passed on to Major A. N. Lee's hands, which had not undergone the same softening as his predecessor's. To him fell the thankless job of censor and supervising the lodging, transport and safety of the war artists. He was unhindered in this task by any sensitivity to artists or their work; he called Sargent and Tonks " 'such children' ".[8] Yockney's memorandum had had a purpose, though he had not taken into account Sassoon's constant vigilance: "wonderfully kind and useful and watches over my changes of scene like a father, and smoothes my way before me . . .", Sargent wrote to Mrs Hunter (5 September).[9] He spirited Sargent off on "a joy ride in a Tank up and down slopes, over trenches and looping the loop generally. There is a row of obsolete ones", as he wrote to Charteris (24) [July], ". . . that made me think of the ships before Troy."[10]

After ten days' schooling at Haig's headquarters he was passed on to the Guards Division, under Major General Sir Geoffrey Fielding "who is delightful and does all he can to help me get the right sort of thing to paint", Sargent wrote to Mrs Hunter (Saturday, 19) [July]. Crouched low on his stool, protected by his easel, his huge umbrella, and a crowd of onlookers, Sargent's diary-notes reeled off – "we go out on our warpath in several motors. . . . It is very hard to see anything really significant in warfare." At night, after dining in the Officers' Mess he tried to make himself comfortable in the tight fit of "a sort of iron tube, a dug-out . . . very crowded".[11] From Berles au Bois he went on to Arras, and the notes increased – a ruined cathedral, a bombed street, a destroyed factory, more troops. The sightseeing tour continued to Ypres where he at last joined American troops (27th Division) who asked him to camouflage his umbrella, and to Peronne where he went to see hundreds of German prisoners locked in a cage, ankle-deep in mud. Major Lee was appalled when Sargent wrote to him from the prison camp saying "he was very happy, and that bombs are coming from all directions", as Lee passed on to the Ministry (5 October), "which is 'just what he likes'. That particular type of amusement does not appeal to all of us."[12]

Sargent had been given three months to study the war for his epic, and as that allowance slipped away – faster still with three weeks lost to influenza – he was getting no closer to finding his subject. He was perplexed. "For a long time I did not see any means of treating the subject given to me," he wrote to Yockney (4 October), "of 'British and American Troops Working Together'. They do this in the abstract but not in any particular space within the limits of a picture."[13] He needed an extension, because he had taken faulty reconnaissance. "I have wasted lots of time going to the front trenches," he wrote to Mrs Hunter (10 October). "There is nothing to paint there – it is ugly, and meagre & cramped, & one only sees one or two men." His picture needed masses of men, and he was pleased to announce to Mrs Hunter (10 October): "In this Somme country

I have seen what I wanted, roads crammed with troops on the march. It is the finest spectacle the war affords, as far as I can make out. . . ."[14]

Tonks had been asked for a picture on a medical theme, and one evening he and Sargent went to look at the dressing station in the Doullens Road. There, under a perfect autumnal sky, they saw soldiers blinded by mustard gas waiting for treatment. Sargent had at last found *his* picture, though it had nothing whatever to do with the terms of his assignment. Tonks said he did not mind; far from it. Notes were made, and Sargent was back at Tite Street at the end of October.

Gassed was finished in four months, by March 1919, when it was handed over to the Imperial War Commission, which had replaced the Ministry of Information. He was paid £600 and he did not ask for his expenses, explaining to Yockney, "on the contrary, I wish to express my thanks to the Ministry of Information for the opportunity afforded me of the most interesting trip to France. . . ."[15] (Yockney insisted that the Commission at least pay for the frame and canvas. The invoices were passed on.)

The architectural plans for the Hall of Remembrance demanded that the canvas's original height be reduced to seven and a half feet; the length was unchanged, which makes it a very difficult picture to put on a postcard. The picture was, by necessity, worked on the horizontal. It was not what Beaverbrook had ordered, yet it was voted the Picture of the Year at the Academy in 1919. Sargent had wanted less room, doubting his ability to cope with "life size, with a lot of life size buttons and buckles and boots", he wrote to Yockney, " – I think the picture would be infinitely better and much less impossible to execute it if were half size. There will be difficulties at any rate in carrying out my picture away from the scene and a life size scale would increase those difficulties enormously."[16] In the end he gave the Commission approximately sixty-five wounded soldiers, nineteen moving blindly towards the dressing station, the others littering the field waiting for treatment. On the horizon is a football match, a tent encampment and, circling above, tiny biplanes; the sun has nearly set, casting a soft rose-pink glow over the scene. Of course, the picture was indebted to the lessons learnt in Boston. He overcame the limitation of height by filling the bottom half of the canvas and leaving the top vacant. He boldly turned the length into an advantage by editing the scene to suggest it was not long enough for the angle formed by the two columns of wounded soldiers to converge at the unseen dressing station; he replayed the distance by placing the soldiers' destination off the canvas. And he finished off this deft geometric solution by supplying a generous sense of depth. *Gassed* was the achievement of simplicity, the fine understanding of balance – and the mastery of the devices of trickery borrowed from decoration.

Gassed is a remarkable picture, Sargent's most ambitious and, alas, not his last excursion into war. That place was reserved for his portrait of twenty-two general officers of the war, finished three years later. He loathed every minute of that commission he was not allowed to refuse. He did everything he could to avoid or postpone it. The officers were difficult to arrange, sittings were an ordeal of complication, and the result looks as if the heads do not match the correct bodies, which were painted first.

The necrology of the war was more generous to Sargent than to most; apart from Rose Marie and her husband, the war was responsible for very few deletions in his address-book. For many years, however, Nature had been busy removing the population of his history, destroying the links to his past, on both sides of the Atlantic. The year his mother died, Stanford White was murdered in the roof garden of Madison Square Garden, and three years later, in 1909, his partner McKim died. The great firm was gone, unable to help or witness the conclusion of their Library. Other architects – Fox and Benton – were appointed to fill their place at the Library, and at the Museum. The figures who had managed to make England look so attractive in the 1880s were also gone: Abbey in 1911, Millet in 1912, and James in 1916 (the same year Charles Hunter died). The longest thread of all, spinning back to his first day at Boulevard Mont Parnasse, snapped at the end of 1917 with the death of Beckwith. And when both Ralph Curtis and his mother died in 1922 his long-standing connection with Venice as well as two of his closest friendships were at an end. The present was emptier. He was only in his sixties. He drew closer still to Emily, and developed an interest in people he had never known – his antecedents. The phrase "my New England conscience" started to make frequent appearances. He supported his cousin, Charles Sprague Sargent (1841–1927), the great arboriculturist and director of the Arnold Arboretum, in his campaign to compile a Sargent genealogy. He gave the dining-room wallpaper to the Sargent family seat in Gloucester, the Sargent House (now the Sargent-Murray-Gilman-Hough House), as a supporting gesture in the establishment of the storehouse to the memory of his ancestors. Later, his portraits of his mother and father, his father's only surviving consulting-book and examples of his bookplate, one of his palettes, and sundry photographs, among them of the house where he was born, and portraits of him and Emily, were added to the collection. In 1922 the first Sargent genealogy appeared, by another distant cousin, Winthrop Sargent, *Early Sargents of New England*; a year later Charles Sprague Sargent's massive volume appeared, *Epes Sargent of Gloucester, and His Descendants*. The wheel continued to revolve back to FitzWilliam; Sargent was reviving another of his father's interests.

Younger friends took over, filling the vacancy but unable to replace the numerous losses: Sassoon, his sister and Charteris commanded more of his attention, but they were too burdened by awe and the distance of time to achieve the same footing as their predecessors. And Sargent's long disappearances from London made any solid attachment impossible. In any case they were granted insufficient time. The other friends that remained – Mrs Hunter, Steer, Tonks, the Helleus, the de Glehns, the

Harrisons, the Barnards, Miss Wedgwood, Miss Priestley (who moved to Carlyle Mansions in 1920) – were recast largely in a spectatorial role at the mercy of his itinerary, because Sargent was reliving a modified version of his childhood, in notations much larger than his mother ever dreamt of owning. He too did not pause before leaving his friends and home behind. The only indication that age was working on him in any way was an infinitely slight decline in his powers of restraint. His letters to Mrs Hunter began with no salutation whatsoever, saving him the closeness of "Mary" and removing the cool distance of "Mrs Hunter" – though he never wavered from a full signature at the end of every letter.

In May 1919 he returned once more to his own system of dislocation, by submitting willingly to another, but this time self-imposed tyranny – the Museum decorations – which drew him back to Boston. Emily accompanied him, and Violet's place was taken by her daughter Reine, aged twenty-one. Uncle and aunt were following the old precedent by introducing their niece to America, with a slight variation, however; Reine Ormond was only half-American by birth – but like them and her mother she was wholly European by education. Sargent moved into the seven-year-old Copley-Plaza Hotel instead of the Vendôme, where he ceased to stay after Nicola's disgrace (though he was no longer in Sargent's employ). At Copley Square he was further from the Pope Building and uselessly near the Library, once the final sigh of *The Mediaeval Contrast*, the two large staircase panels, were in place, and yet very handy for Emily to have her first glimpse of the Hall. She was the first Londoner to see them complete, liked them, but wished they were better lit. She was also a little baffled, uncertain of his quotations, and had to search out his sources for the rest of her life.

His Boston friends, Emily wrote to Tonks, were pleased to have him back again. His correspondence with Mrs Gardner about engagements was renewed. Emily, who had not been in America for thirty-five years, had no difficulty making herself feel at home. Though she, too, was bathed in the hospitality washing over her brother, she owed more to the memory of Henry James, who, in death, managed to do for her in America what he had done for her brother in England so long ago. When James became her neighbour in Carlyle Mansions, she seemed to take over the long-standing Sargent–James friendship, on a daily basis, make it her own, and their friendship was sustained posthumously, by charting a map of her acquaintance. Emily knew Mrs William James, who behaved splendidly at her uncle's funeral and even more splendidly managed to get his ashes back to America with no fuss during the war. Emily was welcome by her at both Irving Street and the house at Chocorua. She was also welcome in Pride's Crossing, where the Lorings lived. Louisa Loring was Alice James's companion, and had known Sargent from the days she was in England in the 1890s. But it was Emily who inspired these friendships with constancy; she had more time than her brother. She also trod on the wide avenues paved by her brother to Fenway Court, and to

her cousins in Brookline (the Charles Sprague Sargents) and Beacon Hil
(the Richard Hales). When she was in Boston the Copley-Plaza turnec
into another halting station for her family, another Carlyle Mansions. Ii
the summer Reine's elder brother Jean-Louis (1894–) appeared, *en rout*
for Tennessee, where he hoped to improve his knowledge of tobacco fo
Ormond Cigars in Switzerland. Family life was established, in a series o
hotel rooms.

While Emily was harvesting the benefits of the past and Reine enjoyec
herself, when she was not copying at the Museum, Sargent was doing
what he liked best, making himself a prisoner of the Pope Building. "Life
over here is for me", he wrote to Charteris (15 June 1919), "extremely
simplified and monotonous, and whatever one thinks about outside ol
one's work seems to belong to your side of the Atlantic. . . . I go daily to
my skyscraper studio and come back here to meals with dreary
regularity."[17] By the late spring his second and much larger studio in the
Pope Building was ready. Fox was given the run of the smaller one down
the hall for drafting-room, office, and home of the six-foot rotunda model,
and Sargent oscillated between the two, busy with architectural changes
needed to meet his decorations. The undramatic routine was established.
He hated the heat, but stayed throughout the summer, drinking quantities of ginger ale and lime juice, rolling up his sleeves "occasionally taking
a weekend wherever Emily is", he wrote to Tonks (23 June 1919), adding:
". . . This is the beastliest climate – cool when the sun shines and
sweltering hot on grey days." "Nothing like the absence of any other
interest for getting on with a long job," he wrote to Tonks three months
later (14 September), ". . . But all the same I have accomplished three or
four of my Wedgwood bas-reliefs." "They are rough," he added two
months later (27 November 1919), "and meant to be seen a long way off
and at a certain angle of light – and is like so many exercises in
composition."[18]

The rotunda kept him in Boston for a total of twenty-four months
between 1919 and 1921; its offspring, the adornment of the staircase,
detained him for a further sixteen months between 1922 and 1924. He was
a little boy who would not come away from his new toy, and when he was
pulled back he pouted. He was playing in the sandbox of Classical
allegory and the Museum decoration was a new toy, wholly unlike the
full-dress combat of the Library: he was also playing with building-
blocks, each a different sort of decorative element, glued fast in a difficult
arrangement. He used symmetry to counterfeit harmony. Quantity took
over from quality. From the base of the elliptical dome he stacked four
banks, each containing a pedimented frame housing carousing nudes
emerging from the wall, a relief of some energetic god, and on top of them
an oil rondel set into the wall of yet another god, which was surmounted
by modelled figures struggling to get a foothold on their curving perch
and yet not be squashed by the skylight. Between these assemblies, as if
to keep them from falling down, were placed two pairs of oval panels in

oils under heavily encrusted mounts. The pair of smaller, vertical scenes house the sphinx staring up at the impossible posture of the chimera in downward flight and, opposite, Minerva trying to shelter painting and sculpture from Time's scythe. The larger spaces were handed over to Apollo getting dizzy watching the Muses cavort round him, and Classical and Romantic art trying to outdo each other.

This busy hodgepodge was a better reading of the decorative commission than he had granted the Library: it was conceived as a warning of what lay in wait for the visitor beyond the dome; it fitted the purpose of the building. The time-honoured benefactors of art look down. Celestial dictators were given a hall of fame. And in its own way the rotunda propaganda was just as ambitious as the Library, and technically far more difficult. He supplied his own architectural disadvantages when he asked for surfaces diminishing in width as they rose higher, and inclining forward as they went. He had to wrestle with ever-changing sight-lines, opposing sources of light, and the knowledge that the spectators below could enter from four sides. The last obstacle made him close his Bible and open a manual of mythology; he relied on manageable scenes rather than on the sequential but disjointed narrative that had carried him across the Library Hall. It was also an intellectual performance which triumphed over his faulty appreciation of spacial geometry, and Sargent could claim little mastery of that science: "there is a good deal of geometry and simple mathematics in my affair," he explained to Charteris (13 April) [1920], "and it takes me weeks to do sums in addition, subtraction[,] division and these to find out the mistakes I have made. . . ."[19] It was an exhausting callisthenic of trial and error under the governorship of Fox, and when Fox was not around to correct him the work slowed down considerably. Added to this basic ignorance was the annoyance that the very heavy reliefs done in the studio had to be hauled into place on the rotunda walls before they could be judged to be satisfactory, a false floor had to be erected high on scaffolding – for at no time was the area allowed to be closed – thus denying Sargent the actual vantage he needed to decide. His hobby tested his stamina as well as his patience, and in the end his fascination with his toy – architecture – swamped his interest in the content of the building-blocks. He was far keener on the reliefs than on the paintings. " 'I find as I grow old – probably a sign of senile decay,' " he once said to Billy (William) James, Henry James's nephew, " 'that I care less and less about the painting of things "just the way they look", and get more interested in – well, something more the nature of a Wedgwood plaque.' "[20]

His paintings were near-duplicates of the reliefs, in a highly toned-down palette, short on subtlety and an advance on the rehearsal of the Wyndham sisters, two decades before. In the summer of 1921, Anton Kamp, a young art student came to pose for one of the small rondels, Music, and fifty years later remembered with impressive clarity Sargent's speedy dispatch of the paintings.[21] He was made to sit on the high platform in the Pope Building studio, built to simulate the angle of observation from the Museum floor and supply the foreshortening he required. Sargent did three or four charcoal sketches, the final one he used for the oil, within the space of an hour. The six-foot round oil was then done in a morning. The figure of Astronomy was started and finished in a day. The oils were accomplished much faster than the reliefs, for he had dispensed with the problem of colour; he was not interested in that inappropriate refinement.

Sargent's energy made no concession to his age. He again employed no studio assistants. He could not trust them to do the work as well as he. And his idea of a holiday from the back-breaking, knuckle-bruising Museum work was to dash off two enormous arched panels for the staircase of the Widener Memorial Library at Harvard – his memorial to fallen alumni.* On the right he pictured marching ranks of soldiers (all with Anton Kamp's face, an ironic choice because Kamp was at the time still a German citizen). Two doughboys grasp the allegorical figure of France, another reaches out to the figure of Victory, and two grab Death enfolded in Victory's cloak. The panel on the left depicts a soldier embracing both Death and Victory, standing on a field of his dead comrades. (This image was also worked as a sculpture.) Sargent began his celebration in the summer of 1922; the panels were in place by the end of October, and ever since critics have longed for an earthquake to remove them.

His devotion to work was undoing his judgement. His entry into the land of allegory turned into a steep downhill path. His affection for decoration, for permanence, had grown out of a poison that had repelled him from portraiture and had never allowed him to value his private holiday work. He had to conquer a challenge; he was only interested in what he could not easily accomplish. Age might not have affected his energy or his ambition, but it was putting a stranglehold on his perspective. He was winding down in the cruellest possible way which was contradicted by the sheer scale of his efforts, his undiminished physical power. He had no reason to believe there was any decline in his ability. But others could see what he could not: he had come to his bid for immortality (as he saw it) too late to negotiate the necessary abstractions. He had turned from portraiture; later he turned from the recital of what

---

* The Library, the memorial to Widener's son, who went down in the *Titanic*, was complete in 1914. Sargent was paid the standard fee for all decoration – $15,000 – and he suffered the usual fit of wanting to make additions. At the end of 1923 he and President Lowell put their heads together and cooked up the inscription on the tablet:

> They crossed the sea crusaders keen to help
> The nations battling in a righteous cause
> Happy those who with that glowing faith
> In one embrace clasped death and victory.

his eyes saw, and he faced the third contest without sufficient aptitude to succeed. He covered the distance. He surmounted the hardships of technique, but the content totally defeated him. Each essay in decoration brought him closer to this sad truth. Nature might have been kinder to reduce the physical strength that was such a worthy, reliable servant to his ambition, and thus put an end to his non-stop activity. But Sargent had known no other language; he would have been sadly unequal to that novelty as well.

His vanity, never very prominent in any case, retired altogether before the force of his work. He remained completely uninterested in critical opinion, once he had satisfied himself. He did not hang around for the public unveiling of the rotunda icing. He glimpsed at the marzipan and fondant shortly before sailing home on 15 October 1921 and wrote to Mrs Gardner from Tite Street (Monday, 28) [Nov.]:

> (further concealment is useless) . . . they lifted the curtain the day before I left, for a few minutes – and I was relieved to see that my bas-reliefs told quite as much as I wanted them to, and that my empty spaces were not too big, and that the whole thing was better than any separate parts. So my spirits rose and I was ready to meet the accusation of being frivolous, platitudinous and academic.
>
> And behold! the Museum wants more – they want me to decorate the staircase – and I am most willing, but I think that will be even more of a problem, with less likelihood of being able to make architectural changes in case these tempt me. [22]

He harboured no reverence whatever for his work. At the unveiling of the rotunda a spectator asked a Museum official who the three figures in one of the pedimented frames were meant to represent. " 'Ah, I cannot tell you. . . . I asked the artist that same question myself, the other day, and he answered, "Oh, they're three blokes dancing!" ' "[23] He called *El Jaleo* "my gloomy old picture" when Mrs Gardner outlined her plans for hanging it in Fenway Court. "It might be like the mummy at the feast unless I give her 'a new gauze gown all spangles' and pull the sword out of her heart."[24] When, in February 1924, the Grand Central Art Gallery in New York – a co-operative body he was quick to join when it began – mounted a Sargent retrospective exhibition of sixty oils and twelve watercolours, he refused to attend, even after he had spent months helping to arrange the loans and correcting sitters' names in the catalogue. The officials of the Gallery begged him over and over again. " 'Why should I spend my time that way?' " he asked Fox in impatient tones of sarcasm. " 'You must remember that I have already seen all of those canvases at least once and most of them many times more.' "[25] Emily went as his ambassador.

The Museum staircase took over the central place in his interest. He returned to London periodically, and as briefly as possible, to address himself to the dreaded generals' portraits. He seized any excuse for postponement. The coal strikes that were fast dismantling Mrs Hunter's fortune – to an extent that forced her to sell fifty-five drawings and paintings from her London collection in July 1920, a good many of which Sargent managed to steer into American collections – helped him to avoid at least one winter season. And one summer he discovered the sitters had all disappeared. He returned to Boston for all but four months in 1922. When he was in London in 1923 the staircase panels were painted in Fulham Road, and he and Emily took them back to Boston in November of that year, staying on until the beginning of July 1924. There was scarcely anything else to tempt him out of this self-imposed seclusion. "I must go back to my 'occupational therapy' as they say in Boston," he wrote to Mrs Astor (23 September) [1924] within weeks of returning to Tite Street, " – which just now happens to be modelling."[26] He succumbed entirely, offering no resistance, to his god of work. But it was a generous, smiling deity, glancing back to another that had been ignored a generation before. Boston gave Sargent more than a Greek chorus declaiming his greatness; she gave him the opportunity to meet the debt of repatriation FitzWilliam had allowed to burn in his pocket. Sargent became an American at the wrong end of his life, in his mother's style of becoming a European – in repetitive dislocation, in a series of hotel rooms he began to hate, living among transients, surrounded by objects fresh from the hold of a liner. He was finishing his life much in the manner it had begun – a strange philanthropy to an unwanted tradition.

He finished the final essays in mythology and allegory in London in a series of a dozen panels and half a dozen reliefs, his visual upholstery on another vaulted ceiling. " 'Now the American things are done,' " he sighed smiling to Stokes, " 'and so, I suppose, I may die when I like.' "[27] He called on portraiture again, grown rusty with neglect, in need of repair: Lady Curzon sat to him, it was absurdly reported, close on to a hundred times. The Boston panels were rolled, crated, labelled, and Sargent helped to put them on to the removal vans that pulled up outside The Avenue. His friends shook their heads at this idiotic display of strength, and he refused to compromise. He booked his stateroom on the *Baltic*, sailing on Saturday, 18 April 1925, and at Tite Street he was preparing for departure.

Emily arranged another farewell party at Carlyle Mansions on Tuesday. She invited ten guests: Violet, the Barnard sisters, Harrison, Steer, Tonks, her brother's friend and solicitor, Nelson Ward, and James's old friend Fanny Prothero. Sargent was in a high mood, doing what he liked second-best. It was a merry gathering. He was back at Tite Street before 11 p.m.

At eight o'clock the next morning the parlourmaid called him. There was no answer. Alarmed by this irregularity, she went in. The bedside lamp was on, Voltaire's *Dictionnaire philosophique* lay open beside him on the bed, his spectacles pushed from his eyes. He had fallen asleep reading, and suffered a heart-attack in his sleep – a graceful, undramatic departure from life. He was sixty-nine years old, the same age as his father. It was the end of a happy life.*

"End of an Epoch in English Art," *The Times* called his death, taking the first posthumous move in the chronic tug-of-war in the imperialistic greed for his nationality. America staked an equal claim, and the rights of colonization have moved back and forth ever since. His obituary ran for two full columns on Thursday morning, 16 April, with a visual supplement nine pages on: *Ellen Terry*, the 1906 Uffizi self-portrait, *Carnation, Lily, Lily, Rose*, *Asher Wertheimer*, and a watercolour, *The Piazzetta*; the murals were ignored.

The reflex of mourning took customary strides. On Saturday, 18 April, Emily and Violet boarded the special train at Paddington to take his coffin to Brookwood Cemetery. The public was asked to reserve gestures of grief for another week, until the Memorial Service at Westminster Abbey (on Friday, 24 April, at noon).

He was not buried near his parents; he started a new family plot. His grave in the Ring of All Saints was marked with a plain stone, inscribed "Laborare est orare" – "To work is to pray" – half of the motto "Orare est laborare, laborare est orare" taken over by St Benedict. Nothing else could be said. Underneath these words is his name in the style he adopted throughout his life, John S. Sargent, which it has not been allowed to remain; the addition of "Singer" is a modern and *incorrect* style.

The will he made in Boston in 1918 was read. He left £200 to Nicola and £5000 to Alice Barnard, Frederick Barnard's widow and the mother of his *Carnation, Lily, Lily, Rose* models. The remainder of his estate went to his sisters – though Violet's half was bequeathed in the form of a trust giving her and her children the income and making certain her husband could not touch it.

The Memorial Service was a ritual. The Academy was out in force, sharing pews lined with sitters, friends, critics, society, and others from art officialdom. The readings were conventional, the music Bach, Brahms and Basil Harwood's *Requiem aeternam*, producing a high ecclesiastic vapour for a man who possessed no religious feelings whatsoever. The service was for his survivors.

Tributes and wreaths washed over the memory of Sargent in a tidal wave. The posthumous literature made an early bid to equal the existing bibliography. Magazines were full of reminiscences. Casual acquaintances revived memories long faded; his closest friends did their best to honour his sense of privacy. But everyone recognized that Sargent was too famous to move into posterity only on canvas. In life he found the searchlight of biography an unwelcome intrusion on his time. After Mrs

* The death certificate recorded the cause of death as "Fatty degeneration of heart, arterio sclerosis of the coronary & other arteries & chronic inflammation of the kidneys natural causes"

Meynell's book of reproductions of his work in 1903 and the enormous correspondence provoked by the Grand Central Art Gallery's exhibition, he lost his taste for that sort of attention. "As to biographical details," he wrote to one hopeful chronicler (n.d.), "there are none of the least interest to the public. I have left no diary, and am vague about dates marking events in my artistic career. It strikes me, and may strike you, that I am advocating a posthumous volume! That indeed would suit me 'down to the ground'."[28] Within months after his death, his executor was petitioning readers of *The Times* for letters and memoirs for Evan Charteris to use in his biography. He was allowed to travel back across Sargent's life with Violet and Emily's blessing.

Emily dressed in mourning and with her sister filled the role of widow. She did everything in partnership with Violet, but his death was the greatest blow in her life. During her remaining years she warmed herself before the hot glow of his memory. She moved into the past. She relived every phase of her life, drawing up a new blueprint for her future, guiding the draughtsman's pen around her brother.

She inhabited a new architecture, built on his memory, housing his reputation. She and Violet gave one of the Redemption crucifixes for the crypt in St Paul's. She took over her brother's correspondence with Fox, who unpacked the Fulham Road crates in Boston and supervised the installation. (The decorations were unveiled in November.) After the Memorial Service she and Violet attended to the mechanics of finality. They cleared the two studios in Tite Street and the two in Fulham Road. Francis Ormond counselled an enormous sale of pictures, thinking his brother-in-law's reputation would never be higher, and the potential for revenue never higher. Emily resisted, but the sheer number of pictures *was* unmanageable. On 24 and 27 July Christie's held a studio sale; 237 of his oils and watercolours went up for sale, plus nearly 100 pictures – engravings, oils, watercolours and drawings – from his collection: Abbey, Brabazon, de Glehn, Helleu, John, Parsons, Rodin, Tiepolo, Besnard, Boldini, Carolus, Corot, MacEvoy, Lavery, Mancini, Monet, Pryde, Steer, and his much admired Annie Swynnertons all moved over to King Street, turning his private collection into an open exhibition. The viewing-days were a crowded social occasion. The bidding realized Ormond's predictions, earning the best part of £175,000 (the equivalent of £2,400,000 today). The event was too much for Emily and Violet. Sentiment, fond memories and sadness flooded over them making them loathe what they had done, and they bought back a good number of lots.

The same month as the sale, Ena Wertheimer Mathias held an exhibition of twenty of his watercolours at her Claridge Gallery. In the autumn the Walker Art Gallery in Liverpool also remembered him. The Winter Exhibition at the Royal Academy, 1926, was handed over entirely to him (631 works) and later the same year the Metropolitan Museum of Art paid him the same honour.

Carlyle Mansions turned into the Sargent archive, with Violet's house at 94 Cheyne Walk as its annexe. There was still an enormous number of works – notebooks, albums, drawings, watercolours, oils, sketches, sculpture. The sale at Christie's had scarcely made a dent in the collection. Emily became the chief librarian and guardian. The rooms were piled high with his work. And she and Violet began the enormous doling out to major public collections on both sides of the Atlantic. They gave lavishly, to almost any institution expressing an interest. It was a long and generous campaign. After Emily's death, Violet's philanthropy continued and also in her sister's name. Few legatees have cared so little for their pockets and so ardently for the deceased's memory.

Emily attached herself entirely to the Ormonds' routine, her only refuge among the living. Each winter she escaped the cold and stayed with them at Villa Ormond in Tunis. In the spring of 1936 she returned to London by way of Zurich, in order to have new corsets made. One afternoon she and a companion were strolling arm in arm along the street; a bicyclist hit her companion, who lost balance and fell to the ground, taking Emily with her, and causing Emily's death. It was the final irony: after having endured a second-hand life, she was forced to endure a second-hand death.

Posterity has made the appropriate correction. Her body was brought back to England, she was buried next to her brother at Brookwood, and her name was chiselled in his tombstone: "Also his sister Emily Sargent".

Appendix I

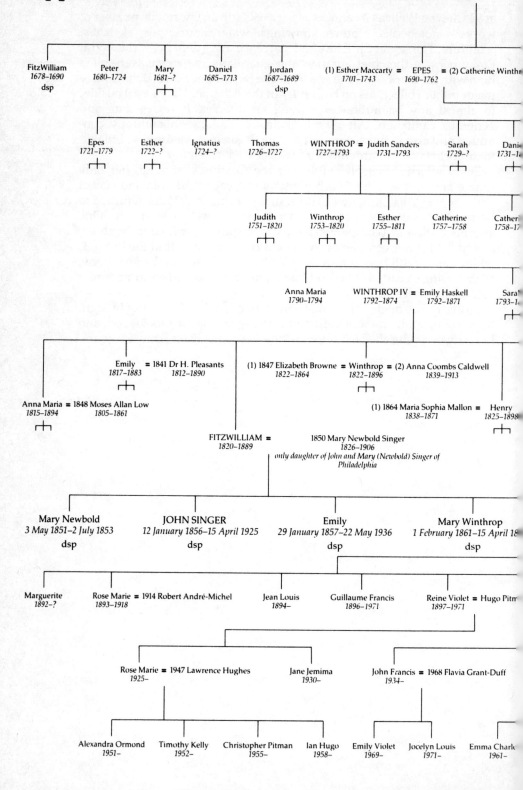

William Sargent
came to Gloucester, Mass., in 1678 = Mary Dunc

FitzWilliam
1678–1690
dsp

Peter
1680–1724

Mary
1681–?

Daniel
1685–1713

Jordan
1687–1689
dsp

(1) Esther Maccarty = EPES = (2) Catherine Winthr
1701–1743   *1690–1762*

Epes
1721–1779

Esther
1722–?

Ignatius
1724–?

Thomas
1726–1727

WINTHROP = Judith Sanders
1727–1793   *1731–1793*

Sarah
1729–?

Dani
1731–1

Judith
1751–1820

Winthrop
1753–1820

Esther
1755–1811

Catherine
1757–1758

Cather
1758–17

Anna Maria
1790–1794

WINTHROP IV = Emily Haskell
1792–1874   *1792–1871*

Sara
1793–1

Emily   = 1841 Dr H. Pleasants
1817–1883   *1812–1890*

(1) 1847 Elizabeth Browne = Winthrop = (2) Anna Coombs Caldwell
1822–1864   *1822–1896*   *1839–1913*

Anna Maria = 1848 Moses Allan Low
1815–1894   *1805–1861*

(1) 1864 Maria Sophia Mallon = Henry
1838–1871   *1825–1898*

FITZWILLIAM = 1850 Mary Newbold Singer
1820–1889   *1826–1906*
only daughter of John and Mary (Newbold) Singer of Philadelphia

Mary Newbold
3 May 1851–2 July 1853
dsp

JOHN SINGER
12 January 1856–15 April 1925
dsp

Emily
29 January 1857–22 May 1936
dsp

Mary Winthrop
1 February 1861–15 April 18
dsp

Marguerite
1892–?

Rose Marie = 1914 Robert André-Michel
1893–1918

Jean Louis
1894–

Guillaume Francis
1896–1971

Reine Violet = Hugo Pitm
1897–1971

Rose Marie = 1947 Lawrence Hughes
1925–

Jane Jemima
1930–

John Francis = 1968 Flavia Grant-Duff
1934–

Alexandra Ormond
1951–

Timothy Kelly
1952–

Christopher Pitman
1955–

Ian Hugo
1958–

Emily Violet
1969–

Jocelyn Louis
1971–

Emma Charl
1961–

The Sargent Family-Tree and Genealogy

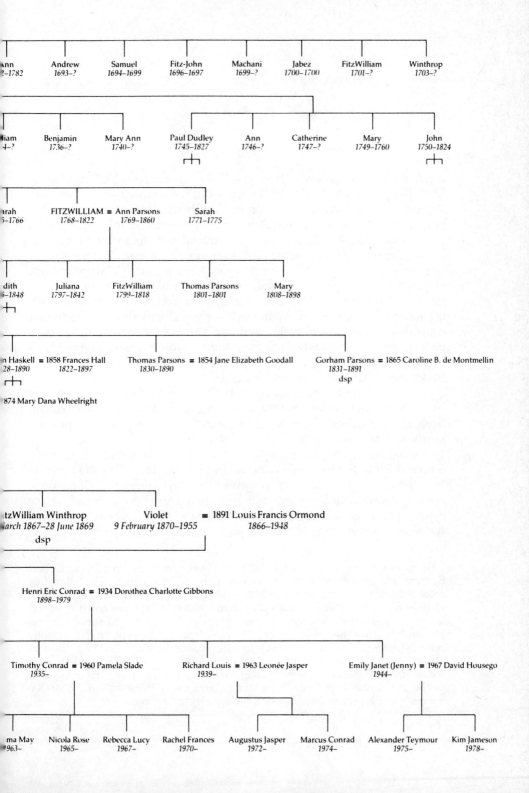

Ann	Andrew	Samuel	Fitz-John	Machani	Jabez	FitzWilliam	Winthrop
2–1782	1693–?	1694–1699	1696–1697	1699–?	1700–1700	1701–?	1703–?

iam	Benjamin	Mary Ann	Paul Dudley	Ann	Catherine	Mary	John
4–?	1736–?	1740–?	1745–1827	1746–?	1747–?	1749–1760	1750–1824

arah	FITZWILLIAM = Ann Parsons	Sarah
5–1766	1768–1822 1769–1860	1771–1775

dith	Juliana	FitzWilliam	Thomas Parsons	Mary
6–1848	1797–1842	1799–1818	1801–1801	1808–1898

n Haskell = 1858 Frances Hall   Thomas Parsons = 1854 Jane Elizabeth Goodall   Gorham Parsons = 1865 Caroline B. de Montmellin
28–1890   1822–1897   1830–1890   1831–1891
dsp

874 Mary Dana Wheelright

tzWilliam Winthrop   Violet   = 1891 Louis Francis Ormond
arch 1867–28 June 1869   9 February 1870–1955   1866–1948
dsp

Henri Eric Conrad = 1934 Dorothea Charlotte Gibbons
1898–1979

Timothy Conrad = 1960 Pamela Slade   Richard Louis = 1963 Leonée Jasper   Emily Janet (Jenny) = 1967 David Housego
1935–   1939–   1944–

ma May	Nicola Rose	Rebecca Lucy	Rachel Frances	Augustus Jasper	Marcus Conrad	Alexander Teymour	Kim Jameson
963–	1965–	1967–	1970–	1972–	1974–	1975–	1978–

Genealogy

When the Sargents boarded their paddle-steamer in New York harbour in 1854, they were also undoing the work of time simply by reviving their ancestors' long-dormant tradition of Continental adventurousness that had turned their families from Europeans to Americans. John S. Sargent's parents waved aside two centuries, retraced near-forgotten steps, and turned themselves, at least in spirit, back into Europeans. But the science of genealogy is blind to desire: Mary and FitzWilliam's European-born children were emphatically, solidly and determinedly American – the products, on both sides, of seven generations of Americans. Both branches had been caught up in the history and growth of their adopted country – it was unavoidable – but on the whole it was a quiet partici-pation. FitzWilliam and Mary gave their children a genealogy rich in number but a bit thin on distinction: their people were the unobtrusive backbone of America, not her blemishes.

Since the seventeenth century FitzWilliam's antecedents were sobered by the cold Atlantic winds that swept into Gloucester, when a William Sargent left England for the Massachusetts Bay Colony.* Much confusion surrounds this otherwise unimportant man, which is compounded by genealogists' zeal that has located at least three other William Sargents who landed in the Bay Colony between 1629 and 1678. One is known to have gone to Salem; another to Ipswich; and yet another to Gloucester, who appeared, disappeared and then reappeared by the end of the century, married and owned land. This last William Sargent has baffled historians. Some claim he was one and the same. Some claim he arrived,

* The family is, of course, much older; the earliest *recorded* Sargent was an Osbert Sargent, a Londoner, who died at the end of the twelfth century. The name, like most surnames, can be traced back to a designation of profession. Each of the forty-seven variations of the name has its root either in the Old French *serjent* or *serjant*, or the Latin *servientam*, present participle of *servire*, "to serve". In the sixteenth century the spelling changed from Sergant to Sargent. In the previous century the name meant "servant" (1450), "common soldier" (1490), "one in service to a knight in the field" (1425). When spelt with a *j* the word denoted a member of the legal profession. The name was very popular in all parts of England in the fourteenth and fifteenth centuries, and today there are well over 300 Sargents or Sergeants listed in the London telephone directory.

left, and sent his son back to take his place. In his extremely erudite study, *The English Ancestors of Epes Sargent*, Lieutenant Colonel H. G. LeMesurier advanced the most plausible solution to the identity of this first American Sargent who was John S. Sargent's great-great-great-great-grandfather. He was the son of William Sargent, purser of the frigate *Griffin* and, like his father, was a mariner by profession. He was at least twenty-one when he became a resident of Gloucester, where he married, settled down, more or less, fathered fifteen children, and drowned *c.*1707. He also started the tedious habit of repeating Christian names, and it is from him the great sprawling family-tree of American Sargents springs.

For generations the Sargents looked to the sea for their livelihood. Their history is woven around the history of Gloucester. They stuck fast to the East Coast. Three generations after William, FitzWilliam Sargent (1768–1818) stayed on land, prospered, sending a fleet of clippers to the far-reaching corners of the globe, to China, Russia and India. His son, Winthrop (1792–1874), took charge of his father's India Company, and expanded the trade routes south to the West Indies, where he dispatched ice in the holds of ships, wrapped in sawdust. But Winthrop's mercantile skills were not of the order of his father's; the fleet's losses were too great for the business to survive, and he moved over into another, less daring profession as Secretary of the Foreign Missions of the Presbyterian Board of Publication. This pious, cautious, sedate man was FitzWilliam's father. He had eight children, six sons, none of whom cast a glance at the sea for their living. Most of them were happier in medicine. Three sons became doctors, one daughter married a doctor (another son went deeper into the church, becoming a Minister; the fourth son became a lawyer, and the fifth worked for the Pennsylvania Railroad). The obsession with health that glazed John S. Sargent's early life had a solid foundation in his father's family.

While the Sargents found a subtle version of evangelicalism once in America, Mary's ancestors came to America for that precise purpose, but because the horticulture of pedigree favours paternal stock – it is easier to cultivate – very little is known of the maternal fertilizer. Mary Sargent (née Singer) could trace her family back to Caspar Singer who left Alsace-Lorraine for fifty acres in Lancaster, Pennsylvania, around 1730. He was a member of the Moravian Brethren, or Moravian Church, a vigorous missionary Protestant sect founded in Bohemia in the fifteenth century.*

---

* Like so many religions, the history of the Moravian Brethren is a story of survival amidst adversity. Once established, the Moravians set about debating their purpose, and after much internal wrangling they settled down, called themselves *Unitas fratum* (the Church of Communion of Brethren), and looked to action rather than to biblical interpretation to satisfy their religious hunger. They were strong on rigid discipline and hierarchy, shunting members into three groups – the Perfect, the Proficient and the Beginners – with a body of lay elders to marshal congregations. Then, in the sixteenth century, the Moravians really got going,

Whether or not Caspar Singer got to work remodelling his fellow-Pennsylvanians' beliefs is not known, but the simple fact that his descendants honoured his religion more than his nationality speaks for a certain, and large, commitment.

Caspar's grandson, another John Singer, was a drummer-boy in the Revolutionary War at the age of thirteen. He was captured, held in a prison-ship in the New York harbour, escaped, and promptly re-enlisted. After his marriage he moved to Philadelphia, fathered eight children, and became a very prosperous merchant in hides and leather. His eldest child, another John Singer (1794–1850) carried on the family business with more success than FitzWilliam's father's involvement in commerce. The Singers never lost their money, though it was never a huge fortune. In 1825 he married Mary Newbold (1804–59), John S. Sargent's grandmother, who, as a widow, boarded the *Arctic* with her only child, Mrs FitzWilliam Sargent, in 1854. Five years later she died in Rome.

The Newbolds furnished Sargent's family-tree with the richest, though highly subtle, nutrient. Much of his character sifted down to him from them, largely because his mother and grandmother must have been very confident and determined women. The Newbolds came from the West Riding of Yorkshire in 1680, settling in Burlington County, New Jersey, where they owned 700 acres. Four generations later they raised their children in a style and atmosphere rare among the settlers of America. They were sufficiently wealthy to ignore the brute necessities of survival. They looked back to Europe. Mary Newbold Singer was the product of money, and refined tastes born of leisure. She was educated in drawing, music, literature and religion. Her days were spent reading aloud, improving her penmanship, playing the piano, and sketching with unexciting conscientiousness. But above all she was schooled in the value of self-discipline.

Her daughter followed in her footsteps unswervingly, and followed her mother's example precisely, improving on but one feature: whereas she and her mother had to content themselves with Europe transplanted in America, she was able to give her children – John, Emily and Violet – the real thing. There the Newbold tradition continued on home ground,

---

opening schools, winning over nobility, spreading into Great Poland, and by the end of the century laying claims to half the Protestants in Bohemia and more than half in Moravia. At the height of their power, with the onset of the Thirty Years War, they were sent flying, to Germany, to England, and even to Texas. They had considerable powers of adaptation. They regrouped most successfully in Germany, scarcely distinguishable from the Lutherans, and there they remained for over a century. Around 1730 persecution sent them emigrating again, which naturally helped to encourage their original missionary zeal, and many fled to America. Perhaps this is why Caspar Singer came to America.

The Moravians were too impatient to wait for the State to issue an invitation to help with the colonial policy; the Church had its own calling, louder than any from the State. For them there was no confusion between Church and State – the Church came first.

so to speak. Safely removed from the influence of Gloucester, her heirs grew more as the true descendants of the Newbolds than either the Singers or the Sargents. She took to Europe as a birthright, her due, and to what had been postponed for too long. It helped to explain her tenacious refusal to return to America, even if she had to employ subterfuge. To her the great end of living abroad justified any means.

The Sargent coat of arms – a chevron between three dolphins haurient Sable – was adopted by the descendants of William Sargent. It was embellished to its highest degree by Paul Revere. FitzWilliam used a more sedate example for his bookplate and, though his son never used it, he did affix examples of dolphins to his Library decorations. The College of Heralds, however, cannot substantiate any claim William's heirs have to the arms, correctly borne by several branches of the Sargent family, dating from the Heralds' Visitation of Wales of 1530, the Staffordshire Visitation of 1639, the Leicestershire Visitation of 1683, and the Gloucestershire Visitation of 1682.

Appendix II

Sargent's Description of His Boston Public Library Decoration

[1893] Argument of Decoration by John S. Sargent for one end of the Special Library Hall of the Boston Public Library.

The surfaces to be decorated are determined by the architectural divisions of the walls and vaulting and are three:
a band between the wainscote and the cornice,
a semicircular lunette, and
a space of vaulted ceiling.
The subject is the religious history of the people of Israel. (Old Testament)

1. The lunette will be occupied by a composition of a severely decorative character representing the Special protection extended by Jehovah to his chosen people. The figures will be larger than life and of an allegorical or abstract nature. The principal elements in this composition are: the people [of] Israel, a group of twelve figures kneeling in prayer in front of an altar of burnt offering; on either side of this group an Assyrian and an Egyptian oppressor; and over this and emerging from a whirl of cherubims' wings and from the smoke of the altar Jehovah's arms seizing the right hands of the ministers of his wrath and staying the punishment of the Israelites. The characteristics of Egyptian and Assyrian art will be recalled in these respective figures, and the motive of a Pharoh about to immolate his victims will be treated in a somewhat similar way to that in which it is seen on many Egyptian temples. This synthetic treatment of the subject will be supplemented by the two other paintings which bear upon it from its opposite poles and between which there will be a strong and intentional contrast.
2 On the *ceiling* the host of false gods, idols, graven images, and symbols of the superstitions of the neighbouring heathen nations whose worship was the principal cause of God's displeasure and the theme of the prophet's remonstrances.
3 In the central position of the *Frieze* Moses will stand with the tables [sic] of the law; on either side of him the four great prophets and the twelve

minor prophets expressive of the highest energies and aspirations of the peoples of Israel.

The lunette measuring 22 feet by 11 is now approaching completion and the rest underway.

[May 1895]

The Triumph of Religion
a mural decoration illustrating certain stages
of Jewish and Christian religious history. by John S. Sargent

Of the portions already completed and which form the beginning of the series, a ceiling, a lunette and a frieze, the subjects are respectively polytheism, monotheism and the Law and the prophets. The ceiling is the first in order as it is the most primitive form of belief represented.

(It will be noticed that, parallel with the progress of belief towards a more spiritual ideal, the material and formulated character of symbolic treatment gives place to a less conventional artistic expression. Thus the ceiling is entirely composed of archaic and definite emblems, the lunette departs somewhat from them to express a more personal relation between the Godhead and humanity, and the third part with the prophets in whom religion became subjective formulas are almost entirely abandoned. The future portions of the decoration will follow historically this aspect of the expression of religion in art.)

THE CEILING groups together some of the more important figures and symbols of the Egyptian, Syrian, Phoenician idolatry, the false Gods 'which were a snare' unto the children of Israel. They are disposed over the black silhouette of the goddess Neith (the vault of heaven, the origin of things, the mother of the Gods) who spans the entire arch, touching the horizon with her hands and with her feet as on Egyptian ceilings and zodiacs.

Beginning on the left over the cornice is the winged globe, symbol of eternity; immediately above is the Egyptian representation of the soul leaving the body; the three black figures are Isis, Osiris, and Horus, the Egyptian trinity. Above them, the bull-headed idol of Baal or Moloch, the destroyer, with his attendant lions typifying fire. In his hands are human offerings. In the centre of the ceiling immediately overhead is the disc of the sun with rays and hands at the end of them, as represented in Egyptian art to denote that the sun is the giver of life. Next come the signs of the zodiac with a representation of the Syrian solar myth. In the autumn the Sungod, Adonis, is overcome by Typhon, the power of darkness, and mourned by the Goddess, and in the spring he rises again and slays Typhon. Below this and concluding the ceiling on the right is the veiled Goddess Astarte or Ashtaroth of the Phoenicians. Her robe is embroidered with the sun and moon, and on the border are lions, birds, fishes and other emblems that are hers in common with Diana of Ephesus and Cybele. Her priestesses dance to the sistrum. The two columns, the serpant, the crescent, the sacred pine-cones of the Tree of Life, are connected with her worship.

The subject of the composition in THE LUNETTE is explained by the inscription taken from Psalm XVI on the moulding that encircles it. The group of twelve kneeling figures in the centre, behind whom is an altar of burnt offerings, represents the children of Israel who are imploring Jehovah to deliver them from their enemies. The arms of Jehovah emerge from a whirl of cherubim that envelope him, and stay the hands of the oppressors who were the instruments of his wrath. Behind the Egyptian and Assyrian are the protecting divinities of each and the sphinx and the lion are advancing over the ruins of the nations whom they have brought low.

THE FRIEZE contains in the central panel alone an element of the abstraction of the preceding portions. Moses still surrounded by the divine presence makes manifest the law of God. Joshua sheathes his sword. Elijah raises his voice as first of the Prophets. The names of the four major and twelve minor prophets can be read over each of the remaining figures.

(Oct. 4th 1919) Description for identification of the two paintings, 'the Church', and 'the Synagogue' occupying the pedimented frames over the staircase in the Sargent Hall of the Boston Public Library.

'The Church'. A seated female figure draped in blue, supporting across her knees the dead figure of Christ. On the yellow background, around the head, the symbols of the four Evangelists with their names on red scrolls. The names of four prophets on scrolls decorating the upright sides of the throne. The signature John S. Sargent © near the bottom left hand corner of picture.

'The Synagogue'. An aged female figure, with white hair, seated on rock rising out of mosaic pavement. She has a black bandage round her eyes, and clasps in her arms the Tablets of the Law and a broken sceptre. She is partly enveloped in the folds of the 'veil of the temple', a red blue and yellow drapery with design of cherubim. Signature John S. Sargent © introduced into mosaic pavement in left hand bottom corner of picture.

Notes

Abbreviations

AAA	Archives of American Art, Smithsonian Institution, Washington, DC
AABPL	Art Archives, Boston Public Library
AAIWM	Art Archives, Imperial War Museum, London
AISGM	Archives of the Isabella Stewart Gardner Museum, Fenway Court, Boston, Massachusetts
ANAD	Archives of the National Academy of Design, New York
BA	Archives of the Boston Athenaeum
CC	The Miller Library, Colby College, Waterville, Maine
Charteris	Evan Charteris, *John Sargent* (1927)
ES	Emily Sargent
FARL	Frick Art Reference Library, New York
FWS	FitzWilliam Sargent
ISG	Isabella Stewart Gardner
JH	Julie H. Heyneman Papers, Bancroft Library, University of California
JSS	John Singer Sargent
MHS	Massachusetts Historical Society, Boston, Massachusetts
NYHS	New York Historical Society, New York
PC	Private Collection
RLO	Ormond Family Collection, comprising the late David McKibbin's notes, correspondence and papers
VL	Violet Paget [Vernon Lee]
VLL	*Vernon Lee's Letters*, ed. Irene Cooper Willis (privately printed, 1937)

Book One

I am tired . . . root. FWS/Emily Haskell Sargent, 10 October [1870], AAA.

Chapter I

1 They sailed in the most modern vessel of the day, the Collins paddle-steamer *Arctic*. She boasted steam heat, bathrooms, smoking-room and barber-shop. Alas, with a sad but fitting sense of irony the *Arctic* sank on the return crossing, with the loss of 322 lives, making maritime history.
2 Mrs Singer/sister, [February 1856], AAA.
3 Mrs Singer/sister, [1857], AAA.
4 FWS/brother, 24 November [1869], AAA.
5 FWS/Winthrop Sargent, 20 May 1871, AAA.

Chapter II

1 FWS/Emily Haskell Sargent, 16 September 1861, AAA.
2 FWS/parents, in Charteris, p. 5 [?father, 1863].
3 ibid.
4 FWS/Winthrop Sargent, 27 May 1865, AAA. The drawing of FWS is at the Sargent–Murray–Gilman–Hough House Association, Gloucester, Mass.
5 FWS/Winthrop Sargent, 27 May 1865, AAA.
6 FWS/Emily Haskell Sargent, [July 1864], AAA.

7 JSS/Ben del Castillo, 16 April 1865, in Charteris, p. 7. This is John's first surviving letter and, like all other letters to del Castillo seen by Evan Charteris, it remains untraced. And, for that matter, not a great deal is known about the recipient, save that he lived next door to the Sargents in Nice, was of Spanish descent (though his parents had lived in Cuba), was a naturalized American citizen, was educated in England (at Cambridge), and that he and his parents lived an itinerant European life before settling in San Remo. From various references in letters, his mother eventually went mad and his father was remarkably petulant, though none of this can be confirmed.

8 FitzWilliam Sargent, *England, the United States, and the Southern Confederacy* (London, 1863), p. 71.

9 ibid., p. [ii].

10 FWS/Emily Haskell Sargent, 12 May 1863, AAA.

11 FWS/brother, 24 November [1869], AAA.

12 Peter Gunn, *Vernon Lee; Violet Paget, 1856–1935* (London, 1964), p. 33.

13 Some of John's early drawings were reproduced in an article by Rachel Field, "John Sargent's boyhood sketches", *St Nicholas Magazine* (June 1926), pp. 774–7. The sketchbook Emily gave him in Rome, 1868–9, was later given to the Fogg Art Museum, Harvard, among other things, by Emily and her sister Violet in 1937. Other childhood sketchbooks were also given to the Metropolitan Museum of Art.

14 FWS/Winthrop Sargent, 21 February 1865, AAA.

15 Bemis/brother (Seth Bemis), 18 February 1969, MHS.

16 FWS/Winthrop Sargent, 7 March 1867, AAA.

Chapter III

1 FWS/Winthrop Sargent, 15 November 1868, AAA.

2 Mary Singer Sargent/Emily Haskell Sargent, 20 October 1867, AAA.

3 FWS/sister, 10 May 1869, AAA.

4 Nathaniel Hawthorne, *Transformation [The Marble Faun]* (London, 1860), pp. x–xi.

5 Henry James, *William Wetmore Story, and His Friends* (New York, 1903), pp. 6 and 346.

6 FWS/Bemis, 20 August 1867, MHS.

7 James, *William Wetmore Story*, p. 34. James first aired this claim for Hawthorne in 1879: "Hawthorne's career was probably as tranquil and uneventful a one as ever fell to the lot of a man of letters; it was almost strikingly deficient in incident, in what may be called the dramatic quality." Mrs Henry Adams believed that Story, after seeing his sculpture, displayed a rare gift for ruining marble.

8 Vernon Lee, *The Sentimental Traveller* (London, 1908), pp. 10–11.

9 Lee, in Charteris, pp. 242–3.

10 Vernon Lee's memory might have been at fault; the problem was solved three years later, in Florence.

11 FWS/Winthrop Sargent, 20 May 1871, AAA.

12 Julie Heyneman, unpublished memoir of Sargent, JH. She got her information from Sargent himself when she was his student, which she later incorporated in her entry on Sargent in the *Encyclopaedia Britannica* (1956).

13 FWS/sister, postscript dated 20 September added to a letter begun in Naples, July [1869].

14 FWS/Emily Haskell Sargent, 18 October [1869], AAA.

15 Julie Heyneman memoir, JH.

16 JSS/Vernon Lee, 23 April 1870, CC.

17 Charteris, p. 13.

18 This scholarship is largely the work of the late David McKibbin of the Boston Athenaeum. Also, see Henry James, *The Notebooks of Henry James*, ed. F. O. Matthiessen and Kenneth B. Murdock (New York, 1947), pp. 71–3; Charteris, pp. 13–15; and Richard Holmes, *Shelley: The Pursuit* (London, 1974). Silsbee's papers, containing letters from Jane (Claire) Clairmont, are at the Essex Institute, Mass. Silsbee donated Shelley papers to Harvard and in 1898 gave Shelley's guitar to the Bodleian Library; the following year the Shelley Society and Librarian commissioned Sargent to do a charcoal drawing of Silsbee.

19 Turner Sargent/Bemis, 29 January 1877, MHS.

20 FWS/Emily Haskell Sargent, 17 April 1870, AAA.

21 Metropolitan Museum of Art, New York.

22 FWS/Winthrop Sargent, 3 January 1872, AAA.

23 FWS/Winthrop Sargent, 11 November [1871], AAA.

24 FWS/Winthrop Sargent, 17 January 1872, AAA.

25 FWS/Winthrop Sargent, 18 February [1872], AAA.

26 Lee, in Charteris, p. 248.

27 JSS/Vernon Lee [autumn 1881], CC: reprinted in Vernon Lee, *For Maurice* (London, 1927), p. xxxviii. In her lengthy preface, she explained that the story was the "result of the mystery of history and longing to hear a singer long dead".

28 Lee, in Charteris, p. 249.

29 Lee, *For Maurice*, pp. xxxi–xxxii. Vernon Lee was wrong about the year they met in Bologna; it was 1873, not 1872.

30 FWS/Bemis, 1 November [1873], MHS.

Chapter IV

1 FWS/Bemis, 23 April 1874, MHS.

2 JSS/Mrs Austin, 22 March 1874, in Charteris, p. 18.

3 JSS/Mrs Austin, 25 April 1874, in Charteris, p. 19. The order in which John reported these facts is noteworthy: it was as if "Cholera in Venice" sent them in the direction of Paris. Cholera did, however, kill their natural propensity for procrastination.

4 Palmer wrote in his diary (20 May 1874): "Went to talk to Sargent about studios . . ." (courtesy of Mrs Maybelle Mann).

5 JSS/Heath Wilson, 23 May 1874. The history of John's vital letters to Heath Wilson is not a happy one: they were sold by Maggs Brothers (London) in the 1930s and thereafter disappeared until 1984 when they again appeared for sale by a dealer in Philadelphia, and were sold to the Morgan Library. Then they were lost in the post. Mercifully, both Maggs Brothers and Miss Catherine Barnes on behalf of William H. Allen, Bookseller, Philadelphia, made lengthy extracts in the respective sales catalogues, and these extracts are my only reference.

6 W. H. Low, *A Painter's Progress* (New York, 1910), p. 89.

7 James Carroll Beckwith in William Coffin, "Sargent and his painting, with special reference to his decorations in the Boston Public Library", *Century Magazine*, vol. 52, no. 2 (June 1896), p. 172.

8 FWS/Winthrop Sargent, 30 May [1874], AA.

9 JSS/Heath Wilson, 12 June 1874, Maggs and Barnes.

10 Scholarship, like fashion, has also been disparaging about him; encyclopaedias and dictionaries of artists cannot even agree on his date of

birth. The best account of Carolus' life, though brief, is Dr Gabriel P. Weisberg, *The Realist Tradition: French Painting and Drawing, 1830–1900* (Cleveland, Ohio, 1980), pp. 279–80, 168 and 249. There has been no biography of Carolus.

11 For the history of the foundation of the studio, see James Carroll Beckwith's autobiographical sketch, pp. 88–9, ANAD.

12 FWS/Winthrop Sargent, 30 May [1874], AAA.

13 JSS/Heath Wilson, 12 June 1874, Maggs and Barnes. The reigning professors were Isadore Pils, Alexandre Cabanel, Jean Léon Gérôme and Henri Frédéric Yvon. The neatest survey of the Ecole's near-unintelligible organization can be found in Dr H. Barbara Weinberg, "Nineteenth century American painters at the Ecole des Beaux Arts", *American Art Journal*, vol. 13, no. 4 (Autumn 1981).

14 Beckwith diary, 6 December 1874, ANAD.

15 Carolus-Duran, "A French painter and his pupils", *Century Magazine*, vol. 31, no. 38 (January 1886), p. 373.

16 Charteris, pp. 28–9.

17 JSS/Heath Wilson, 12 June 1874, Maggs and Barnes.

18 JSS/Heath Wilson, 23 May 1874, Maggs and Barnes.

19 JSS/Heath Wilson, 12 June 1874, Maggs and Barnes.

20 FWS/sister Anna Maria, 25 June 1874, AAA.

Chapter V

1 FWS/Bemis, 25 June [1874], MHS.

2 Mary Singer Sargent's Will, London 1906 (St Catherine's House, London).

3 FWS/Bemis, 18 September [1874], MHS.

4 JSS/Heath Wilson, 12 June 1874, Maggs and Barnes.

5 JSS/Ben del Castillo, 4 October 1874, in Charteris, p. 22.

6 Julian Alden Weir/mother, 4 October 1874, AAA. Also in Dorothy Weir Young, *The Life and Letters of J. Alden Weir* (New York, 1910), pp. 90–2.

7 W. H. Low, *A Painter's Progress* (New York, 1910), pp. 90–2.

8 The best and most cogent account of the varying fortunes of the Academy Schools during the 1870s can be found in Dr Lois M. Fink, *Academy: The Academic Tradition in American Art* (Washington, DC, 1975).

9 Charteris, p. 37.

10 Julian Alden Weir/mother, 10 April [1875], AAA.

11 Julian Alden Weir/mother, 1 May 1875, AAA.

12 Julian Alden Weir/mother, 17 May 1875, AAA.

13 Albert Edelfeldt/mother, 10 January 1877, in Albert Edelfeldt, *Drottning Blanca och Hertig Carl*, samt Nagra Andra Tavlor (Helsingfors, 1917), p. 12.

14 Sydney Colvin, in *The Dictionary of National Biography*.

15 R. A. M. Stevenson, "J. S. Sargent", *Art Journal*, March 1888, p. 66.

16 JSS/Fanny Watts, 10 March 1876, RLO.

17 FWS/Bemis, 24 March [1877], MHS.

18 Mary Singer Sargent/sister-in-law, 13 December 1875, AAA.

19 FWS/sister-in-law, Mrs Thomas Sargent, 31 August 1875, AAA.

20 FWS/sister, 1 March 1877, AAA.

21 ES/Violet Paget (later VL), 24 September 1876, RLO.

22 Mary Hale, "The Sargent I knew", *The World Today*, November 1927, p. 566.

23 Metropolitan Museum of Art, New York.

24 Eliot Gregory, *Worldly Ways and Byways* (New York, 1898), p. 44.

25 Beckwith diary, 6 December 1874, ANAD.

26 Julian Alden Weir/mother, 1 December 1874, AAA.

27 William Coffin, "Sargent and his painting, with special reference to his

decorations in the Boston Public Library", *Century Magazine*, vol. 52, no. 2 (June 1896), p. 172.

28 Carolus-Duran, "A French painter and his pupils", *Century Magazine*, vol. 31, no. 38 (January 1886), pp. 374–5.

29 FWS/sister, 1 March 1877, AAA.

30 FWS/brother, 3 April 1877.

Book Two

I must . . . place. JSS/Charles Deering, 2 May 1878, Chicago Art Institute.

Yes . . . will do. Henry James/Thomas Bailey Aldrich, 5 March 1888, in Henry James, *Letters*, ed. Leon Edel, Vol. 3 (London, 1980), p. 223.

Chapter VI

1 See Paulette Howard-Johnston, "Helleu et ses modèles", *La Nouvelle Revue des deux mondes*, December 1974, p. 605.

2 Charteris, p. 45.

3 Jean Vallery-Radoit, "Au temps de Montesquiou et Proust", preface, *Helleu* (Paris: Bibliothèque Nationale, 1957), p. 7 (Jean Adhemar).

4 Helleu/Paulette Helleu [December 1922], Collection Mme Paulette Howard-Johnston.

5 Beckwith, untitled autobiographical fragment, n.d., pp. 93–4, ANAD.

6 ibid., pp. 84–6, 89.

7 *Atlantic Monthly*, January 1878, p. 785.

8 DuBois/J. Alden Weir, 2 March 1878, AAA. "You will see a good sketch by Sargent in the AAA [Association of American Artists] some Cancale women on the beach, very luminous."

9 ES/Violet Paget, 24 July 1878, CC.

10 Helena Modjeska, *Memories and Impressions of Helena Modjeska: An Autobiography* (New York, 1910), p. 368.

11 FWS/brother, 15 August [1879], AAA.

12 DuBois/Weir, 14 May 1879, AAA.

13 ES/Julie Heyneman, 27 September [1912], J.H.

14 JSS/Ben del Castillo, [10 August 1878], in Charteris, p. 47.

15 FWS/Tom Sargent, 15 August [1879], AAA.

16 Charteris, p. 51; and, again, JSS/Julie Heyneman, [20 September 1897]: "I hope you'll have some copies of Franz Hals to show. [Jacomb] Hood tells me that you have come back charged with enthusiasm and spirit of knowledge – there is certainly no place like Haarlem to key one up." JH.

17 Now at the Isabella Stewart Gardner Museum. The sketchbook was given by JSS to Mrs Gardner in 1919. See *Drawings, Isabella Stewart Gardner Museum*, ed. Rollin van N. Hadley (Boston, Mass., 1968), p. 46.

18 Charteris, p. 147.

19 ibid., p. 148.

20 JSS/VL, 9 July [1880], CC.

21 I am indebted to Señor Don Jaime Parladé for this information.

22 JSS/Ben del Castillo, 4 January 1880, in Charteris, p. 50.

23 cf. *Larousse gastronomique* and *Encyclopaedia Britannica* (1911) for the definition of *ambre gris*.

24 FWS/brother, 15 August [1879], AAA.

25 Marie-Louise Pailleron, *Le Paradis perdu* (Paris, 1947), p. 150.

26 Marie-Louise Pailleron's text reads: "Dans le portrait d'Edouard Pailleron,

cette chemise de soie souple, ce veston un peu débraillé à une époque de conformisme, étonna, parait-il, le public du Salon des Artistes français habitué au protocole de Bonnat, aux redingotes noires sur fond de bitume. Malgré cette infraction aux règles, le portrait plût et fut reproduit avec abondance dans les journaux illustrés" (ibid., p. 15).

27 ibid., p. 152.
28 ES/VL, 3 September 1879, CC.
29 Pailleron, *Le Paradis perdu*, p. 152.
30 ibid., p. 157.
31 Henry St John Smith diary, RLO.
32 In 1925 a fellow-student from *atelier* Duran recalled John's domestic arrangements in austere terms – he merely *slept* at a hotel, the Hôtel des Etats-Unis. See Hamilton Minchin, "Some early recollections of Sargent", *Contemporary Review*, June 1925. (The only Hôtel des Etats-Unis this author has been able to identify was in the rue d'Antin, the other side of the Seine, and not at all close to rue Notre-Dame-des-Champs.) After Beckwith returned to New York his share of the rent – still 1,000 fr. in 1880 – was taken over by Leopold Hirsch.
33 Ramon Subercaseaux, *Memorias de Ochenta Anos; Recuerdos Personales, Criticas, Reminiscencias Historicas, Viajes, Anecdotas*, Vol. 1 (Santiago, 1936), pp. 388–9: "Pasado el verano, nos juntamos en Venecia con el mismo Sargent y su familia. Entre ocupaciones de arte y excursiones en tan buena compania se onterarons los meses de septiembre y octubre."
34 ES/VL, 23 May 1880, CC.

Chapter VII

1 Bemis left FitzWilliam $10,000.
2 FWS/sister, 12 August [1882], AAA.
3 FWS/brother, 13 November [1883 or 1884], AAA.
4 FWS/brother, 16 November [1883], AAA.
5 Charteris, p. 246.
6 VLL, pp. 60–1.
7 ibid., p. 63.
8 FWS/brother, 19 December 1884, AAA.
9 Beckwith diary, ANAD.
10 ibid.
11 ibid.
12 ibid.
13 cf. VL/E. Lee-Hamilton, 3 July 1882: "It appears that he is at present the victim of fresh matrimonial cabals on the part of Mrs Burckhardt" (VLL, p. 96).
14 Beckwith diary, ANAD.
15 Richard Ormond disagrees.
16 Albert Edelfeldt/mother, 25 May 1882, in Albert Edelfeldt, *Resor och Intryck* (Helsingfors, 1921), p. 176.
17 ibid., p. 165.
18 VLL, p. 87.
19 Richard Ormond disagrees.
20 ES/VL, 25 August 1880, CC.
21 JSS/Mrs Paget, 27 September [1880], CC.
22 JSS/VL, 22 October [1880], CC; Warren Adelson and Donna Seldin, *Americans in Venice, 1879–1913*, exhibition catalogue, the Coe Kerr Gallery (New York, 1983); Margaretta M. Lovell, *Venice: The American View, 1860–1920*, exhibition catalogue (San Francisco, Calif., 1984).

23 Martin Brimmer/Sarah Whitman, 26 October [18]82, from Venice, AAA. (Brimmer was later a Trustee of the Museum of Fine Arts, Boston, Mass.)

24 L. V. Fildes, *Luke Fildes, RA: A Victorian Painter* (London, 1968), p. 67.

25 E. R. and J. Pennell, *The Life of James McNeill Whistler* (London, 1928). First edition 1908.

26 *The Whistler Journal*, ed. E. R. and J. Pennell (Philadelphia, Pa, 1921), p. 34.

27 ibid., p. 39.

28 MS draft of "How to Paint", p. 4: Edward Darley Boit Papers, AAA.

29 ES/Julie Heyneman, 11 February 1909, JH.

30 See Donelson F. Hoopes, *Sargent Water-Colors* (New York, 1970).

31 Robert Apthorp Boit (EDB's brother), *Chronicles of the Boit Family and Their Descendants and of Other Allied Families* (Boston, Mass., 1915), AAA; and Boit diaries, AAA.

32 Henry James, in *Harper's New Monthly Magazine*, October 1887, p. 688; *Picture and Text* (New York, 1893), pp. 104–5; *The Painter's Eye*, ed. J. Sweeney (London, 1956), pp. 222–3.

33 See Allan Nevins, *Henry White: Thirty Years of American Diplomacy* (New York, 1930); *Dictionary of American Biography*; Mrs White's diaries, Columbia University Library and Library of Congress.

34 Henry James, *Letters*, ed. Leon Edel, Vol. 3 (London, 1980), p. 215.

35 JSS/Russell, Tate Gallery.

36 VLL, pp. 116–17.

37 See Mettha Westfeldt Eshleman (ed.), *Madame Gautreau (née Virginie Avengo), 1898, Antonio de la Gandara* (New Orleans, La, 1984; revised 1985); Metropolitan Museum of Art, New York, Archives (for letter from George E. Jordan to Doreen Bolger Burke, 6 December 1975); Sargent entry in *Encyclopaedia Britannica* (New York, 1956).

38 I am indebted to Mrs T. Monroe for pointing this fact out to me.

39 See Paulette Howard-Johnston, "Helleu et ses modèles", *La Nouvelle Revue des deux mondes* (Paris: December 1974), p. 605.

40 Charteris, p. 59.

41 ibid.; and CC.

42 Metropolitan Museum of Art, New York; Fogg Art Museum, Harvard University; private collections.

43 Fogg Art Museum, Harvard University.

44 *Madame Gautreau Drinking a Toast* at the Isabella Stewart Gardner Museum; originally given by John to Mme Avegno; from her it went to Dr Pozzi; and on Dr Pozzi's death it was sold at auction to Mrs Gardner.

45 Charteris, pp. 59–60.

46 See Trevor Fairbrother, "The Shock of John Singer Sargent's 'Madame Gautreau'", *Arts Magazine*, January 1981, pp. 90–7, for a discussion of the change in her dress and a detailed account of contemporary criticism.

47 Charteris, p. 61; original BA.

Chapter VIII

1 Rebecca West, *1900* (London, 1982), p. 100.

2 Henry James, *Letters*, ed. Leon Edel, Vol. 3 (London, 1980), p. 32.

3 Leon Edel, *Henry James: The Middle Years, 1884–1894* (London, 1963), p. 46.

4 ibid., p. 45.

5 ibid., p. 47.

6 James, *Letters*, Vol. 3, p. 43; and Edel, *James: The Middle Years*, p. 48.

7 James, *Letters*, Vol. 3, pp. 43 and 42.

8 JSS/VL, CC.
9 VLL, p. 149.
10 ibid., p. 143.
11 JSS/Henry James, Houghton Library, Harvard University.
12 JSS/Edward Russell, Tate Gallery Archives.
13 W. Graham Robertson, *Time Was* (London, 1931), pp. 45 and 47.
14 James, *Letters*, Vol. 3, p. 43.
15 Lord Newton, *Retrospection* (London, 1941), p. 24.
16 James, *Letters*, Vol. 3, p. 50.
17 Stevenson/Henley, [17 December 1884], National Library of Scotland, Edinburgh.
18 JSS/Stevenson, the Beinecke Rare Book and Manuscript Library, Yale University.
19 Alice Strettell Carr, *Mrs J. Comyns Carr's Reminiscences*, ed. Eve Adam (London, [1926]), p. 302.
20 Stevenson/Henley, [17 December 1884], National Library of Scotland, Edinburgh.
21 JSS/James, 29 June [1885], Houghton Library, Harvard University.
22 Stevenson/parents, 31 July 1885, in R. L. Stevenson, *Letters*, Vol. 2 (London, 1923), p. 355.
23 Fanny Osborne Stevenson/mother-in-law, 13 August 1885, Silverado Museum, St Helena, Calif.
24 Charteris, p. 80.
25 VLL, p. 176.
26 ibid., p. 177.
27 ibid., p. 177.
28 JSS/Edward Russell, Tate Gallery Archives.
29 Charteris, p. 76.
30 Carr, *Reminiscences*, p. 299.
31 E. V. Lucas, *Edwin Austin Abbey, Royal Academician: The Record of His Life and Work* (London, 1921), p. 47.
32 JSS/Mrs Mahlon Sands, n.d. [1890], PC.
33 ibid.
34 Lucas, *Abbey*, p. 151.
35 Henry James, *Picture and Text* (New York, 1893), pp. 4, 5, 7, 5, 6.
36 See Joyce Sharpey-Schafer, *Soldier of Fortune: F. D. Millet, 1846–1912* (Utica, NY, 1984).
37 JSS/ES, n.d. [August/September 1885], PC. Facsimile in Charteris, between pp. 76 and 77.
38 See Mary Anderson [de Navarro], *A Few More Memories* (London, 1896), p. 202, for an exceedingly unhelpful quote.
39 James, *Letters*, Vol. 3, p. 338.
40 Charteris, p. 77.
41 Lucas, *Abbey*, p. 152.
42 Charteris, pp. 76–7.
43 Evan Charteris, *Life and Letters of Sir Edmund Gosse* (London, 1931), p. 192.
44 A. Lucia Millet to her parents, 22 September 1885, PC.
45 Charteris, p. 192.
46 Lucas, *Abbey*, p. 152.
47 JSS/Edward Russell, Tate Gallery Archive.
48 Charteris, pp. 74–5.
49 In Francis D. Millet Papers, AAA; written in JSS hand, with caricature of

Sargent at work by Millet. I am grateful to Miss Claudia T. Esko for bringing this to my attention.
50 JSS/ES n.d. [August/September 1885], RLO. Facsimile in Charteris between pp. 76 and 77.

Chapter IX

1 William Rothenstein, *Men and Memories: A History of the Arts, 1872–1922* (New York, 1938), p. 196.
2 Caroline Burch diary, McKibbin files, RLO.
3 Lucia Millet/parents, 9 and 22 November 1886, PC.
4 Rothenstein, *Men and Memories*, p. 192.
5 Frederick Sumner Platt, "J. S. Sargent (his views)", unpublished memoir, written after meeting Sargent in Worcester, Mass., August 1890, PC; quoted in Susan E. Strickler, "John Singer Sargent and Worcester", *Worcester Art Museum Journal* (1982–3), p. 26. I am grateful to Miss Strickler for this reference and Platt's other memories of Sargent.
6 Osbert Sitwell, *Left Hand, Right Hand!* (London, 1944), p. 222. See also George Henschel, *Musings and Memories of a Musician* (London, 1918), p. 333.
7 Julie Heyneman, private memoir [1941], "Tite Street and around the corner", JH.
8 The aggregate of American sitters reads:
1880: Gordon Greenough, Brooks Chadwick, Ralph Curtis, Mrs Charles Clifford Dyer, Henry St John Smith and Valerie Burckhardt (who counts as half-American);
1881: Mrs Joseph Jay Townsend;
1882: Joseph Jay Townsend, his daughters, Isabel Valle, the Boit sisters, Mrs Curtis, Mr and Mrs John W. Field, Misses Beatrice and Eleanor Chapman;
1883: Mrs Waldo Story, Mrs Henry White, Mme Gautreau, Miss Olivia Richardson;
1884: Mrs Kate Moore, Mrs Wilton Phipps, Lady Playfair (from Boston);
1885: Mrs Alice Mason, Mrs Burckhardt and Louise Burckhardt (who together count as three-quarters American), Teresa Gosse (half-American);
1886: Mrs Archibald Douglas Dick, Mrs Frank Millet, her son, Violet Sargent – and a self-portrait.
9 Edwin H. Blashfield, "John Sargent", *Academy Notes and Monographs* (1927), p. 36.
10 Charteris, p. 78.
11 Blashfield Papers, NYHS.
12 ibid.
13 Millet Papers, AAA (written in JSS's hand).
14 Alice Strettell Carr, *Mrs J. Comyns Carr's Reminiscences*, ed. Eve Adam (London, [1926]), p. 302.
15 JSS/Marquand, Princeton University Library.
16 Henry Marquand, Metropolitan Museum of Art, New York, Archives; quoted in Doreen Bolger Burke, *American Paintings in the Metropolitan Museum of Art*, Vol. 3 (New York, 1980), p. 252.
17 Martin Birnbaum, *John Singer Sargent: A Conversation Piece* (New York, 1941), pp. 41–2.
18 Charles C. Baldwin, *Stanford White* (New York, 1931), p. 173.
19 White dinner, 3 November and again in February; *Tristan*, 2 November; wedding-present painting, 6 November.
20 Countess Palffy, *The Lady and the Painter* (Boston, Mass., 1951), p. viii.

21 Louise Hall Tharp, *Mrs Jack* (Boston, Mass., 1965), p. 123.
22 Theodore Robinson diaries, FARL.
23 JSS/ISG, AISGM.
24 Gorham Bacon, *Recollections: Gorham Bacon*, ed. Ruth Bacon Cheney (Boston, Mass., 1971), p. 54. Also see Trevor Fairbrother, "Notes on John Singer Sargent in New York, 1888–1890", *Archives of American Art Journal*, vol. 22, no. 4 (1982), pp. 27–32, for the complete guest-list.
25 Bunker/ISG, 9 April 1888, AISGM.
26 JSS/ISG, AISGM.
27 Quoted in Richard Ormond, *John Singer Sargent: Paintings, Drawings, Watercolors* (New York, 1970), p. 41.
28 Henry James, *Letters*, ed. Leon Edel, Vol. 3 (London, 1980), p. 231.
29 Bunker/ISG, 1 August [1888], AISGM.
30 Bunker/ISG, 25 June [1888], AISGM.
31 ibid.
32 R. H. Ives Gammell, *Dennis Miller Bunker* (New York, 1953), p. 26.

Chapter X

1 Bunker/ISG, 2 September 1888, AISGM.
2 Paulette Howard-Johnston, "Une visite à Giverny en 1924", *L'Oeil* (March 1969), p. 28.
3 Monet wrote to Helleu, in an undated letter (Bibliothèque Nationale) saying he had just spent two days with Sargent in the country. This letter has been dated July 1888, based on internal evidence. Other sources, among them John Rewald's *The History of Impressionism* (New York, 1961) give an 1889 date; the latter date seems correct as Sargent was in Paris for most of June.
4 JSS/Monet, n.d. [1887]; French text in Charteris, p. 97. This translation in Donelson F. Hoopes, "John S. Sargent: the Worcestershire interlude, 1885–1889", *Brooklyn Museum Annual* (1965–6), p. 81.
5 Beckwith diary, ANAD.
6 JSS/Mrs Hunter, 9 January 1917, AAA.
7 Monet/Helleu, 16 April 1925, Collection Mme Paulette Howard-Johnston.
8 Charteris, p. 130.
9 Sir George Henschel, *Musings and Memories of a Musician* (London, 1918), p. 331.
10 E. V. Lucas, *Edwin Austin Abbey, Royal Academician: The Record of His Life and Work* (London, 1921), p. 210.
11 Charteris, p. 107.

Book Three

Voilà . . . l'époque. William Horre Downes, *John S. Sargent: His Life and Work* (Boston, Mass., 1925), p. 58.
I have . . . free man. JSS/Mrs Curtis, 13 June [1907], BA.
I will . . . human being. . . . JSS/Lady Radnor, Longford Castle and in the Dowager Countess of Radnor, *From a Great Grandmother's Armchair* (London, ?1927), p. 181.

Chapter XI

1 JSS/Mrs Mahon Sands, n.d. [?1893/4], PC.
2 Beckwith diary, 1 March 1890, ANAD.
3 Beckwith diary, 17 February 1890, ANAD.
4 JSS/ISG, n.d. [March 1890], AISGM.

5 Dora Wheeler Keith interview, AAA.
6 See William Howe Downes, *John S. Sargent: His Life and Works* (London, 1925), where newspaper reports are quoted, and Leda Rose McCabe, "Carmencita and her painters", *New York Times Book Review and Magazine*, 8 July 1923.
7 JSS/ISG, n.d. [spring 1890], AISGM.
8 Charteris, p. 113.
9 Charles C. Baldwin, *Stanford White* (New York, 1931; reprinted 1976), p. 16.
10 C. H. Reilly, *McKim, Mead & White* (London, 1924), p. 10.
11 ibid., p. 11.
12 Baldwin, *White*, p. 176.
13 Contract dates given in ibid.; Charles Moore, *The Life and Times of Charles Follen McKim* (New York, 1970); and Walter Muir Whitehill, *Boston Public Library: A Centennial History* (Cambridge, Mass., 1956).
14 E. V. Lucas, *Edwin Austin Abbey, Royal Academician: The Record of His Life and Work* (London, 1921), p. 230.
15 Charteris, p. 105, and Moore, *McKim*, p. 73.
16 Lucas, *Abbey*, pp. 231–2.
17 JSS/Flora Priestley, BA.
18 JSS/Ralph Curtis, BA.
19 JSS/Ralph Curtis, BA.
20 JSS/Fairchild, BA.
21 JSS/Ralph Curtis, BA.
22 Charteris, p. 115.
23 JSS/ISG, AISGM.
24 VLL, pp. 334–5.
25 JSS/Charles Derring, n.d., JH.
26 VLL, p. 354.
27 JSS/McKim, AABPL; Moore, *McKim*, p. 78 (incomplete).
28 JSS/Whistler, Glasgow University Library.
29 Moore, *McKim*, p. 85.
30 Lucas, *Abbey*, p. 183.
31 JSS/Helleu, Collection Mme Paulette Howard-Johnston.
32 JSS/Mrs Fairchild, BA.
33 JSS/Helleu, Collection Mme Paulette Howard-Johnston.
34 G. P. Jacomb-Hood, "John Sargent", *Cornhill*, September 1925, p. 284.
35 Charteris, p. 119.
36 JSS/Henry James, Houghton Library, Harvard University.
37 JSS/Helleu, 5 June [1890], PC.
38 JSS/Helleu, [winter 1891–2], Collection Mme Paulette Howard-Johnston.

Chapter XII

1 Charles Moore, *The Life and Times of Charles Follen McKim* (New York, 1970), p. 76.
2 JSS/Charles Fairchild, 7 March 1982, BA.
3 E. V. Lucas, *Edwin Austin Abbey, Royal Academician: The Record of His Life and Work* (London, 1921), p. 255.
4 The best and most thorough account of *The Triumph of Religion* was written by Sylvester Baxter, with Sargent's guidance, in *The Boston Public Library: A Handbook to the Library Building, Its Mural Decorations and Its Collections* (Boston, Mass., 1921), pp. 38–58. Three previous editions appeared in 1916, and 1920. All titles quoted hereafter come from this source, and in many cases are not the titles now generally applied. An edited account is given in Peter A. Wick, *A*

Handbook to the Art and Architecture of the Boston Public Library (Boston, Mass., 1978), pp. 47–52, wherein the chronology is listed.

5 See Appendix II.
6 William Howe Downes, *John S. Sargent: His Life and Works* (London, 1925), pp. 38–9.
7 Beckwith diary, ANAD.
8 Nicola d'Inverno, "The Real John Singer Sargent", *Boston Sunday Advertiser*, 7 February 1926.
9 W. Graham Robertson, *Time Was* (London, 1931), p. 233.
10 VLL, p. 352.
11 Charteris, p. 141.
12 JSS/Mrs Mahlon Sands, 26 February [1894], Wendy Baron, RLO.
13 Camille Pissaro, *Letters to His Son Lucien*, ed. with the assistance of Lucien Pissaro by John Rewald (London, 1980), p. 183.
14 William Rothenstein, *Men and Memories: A History of the Arts, 1872–1922* (New York, 1938), pp. 191 and 194.
15 Charteris, p. 124.
16 JSS/Secretary of the Council of the Royal Academy, Royal Academy Archives.
17 Charteris, p. 144.
18 JSS/Curtis, n.d. [May 1894], BA.
19 Henry James, *Letters*, ed. Leon Edel, Vol. 3 (London, 1980), p. 156.
20 JSS/Mrs Mahlon Sands, PC. Also see Wendy Baron, *Miss Ethel Sands and Her Circle* (London, 1977), p. 26.
21 Robertson, *Time Was*, p. 235.
22 ibid., pp. 238 and 236.
23 Catalogue Raisonnée (unpublished).
24 See Charteris, p. 142.
25 Quoted in James Lomax and Richard Ormond, *John Singer Sargent and the Edwardian Age*, exhibition catalogue (Leeds, 1979), p. 57.
26 JSS/Abbott, 18 January [1895], AABPL.
27 Lucas, *Abbey*, p. 284.
28 Downes, *Sargent*, p. 38.
29 JSS/Mrs Curtis, BA.
30 JSS/Mrs Sears [May/June 1895], PC.
31 Henry James/Mrs Sands, see Baron, *Ethel Sands*, p. 25.
32 JSS/George Vanderbilt, Biltmore House Archives.
33 Charteris, p. 223.
34 Sir George Henschel, *Musings and Memories of a Musician* (London, 1918), pp. 331–2.
35 Flora Priestley/Vernon Lee, n.d. [1899], CC.
36 Jane von Glehn/mother, Mrs Emmet, 23 December 1904 and [January 1905], PC.
37 ES/ISG, 9 November 1921, AISGM.
38 ES/ISG, 13 March 1923, AISGM.
39 JSS/Mrs Charles Hunter, 9 January 1917, AAA.
40 Thomas Bodkin, *Hugh Lane and His Pictures* (Dublin, 1956), p. 17.
41 *The Letters of W. B. Yeats*, ed. Richard Finneran and others, Vol. 1 (London, 1977), p. 196.
42 Rothenstein, *Men and Memories*, p. 244.
43 The Dowager Marchioness of Cholmondeley to the author, 21 August 1980.
44 Charteris, p. 145.
45 The Dowager Marchioness of Cholmondeley to the author.

Chapter XIII

1 William Howe Downes, *John S. Sargent: His Life and Works* (London, 1925), p. 180.
2 Dartmouth College Library, and Doreen Bolger Burke, *American Paintings in the Metropolitan Museum of Art*, Vol. 3 (New York, 1980), p. 252.
3 I. N. Phelps Stokes, *Random Recollections of a Happy Life* (New York, 1932), pp. 115–18.
4 Henry James, *The Painter's Eye*, ed. John L. Sweeney (London, 1956), pp. 254 and 257.
5 D. H. Cater (ed.), *Henry Adams and His Friends* (London, 1947), p. 404; quoted in James Lomax and Richard Ormond, *John Singer Sargent and the Edwardian Age*, exhibition catalogue (Leeds, 1979), p. 57.
6 Wilfred Scawen Blunt, *My Diaries* (London, 1922), Vol. 2, p. 171.
7 Charteris, p. 164.
8 John Russell, "Art", in *Edwardian England, 1901–1914*, ed. Simon Nowell-Smith (London, 1964), pp. 332–3.
9 Max Beerbohm, *Letters to Reggie Turner*, ed. Rupert Hart-Davis (London, 1964), p. 232: letter dated 14 April 1914.
10 Maurice Baring, *Half a Minute's Silence and Other Stories* (London, 1925), pp. 103–4.
11 JSS/Julie Heyneman, JH.
12 JSS/Julie Heyneman, [15 March 1897], JH.
13 JSS/Mrs Swinton [26 May 1898], PC.
14 JSS/Mrs Swinton [August 1898], PC. Fauré was staying with them in Wales.
15 Ethel Smyth, *What Happened Next* (London, 1940), p. 146.
16 In a letter from Harry Brewster to Ethel Smith, [January/February 1897], PC.
17 Ethel Smyth, *Impressions That Remained* (London, 1919), Vol. 2, p. 5.
18 Smyth, *What Happened Next*, p. 118.
19 Curtis/ISG, AISGM.
20 See Lady Cynthia Asquith, *Diaries, 1915–1918* (London, 1968), p. 177, for edited version; I am grateful to Mrs Nicola Beauman, Lady Cynthia Asquith's biographer, for the complete text.
21 Courtesy of Mrs Nicola Beauman.
22 See Gabriel Fauré, *Correspondance*, ed. Jean-Michel Nectoux (Paris, 1980), pp. 156–7.
23 Robert Orledge, *Gabriel Fauré* (London, 1979), p. 17.
24 Jean-Michel Nectoux, "Gabriel Fauré", in *The New Grove Dictionary of Music and Musicians* (London, 1981), Vol. 6, p. 419. Also see Anthony Hopkins, "Talking about music", BBC Radio 4, 16 August 1983.
25 Fauré, *Correspondance*, p. 310.
26 JSS/Mrs Swinton, PC.
27 Harry Brewster/Ethel Smyth, PC.
28 JSS/Mrs Curtis, BA.
29 JSS/Augustus Saint-Gaudens, Dartmouth College Library.
30 JSS/Augustus Saint-Gaudens, Dartmouth College Library.
31 JSS/Mrs Curtis, BA.
32 Blunt, *My Diaries*, Vol. 1, p. 315: 9 March 1899.
33 D. S. MacColl, review in *Saturday Review*, May 1900, pp. 583–4.
34 Downes, *Sargent*, p. 189.
35 Osbert Sitwell, *Left Hand, Right Hand!* (London, 1944), p. 216.
36 JSS/Curtis [?October 1900], BA.

37 W. Graham Robertson, *Time Was* (London, 1931), p. 233.
38 Royal Archives, Windsor, courtesy of Miss Jane Langton.
39 Sir Sidney Lee, *Edward VII: The Reign* (London, 1927), p. 469, courtesy of Miss Jane Langton.
40 The Duke of Portland, *Men, Women and Things* (London, 1937), pp. 219–20.
41 Lord Ribblesdale, *Impressions and Memories* (London, 1927), with a preface by his daughter, Lady Wilson, p. xvii.
42 C. V. Balsan, *The Glitter and the Gold* (London, 1953), p. 145.
43 JSS/Helleu [?March 1909], Collection Mme Paulette Howard-Johnston.
44 JSS/Evan Charteris, PC.
45 JSS-Mrs Cazalet, PC.
46 Lomax and Ormond, *Sargent*, p. 77.
47 Royal Cortissoz, in *The Johns Hopkins University Circular*, February 1907, pp. 20–2; Oxford robe story repeated in Charteris, p. 159.
48 JSS/Augustus Saint-Gaudens, Dartmouth College Library.
49 JSS/Thomas Fox, [1903], BA.
50 See Dr Martha Kingsbury, "Sargent's murals in the Boston Public Library", *Winterthur Portfolio II* (University of Virginia, 1976), pp. [153]–[172].
51 *Letters of Henry Adams (1892–1918)*, ed. W. C. Ford (Boston, Mass., 1938), p. 398.
52 JSS/ISG, AISGM.
53 Jacques-Emile Blanche, *Portraits of a Lifetime*, trans. Edward Clement (London, 1937), p. 158.
54 JSS/Mrs Curtis, BA.
55 JSS/Curtis, in Charteris, p. 155.
56 *L'Oeuvre de John S. Sargent*, with an introduction by Mrs Alice Meynell (Paris, 1905).
57 Marieli Benziger, *August Benziger, Portrait Painter* (Glendale, Calif., 1958), p. 358.

Chapter XIV

1 JSS/Mrs Curtis, 25 January [1906], BA.
2 JSS/Mrs Hunter, 24 January [1906], AAA.
3 JSS/Mrs Curtis, BA.
4 JSS/Mrs Hunter, AAA.
5 JSS/Mrs Hunter, [3 February 1906], AAA.
6 Eliza Wedgwood/Evan Charteris, 22 November 1925, RLO.
7 JSS/Mrs Curtis, [31 August 1913], BA.
8 Royal Academy Visitor's Report, 1 December 1907; the other 1910, Royal Academy Archives.
9 Charteris, p. 186.
10 ibid., pp. 182–3.
11 ibid., p. 182.
12 ibid., p. 188.
13 Vanessa Bell/Margery Snowden, 4 January [1902], Kings College Library, Cambridge; and in Frances Spalding, *Vanessa Bell* (London, 1983), p. 35.
14 ibid., p. 35.
15 *Nation*, 7 January 1911, p. 610; letter dated 29 December 1910.
16 ibid.
17 JSS/D. S. MacColl, 21 [January 1912], Glasgow University Library; and Charteris, pp. 192–3.
18 See Joseph Hone, *The Life of Henry Tonks* (London, 1939), p. 142.

19 JSS/D. S. MacColl, Glasgow University Library.
20 Charteris, p. 221.
21 JSS/Evans Charteris, PC; and Charteris, p. 221.
22 Eliza Wedgwood/Evans Charteris, RLO.
23 Edward Speyer, *My Life and Friends* (London, 1937), p. 158.
24 Typescript, preface, Albany Gallery; RLO.
25 Ralph Curtis/ISG, 2 July [1910], AISGM.
26 Cynthia Asquith, *Haply I May Remember* (London, 1950), p. 63, and see her diaries.
27 JSS/Mrs Nancy Potter, [1921], PC.
28 Max Beerbohm, *Letters to Reggie Turner*, ed. Rupert Hart-Davis (London, 1964), p. 222.
29 Henry James, *Letters*, ed. Leon Edel, Vol. 4 (Cambridge, Mass., 1984), p. 660.
30 Leon Edel, *Henry James: The Master, 1901–1916* (New York, 1972), p. 485.
31 JSS/Edith Wharton, 28 March [1912], Beinecke Rare Book and Manuscript Library, Yale University.
32 James, *Letters*, Vol. 4, pp. 674–5 (the date is in question: the letter is dated the thirteenth, but the editor, in a note to the previous letter, says the sittings began on the eighth).
33 Henry James/the Ranee of Sarawak, 8 December [1913], sold at Christie's, 18 December 1968, Lot 33 – the quotation is taken from the published extract in the catalogue for that sale.
34 Charteris, p. 161.
35 ibid., p. 195.
36 JSS/Mrs Hunter, 18 October [1914], AAA.
37 Henry James/Jessie Allen, 27 December 1914, Houghton Library, Harvard University.
38 JSS/Edith Wharton, 6 August [1915], the Beinecke Rare Books and Manuscripts Library, Yale University.
39 JSS/Whistler, n.d., Glasgow University Library.
40 JSS/Abbott Thayer, 12 November 1915, AAA.
41 JSS/Abbott Thayer, 31 January 1916, AAA.
42 JSS/Evan Charteris, 6 [February 1916], PC.
43 JSS/Mrs Hunter, 24 [March 1916], AAA.
44 JSS/Mrs Hunter, 13 April [1916], AAA.
45 JSS/Charteris, 8 June [1916], PC.
46 Charteris, p. 204.
47 JSS/Mrs Hunter, 31 August [1916], AAA.
48 JSS/Fox, 28 August [1916], BA.
49 JSS/Charteris, 25 July [1916], PC; and Charteris, p. 207.
50 JSS/Mrs Hunter, 9 January 1917, AAA.
51 JSS/Evan Charteris, 24 October [1919], PC; and Charteris, p. 209.
52 JSS/Fox, 22 November 1915, BA.
53 JSS/Charteris, 7 June 1917, PC.
54 JSS/Mrs Curtis, 26 February [1917], BA.
55 Mary Hale, "The Sargent I Knew", *The World Today* (November 1927), p. 569.
56 JSS/Mrs Hunter, 21 April 1917, AAA.
57 JSS/Charteris, 14 September [1917], PC.
58 JSS/Charteris, 7 June 1917, PC.
59 JSS/ISG, n.d. [1917], AISGM.
60 JSS/ISG, 28 [October 1917], AISGM.
61 JSS/Violet Ormond, 31 March 1918, RLO.

62 JSS/Violet Ormond, 3 April [1918], RLO.
63 ibid.

Chapter XV

1 JSS/ISG, AISGM.
2 JSS/Charteris, PC; and Charteris, p. 217.
3 JSS/ISG, 31 May 1918, AISGM.
4 Yockney/JSS, AAIWM (two letters).
5 Memorandum, 18 June 1918, AAIWM.
6 Memorandum, 11 June 1918, AAIWM.
7 Martin Birnbaum, *John Singer Sargent: A Conversation Piece* (New York, 1941), p. 8.
8 Meirion and Susie Harries, *The War Artists: British Official War Art of the Twentieth Century* (London, 1983), p. 34.
9 JSS/Mrs Hunter, AAA.
10 JSS/Charteris, PC; and Charteris, p. 212.
11 JSS/Mrs Hunter, AAA.
12 AAIWM. See O'Ryan's letter to David McKibbin, 1948, about Sargent with 27th Division, RLO.
13 JSS/Yockney, AAIWM.
14 JSS/Mrs Hunter, 10 October 1918, AAA.
15 JSS/Yockney, AAIWM.
16 JSS/Yockney, AAIWM.
17 JSS/Charteris, 15 June 1919, PC.
18 JSS/Tonks, three letters, RLO.
19 JSS/Charteris, 13 April [1920], PC.
20 Charteris, p. 199.
21 Anton Kamp, "John Singer Sargent – As I Remember Him", unpublished memoir, 1973.
22 JSS/ISG, AISGM.
23 William Howe Downes, *John S. Sargent: His Life and Works* (London, 1925).
24 JSS/ISG, AISGM.
25 Fox memoir, typescript, BA.
26 JSS/Mrs Astor, 23 September [1924], Library of the University of Reading.
27 Adrian Stokes, "John Singer Sargent, RA, RWS", *The Old Water-Colour Society's Club* (1925–6), Vol. 3, ed. Randall Davies (London, 1926).
28 Fox memoir, typescript, BA.

Bibliography

Abdy, Jane, and Gere, Charlotte, *The Souls* (London, 1983).
Ackerley, J. R., *My Father and Myself* (London, 1968).
Adams, Henry, *The Letters of Henry Adams*, ed. J. C. Levenson and others (Cambridge, Mass., 1982), Vol. 2, *1868–1885*, and Vol. 3, *1886–1892*.
Adams, Marian Hooper, *The Letters of Mrs Henry Adams, 1865–1883*, ed. Ward Thoron (Boston, Mass., 1936).
Adelson, Warren, *John Singer Sargent: His Own Work* (New York, 1981).
Aldrich, Mrs Thomas Bailey, *Crowding Memories* (London, 1921).
Anderson, Mary [de Navarro], *A Few Memories* (London, 1896).
—, *A Few More Memories: People and Things as I Have Seen Them* (London, 1936).
Anstruther-Thomson, Clementina, *Art and Man: Essays and Fragments* (London, 1924).
Asquith, Lady Cynthia, *Diaries, 1915–1918* (London, 1968).
—, *Haply I May Remember* (London, 1950).
Babson, John L., *History of the Town of Gloucester* (Boston, Mass., 1860).
Bacon, Gorham, *Recollections: Gorham Bacon*, ed. Ruth Bacon Cheney (New York, 1971).
Bacon, Henry, *Parisian Art and Artists* (Boston, Mass., 1883).
Baldwin, Charles C., *Stanford White* (New York, 1931).
Balson, C. V., *The Glitter and the Gold* (New York, 1953).
Baring, Maurice, *Half a Minute's Silence and Other Stories* (London, 1925).
Baron, Wendy, *Miss Ethel Sands and Her Circle* (London, 1977).
Bashkirtseff, Marie, *Further Memoirs, together with Her Correspondence with Guy de Maupassant* (London, 1901).
—, *Journal of Marie Bashkirtseff*, 2 vols (Paris, 1890).
—, *Letters of Marie Bashkirtseff*, trans. Mary J. Serviano (London, [1891]).
Beaux, Cecilia, *Background with Figures: Autobiography of Cecilia Beaux* (Boston, Mass., 1930).
Beerbohm, Max, *Letters to Reggie Turner*, ed. Rupert Hart-Davis (London, 1964).
Bell, Gertrude, *The Letters of Gertrude Bell* (London, 1903).
Belleroche, Albert de, "The lithographs of Sargent", *Print Collector's Quarterly* (March 1926).
Benson, A. C., *The Diaries of A. C. Benson*, ed. Percy Lubbock (London, 1926).
Benziger, Maridi and Peter, *August Benziger, Portrait Painter* (Glendale, Calif., 1958).
Bird, John, *Percy Grainger* (London, 1976).
Birnbaum, Martin, *John Singer Sargent: A Conversation Piece* (New York, 1941).
Blanche, Jacques-Emil, "Un grand américain: l'exposition John Sargent à Londres", *Revue de Paris*, 1 avril 1926, pp. 559–78; 1 juillet 1926, pp. 65–84.
—, *More Portraits of a Lifetime, 1918–1938*, trans. and ed. Walter Clement (London, 1939).
—, *Portraits of a Lifetime; The Late Victorian Era; The Edwardian Pageant, 1870–1914*, trans. and ed. Walter Clement (London, 1937).
Blashfield, Edwin H., *Mural Painting in America* (New York/London, 1914).
Blunt, Wilfred Scawen, *My Diaries*, 2 vols (London, 1919–20).
Bodkin, Thomas, *Hugh Lane and His Pictures* (Dublin, 1956).
Boime, Albert, *The Academy and French Painting in the Nineteenth Century* (London, 1971).
Boit, Robert Apthorp, *Chronicles of the Boit Family* (privately printed Boston, Mass., 1915).
Brooks, Van Wyck, *The Dream of Arcadia: American Writers and Artists in Italy, 1760–1915* (New York, 1958).
—, *New England: Indian Summer, 1865–1915* (Cleveland, Ohio, 1946).
Brown, Oliver, *Exhibition: The Memoirs of Oliver Brown* (London, 1968).
Burke, Doreen Bolger, *American Paintings in the Metropolitan Museum of Art*, Vol. 3 (New York, 1980).
Carr, Mrs J. Comyns, *Mrs J. Comyns Carr's Reminiscences*, ed. Eve Adam (London, 1926).
Carter, Morris, *Isabella Stewart Gardner and Fenway Court* (Boston, Mass., 1926).
Cater, D. H. (ed.), *Henry Adams and His Friends* (London, 1947).
Cecchi, Dario, *Giovanni Boldini* (Milan, 1962).
Cecil, Lord David, *Max: A Biography* (London, 1964).
Champneys, B., *Memoir and Correspondence of Coventry Patmore*, 2 vols (London, 1920).

Chanler, Mrs Winthrop, *Autumn in the Valley* (Boston, Mass., 1936).

—, *Roman Spring: Memoirs* (London, 1935).

Charteris, Evan, *John Sargent* (London, 1927).

—, *The Life and Letters of Edmund Gosse* (London, 1931).

Chase, Frank H., *The Boston Public Library: A Handbook to the Library Building, Its Mural Decorations and Its Collections* (Boston, Mass., 1921).

Clark, Walter, *Memories* (New York, 1924).

Cortissoz, Royal, *American Artists* (New York, 1923).

—, *Augustus Saint-Gaudens* (New York, 1907).

—, *Personalities in Art* (New York, 1925).

Cossart, Michael de, *The Food of Love: Princesse Edmond de Polignac (1865–1943) and Her Salon* (London, 1978).

Cox, Kenyon, *Artist and Public, and Other Essays on Art Subjects* (London, 1914).

—, *The Classic Point of View* (London/[New York], [1911]).

Dentler, Clara Louise, *Famous Foreigners in Florence, 1400–1900* (Florence, 1964).

Dormer, Heston, *The Life of Marie Bashkirtseff* (London, 1943).

Downes, William Howe, *John S. Sargent: His Life and Works* (London, 1925).

Easton, Malcolm, *Artists and Writers in Paris* (London, 1964).

Edel, Leon, *Henry James: The Middle Years, 1884–1894* (London, 1963).

—, *Henry James: The Treacherous Years, 1895–1901* (London, 1969).

—, *Henry James: The Master, 1901–1916* (London, 1972).

Fairbrother, Trevor, "John Singer Sargent and America", PhD thesis, Boston University, 1981.

—, *Sargent; Portrait Drawings* (New York, 1983).

Farr, Dennis, *English Art, 1870–1940* (Oxford, 1978).

Fauré, Gabriel, *Correspondance*, ed. Jean-Michel Nectoux (Paris, 1980).

Fauré, G. A., *Gabriel Urbain Fauré* (Paris, 1945).

Field, Isobel, *The Life I've Loved* (London, 1937).

Fildes, L. V., *Luke Fildes, RA: A Victorian Painter* (London, 1968).

Fink, Lois Marie, and Taylor, Joshua C., *Academy: The Academic Tradition in American Art* (Washington, DC, 1975).

Finneran, Richard, Harper, George Mills, and Murphy, W. M. (eds), *Letters to W. B. Yeats* (London, 1977).

Fraser, Mrs Hugh, *A Diplomat's Wife in Many Lands*, 2 vols (London, 1911).

Fry, Roger, *Transformations* (London, 1926).

Fuchs, Emil, *With Pencil, Brush and Chisel: The Life of an Artist* (New York, 1925).

Gammell, R. H. Ives, *Dennis Miller Bunker* (New York, 1953).

Gregory, Eliot, *Worldly Ways and Byways* (London, 1898).

Gunn, Peter, *Vernon Lee; Violet Paget, 1856–1935* (London, 1964).

Hamilton, James, *The Misses Vickers: The Centenary of the Painting by John Singer Sargent* (Sheffield, 1984).

Harper, Henry J., *The House of Harper: A Century of Publishing in Franklin Square* (New York, 1912).

Harries, Meirion and Susie, *The War Artists: British Official War Art of the Twentieth Century* (London, 1983).

Hart-Davis, Sir Rupert, *Catalogue of the Caricatures of Max Beerbohm* (London, 1972).

Hawthorne, Nathaniel, *Transformation; or, The Romance of Monte Beni* [*The Marble Faun*], 3 vols (London, 1860).

Helleu, Paul, *Gallery of Portraits* (Paris, 1907).

Henschel, Sir George, *Musings and Memories of a Musician* (London, 1918).

Henschel, Helen, *When Soft Voices Die: A Musical Biography* (London, 1949).

Hone, Joseph, *The Life of Henry Tonks* (London, 1939).

Hoopes, Donelson F., *The Private World of John Singer Sargent* (Washington, DC, 1964).

Hosmer, Harriet, *Letters and Memories*, ed. Cornelia Carr (London, 1913).

Houghton, C. C., *A Walk about Broadway* (Shepperton, 1980).

Howe, M. A. de Wolfe, *John Jay Chapman and His Letters* (Boston, Mass., 1937).

Howe, Maud, *My Cousin F. Marion Crawford* (London, 1934).

Howells, W. D., *Venetian Life*, 2 vols (Boston, Mass., 1881).

Isham, Samuel, *The History of American Art* (New York, 1936). With supplemental chapters by Royal Cortissoz.

Jackson, Stanley, *The Sassoons* (London, 1928).

Jacomb-Hood, G. P., *With Brush and Pencil* (London, 1925).

James, Henry, *Letters*, ed. Leon Edel, Vol. 2, *1875–1883* (London, 1978); Vol. 3, *1883–1895* (London, 1980); Vol. 4, *1895–1916* (Cambridge, Mass., 1984).

—, *Letters*, ed. Percy Lubbock, 2 vols (London, 1920).

—, *The Painter's Eye*, ed. John L. Sweeney (London, 1956).

—, *Picture and Text* (New York, 1983).

—, *William Wetmore Story and His Friends from Letters, Diaries and Recollections*, 2 vols (London, 1903).

Karsavina, Tamara, *Theatre Street: The Reminiscences of Tamara Karsavina* (London, 1930).

Kingsbury, Martha, "John Singer Sargent: aspects of his work", PhD thesis, Harvard University, 1979.

Bibliography

Lamb, Sir Walter R. M., *The Royal Academy: A Short History of Its Foundation and Development* (London, 1951).

Le Mesurier, H. G., *The English Ancestors of Epes Sargent* [c.1930].

Lee, Sir Sidney, *King Edward VII*, 2 vols (London, 1931).

Lee, Vernon, *Belcaro, Being Essays on Sundry Aesthetical Questions* (London, 1883).

—, *For Maurice: Five Unlikely Stories* (London, 1927).

—, *Sentimental Traveller: Notes on Places* (London, 1908).

—, *Vernon Lee's Letters*, ed. Irene Cooper Willis (privately printed London, 1937).

Lethère, Jacques, *Daily Life of French Artists in the Nineteenth Century*, trans. Hilary Paddon (New York, 1972).

Lewis, R. W. B., *Edith Wharton: A Biography* (New York, 1975).

Lister, Thomas, Lord Ribblesdale, *Impressions and Memories* (London, 1927).

Lomax, James, and Ormond, Richard, *John Singer Sargent and the Edwardian Age* (Leeds, 1979).

Low, W. H., *Chronicle of Friendships, 1873–1900* (London, 1908).

—, *A Painter's Progress* (New York, 1910).

Lucas, E. V., *Edwin Austin Abbey, Royal Academician: The Record of His Life and Work*, 2 vols (London, 1921).

—, *The Colvins and Their Friends* (London, 1928).

MacColl, D. S., *The Administration of the Chantry Bequest* (London, 1904).

—, *Life, Work and Setting of Philip Wilson Steer* (London, n.d.).

—, *What Is Art?* (London, 1940).

McKibbin, David, *Sargent's Boston* (Boston, Mass., 1956).

Mann, C. C., *The Sargent Family* (Boston, Mass., 1919).

Mayor, A. Hyatt, and Davis, Mark, *American Art at the Century* (New York, 1977).

Meadmore, N. S., *Lucien Pissaro: Un Cœur Simple* (London, 1962).

Meynell, Alice, *John Sargent* (London, 1903).

Millet, Francis Davis, "Frank Millet – a sketch" [1940], typescript, Archives of American Art, Smithsonian Institution, Washington, DC.

Mix, Katherine Lyon, *Max and the Americans* (Brattleboro, Vt, 1974).

Modjeska, Helena, *Impressions and Memories of Helena Modjeska: An Autobiography* (New York, 1910).

Montesquiou, Comte Robert de, *Paul Helleu* (Paris, 1913).

Moore, Charles, *The Life and Times of Charles Follen McKim* (New York, 1970).

Morisot, Berthe, *The Correspondence of Berthe Morisot*, ed. Denis Rouard, trans. Betty W. Hubbard (London, 1957).

Mount, Charles Merrill, *John Singer Sargent* (London, 1957).

Nectoux, Jean-Michel, *Gabriel Fauré; His Life Through His Letters*, trs J. A. Underwood (London, 1982).

Newton, Lord, *Retrospection* (London, 1941).

Nocklin, Linda, *Realism* (Harmondsworth, 1970).

Nowell-Smith, Simon (ed.), *Edwardian England, 1901–1914* (London, 1964).

Orledge, Robert, *Gabriel Fauré* (London, 1979).

Ormond, Richard, *John Singer Sargent: Paintings, Drawings, Watercolours* (London, 1970).

Pailleron, Marie-Louise, *Le Paradis perdu: souvenirs d'enfance* (Paris, 1947).

Palffy, Eleanor Countess, *The Lady and the Painter* (Boston, Mass., 1951).

Pennell, E. R. and J., *The Life of James McNeill Whistler*, revised edn (London, 1911).

——, *The Whistler Journal* (Philadelphia, Pa, 1921).

Perry, Bliss, *The Life and Letters of Henry Lee Higginson* (Boston, Mass., 1911).

Phillips, Olga Somech, *Solomon J. Solomon: A Memoir of Peace and War* (London, [1933]).

Pissaro, Camille, *Letters to His Son Lucien*, ed. John Rewald with the assistance of Lucien Pissaro (London, 1980).

Portland, Duke of, *Men, Women and Things: The Memoirs of the Duke of Portland* (London, 1937).

Ratcliff, Carter, *John Singer Sargent* (New York, 1982).

Reilly, C. H., *McKim, Mead & White* (London, 1924).

Robertson, W. Graham, *Letters of Graham Robertson* (London, 1952).

—, *Time Was* (London, 1931).

Roth, Cecil, *The Sassoon Dynasty* (London, 1940).

Rothenstein, William, *Men and Memories: A History of the Arts, 1872–1922; Being the Recollections of William Rothenstein*, two volumes in one (New York, 1938).

—, *Men and Memories: Recollections, 1872–1938, of William Rothenstein*, ed. Mary Lago (London, 1978).

—, *Since Fifty: Men and Memories, 1922–1938. Recollections of William Rothenstein* (London, 1939).

Saint-Gaudens, Augustus, *Reminiscences of Augustus Saint-Gaudens*, ed. H. Saint-Gaudens, 2 vols (New York, 1913).

Sargent, FitzWilliam, *England, the United States and the Southern Confederacy* (London, 1863).

—, *On Bandaging, and Other Operations of Minor Surgery* (Philadelphia, Pa, 1848).

Sari, Guido, *Boldini a Parigi* (Alghero, 1980).

Schiekeritch, Marie, *Time Past*, trans. Gaucoise Deliste (London, 1936).

Sharpey-Schafer, Joyce, *Soldier of Fortune: F. D. Millet* (Utica, NY, 1984).

Sitwell, Osbert, *Left Hand, Right Hand!* (London, 1944).

Bibliography

Smith, Janet Adam (ed.), *Henry James and Robert Louis Stevenson: A Record of Friendship and Criticism* (London, 1948).

Smith, Joseph Lindon, *Tombs, Temples and Ancient Art*, ed. Corinna Lindon Smith (Norman, Okla., 1956).

Smyth, Ethel, *Impressions That Remain* (London, 1919).

—, *What Happened Next* (London, 1940).

Söderhjelm, J., *Profiler ur finski Kulturtir* (Helsinki, 1913).

Soria, Regina, *Dictionary of Nineteenth-Century American Artists in Italy, 1760–1914* (London, 1982).

Speyer, Edward, *My Life and Friends* (London, 1937).

Stevenson, R. A. M., *Velazquez*, ed. Denys Sutton and T. Crombie (London, 1962).

Stevenson, Robert Louis, *The Letters of Robert Louis Stevenson*, ed. Sidney Colvin, 4 vols (London, 1921).

Stokes, L. N. Phelps, *Random Recollections of a Happy Life* (New York, 1932).

Strettell, Alma (trans.), *Spanish and Italian Folk Songs* (London, 1887).

Strouse, Jean, *Alice James: A Biography* (Boston, Mass., 1980).

Subercaseaux, Ramon, *Memorias de Ochenta Anos, Recuerdos personales riticas, Reminiscencias Historicas Viajes, Anecdotas* (Santiago, 1936).

Suckling, Norman C., *Gabriel Urbain Fauré* (London, 1946).

Suthu, S. B., *Charles Spraque Sargent* (Boston, Mass., 1920).

Tharp, Louise Hall, *Augustus Saint-Gaudens and the Gilded Era* (Boston, Mass., 1968).

—, *Mrs Jack* (Boston, Mass., 1965).

Thwaite, Ann, *Edmund Gosse: A Literary Landscape, 1849–1928* (London, 1984).

Tuchman, Barbara, *The Proud Tower* (New York, 1966).

Van Dyke, John C. (ed.), *Modern French Masters: A Series of Biographical and Critical Reviews by American Artists* (New York, 1896).

Weisberg, Gabriel P., *The Realist Tradition: French Painting and Drawing, 1830–1900* (Cleveland, Ohio, 1980).

Wemyss, Lady, *A Family Record* (privately printed London, 1932).

West, Rebecca, *1900* (London, 1981).

—, *The Thinking Reed* (London, 1936).

Wharton, Edith, *A Backward Glance* (New York, 1934).

Widmore, Fred, *Hercules Brabazon Brabazon*, with a preface by John Singer Sargent (London, 1906).

Wildenstein, Daniel, *Claude Monet: biographie et catalogue raisonné*, 3 vols (Lausanne/Paris, 1974–9).

Winthrop, J., *History of New England* (Boston, Mass., 1825).

Young, Dorothy Weir, *The Life and Letters of J. Alden Weir*, ed. and with an introduction by Lawrence W. Chisolm (New Haven, Conn., 1960; reissued New York, 1971).

Index

Index

302

Credits

The author would like to thank the following for their kind permission to reprint extracts: Bancroft Library, University of California; the Collection of American Literature, Beinecke Rare Book and Manuscripts Library, Yale University; Ernest Benn for *McKim, Mead and White* by R. H. Ives Gammell; the Boston Athenaeum; the Trustees of the Boston Public Library; Marion Boyars for *Correspondence* by Gabriel Fauré; Cassell for *Impressions and Memories* by Lord Ribblesdale; Chatto & Windus for *Men and Memories: A History of the Arts, 1872–1922* by William Rothenstein; Colby College Library, Waterville, Maine; Coward McCann for *Portraits of a Lifetime* by J. E. Blanche; Dartmouth College Library, Hanover, New Hampshire; De Capo Press for *The Life and Letters of J. Alden Weir* by Dorothy Weir Young, Stanford White by Charles C. Baldwin and *The Life and Times of Charles Follen McKim* by Charles Moore; Eulenburg Books for *Gabriel Fauré* by Robert Orledge; Faber & Faber for *Men, Women & Things* by the Duke of Portland; Frick Art Reference Library, New York; Grafton Books, a division of the Collins Publishing Group, for *The Selected Letters of Henry James* (ed. Leon Edel); Harper & Row for *The Glitter and the Gold* by C. V. Bodsan; Heinemann for *John Sargent* by Evan Charteris, *Half a Minute's Silence and Other Stories* by Maurice Baring and *Life and Letters of Sir Edmund Gosse* by Evan Charteris; David Higham Associates for *What Happened Next* by Ethel Smyth and *Impressions That Remained* by Ethel Smyth; the Houghton Library, Harvard University; Hutchinson Books for *Mrs J. Comyns Carr's Reminiscences* by Alice Strettell Carr; the Imperial War Museum, London; the Isabella Stewart Gardner Museum, Boston; Michael Joseph for *The War Artists: British Official War Art of the Twentieth Century* by Meiron and Susie Harries and *Luke Fildes, RA: A Victorian Painter* by L. V. Fildes; Little, Brown for *Mrs Jack* by Louise Hall Tharp, *Recollections: Gorham Bacon* by Gorham Bacon and *John Singer Sargent: His Life and Work* by William Howe Downes; Massachusetts Historical Society; Methuen London Ltd. for *Edwin Lucas Abbey* by E. V. Lucas; John Murray for *Retrospection* by Lord Newton; the National Library of Scotland, Edinburgh; the New York Historical Society, New York; the Ormond family; Oxford University Press for *Edwardian England* (ed. Simon Nowell-Smith); Quartet for *Time Was* by W. Graham Robertson; Routledge & Kegan Paul for *Letters to His Son Lucien* by Camille Pissarro; Rupert Hart-Davis for *Henry James: The Middle Years 1884–1894* by Leon Edel and *Letters to Reggie Turner* by Max Beerbohm; Rosamond Sherwood; the Smithsonian Institution, Washington; Weidenfeld & Nicolson for *1900* by Rebecca West and *Vanessa Bell* by Francis Spalding.

Picture Acknowledgements

Endpapers: Letter from John Singer Sargent to his sister Emily from a Private Collection. Archives of American Art, Smithsonian Institution, *Photographs of Artists in Paris Studios*, original photograph owned by R. P. Tolman: XI above; *Francis Davis Millet Papers*: XV above right. Ashmolean Museum, Oxford (Department of Western Art): IV below. Courtesy of the Art Institute of Chicago, Friends of American Art Gift: XXX right. Brooklyn Museum, New York, Museum Collection Fund: XVIII above. Courtesy of the Associates of the Boston Public Library: XXV photograph by Richard Cheek, XXVI below. Fogg Art Museum: XV above left. Dr C. C. Houghton: XIV. Isabella Stewart Gardner Museum, Boston: VII below, IX below, XVI. Imperial War Museum, London: XXVIII. Percy Lubbok, *The Letters of Henry James*, Vol. I, Macmillan and Co., 1920: XIII below left. E. V. Lucas, *Edwin Austin Abbey*, Vol. I, Methuen and Co., London, and Charles Scribner's Sons, New York, 1921: XIII below right, XXI. Metropolitan Museum of Art, New York, Arthur H. Hearn Fund: X; Bequest of Mrs Valerie B. Hadden: XII below. Courtesy Museum of Fine Arts, Boston: IX above, XXIX, XXXI left. National Academy of Design, New York: VII below right. National Monuments Record, London: XXII. Courtesy Ormond Family: I, IV above, V, VI below, VIII, XI, XVII, XIX above, XIX below right, XXIII, XXIV above left, XXVI above, XXXI right, XXXII. Private Collections: XII above, XIII above. Private Collection, photograph courtesy of the Worcester Art Museum, Massachusetts: XX. Courtesy Mme Paulette Howard-Johnston: VII below left, XVIII below. *Epes Sargent of Gloucester and his Descendants*, 1923, Houghton Mifflin Co., Boston and New York: II above, III above. Sargent-Murray-Gilman-Hough House Association: II below, III below. Sterling and Francine Clark Art Institute, Williamstown, Massachusetts: VI above. Tate Gallery, London: XV below, XIX below left, XXIV below right, XXVII, XXX left.

bright enough. & then
the effect only lasts ten
minutes.

I am sorry
I again have been
long without writing.
shall try to mend.

Heard from Profh
or Klein Vienna &
Cooh —

Best love
Yours loving
John Blackie